THE Barbecue COLLECTION

TRANSCONTINENTAL BOOKS
5800 Saint-Denis St.
Suite 900
Montreal, Que. H2S 3L5
Telephone: (514) 273-1066
Toll-free: 1-800-565-5531
www.canadianliving.com

Bibliothèque et Archives nationales du
Québec and Library and Archives Canada
cataloguing in publication

Main entry under title:
The barbecue collection
Updated ed.
Includes index.
ISBN 978-0-9877474-0-2
1. Barbecuing. I. Canadian Living Test
Kitchen.

TX840.B3C42 2012   641.5'784
C2012-940418-7
Project editor: Christina Anson Mine
Copy editors: Lisa Fielding,
Austen Gilliland
Indexer: Gillian Watts
Art direction and design: Chris Bond
Front cover design: Michael Erb

Printed in Canada
© Transcontinental Books, 2012
Legal deposit – 2nd quarter 2012
National Library of Quebec
National Library of Canada
ISBN 978-0-9877474-0-2

We acknowledge the financial support of
our publishing activity by the Government
of Canada through the Canada Book Fund.

For information on special rates for
corporate libraries and wholesale
purchases, please call 1-866-800-2500.

Canadian Living

THE
Barbecue
COLLECTION

By The Canadian Living Test Kitchen

Transcontinental Books

contents

the basics — 6

brochettes
& kabobs — 10

burgers,
sandwiches
& sausages — 78

steaks, chops
& ribs — 150

roasts — 234

poultry — 278

fish & seafood — 348

grilled vegetables,
cheeses & breads — 426

salads & sides — 472

sauces,
marinades
& rubs — 514

index — 538

the basics

Charcoal or Gas?

Grilling is enormously popular in Canada. Many dedicated cooks even grill throughout the winter, bundled in parkas and tuques. Perhaps because of our relatively cold climate, we prefer gas grilling by a large margin (compared to Americans, who are almost evenly split).

While nothing can quite compare to open-fire wood grilling, charcoal gives a natural smoky flavour and intense heat. Lump charcoal burns hot and quickly, but many cooks prefer charcoal briquettes because they maintain a more even, longer-burning heat.

Gas burns clean, so you don't get a natural smoky flavour from it. But a handful of soaked wood chips can do the trick, adding a taste of natural smoke to your grilled dishes. Follow the manufacturer's instructions for using wood chips, as gas grills come in all shapes and sizes and have different specifications.

Cooking Temperatures

Grilling isn't an exact science. Because it's done outdoors, the temperature and wind – even humidity – can change cooking conditions, which affects timing and even appropriate grilling heat. So take the recommended times and temperatures in this cookbook as guidelines, not as scripture, and use common sense. If, for example, a recipe doesn't call for a covered grill but the weather is inclement, then close the lid anyway. Just remember that it's heat that cooks food, and anything that takes heat away from the grill will change the grilling results.

Always preheat your grill to the right temperature. Many come with temperature gauges attached to the lid, which makes preheating easy. You can set an ovenproof thermometer inside the grill (try to keep it slightly above the grates) or use the easy and surprisingly accurate hand test (right) to gauge.

Heat Hand Test

Hold your hand, palm down, 2 to 3 inches (5 to 8 cm) above the hot grill. Count how many seconds you can keep it there comfortably to determine the heat level.

5 seconds	Low
4 seconds	Medium
3 seconds	Medium-High
2 seconds	High

Grilling Temperatures

Low	325 to 350°F (160 to 180°C)
Medium	350 to 375°F (180 to 190°C)
Medium-High	375 to 400°F (190 to 200°C)
High	425 to 450°F (220 to 230°C)

Essential Barbecue Tools

- If you have a charcoal grill, a **chimney charcoal starter** is indispensable. You just crumple up a few sheets of newspaper on the bottom of the starter, pile charcoal over them, light the paper and, in 15 to 20 minutes, you have perfect glowing coals.

- Heat-resistant **grilling gloves** are a must for safety.

- Short **tongs** are much easier to use, but long tongs keep your hands away from the heat, so both are nice to have.

- A **long-handled fork** is useful, especially for large cuts of meat or poultry.

- A couple of **wide spatulas** make turning fish an easy task.

- A solid **wire brush** keeps the grates clean.

- An **instant-read thermometer** takes the guesswork out of determining the doneness of grilled meats and poultry. It helps you avoid cutting into the food and wasting delicious juices.

- **Grill pans and baskets** are useful for vegetables and small pieces of meat or poultry, and for grilling whole fish.

- If you're a rib lover, you might want to invest in a simple **rib rack,** which holds multiple racks of ribs at one time over indirect heat.

- **Silicone brushes** don't burn, and let you baste foods easily without leaving nasty bristles behind.

Avoid Flare-Ups

Minimize barbecue flare-ups, which can scorch and char food, by keeping a clean grill. Turn heat to high after each use or when preheating until grease and residue have burned off, then scrub with a wire brush. Always keep a squirt bottle of water handy to douse flames. An even more effective way of putting out flare-ups is to use baking soda instead of water, but you must be extremely careful not to get it on your food – it tastes terrible. Most people prefer the water method.

Marmalade-Glazed
Chicken Thighs (page 59)

brochettes & kabobs

Beef Satays | 13

Spicy Steak Kabobs | 15

Steak Shish Kabobs | 16

Deli-Spiced Steak Kabobs
    With Pearl Onions | 17

Beef Bulgogi Skewers | 20

Beef Kabobs With
    Horseradish Sauce | 21

Grilled Veal Saltimbocca | 22

Island Pork Loin &
    Pineapple Brochettes | 23

Pork Souvlaki | 25

Italian Pork Tenderloin Brochettes | 27

Honey-Mustard Pork Kabobs | 28

Pork & Poblano Kabobs | 30

Philippine Pork Kabobs | 31

Coriander Pork Skewers
    With Red Onion Salsa | 33

Thai Minced Pork Kabobs | 34

Tofu Skewers With
    Jerk Barbecue Sauce | 35

Sweet & Tangy Sausage
    Pepper Kabobs | 36

Grilled Sausage Spiedini | 38

Adana Lamb Kabobs | 39

Lamb Koftas on Rosemary | 40

Sage Lamb Kabobs | 42

Herbed Lamb Kabobs | 43

Lamb Kabobs With
    Kachumber Salad | 45

Ginger Soy Chicken Skewers | 46

Chicken Teriyaki Skewers | 47

Lemon Chicken Kabobs | 49

Chicken & Mango Kabobs | 50

Chicken Tikka | 52

Chicken Bacon Brochettes | 54

Chinese Seasoned Chicken Kabobs | 55

Peanut & Coconut Chicken Skewers | 56

Marmalade-Glazed Chicken Thighs | 59

Caesar Turkey Brochettes | 60

Ancho Turkey Waves | 62

Salmon Kabobs With Baby Bok Choy | 63

Tamarind-Glazed Salmon Kabobs | 64

Soy-Glazed Halibut Kabobs | 65

Pickerel With Charmoula | 66

Glazes | 68

Glazed Fish Kabobs | 69

Greek-Style Seafood Kabobs | 70

Sweet & Sour Shrimp Kabobs | 72

Shrimp Skewers With
    Cilantro & Almond Relish | 73

Seafood Kabobs With Saffron Aioli | 74

Shrimp & Mango Brochettes | 76

Miso-Orange Grilled Scallops | 77

Beef Satays

In Indonesia and Malaysia, beef and mutton satays are usually served with a sauce made from kecap manis, a sweet soy sauce. You can buy kecap manis at Chinese or southeast Asian grocery stores and large grocery stores with Asian sections. Serve the satays with sliced cucumber and red onion.

1 tsp finely grated or minced **fresh ginger**

1 clove **garlic,** pressed or minced

1 tsp **salt**

½ tsp **pepper**

½ tsp **ground coriander**

½ tsp **turmeric**

¼ tsp **cayenne pepper**

¼ tsp **ground cumin**

1 lb (450 g) **beef sirloin grilling steak** or lamb or pork loin, cut into 3- x 1- x ¼-inch (8 x 2.5 x 0.5 cm) strips

SWEET SOY SATAY SAUCE:

¼ cup **peanut oil** or vegetable oil

¼ cup thinly sliced **shallots**

3 cloves **garlic,** thinly sliced

1 tbsp chopped **Thai bird's-eye peppers** or other hot peppers

⅓ cup **kecap manis**

¼ cup **lime juice**

3 tbsp finely chopped **roasted peanuts**

Sweet Soy Satay Sauce: In small saucepan, heat oil over medium-high heat; fry shallots until golden. Remove with slotted spoon. Add garlic to pan; fry until golden. Remove with slotted spoon, reserving oil. In mortar with pestle, pound Thai peppers to paste; add shallots and garlic and pound until almost smooth. (Or finely mince Thai peppers; add shallots and garlic and mince until almost smooth.) Mix in kecap manis, lime juice and peanuts.

Mix together 1 tbsp of the reserved oil (save remainder for another use), ginger, garlic, salt, pepper, coriander, turmeric, cayenne and cumin; toss with beef until coated. Marinate for 30 minutes or, covered and refrigerated, up to 8 hours.

Thread onto skewers. Grill on greased grill over high heat, turning once, until desired doneness, about 4 minutes for medium. Serve with sweet soy satay sauce.

Makes 4 to 6 main-course servings.

TIP

If you can't find kecap manis for this recipe, boil together ⅓ cup granulated sugar, ¼ cup soy sauce and 1½ tbsp fancy molasses until sugar is dissolved.

PER EACH OF 6 SERVINGS: about 224 cal, 17 g pro, 9 g total fat (2 g sat. fat), 20 g carb, 1 g fibre, 35 mg chol, 1,036 mg sodium, 370 mg potassium. % RDI: 3% calcium, 17% iron, 1% vit A, 5% vit C, 6% folate.

Spicy Steak Kabobs

Asian chili pastes vary in intensity from just a bit spicy to fiery. Experiment with a variety of them on these simple steak kabobs until you find your favourite.

Half **white onion,** chopped

2 cloves **garlic,** chopped

1 piece (1 inch/2.5 cm) **fresh ginger,** chopped

3 tbsp **tomato paste**

1 tbsp **red wine vinegar**

2 tsp **chili paste** (such as sambal oelek)

1 tsp packed **brown sugar**

½ tsp **salt**

1 lb (450 g) **beef top sirloin grilling steak,** cut into 24 cubes

1 each **sweet red and green pepper,** each cut into 24 pieces

In food processor, pulse together onion, garlic and ginger until coarse paste. Add tomato paste, vinegar, chili paste, sugar and salt; pulse until smooth.

Transfer onion mixture to bowl; toss with steak until coated. Marinate for 10 minutes.

Discarding tomato mixture, alternately thread beef and red and green pepper pieces onto 8 skewers.

Grill, covered, on greased grill over medium-high heat, turning occasionally, until medium-rare, 10 to 12 minutes.

Makes 4 main-course servings.

Soak wooden or bamboo skewers in water for about 30 minutes before using to keep them from charring or catching fire.

PER SERVING: about 177 cal, 24 g pro, 5 g total fat (2 g sat. fat), 9 g carb, 2 g fibre, 53 mg chol, 225 mg sodium, 477 mg potassium. % RDI: 2% calcium, 19% iron, 14% vit A, 120% vit C, 8% folate.

Steak Shish Kabobs

A rib eye is a particularly flavourful steak that makes wonderful kabobs. Here, it is made even more interesting with the addition of fragrant Middle Eastern spices.

Half **onion,** grated

2 tbsp **extra-virgin olive oil**

4 tsp **lemon juice**

2 cloves **garlic,** pressed or minced

½ tsp **ground allspice**

½ tsp **ground cumin**

¼ tsp **pepper**

Generous pinch **cinnamon**

Generous pinch **cayenne pepper**

1½ lb (675 g) **beef rib eye grilling steak** or strip loin grilling steak, cut into 1-inch (2.5 cm) cubes

1 lb (450 g) **cherry tomatoes**

½ tsp **salt**

Mix together onion, oil, lemon juice, garlic, allspice, cumin, pepper, cinnamon and cayenne; toss with beef until coated. Marinate for 20 minutes or, covered and refrigerated, up to 4 hours.

Alternately thread beef and tomatoes onto skewers; sprinkle with salt. For rare, grill on greased grill over high heat, turning once, for about 6 minutes; for medium-rare to well-done, grill over medium-high heat until desired doneness, 10 to 12 minutes for medium.

Makes 4 to 6 main-course servings.

When threading meat onto skewers, don't cram the pieces up against one another. Leave a little space for even cooking.

PER EACH OF 6 SERVINGS: about 252 cal, 20 g pro, 17 g total fat (6 g sat. fat), 4 g carb, 1 g fibre, 48 mg chol, 234 mg sodium. % RDI: 2% calcium, 19% iron, 6% vit A, 17% vit C, 6% folate.

Deli-Spiced Steak Kabobs With Pearl Onions

Grilling the onions on separate skewers ensures both the steak kabobs and the onions are cooked perfectly.

1½ lb (675 g) **beef grilling steak** or bison grilling steak, cut into 1-inch (2.5 cm) cubes

1 tbsp **Deli-Style Steak Spice Mix** (right)

1 tbsp **vegetable oil**

PEARL ONION SKEWERS:

2 cups **pearl onions,** about 10 oz (280 g)

1 tbsp **vegetable oil**

2 tsp **Deli-Style Steak Spice Mix** (right)

Pearl Onion Skewers: In saucepan of boiling water, boil unpeeled onions for 2 minutes; drain. Slip off skins; toss onions with oil. Thread onto skewers; sprinkle with spice mix.

Toss together beef, spice mix and oil; thread onto skewers. For rare, grill beef on greased grill over high heat, turning once, for about 6 minutes; for medium-rare to well-done, grill over medium-high heat until desired doneness, 10 to 12 minutes for medium. Meanwhile, grill onions on greased grill over high or medium-high heat until lightly charred and tender, 3 to 5 minutes.

Makes 6 main-course servings.

Deli-Style Steak Spice Mix

Coarsely grind together 1 tbsp lightly toasted coriander seeds, 1 tbsp black peppercorns and 1 tsp dillseed. Mix in 4 tsp coarse sea salt or kosher salt, 2 tsp each sweet paprika and hot pepper flakes, and 1½ tsp granulated garlic (or 1 tsp garlic powder). *(Make-ahead: Store in airtight container.)*

Makes about 5 tbsp.

PER SERVING (WITHOUT ONIONS): about 186 cal, 26 g pro, 8 g total fat (2 g sat. fat), 1 g carb, 1 g fibre, 56 mg chol, 252 mg sodium, 264 mg potassium. % RDI: 18% iron, 2% vit A, 2% folate.

From left: Beef Bulgogi
Skewers (page 20)
and Grilled Veal
Saltimbocca (page 22)

Beef Bulgogi Skewers

Serve these colourful kabobs over Boston lettuce leaves with steamed white rice. For more authentic Korean flavour, offer assorted pickles and kimchi alongside.

6 cloves **garlic,** minced

¼ cup **soy sauce**

2 tbsp packed **brown sugar**

1 tbsp grated **fresh ginger**

1 tbsp **sesame oil**

½ tsp **hot pepper flakes**

1 lb (450 g) **beef grilling steak,** cut into 1-inch (2.5 cm) cubes

1 **red onion,** cut into 1-inch (2.5 cm) pieces

1 **sweet green pepper,** cut into 1-inch (2.5 cm) pieces

Whisk together garlic, soy sauce, brown sugar, ginger, sesame oil and hot pepper flakes.

Place beef in bowl; place onion and green pepper in separate bowl. Divide marinade between bowls. Marinate for 15 minutes or, covered and refrigerated, up to 1 day.

Reserving any remaining marinade, alternately thread beef, onion and peppers onto skewers; brush with marinade. Grill on greased grill over high heat, turning once, until desired doneness, about 8 minutes for medium-rare.

Makes 4 main-course servings.

Photo, page 18

Two categories of boneless beef steaks work for kabobs. The first is grilling steak. For unmarinated or briefly marinated kabobs, the most luxurious choices are rib eye (well-marbled, tender and tasty) and strip loin or New York (leaner and denser). Tenderloin is ultratender but can lack flavour unless well-aged. Top sirloin, tri-tip and wing grilling steaks are lean and flavourful but not as tender, and are suited to longer marinating. The second type is marinating grilling steak, which needs long marinating. We recommend inside or outside round or sirloin tip for long-marinated kabobs.

PER SERVING: about 197 cal, 20 g pro, 5 g total fat (2 g sat. fat), 18 g carb, 3 g fibre, 43 mg chol, 410 mg sodium, 511 mg potassium. % RDI: 3% calcium, 18% iron, 3% vit A, 110% vit C, 14% folate.

Beef Kabobs With Horseradish Sauce

These well-seasoned bites are satisfying and packed with flavour. We used Greek yogurt to lighten up and add some zip to the horseradish sauce. You could also grill the beef cubes on soaked toothpicks to make a delicious appetizer.

2 cloves **garlic**

½ tsp **coarse sea salt**

4 tsp minced **fresh rosemary**

1 tbsp **olive oil**

1 tsp **pepper**

1 lb (450 g) **beef top blade flatiron grilling steak** or beef flank marinating steak, cut into 1-inch (2.5 cm) cubes

HORSERADISH SAUCE:

2 tbsp each **sour cream** and **2% Greek yogurt**

1 tbsp minced **fresh chives**

1 tbsp **extra-hot prepared horseradish**

On cutting board, coarsely chop garlic; sprinkle with salt. With flat side of knife or fork, mash into paste.

In large bowl, stir together garlic paste, rosemary, oil and pepper; toss with beef until coated. Marinate for 30 minutes.

Thread onto skewers. Grill on greased grill over high heat, turning once, until desired doneness, about 7 minutes for medium-rare.

Horseradish Sauce: Stir together sour cream, yogurt, chives and horseradish. Serve with kabobs.

Makes 4 main-course servings.

PER SERVING: about 211 cal, 24 g pro, 11 g total fat (4 g sat. fat), 2 g carb, trace fibre, 52 mg chol, 246 mg sodium, 251 mg potassium. % RDI: 3% calcium, 16% iron, 2% vit A, 2% vit C, 3% folate.

Grilled Veal Saltimbocca

Saltimbocca is Italian for "jumps in your mouth" – the perfect name for this irresistibly tasty, simple dish, which has just a few ingredients that pack so much flavour. If you like, serve the slices as individual appetizers.

8 thin slices **prosciutto**

8 pieces **veal scaloppine,**
   about 1 lb (450 g)

8 oz (225 g) **soft goat cheese**

1 tsp **pepper**

24 to 32 **fresh basil leaves**

Arrange prosciutto slices on work surface; top each with 1 of the veal pieces, matching edges as closely as possible. Spread goat cheese evenly over veal; sprinkle with pepper. Arrange 3 or 4 basil leaves in single layer on top; starting at 1 short end, roll up. Thread each roll diagonally onto 2 soaked wooden toothpicks.

Grill, covered, on greased grill over medium-high heat, turning once, until just a hint of pink remains inside veal and edges of prosciutto are crisp, about 12 minutes.

To serve, cut rolls in half between toothpicks.

Makes 4 main-course servings.

Photo, page 19

PER SERVING: about 321 cal, 42 g pro, 15 g total fat (9 g sat. fat), 1 g carb, trace fibre, 19 mg chol, 982 mg sodium, 636 mg potassium. % RDI: 9% calcium, 18% iron, 18% vit A, 10% folate.

Island Pork Loin & Pineapple Brochettes

The citrus marinade, laced with hot peppers, offsets the sweet, fresh pineapple in this West Indian–inspired grill.

2 or 3 **Scotch bonnet peppers**
 or habanero peppers, halved
 and seeded

4 cloves **garlic,** smashed

⅓ cup chopped **onion**

2 tbsp each **lime juice** and
 orange juice

1 tbsp **tomato paste**

2 tsp chopped **fresh ginger**

¾ tsp **ground cumin**

¾ tsp **dried oregano,** crumbled

¾ tsp **salt**

½ tsp **ground allspice**

¼ tsp **pepper**

1¼ lb (565 g) **pork loin** or shoulder,
 cut into 1-inch (2.5 cm) cubes

3 cups cubed (1 inch/2.5 cm)
 fresh pineapple

1 tbsp **vegetable oil**

Fresh cilantro sprigs

Lime wedges

In blender or food processor, purée together peppers, garlic, onion, lime and orange juices, tomato paste and ginger; transfer to bowl. Stir in cumin, oregano, ½ tsp of the salt, allspice and pepper; toss with pork until coated. Cover and marinate, refrigerated, for 3 to 8 hours.

Toss pineapple with remaining salt. Reserving any remaining marinade, alternately thread pork and pineapple onto skewers. Stir oil into marinade; brush over skewers.

Grill, covered, on greased grill over medium-high heat, turning once, until just a hint of pink remains inside for loin or until no longer pink inside for fattier shoulder, 12 to 15 minutes. Garnish with cilantro; serve with lime wedges.

Makes 4 to 6 main-course servings.

PER EACH OF 6 SERVINGS (WITHOUT LIME WEDGES): about 198 cal, 24 g pro, 5 g total fat (1 g sat. fat), 15 g carb, 2 g fibre, 47 mg chol, 333 mg sodium. % RDI: 3% calcium, 10% iron, 16% vit A, 93% vit C, 7% folate.

Pork Souvlaki

Everyone loves this classic Greek kabob. It's delicious on a pita as a sandwich, but it's equally at home with rice and Greek Village Salad (page 505).

2 tbsp **lemon juice**

1 tbsp **extra-virgin olive oil**

1 large clove **garlic,** minced

½ tsp **dried oregano**

½ tsp **salt**

¼ tsp **pepper**

1½ lb (675 g) **pork tenderloin,** trimmed and cut into 1-inch (2.5 cm) cubes

2 **plum tomatoes,** sliced

Half **red onion,** sliced

1 cup shredded **romaine lettuce**

4 **Greek-style pocketless pitas**

TZATZIKI:

1 cup shredded **cucumber**

½ tsp **salt**

¾ cup **Balkan-style plain yogurt**

2 cloves **garlic,** minced

2 tbsp chopped **fresh dill** (optional)

1 tbsp **lemon juice**

Tzatziki: Mix cucumber with salt; let stand for 10 minutes. Squeeze out moisture. Stir together cucumber, yogurt, garlic, dill (if using) and lemon juice.

Meanwhile, whisk together lemon juice, oil, garlic, oregano, salt and pepper; toss with pork until coated. Marinate for 10 minutes or, covered and refrigerated, up to 6 hours.

Reserving any remaining marinade, thread pork onto skewers; brush with marinade. Grill, covered, on greased grill over medium-high heat, turning halfway through, until juices run clear when pork is pierced and just a hint of pink remains inside, about 12 minutes. Remove skewers. Serve with tomatoes, onion, lettuce and tzatziki on pitas.

Makes 4 main-course servings.

PER SERVING: about 463 cal, 46 g pro, 10 g total fat (4 g sat. fat), 44 g carb, 3 g fibre, 100 mg chol, 863 mg sodium, 910 mg potassium. % RDI: 14% calcium, 28% iron, 12% vit A, 22% vit C, 49% folate.

Italian Pork Tenderloin Brochettes

This Italian dish (called spiedini*) showcases perfectly cooked pork tenderloin and crispy seasoned bread.*

1½ lb (675 g) **pork tenderloin,** cut into sixteen ¾-inch (2 cm) thick slices

8 slices **pancetta,** halved

Half **baguette,** cut into twelve ¾-inch (2 cm) slices

8 **fresh bay leaves** or sage leaves

¼ tsp each **salt** and **pepper**

3 tbsp **extra-virgin olive oil**

Wrap each pork slice in pancetta. Onto each of 4 skewers, thread in order: bread, pork, bay leaf, pork, bread, pork, bay leaf, pork, bread. Sprinkle with salt and pepper; drizzle with oil.

Grill, covered, on greased grill over medium-high heat, turning once, until just a hint of pink remains inside pork, about 12 minutes.

Makes 4 main-course servings.

PER SERVING: about 406 cal, 45 g pro, 15 g total fat (5 g sat. fat), 19 g carb, 1 g fibre, 108 mg chol, 512 mg sodium. % RDI: 4% calcium, 24% iron, 1% vit A, 2% vit C, 15% folate.

Honey-Mustard Pork Kabobs

The tang of hot mustard and the sweetness of honey give this pork loin kabob a bit of zip. Try it with corn on the cob and one of our tasty corn butters (page 431).

2 tbsp **hot mustard** or
    Dijon mustard

2 tbsp **liquid honey**

1 tbsp **vegetable oil**

3 cloves **garlic,** pressed or minced

½ tsp **ground ginger**

¼ tsp each **salt** and **pepper**

1 lb (450 g) **pork loin** or tenderloin,
    cut into 1-inch (2.5 cm) cubes

Mix together mustard, honey, oil, garlic, ginger, salt and pepper; toss with pork until coated. Marinate for 10 minutes.

Reserving remaining marinade, thread pork onto skewers; brush with marinade. Grill, covered, on greased grill over medium-high heat, turning once, until just a hint of pink remains inside, about 12 minutes.

Makes 4 main-course servings.

When choosing pork to marinate, check the label and choose meat that hasn't been seasoned, a brining method now common in supermarket pork. So much fat has been bred out of modern pigs that the meat is dry when even slightly overcooked. Producers compensate by injecting it with a saline solution and labelling it "seasoned." In our experience, this procedure prevents the pork from absorbing marinades or browning properly, resulting in moist but less flavourful meat.

PER SERVING: about 199 cal, 22 g pro, 8 g total fat (2 g sat. fat), 8 g carb, 0 g fibre, 60 mg chol, 247 mg sodium. % RDI: 3% calcium, 7% iron, 2% vit C, 1% folate.

Pork & Poblano Kabobs

Poblano peppers have just a hint of heat and a full, dark flavour that pairs nicely with mild-tasting pork loin.

2 cloves **garlic,** pressed or minced

3 tbsp **tomato-based chili sauce** or ketchup

2 tbsp + 2 tsp **olive oil** or vegetable oil

2 tsp **lime juice**

1½ tsp **chipotle chili powder**

¾ tsp **salt**

½ tsp crumbled **dried marjoram**

1½ lb (675 g) **pork loin** or shoulder, cut into 1-inch (2.5 cm) cubes

2 **poblano peppers** or 1 sweet green pepper, cut into 1-inch (2.5 cm) pieces

Half **red onion,** cut into 1-inch (2.5 cm) pieces

Lime wedges

Mix together garlic, chili sauce, 2 tbsp of the oil, lime juice, chipotle chili powder, ½ tsp of the salt and marjoram; toss with pork until coated. Marinate for 20 minutes or, covered and refrigerated, up to 8 hours.

Stir together peppers, onion, and remaining oil and salt until coated. Alternately thread pork, peppers and onion onto skewers.

Grill, covered, on greased grill over medium heat, turning once, until just a hint of pink remains inside for loin or until no longer pink inside for fattier shoulder, about 15 minutes. Serve with lime wedges.

Makes 4 to 6 main-course servings.

PER EACH OF 6 SERVINGS: about 226 cal, 23 g pro, 12 g total fat (3 g sat. fat), 6 g carb, 1 g fibre, 60 mg chol, 394 mg sodium. % RDI: 2% calcium, 9% iron, 3% vit A, 27% vit C, 4% folate.

Philippine Pork Kabobs

Garlic, bay leaf, pepper and cloves is such a popular combination of seasonings in the Philippines that packages of it are sold at every corner store.

¼ cup **soy sauce**

2 tbsp minced **fresh cilantro**

2 tbsp **unseasoned rice vinegar**

2 cloves **garlic,** pressed or minced

1 tbsp minced **fresh ginger**

1 **bay leaf**

½ tsp **pepper**

Generous pinch **ground cloves**

Generous pinch **cayenne pepper**

1½ lb (675 g) **boneless pork shoulder** or loin, cut into 1½-inch (4 cm) cubes

BASTING SAUCE:

3 tbsp **ketchup**

2 tbsp **lime juice**

1 tbsp **granulated sugar**

1 tbsp **vegetable oil**

Mix together soy sauce, cilantro, vinegar, garlic, ginger, bay leaf, pepper, cloves and cayenne; toss with pork until coated. Cover and marinate, refrigerated, for 2 hours or up to 1 day. Thread onto skewers.

Basting Sauce: Mix together ketchup, lime juice, sugar and oil.

Grill pork, covered, on greased grill over medium-high heat, turning often and brushing with basting sauce, until no longer pink inside for fattier shoulder or until just a hint of pink remains inside for loin, 12 to 15 minutes.

Makes 4 main-course servings.

PER SERVING: about 270 cal, 28 g pro, 13 g total fat (4 g sat. fat), 9 g carb, trace fibre, 80 mg chol, 877 mg sodium. % RDI: 3% calcium, 13% iron, 2% vit A, 5% vit C, 5% folate.

Coriander Pork Skewers With Red Onion Salsa

Bay leaves are just for flavour; they're too hard to eat, so discard them after grilling. If you don't have hot paprika, mix ¾ tsp sweet paprika with ¼ tsp cayenne pepper.

1 lb (450 g) **pork tenderloin,** cut into 1-inch (2.5 cm) cubes

2 cloves **garlic,** minced

1 tbsp **ground coriander**

1 tbsp **olive oil**

1 tsp **ground cumin**

1 tsp **hot paprika**

½ tsp **salt**

12 **fresh bay leaves** (approx)

RED ONION SALSA:

1 **tomato**

1 cup thinly sliced **red onion**

1½ tbsp **red wine vinegar**

Pinch each **salt** and granulated sugar

2 tbsp chopped **fresh mint**

Toss together pork, garlic, coriander, oil, cumin, paprika and salt until coated; marinate for 10 minutes.

Red Onion Salsa: Meanwhile, cut tomato into quarters; seed, core and slice. Toss together tomato, onion, vinegar, salt and sugar. Stir in mint.

Alternately thread pork and bay leaves onto skewers, using more bay leaves if desired. Grill, covered, on greased grill over medium-high heat, turning once, until just a hint of pink remains inside pork, about 12 minutes. Serve with red onion salsa.

Makes 4 main-course servings.

PER SERVING: about 397 cal, 31 g pro, 17 g total fat (3 g sat. fat), 33 g carb, 6 g fibre, 61 mg chol, 501 mg sodium, 672 mg potassium. % RDI: 6% calcium, 31% iron, 13% vit A, 33% vit C, 27% folate.

Thai Minced Pork Kabobs

These minced meat skewers have the ideal Thai balance of sweet, salty, sour and hot notes. Serve with a simple salad and sliced mangoes for dessert.

2 **shallots** (or 1 green onion), minced

2 cloves **garlic,** pressed or minced

4 **Thai bird's-eye peppers** (optional), minced

½ cup minced **fresh cilantro**

¼ cup ground **roasted peanuts**

1 **egg**

4 tsp **fish sauce** or soy sauce

2 tsp minced **fresh lemongrass**

2 tsp packed **brown sugar**

2 tsp **lime juice**

2 to 4 tsp **Thai red curry paste**

1 lb (450 g) **lean ground pork**

Fresh cilantro sprigs

Lime wedges

Stir together shallots, garlic, peppers (if using), cilantro, 3 tbsp of the peanuts, egg, fish sauce, lemongrass, sugar, lime juice and curry paste; mix in pork.

Using heaping 1 tbsp each, shape into small sausages; thread lengthwise onto skewers. Cover and refrigerate for 1 to 12 hours.

Grill, covered, on greased grill over medium heat, turning once, until no longer pink inside or instant-read thermometer registers 160°F (71°C), about 12 minutes. Sprinkle with remaining peanuts; garnish with cilantro sprigs. Serve with lime wedges.

Makes 4 to 6 main-course servings.

PER EACH OF 6 SERVINGS (WITHOUT LIME WEDGES): about 195 cal, 17 g pro, 12 g total fat (4 g sat. fat), 4 g carb, 1 g fibre, 80 mg chol, 360 mg sodium. % RDI: 3% calcium, 7% iron, 3% vit A, 9% folate.

Tofu Skewers With Jerk Barbecue Sauce

Tofu on its own is nearly flavourless, but it readily absorbs strong flavours, such as the ones in this deliciously simple jerk barbecue sauce.

1 pkg (454 g) **firm tofu** or extra-firm tofu, cut into 24 cubes

2 cloves **garlic,** minced

2 tbsp **sodium-reduced soy sauce**

1 tbsp **vegetable oil**

1 each **sweet red, orange** and **yellow pepper,** each cut into 24 pieces

6 **green onions** (white parts only), halved

Grilled Coleslaw (right)

JERK BARBECUE SAUCE:

1 cup **bottled strained tomatoes** (passata)

2 tbsp **fancy molasses**

1 to 2 tbsp **prepared jerk sauce**

2 tsp **malt vinegar**

¼ tsp **dried thyme**

Jerk Barbecue Sauce: In saucepan, bring tomatoes, molasses, jerk sauce, vinegar and thyme to boil. Reduce heat; simmer until reduced to ½ cup, 10 to 15 minutes.

Meanwhile, gently toss together tofu, garlic, soy sauce and oil until coated; marinate for 10 minutes.

Alternately thread peppers, onions and tofu onto skewers; brush with some of the jerk barbecue sauce.

Grill, covered, on greased grill over medium-high heat, turning and brushing with remaining jerk barbecue sauce, until vegetables are tender and slightly browned. Serve with grilled coleslaw.

Makes 4 to 6 main-course servings.

Grilled Coleslaw

Cut 1 small cabbage into sixths; core. Cut half red onion into 3 wedges. Grill cabbage and onion on greased grill over medium heat until outer layers start to soften, about 10 minutes. Thinly slice. Toss together cabbage; onion; 1 large carrot, grated; 2 tbsp each mayonnaise and cider vinegar; and ¼ tsp each salt, pepper and celery seed.

Makes 4 to 6 side-dish servings.

PER EACH OF 6 SERVINGS WITH GRILLED COLESLAW: about 201 cal, 9 g pro, 10 g total fat (2 g sat. fat), 23 g carb, 4 g fibre, 2 mg chol, 639 mg sodium, 575 mg potassium. % RDI: 22% calcium, 24% iron, 31% vit A, 197% vit C, 28% folate.

Sweet & Tangy Sausage Pepper Kabobs

You can use any type of sausage for these glazed kabobs – make sure to try them with Hot Italian Sausages (page 141) or Pork, Apple, Sage & Stilton Sausages (page 144). Using metal skewers saves you the 30 minutes it would take to soak bamboo skewers.

1 lb (450 g) **mild Italian sausages,** cut into 24 pieces

2 **Cubanelle peppers,** seeded and cut into 32 pieces

1 **sweet red pepper,** seeded and cut into 32 pieces

1 **red onion,** cut into chunks

2 tbsp **extra-virgin olive oil**

2 tbsp **balsamic vinegar**

1½ tsp packed **brown sugar**

½ tsp each **salt, pepper** and **dried oregano**

Alternately thread pieces of sausage, Cubanelle peppers, red pepper and onion onto 8 metal skewers.

Whisk together oil, vinegar, sugar, salt, pepper and oregano; brush half over skewers.

Grill, covered, on greased grill over medium-high heat, turning once and brushing with remaining oil mixture, until sausages are no longer pink in centre, 12 to 15 minutes.

Makes 4 main-course servings.

PER SERVING: about 335 cal, 18 g pro, 23 g total fat (7 g sat. fat), 15 g carb, 2 g fibre, 48 mg chol, 863 mg sodium, 354 mg potassium. % RDI: 4% calcium, 13% iron, 12% vit A, 110% vit C, 10% folate.

Grilled Sausage Spiedini

Serve these brochettes with mustard, Balsamic Grilled Peppers (below) and a juicy tomato salad. Grill the peppers first so that they cool down enough to allow peeling.

1 lb (450 g) **Hot Italian Sausages** (page 141) or other Italian sausages

1 piece (8 inches/20 cm) **baguette,** cut into 1-inch (2.5 cm) cubes

Half **red onion,** cut into 1-inch (2.5 cm) pieces

2 tbsp **extra-virgin olive oil**

1 clove **garlic,** pressed or minced

Pinch each **salt** and **pepper**

Prick sausages with fork. Microwave, covered, at high until no longer pink, about 5 minutes. Cut into 1½-inch (4 cm) pieces.

Alternately thread sausage, bread and onion onto skewers. Mix together oil, garlic, salt and pepper; brush over bread. Grill, covered, on greased grill over medium heat, turning often, until browned and onion is tender, about 10 minutes.

Makes 4 main-course servings.

Balsamic Grilled Peppers

Seed, core and cut 3 sweet peppers into eighths. Grill, covered, on greased grill over medium-high heat, turning once, until tender, about 10 minutes. Peel if desired. Toss together peppers, 2 tbsp balsamic vinegar, 1 tbsp each chopped fresh basil and extra-virgin olive oil, and pinch each granulated sugar, salt and pepper.

Makes 4 side-dish servings.

PER SERVING (WITHOUT PEPPERS): about 354 cal, 19 g pro, 23 g total fat (7 g sat. fat), 17 g carb, 1 g fibre, 48 mg chol, 854 mg sodium. % RDI: 4% calcium, 14% iron, 5% vit C, 11% folate.

Adana Lamb Kabobs

These beautifully spiced kabobs, from the Turkish city of Adana, are typically grilled on long metal skewers and served with Turkish Onion Salad (below), and sliced cucumbers and tomatoes drizzled with extra-virgin olive oil.

1 lb (450 g) **ground lamb**

1 **small onion,** minced

1 large clove **garlic,** pressed or minced

½ cup finely chopped **fresh parsley**

⅓ cup puréed **roasted red pepper**

1½ tsp **ground coriander**

1 tsp **ground cumin**

1 tsp **salt**

1 tsp **hot paprika,** or ¾ tsp sweet paprika and ¼ tsp cayenne pepper

¼ tsp **pepper**

1 tbsp **olive oil** (approx)

Mix together lamb, onion, garlic, parsley, red pepper purée, coriander, cumin, salt, paprika and pepper until well combined. Cover and refrigerate for 2 hours or, preferably, overnight.

With hands, knead meat and shape into tight 1-inch (2.5 cm) diameter cylinders around long metal skewers, each about two-thirds length of skewer. Brush with oil to coat lightly. Grill, covered, on greased grill over medium heat, turning occasionally, until no longer pink inside or instant-read thermometer registers 160°F (71°C), about 10 minutes.

Makes 4 to 6 main-course servings.

Turkish Onion Salad

Mix 3 cups thinly sliced Spanish onion, sweet onion or white onion with ½ tsp salt, using hands to rub in; let stand for 30 minutes. Rinse; drain well, squeezing out excess moisture. Toss together onions, 1 tbsp lemon juice, 1½ tsp ground sumac and pinch salt until coated. Toss in 3 tbsp chopped fresh parsley or dill and 1 tsp extra-virgin olive oil. Let stand for 5 minutes before serving.

Makes 4 to 6 side-dish servings.

PER EACH OF 6 SERVINGS WITH ONION SALAD: about 208 cal, 14 g pro, 14 g total fat (5 g sat. fat), 8 g carb, 2 g fibre, 51 mg chol, 626 mg sodium, 348 mg potassium. % RDI: 4% calcium, 14% iron, 12% vit A, 58% vit C, 17% folate.

Lamb Koftas on Rosemary

Serve these fabulous herb-infused koftas with thick plain yogurt and grilled pitas.

4 branches (each 10 inches/25 cm)
    fresh rosemary

1 tbsp **coriander seeds**

2 tsp **cumin seeds**

¼ cup **pine nuts**

½ cup chopped **fresh mint**

2 tsp grated **lemon zest**

4 tsp **lemon juice**

2 cloves **garlic,** minced

½ tsp each **salt** and **pepper**

1 **egg,** lightly beaten

1 lb (450 g) **ground lamb**

Soak rosemary in cold water for 30 minutes.

Meanwhile, in dry skillet over medium heat, toast coriander and cumin seeds until fragrant, about 1 minute. Transfer to mortar and pestle or spice grinder; crush until fine. Transfer to large bowl.

In same skillet, toast pine nuts over medium heat until golden, about 2 minutes. Transfer to mortar and pestle or spice grinder and lightly crush; add to bowl. Stir in mint, lemon zest and juice, garlic, salt, pepper and egg; mix in lamb. Divide into 8 portions; shape 2 around each rosemary branch, pressing to form two 4-inch (10 cm) long sausage-shaped ovals. Refrigerate for 30 minutes.

Grill, covered, on greased grill over medium-high heat, turning once, until no longer pink inside or instant-read thermometer inserted in centre registers 160°F (71°C), 12 to 15 minutes.

Makes 4 main-course servings.

PER SERVING: about 267 cal, 25 g pro, 18 g total fat (5 g sat. fat), 5 g carb, 2 g fibre, 102 mg chol, 476 mg sodium, 454 mg potassium. % RDI: 6% calcium, 28% iron, 5% vit A, 8% vit C, 20% folate.

Sage Lamb Kabobs

Cubes of richly flavoured lamb shoulder really soak up simple Italian seasonings.

2 tbsp **olive oil**

2 tbsp thinly sliced **fresh sage leaves**

1 tsp minced **garlic**

½ tsp **salt**

½ tsp **pepper**

1 lb (450 g) **lamb shoulder,** cut into 1-inch (2.5 cm) cubes

Mix together oil, sage, garlic, salt and pepper; toss with lamb until coated. Cover and marinate, refrigerated, for 4 hours or overnight.

Thread onto skewers. Grill, covered, on greased grill over medium-high heat, turning often, until medium-rare, 8 to 10 minutes.

Makes 4 main-course servings.

PER SERVING: about 244 cal, 22 g pro, 17 g total fat (4 g sat. fat), 1 g carb, trace fibre, 78 mg chol, 362 mg sodium, 327 mg potassium. % RDI: 3% calcium, 12% iron, 8% folate.

Herbed Lamb Kabobs

Anchovies add a salty, savoury note to these kabobs, and even people who don't like seafood won't be able to discern any fishy taste.

2 cloves **garlic,** smashed

2 **anchovy fillets**

1 **green hot pepper,** seeded and chopped

½ cup chopped **fresh cilantro**

⅓ cup packed **fresh mint**

¼ cup chopped **onion**

3 tbsp **extra-virgin olive oil**

2 tbsp **lemon juice** or lime juice

1 tbsp chopped **fresh ginger**

2 tsp **fennel seeds**

1 tsp **salt**

½ tsp **ground cumin**

¼ tsp **pepper**

Pinch **ground cloves**

12 **mushrooms**

1½ lb (675 g) **boneless lamb leg** or shoulder, cut into 1-inch (2.5 cm) cubes

In food processor, purée together garlic, anchovies, hot pepper, cilantro, mint, onion, half of the oil, the lemon juice, ginger, fennel seeds, salt, cumin, pepper and cloves. Transfer 1 tbsp to bowl; toss with mushrooms and remaining oil. In separate bowl, toss lamb with remaining garlic mixture. Marinate for 20 minutes or, covered and refrigerated, up to 8 hours.

Alternately thread lamb and mushrooms onto skewers. Grill, covered, on greased grill over medium-high heat, turning often, until medium-rare, 8 to 10 minutes.

Makes 4 to 6 main-course servings.

PER EACH OF 6 SERVINGS: about 213 cal, 22 g pro, 12 g total fat (3 g sat. fat), 4 g carb, 1 g fibre, 76 mg chol, 452 mg sodium. % RDI: 3% calcium, 20% iron, 2% vit A, 7% vit C, 4% folate.

Lamb Kabobs With Kachumber Salad

An uncomplicated Indian marinade flavours and tenderizes these lamb kabobs. Serve with yogurt and warm naan.

1 cup **Balkan-style plain yogurt**

2 cloves **garlic,** minced

1 tbsp grated **fresh ginger**

1 tbsp **vegetable oil**

1 tsp **ground cumin**

1 tsp **ground coriander**

1 tsp **turmeric**

1 tsp **lime juice**

½ tsp **salt**

2½ lb (1.125 kg) **boneless lamb leg** or shoulder, cut into 1½-inch (4 cm) cubes

KACHUMBER SALAD:

1 cup coarsely chopped **cucumber**

1 cup coarsely chopped **red onion**

1 cup coarsely chopped **tomato**

2 tbsp coarsely chopped **fresh cilantro**

2 tbsp **lime juice**

1 **green hot pepper,** chopped

¼ tsp **granulated sugar**

¼ tsp **salt**

¼ tsp **cayenne pepper**

Drain yogurt in cheesecloth-lined sieve set over bowl for 30 minutes. Transfer yogurt to clean bowl, discarding whey. Stir in garlic, ginger, oil, cumin, coriander, turmeric, lime juice and salt; toss with lamb until coated. Cover and marinate, refrigerated, for 15 minutes or up to 8 hours.

Kachumber Salad: Toss together cucumber, onion, tomato, cilantro, lime juice, hot pepper, sugar, salt and cayenne pepper.

Thread lamb onto skewers. Grill, covered, on greased grill over medium-high heat, turning once, until medium-rare, about 10 minutes. Serve with kachumber salad.

Makes 6 to 8 main-course servings.

PER EACH OF 8 SERVINGS: about 227 cal, 27 g pro, 10 g total fat (4 g sat. fat), 6 g carb, 1 g fibre, 97 mg chol, 269 mg sodium, 335 mg potassium. % RDI: 6% calcium, 18% iron, 4% vit A, 10% vit C, 5% folate.

Ginger Soy Chicken Skewers

Ginger and soy sauce are the perfect partners for tender, moist chicken thighs. Serve with steamed rice and a simple green salad.

¼ cup **sodium-reduced soy sauce**

4 tsp **granulated sugar**

4 tsp **sesame oil**

2 cloves **garlic,** pressed or minced

1 tbsp minced **fresh ginger**

¼ tsp **hot pepper flakes**

8 **boneless skinless chicken thighs,** quartered

1 **sweet onion,** quartered

8 **green onions,** cut into 1½-inch (4 cm) pieces

Mix together soy sauce, sugar, sesame oil, garlic, ginger and hot pepper flakes until sugar is dissolved; toss with chicken until coated. Marinate for 20 minutes.

Separate sweet onion quarters into pieces 3 layers thick; toss together sweet onion, green onions, chicken and marinade until coated. Alternately thread chicken, onion and green onions onto skewers.

Grill, covered, on greased grill over medium heat, turning once, until juices run clear when chicken is pierced, 12 to 15 minutes.

Makes 4 main-course servings.

PER SERVING: about 236 cal, 24 g pro, 11 g total fat (2 g sat. fat), 11 g carb, 1 g fibre, 95 mg chol, 636 mg sodium. % RDI: 4% calcium, 15% iron, 5% vit A, 13% vit C, 13% folate.

Chicken Teriyaki Skewers

This recipe makes more teriyaki sauce than you need. Refrigerate the extra for later. If you aren't fond of chicken livers, omit them and use double the amount of thighs.

8 oz (225 g) **boneless skinless chicken thighs,** cut into bite-size pieces

1 bunch **green onions,** cut into 1½-inch (4 cm) pieces

8 oz (225 g) **chicken livers**

QUICK TERIYAKI SAUCE:

½ cup **soy sauce**

⅓ cup **mirin**

2 tbsp **granulated sugar**

2 tbsp **sake** (optional)

2 slices **fresh ginger**

1 tbsp **cornstarch**

Quick Teriyaki Sauce: In saucepan, bring soy sauce, mirin, sugar, sake (if using), ginger and ¾ cup water to boil. Reduce heat and simmer until reduced to about 1 cup, about 10 minutes. Whisk 2 tbsp cold water with cornstarch; add to pan and cook, stirring, until thickened. Discard ginger. Let cool.

Alternately thread chicken and half of the onions onto 4 skewers. Repeat with livers and remaining onions.

Grill, covered, on greased grill over medium-high heat, turning halfway through and brushing with about half of the teriyaki sauce, until juices run clear when chicken is pierced, about 8 minutes for thighs and 4 minutes for livers. Brush with more teriyaki sauce, if desired.

Makes 4 main-course servings.

PER SERVING: about 178 cal, 22 g pro, 5 g total fat (2 g sat. fat), 8 g carb, 1 g fibre, 306 mg chol, 963 mg sodium, 268 mg potassium. % RDI: 3% calcium, 34% iron, 209% vit A, 15% vit C, 155% folate.

Lemon Chicken Kabobs

This brightly flavoured chicken is a cinch to put together – even for a quick weeknight meal. Or make it the night before and refrigerate it to grill in a flash.

2 tbsp **olive oil**

2 tbsp **lemon juice**

3 cloves **garlic,** pressed or minced

½ tsp **dried thyme**

½ tsp **salt**

¼ tsp **pepper**

1 lb (450 g) **boneless skinless chicken breasts,** cut into 1-inch (2.5 cm) cubes

1 **sweet green pepper** or 2 banana peppers, cut into 1-inch (2.5 cm) pieces

Mix together oil, lemon juice, garlic, thyme, salt and pepper; toss with chicken until coated. Marinate for 15 minutes or, covered and refrigerated, up to 1 day.

Alternately thread chicken and green pepper onto skewers. Grill, covered, on greased grill over medium-high heat, turning occasionally, until chicken is browned and no longer pink inside, about 12 minutes.

Makes 4 main-course servings.

PER SERVING: about 189 cal, 26 g pro, 8 g total fat (1 g sat. fat), 3 g carb, 1 g fibre, 66 mg chol, 303 mg sodium. % RDI: 1% calcium, 6% iron, 2% vit A, 40% vit C, 4% folate.

Chicken & Mango Kabobs

These pretty tropical kabobs are slightly sweet, mildly tart and just a little bit spicy.

1 tsp grated **lime zest**

¼ cup **lime juice**

2 tbsp **peanut oil** or vegetable oil

3 cloves **garlic,** minced

2 tsp **chili powder**

½ tsp **salt**

¼ tsp **cayenne pepper**

1 lb (450 g) **boneless skinless chicken breasts,** cut into 1-inch (2.5 cm) cubes

2 tsp **liquid honey**

12 red or white **pearl onions,** or 1 small red or sweet onion, cut into 1-inch (2.5 cm) pieces

2 **mangoes,** cut into ¾-inch (2 cm) cubes

1 **sweet red pepper,** cut into ¾-inch (2 cm) pieces

Mix together lime zest and juice, oil, garlic, chili powder, salt and cayenne; toss half with chicken until coated. Stir honey into remaining marinade; set aside. Marinate chicken for 20 minutes or, covered and refrigerated, up to 4 hours.

Meanwhile, in saucepan of boiling water, boil unpeeled pearl onions for 2 minutes; drain. Slip off skins.

Alternately thread mango and red pepper onto skewers; brush with half of the reserved marinade. Alternately thread chicken and onions onto separate skewers. Grill, covered, on greased grill over medium-high heat, turning once and basting with remaining honey marinade, until mango is softened and chicken is no longer pink inside, about 8 minutes.

Makes 4 main-course servings.

PER SERVING: about 291 cal, 26 g pro, 8 g total fat (1 g sat. fat), 31 g carb, 4 g fibre, 63 mg chol, 308 mg sodium. % RDI: 4% calcium, 7% iron, 45% vit A, 128% vit C, 12% folate.

Chicken Tikka

Compete with the best Indian restaurants with these authentic, ever-popular kabobs. The ingredient list might seem long, but the method is simple and straightforward.

¼ cup chopped **fresh cilantro**

¼ cup chopped **fresh mint**

¼ cup **lemon juice**

¼ cup **full-fat plain yogurt**

3 tbsp chopped **fresh ginger**

2 tbsp **chickpea flour** (optional)

8 cloves **garlic,** smashed

1½ tsp **salt**

1 tsp **ground coriander**

½ tsp each **ground cardamom, cayenne pepper, ground cumin, turmeric** and **pepper**

½ tsp each **ground mace** and **nutmeg** (or ¾ tsp nutmeg)

3 tbsp **peanut oil** or vegetable oil

4 **boneless skinless chicken breasts,** cut into 8 cubes each, or 12 boneless skinless chicken thighs, cut into 3 pieces each

GARNISH:

1 **small red onion,** thinly sliced

½ tsp **salt**

¼ cup **lemon juice**

Fresh cilantro sprigs

In blender or food processor, purée together cilantro, mint, lemon juice, yogurt, ginger, chickpea flour (if using), garlic, salt, coriander, cardamom, cayenne, cumin, turmeric, pepper, mace and nutmeg; mix in oil. Toss with chicken until coated. Cover and marinate, refrigerated, for 3 to 4 hours.

Garnish: Meanwhile, mix onion with salt; pour lemon juice over top. Let stand for 30 minutes; drain.

Thread chicken onto skewers, leaving about ½ inch (1 cm) between pieces. Grill, covered, on greased grill over medium-high heat, turning once, until no longer pink inside, 8 to 10 minutes.

Garnish chicken with onion mixture and cilantro.

Makes 4 main-course servings.

PER SERVING: about 288 cal, 32 g pro, 13 g total fat (3 g sat. fat), 10 g carb, 2 g fibre, 82 mg chol, 924 mg sodium. % RDI: 6% calcium, 11% iron, 3% vit A, 20% vit C, 7% folate.

Chicken Bacon Brochettes

Traditional English flavourings and crisp bacon give a boost to mild chicken breast.

2 tbsp **vegetable oil**

2 tsp **Worcestershire sauce**

2 tsp **soy sauce**

½ tsp **malt vinegar** or other vinegar

¼ tsp **pepper**

1 lb (450 g) **boneless skinless chicken breasts,** cut into twelve 1½-inch (4 cm) cubes

12 **large mushrooms**

2 tsp **lemon juice**

¼ tsp **salt**

4 slices **bacon,** cut into thirds

4 **green onions,** cut into thirds

Mix together half of the oil, the Worcestershire sauce, soy sauce, vinegar and pepper; toss with chicken until coated. Marinate for 20 minutes.

Meanwhile, toss together mushrooms, remaining oil, lemon juice and salt; let stand for 20 minutes. Reserving remaining marinade, wrap each chicken cube in bacon; thread onto skewers alternately with mushrooms and green onions.

Grill, covered, on greased grill over medium-high heat for 5 minutes. Turn and brush with marinade. Grill until chicken is no longer pink inside, 5 to 7 minutes.

Makes 4 main-course servings.

PER SERVING: about 245 cal, 29 g pro, 12 g total fat (3 g sat. fat), 5 g carb, 1 g fibre, 72 mg chol, 509 mg sodium. % RDI: 2% calcium, 13% iron, 1% vit A, 7% vit C, 9% folate.

Chinese Seasoned Chicken Kabobs

A base of seasoned oil in the marinade gives this chicken a rich yet subtle flavour.

1½ lb (675 g) **boneless skinless chicken breasts** or thighs, cut into 1-inch (2.5 cm) cubes

2 **Cubanelle peppers,** cut into 1½-inch (4 cm) pieces

Half **sweet onion,** cut into 1½-inch (4 cm) pieces

MARINADE:

3 tbsp **peanut oil** or vegetable oil

4 tsp **coriander seeds**

4 tsp **black peppercorns**

4 **dried hot peppers**

3 cloves **garlic,** smashed

8 slices **fresh ginger**

1 tbsp **soy sauce**

2 tsp **Chinese black vinegar** or balsamic vinegar

2 tsp **sesame oil**

Marinade: In small skillet, heat oil over medium-low heat; fry coriander seeds, peppercorns and hot peppers until hot peppers darken. Add garlic and ginger; fry until garlic turns golden. Strain oil through fine sieve into large heatproof bowl; discard solids. Let cool until warm. Whisk in soy sauce, vinegar and sesame oil.

Toss together marinade, chicken, peppers and onion until coated. Marinate for 30 minutes or, covered and refrigerated, up to 12 hours.

Alternately thread chicken, peppers and onion onto skewers. Grill, covered, on greased grill over medium-high heat until chicken is no longer pink inside, about 12 minutes.

Makes 4 to 6 main-course servings.

PER EACH OF 6 SERVINGS: about 208 cal, 26 g pro, 10 g total fat (2 g sat. fat), 3 g carb, trace fibre, 67 mg chol, 211 mg sodium. % RDI: 1% calcium, 4% iron, 1% vit A, 5% vit C, 5% folate.

Peanut & Coconut Chicken Skewers

Sliced cucumber, jicama and red onions tossed with lime juice, and a touch of sugar and salt, is a crispy and fresh accompaniment to these tropical skewers.

1½ lb (675 g) **boneless skinless chicken breasts,** cut into 1-inch (2.5 cm) cubes

¼ cup **shredded coconut**

6 **long hot peppers,** cut into 1-inch (2.5 cm) lengths

1 **lime,** cut into wedges

PEANUT SAUCE:

1½ tsp **peanut oil** or vegetable oil

4 cloves **garlic,** minced

½ cup chopped **shallots** or onion

2 tsp **ground coriander**

1 tsp **ground cumin**

¾ tsp **salt**

½ tsp each **ground ginger, turmeric** and **sweet paprika**

¼ tsp **cayenne pepper**

¾ cup **coconut milk**

2 tsp packed **brown sugar**

½ tsp grated **lime zest** or lemon zest

3 tbsp **crunchy natural peanut butter**

1 tbsp **lime juice** or lemon juice

Peanut Sauce: In small saucepan, heat oil over medium heat; fry garlic and shallots until softened, about 2 minutes. Stir in coriander, cumin, salt, ginger, turmeric, paprika and cayenne; cook, stirring, until fragrant, about 2 minutes. Stir in coconut milk, sugar and lime zest; cook, stirring, just until boiling. Reduce heat and simmer for 2 minutes. Stir in peanut butter and lime juice; let cool.

Toss chicken with ⅓ cup of the peanut sauce until coated. In skillet, toast coconut over medium-low heat until golden, about 6 minutes.

Alternately thread chicken and hot peppers onto skewers. Grill, covered, on greased grill over medium-high heat, turning often, until chicken is no longer pink inside, about 10 minutes.

Transfer skewers to serving platter along with lime wedges. Brush with ¼ cup of the remaining peanut sauce; sprinkle with some of the toasted coconut.

Transfer remaining peanut sauce to serving bowl; sprinkle with remaining coconut. Serve with chicken.

Makes 6 main-course servings.

PER SERVING: about 281 cal, 29 g pro, 14 g total fat (8 g sat. fat), 10 g carb, 1 g fibre, 67 mg chol, 401 mg sodium. % RDI: 3% calcium, 16% iron, 3% vit A, 8% vit C, 9% folate.

Marmalade-Glazed Chicken Thighs

Orange marmalade is delightfully sweet-tart and makes a delicious glaze on tender grilled chicken thighs.

2 tbsp **lemon juice**

1 tbsp **extra-virgin olive oil**

2 tsp chopped **fresh rosemary**

1 clove **garlic,** minced

¼ tsp each **salt** and **pepper**

8 **boneless skinless chicken thighs,** halved crosswise

2 tbsp **orange marmalade**

Whisk together lemon juice, oil, rosemary, garlic, salt and pepper; toss with chicken until coated. Marinate for 15 minutes or, covered and refrigerated, up to 8 hours.

Reserving any remaining marinade, thread chicken onto double-pronged bamboo skewers or 8 pairs of soaked wooden skewers; brush with marinade. Grill, covered, on greased grill over medium heat, turning once, until juices run clear when chicken is pierced, 12 to 15 minutes.

Meanwhile, microwave marmalade, covered, at high until melted, about 30 seconds. (Or heat in small saucepan over low heat until melted.) Brush skewers with marmalade; grill, turning once, for 1 minute.

Makes 4 main-course servings.

PER SERVING: about 204 cal, 22 g pro, 9 g total fat (2 g sat. fat), 8 g carb, trace fibre, 95 mg chol, 248 mg sodium, 285 mg potassium. % RDI: 2% calcium, 9% iron, 2% vit A, 12% vit C, 5% folate.

Caesar Turkey Brochettes

The clam and tomato juices of one of Canada's favourite drinks are mimicked in this marinated turkey that's basted with an oyster sauce–flavoured barbecue sauce.

2 tbsp **lime juice**

2 tbsp **vodka**

1 tbsp **sesame oil**

¾ tsp **celery salt**

¼ tsp **pepper**

1 **boneless turkey breast,** skinned, or 4 turkey thighs, skinned and boned, cut into 1½-inch (4 cm) cubes

2 ribs **celery** or banana peppers, cut into 1½-inch (4 cm) chunks

1 **red onion,** cut into 1½-inch (4 cm) chunks

BASTING SAUCE:

⅓ cup **ketchup**

3 tbsp **oyster sauce**

1 tsp **Worcestershire sauce**

½ tsp **hot pepper sauce**

Mix together lime juice, vodka, sesame oil, celery salt and pepper; toss with turkey until coated. Marinate for 30 minutes or, covered and refrigerated, up to 8 hours.

Alternately thread turkey, celery and red onion onto skewers.

Basting Sauce: Mix together ketchup, oyster sauce, Worcestershire sauce and hot pepper sauce.

Grill skewers, covered, on greased grill over medium heat, turning often and brushing with basting sauce during last 5 minutes, until glazed and turkey is no longer pink inside, about 18 minutes.

Makes 6 to 8 main-course servings.

PER EACH OF 8 SERVINGS: about 186 cal, 30 g pro, 3 g total fat (1 g sat. fat), 9 g carb, 1 g fibre, 79 mg chol, 489 mg sodium. % RDI: 3% calcium, 14% iron, 3% vit A, 42% vit C, 8% folate.

From top: Mojito Rack of Lamb (page 225) and Caesar Turkey Brochettes (opposite)

Ancho Turkey Waves

Sweet and moderately hot ancho chili powder adds good flavour to mild turkey breast. Bonus: The long, thin waves cook more quickly than cubes.

1 lb (450 g) **boneless skinless turkey breast**

2 tbsp **vegetable oil**

2 tbsp **red wine vinegar**

2 cloves **garlic,** minced

2 tsp **ancho chili powder**

½ tsp **dried oregano**

½ tsp **salt**

Pinch **granulated sugar**

Slice turkey crosswise into ¼-inch (5 mm) thick strips. Mix together oil, vinegar, garlic, ancho chili powder, oregano, salt and sugar; toss with turkey until coated. Cover and marinate, refrigerated, for 2 to 6 hours.

Thread into wave shapes on skewers. Grill, covered, on greased grill over medium-high heat, turning once, until no longer pink inside, about 6 minutes.

Makes 4 main-course servings.

VARIATION
Chipotle Turkey Waves
Substitute 1½ tsp chipotle chili powder for the ancho chili powder.

PER SERVING: about 170 cal, 27 g pro, 6 g total fat (1 g sat. fat), 1 g carb, trace fibre, 74 mg chol, 269 mg sodium. % RDI: 1% calcium, 11% iron, 3% vit A, 2% vit C, 3% folate.

Salmon Kabobs With Baby Bok Choy

Serve these sweet and succulent kabobs with brown or wild rice. If the bok choy are tiny, you'll need eight instead of four.

4 tsp **soy sauce**

1 tbsp **oyster sauce**

2 tsp each **lemon juice** and **sesame oil**

1 tsp **liquid honey**

¼ tsp **hot pepper flakes**

4 **skinless salmon fillets,** each about 6 oz (170 g), quartered crosswise

BABY BOK CHOY:

1 tbsp **butter**

1 **shallot,** minced

2 tsp minced **fresh ginger**

1 clove **garlic,** minced

4 **baby bok choy,** halved lengthwise

¼ tsp **salt**

1 tsp **sesame oil**

In shallow dish, mix together soy sauce, oyster sauce, lemon juice, sesame oil, honey and hot pepper flakes. Add salmon, turning to coat; marinate for 10 minutes.

Thread salmon onto skewers. Grill, covered, on greased grill over medium-high heat, turning once, until grill marked and fish flakes easily when tested, 8 to 10 minutes.

Baby Bok Choy: Meanwhile, in skillet, melt butter over medium-high heat; sauté shallot, ginger and garlic for 1 minute. Add bok choy, ¼ cup water and salt; cover and steam for 2 minutes. Uncover and cook until tender-crisp, 2 to 3 minutes. Drizzle with sesame oil. Serve with salmon.

Makes 4 main-course servings.

PER SERVING: about 338 cal, 31 g pro, 22 g total fat (6 g sat. fat), 4 g carb, 1 g fibre, 91 mg chol, 483 mg sodium, 835 mg potassium. % RDI: 9% calcium, 10% iron, 39% vit A, 43% vit C, 36% folate.

Tamarind-Glazed Salmon Kabobs

Rich Canadian salmon takes as naturally to a tasty sweet-and-sour southeast Asian–style glaze as a hot dog does to mustard.

1 lb (450 g) **skinless salmon fillet,** cut into 1½-inch (4 cm) cubes

1 clove **garlic,** pressed or minced

1 tbsp minced **fresh cilantro**

1 tbsp **peanut oil** or vegetable oil

¼ tsp each **salt** and **pepper**

4 **green onions,** cut into 1½-inch (4 cm) lengths

Fresh cilantro sprigs

TAMARIND GLAZE:

1 tbsp **peanut oil** or vegetable oil

3 tbsp **seedless tamarind paste**

2 tbsp **palm sugar** or packed brown sugar

1 tbsp **soy sauce**

1 tsp grated **fresh ginger**

¾ tsp **chili paste** (such as sambal oelek)

2 tsp **lemon juice**

Toss together salmon, garlic, cilantro, oil, salt and pepper until coated. Marinate for 15 minutes.

Tamarind Glaze: Meanwhile, in small saucepan, heat oil over medium heat; add tamarind, sugar, soy sauce and ginger. Bring to boil, stirring until sugar is dissolved; reduce heat to low and simmer, stirring, for 3 minutes. Remove from heat; stir in chili paste. Let cool; stir in lemon juice.

Alternately thread salmon and onion onto skewers. Grill on greased grill over medium-high heat, turning occasionally, until just a hint of pink remains in centre of salmon, about 3 minutes. Turn, brushing both sides with some of the tamarind glaze; grill for 1 minute. Turn, brushing both sides with remaining tamarind glaze; grill for 1 minute. Garnish with cilantro sprigs.

Makes 4 main-course servings.

PER SERVING: about 291 cal, 20 g pro, 18 g total fat (3 g sat. fat), 12 g carb, 1 g fibre, 56 mg chol, 431 mg sodium, 463 mg potassium. % RDI: 3% calcium, 7% iron, 3% vit A, 10% vit C, 18% folate.

Soy-Glazed Halibut Kabobs

Pacific halibut is one of North America's finest sustainable fishes. It has a rich yet subtle flavour, so a simple glaze is all it needs.

5 tsp **peanut oil** or vegetable oil

1 clove **garlic,** minced

1 tsp minced **fresh ginger**

1 **fresh bay leaf** or dried bay leaf

¼ cup **soy sauce**

1 tbsp **liquid honey**

1 tbsp **lemon juice**

1 tsp **cornstarch**

1 lb (450 g) **skinless halibut fillet,** cut into 1-inch (2.5 cm) cubes

1 **Asian (long) eggplant,** cut into 1-inch (2.5 cm) slices

⅓ cup **sweet onion** pieces (1 inch/2.5 cm)

½ tsp each **five-spice powder** and **salt**

1 tbsp toasted **sesame seeds**

1 tbsp thinly sliced **green onion**

In small saucepan, heat 2 tsp of the oil over medium heat; fry garlic, ginger and bay leaf until fragrant, about 1 minute. Stir in soy sauce, 3 tbsp water, honey and lemon juice; simmer for 3 minutes. Mix cornstarch with 2 tsp water; stir into sauce. Simmer for 2 minutes. Let cool.

Toss together halibut, eggplant, sweet onion, five-spice powder, salt and remaining oil until coated; thread onto skewers. Grill on greased grill over medium-high heat, turning occasionally, until fish flakes easily and eggplant is tender, 6 to 7 minutes. Brush with glaze; grill, brushing and turning often, until well glazed, about 3 minutes. Garnish with sesame seeds and green onion.

Makes 4 main-course servings.

PER SERVING: about 234 cal, 26 g pro, 10 g total fat (2 g sat. fat), 11 g carb, 2 g fibre, 36 mg chol, 1,251 mg sodium, 630 mg potassium. % RDI: 6% calcium, 12% iron, 5% vit A, 3% vit C, 11% folate.

Pickerel With Charmoula

Charmoula is a green sauce from Morocco that's often used to flavour fish. Its fresh herbal notes and spicy undertones are a good match for sweet Canadian pickerel.

1½ lb (675 g) **skin-on pickerel fillets,** or perch or other freshwater fish fillets

¼ tsp each **salt** and **pepper**

CHARMOULA:

½ cup finely chopped **fresh parsley**

½ cup finely chopped **fresh cilantro**

2 **green onions,** finely chopped

¼ cup **extra-virgin olive oil**

3 tbsp **lemon juice**

2 cloves **garlic,** minced

1 tsp **ground cumin**

1 tsp **sweet paprika**

¼ tsp **cayenne pepper**

¼ tsp each **salt** and **pepper**

Charmoula: Mix together parsley, cilantro, green onions, oil, lemon juice, garlic, cumin, paprika, cayenne pepper, salt and pepper; set aside.

Divide fish into 4 servings. Thread each crosswise onto 2 skewers; sprinkle with salt and pepper.

Grill, covered and skin side down, on greased grill over medium-high heat, turning once, until fish flakes easily, about 5 minutes per ½ inch (1 cm) thickness. Top with some of the charmoula; serve remainder on side.

Makes 4 main-course servings.

PER SERVING: about 274 cal, 30 g pro, 16 g total fat (2 g sat. fat), 3 g carb, 1 g fibre, 129 mg chol, 374 mg sodium. % RDI: 18% calcium, 24% iron, 15% vit A, 27% vit C, 18% folate.

Glazes

Ginger Teriyaki Glaze

¼ cup **chicken broth** or vegetable broth

2 tbsp **soy sauce**

2 tbsp **sake,** dry sherry or apple juice

2 tbsp **corn syrup**

1 tbsp minced **fresh ginger**

2 tsp **cornstarch**

In small saucepan, bring broth, soy sauce, sake, corn syrup and ginger to boil; reduce heat and simmer for 5 minutes. Mix cornstarch with 2 tsp water; stir into sauce. Cook until thickened, about 30 seconds.

Makes about ⅓ cup.

Curry Glaze

2 tsp **vegetable oil**

2 tbsp minced **onion**

2 tbsp minced **fresh cilantro**

1 clove **garlic,** minced

2 tbsp **tomato paste**

4 tsp **curry paste**

1 tsp packed **brown sugar**

¼ cup **chicken broth** or vegetable broth

1 tbsp **cider vinegar**

2 tsp **cornstarch**

In small saucepan, heat oil over medium heat; fry onion, cilantro and garlic, stirring, until fragrant, about 1 minute. Stir in tomato paste, curry paste and sugar; cook for 1 minute. Stir in broth and vinegar; bring to boil. Reduce heat and simmer for 5 minutes. Mix cornstarch with 2 tsp water; stir into sauce. Cook until thickened, about 30 seconds.

Makes about ½ cup.

Glazed Fish Kabobs

Use saltwater fish, such as swordfish, Pacific halibut, kingfish or salmon, for these kabobs. Ask your fishmonger for sustainable choices caught in North America.

1 lb (450 g) **thick fish fillets,** cut into 1½-inch (4 cm) cubes

½ tsp **salt**

¼ tsp **pepper**

Half **onion,** cut into bite-size pieces

1 **sweet red pepper,** or sweet green or yellow pepper, cut into bite-size pieces

1 tbsp **vegetable oil**

Ginger Teriyaki Glaze or **Curry Glaze** (opposite)

Lemon wedges

Sprinkle fish with salt and pepper. Alternately thread fish, onion and red pepper onto skewers; brush with oil.

Grill, covered, on greased grill over medium-high heat, turning once, until fish is firm but starting to flake, about 7 minutes. Brush with glaze; grill for 2 minutes. Turn and brush with glaze; grill until fish flakes easily when tested, about 1 minute. Serve with lemon wedges.

Makes 4 main-course servings.

PER SERVING WITH GINGER TERIYAKI GLAZE: about 180 cal, 18 g pro, 5 g total fat (trace sat. fat), 14 g carb, 1 g fibre, 28 mg chol, 887 mg sodium. % RDI: 2% calcium, 6% iron, 12% vit A, 85% vit C, 7% folate.

PER SERVING WITH CURRY GLAZE: about 195 cal, 18 g pro, 19 g total fat (1 g sat. fat), 9 g carb, 1 g fibre, 29 mg chol, 364 mg sodium. % RDI: 2% calcium, 8% iron, 15% vit A, 92% vit C, 7% folate.

Greek-Style Seafood Kabobs

Ultrafresh seafood, simply seasoned, is a hallmark of Greek cuisine. Serve these simple skewers with Greek Village Salad (page 505) for a refreshing meal.

¼ cup **extra-virgin olive oil**

2 cloves **garlic,** minced

2 tsp minced **fresh thyme**

¼ tsp each **salt** and **pepper**

¼ tsp **dried marjoram** or oregano

6 oz (170 g) **skinless centre-cut salmon fillets,** cut into 1-inch (2.5 cm) cubes

6 oz (170 g) **sea scallops**

Half **sweet green pepper,** cut into 1-inch (2.5 cm) pieces

8 **raw extra jumbo shrimp** (size 16 to 20), peeled and deveined

Lemon wedges

Mix together oil, garlic, thyme, salt, pepper and marjoram; toss with salmon, scallops, green pepper and shrimp until coated. Marinate for 15 minutes.

Reserving any remaining marinade, alternately thread salmon, scallops, green pepper and shrimp loosely onto skewers; brush with marinade. Grill, covered, on greased grill over medium heat, turning once, until fish flakes easily when tested, 6 to 8 minutes. Serve with lemon wedges.

Makes 4 main-course servings.

PER SERVING: about 323 cal, 26 g pro, 22 g total fat (4 g sat. fat), 3 g carb, trace fibre, 88 mg chol, 414 mg sodium. % RDI: 4% calcium, 10% iron, 3% vit A, 25% vit C, 14% folate.

Sweet & Sour Shrimp Kabobs

A Malay-style tamarind glaze makes these shrimp-and-pineapple kabobs simply irresistible. Tamarind concentrate is seedless tamarind pulp mixed with a little water to make a thin paste. It's available in jars in the Asian-food section of some supermarkets and at most southeast Asian and Chinese grocery stores.

1½ lb (675 g) **raw extra jumbo shrimp** (size 16 to 20) or raw jumbo shrimp (size 21 to 25), peeled and deveined

Half **pineapple,** cut into 1-inch (2.5 cm) cubes

4 **green onions,** cut into 1½-inch (4 cm) pieces

2 tbsp ground **roasted peanuts**

GLAZE:

2 tbsp packed **brown sugar**

2 tbsp **tamarind concentrate**

2 tsp **Thai red curry paste**

2 tsp **peanut oil** or vegetable oil

2 tsp **fish sauce**

1½ tsp **curry powder**

Glaze: Mix together sugar, tamarind, curry paste, oil, fish sauce and curry powder until smooth.

Alternately thread shrimp, pineapple and onions onto skewers; brush with glaze. Grill on greased grill over high heat, turning once and brushing with remaining glaze, until shrimp are pink and opaque in centre, about 5 minutes. Sprinkle with peanuts.

Makes 4 to 6 main-course servings.

TIP

If you can't find tamarind concentrate, you can make your own for this recipe. Soak 2 tbsp seedless tamarind pulp in 2 tbsp boiling water until softened, then press through fine sieve, discarding solids.

PER EACH OF 6 SERVINGS: about 173 cal, 19 g pro, 5 g total fat (1 g sat. fat), 13 g carb, 1 g fibre, 129 mg chol, 287 mg sodium. % RDI: 6% calcium, 19% iron, 5% vit A, 22% vit C, 8% folate.

Shrimp Skewers With Cilantro & Almond Relish

Both the colour and flavour of these simply seasoned shrimp balance nicely with the lovely green relish.

1 lb (450 g) **raw extra jumbo shrimp** (size 16 to 20), peeled and deveined

1½ cloves **garlic,** pressed

1 tbsp **extra-virgin olive oil**

¼ tsp **salt**

¼ tsp **smoked paprika**

CILANTRO & ALMOND RELISH:

1 cup lightly packed chopped **fresh cilantro**

⅓ cup toasted **almonds**

¼ cup chopped **sweet onion**

½ tsp **salt**

Pinch **ground cumin**

Pinch **cayenne pepper**

¼ cup **extra-virgin olive oil**

2 tbsp **lemon juice**

Toss together shrimp, garlic, oil, salt and paprika until coated. Tail first, thread shrimp lengthwise through centre onto skewers. Marinate for 10 minutes or, covered and refrigerated, up to 8 hours.

Cilantro & Almond Relish: In food processor, pulse together cilantro, almonds, onion, salt, cumin and cayenne until finely minced; pulse in oil and lemon juice. Transfer to serving dish.

Grill shrimp on greased grill over high heat, turning once, until pink and opaque in centre, about 5 minutes. Serve with relish.

Makes 4 main-course servings.

PER SERVING: about 330 cal, 23 g pro, 25 g total fat (3 g sat. fat), 5 g carb, 2 g fibre, 150 mg chol, 583 mg sodium. % RDI: 8% calcium, 23% iron, 8% vit A, 8% vit C, 8% folate.

Seafood Kabobs With Saffron Aioli

If you make these kabobs with fish, choose a fairly firm-fleshed variety. Salmon is also nice – just cube the fillets with the skin on to help hold the pieces together on the grill.

12 oz (340 g) **raw jumbo shrimp** (size 21 to 25), peeled and deveined

12 oz (340 g) **sea scallops** (or firm-fleshed fish, cut into 1½-inch/4 cm cubes)

¼ cup **lemon juice**

½ tsp **salt**

2 tbsp **olive oil**

¼ tsp **pepper**

2 tbsp finely chopped **fresh parsley** or cilantro

SAFFRON AIOLI:

Pinch **saffron threads**

2 tbsp **extra-virgin olive oil**

2 tsp **lemon juice**

1 clove **garlic,** pressed or pounded into paste

Pinch **salt**

½ cup **mayonnaise**

Saffron Aioli: In dry small skillet over medium-low heat, toast saffron until fragrant and dried, 10 to 20 seconds; crumble finely into small bowl. Pour in 1 tsp boiling water; let cool. Whisk in oil, lemon juice, garlic and salt. In separate bowl, slowly whisk saffron mixture into mayonnaise.

Toss together shrimp, scallops, lemon juice and salt; marinate for 15 minutes. Drain; toss with oil and pepper until coated.

Alternately thread shrimp and scallops onto skewers. Grill on greased grill over high heat, turning once, until shrimp and scallops are opaque, about 6 minutes. Garnish with parsley and serve with saffron aioli.

Makes 4 to 6 main-course servings.

PER EACH OF 6 SERVINGS: about 304 cal, 20 g pro, 24 g total fat (4 g sat. fat), 2 g carb, trace fibre, 92 mg chol, 359 mg sodium, 306 mg potassium. % RDI: 3% calcium, 12% iron, 6% vit A, 5% vit C, 5% folate.

Shrimp & Mango Brochettes

If you like a little heat with your sweet, dip these simply spiced kabobs into Thai Sweet Chili Sauce (below). It's a perfect match for all kinds of grilled and fried foods.

1 firm **mango,** peeled, pitted and
　　cut into sixteen 1-inch (2.5 cm)
　　chunks

1 **sweet red pepper,** cut into
　　16 triangles

8 **okra pods,** trimmed and halved

8 **red pearl onions,** peeled
　　and halved

16 **raw jumbo shrimp** (size 21 to 25),
　　peeled and deveined

2 **limes,** each cut into 8 wedges

¼ cup **extra-virgin olive oil**

1 tsp **ground coriander**

½ tsp **ground cumin**

½ tsp **cayenne pepper**

½ tsp **salt**

Thread 1 piece each mango, red pepper, okra, onion, shrimp and lime onto each of 16 skewers.

Mix together oil, coriander, cumin, cayenne and salt; brush over skewers. Grill, covered, on greased grill over medium-high heat, turning once, until shrimp are pink and opaque in centre and vegetables are tender-crisp, about 5 minutes.

Makes 4 to 6 main-course servings.

Thai Sweet Chili Sauce

In saucepan, stirring constantly, bring ¾ cup unseasoned rice vinegar, ½ cup granulated sugar, ¼ cup water, 1 tbsp fish sauce and ¼ tsp salt to boil; reduce heat to medium and simmer, stirring often, until as thick as maple syrup, 10 to 15 minutes. Stir in 3 red finger hot peppers or 10 Thai bird's-eye peppers, seeded and chopped; and 3 cloves garlic, minced. Simmer for 3 minutes. Let cool. *(Make-ahead: Refrigerate for up to 1 month.)*

Makes about 1 cup.

PER EACH OF 6 SERVINGS (WITHOUT SAUCE): about 151 cal, 7 g pro, 10 g total fat (1 g sat. fat), 11 g carb, 2 g fibre, 43 mg chol, 236 mg sodium. % RDI: 3% calcium, 7% iron, 20% vit A, 78% vit C, 7% folate.

Miso-Orange Grilled Scallops

Japanese miso blended with orange makes a vibrant glaze and creates a beautiful contrast to the delicate ivory flesh of the scallops.

¼ cup red or white **miso paste**

2 tbsp **granulated sugar**

1 tsp grated **orange zest**

2 tbsp **orange juice**

12 oz (340 g) **sea scallops**

2 **green onions**

In small saucepan, heat miso, sugar, and orange zest and juice, stirring, over medium-low heat until smooth and sugar is dissolved, about 2 minutes. Set aside.

Pat scallops dry. Cut green onions into green and white parts; cut white parts into 8 pieces.

Alternately thread scallops and white parts of onions onto skewers; brush with miso mixture.

Grill, covered, on greased grill over medium-high heat, turning once, until miso is caramelized and scallops are opaque, about 6 minutes. Thinly slice green parts of onions; sprinkle over skewers before serving.

Makes 4 main-course servings.

PER SERVING: about 140 cal, 16 g pro, 2 g total fat (trace sat. fat), 14 g carb, 2 g fibre, 28 mg chol, 765 mg sodium. % RDI: 3% calcium, 6% iron, 1% vit A, 5% vit C, 8% folate.

Rosemary Beef Burgers With
Jalapeño Mayo (page 90)

burgers, sandwiches & sausages

Classic Backyard Burgers | 81

Brandy Dijon Beef Burgers | 83

Steak Burgers | 84

Puttanesca Burgers | 85

Stuffed Cheddar Burgers | 86

Shiitake Beef Burgers | 88

Argentine Burgers | 89

Rosemary Beef Burgers With
Jalapeño Mayo | 90

Jalapeño Cheeseburgers With
Tomato Salad | 92

Smoky Beef Burgers With
Chipotle Ketchup | 93

Hamburger Buns | 94

Stuffed Meatball Sliders | 95

Bison Burgers | 98

Veal & Gorgonzola Burgers
With Onions | 99

Italian Stuffed Veal Burgers | 100

Quick-Fix Burger Toppings | 101

Veal Patty Melts | 104

Flank Steak Sandwiches With
Pepper Sauce | 105

Cheesesteak Sandwiches
for Two | 106

Green Onion Pork Burgers | 109

Glazed Cheddar Pork Burgers | 110

Grilled Cubanos | 111

Curried Pork Burgers | 113

Juicy Pork Burgers | 114

Lamb Burgers | 115

Lamb Burgers With Grilled
Vegetables | 116

Herb & Spice Lamb Burgers | 118

Feta & Lamb Burger Pitas | 119

Venison Burgers With Red Wine
Mushrooms | 120

Grilled Prosciutto & Fig Sandwiches | 121

Gourmet Teriyaki Chicken
Sandwiches | 123

Grilled Chicken Banh Mi | 124

Bocconcini Chicken Burgers | 125

Thai-Style Grilled Chicken Wraps | 127

Grilled Salmon Patties | 129

Grilled Whitefish BLTs | 130

Grilled Salmon Sandwiches With
Bok Choy Slaw | 131

Spiced Tilapia Sandwiches With
Onion Salad | 132

Grilled Eggplant & Pepper Panini | 134

Bulgur & Mushroom Burgers | 135

Grilled Portobello & Cheese
Burgers | 136

Grilled Eggplant &
Tomato Sandwiches | 138

Italian Sausage Spiral | 139

Sausage Tips | 140

Hot Italian Sausages | 141

Beef & Pork Bratwurst | 142

Pork, Apple, Sage &
Stilton Sausages | 144

Beef, Caramelized Shallot & Thyme
Sausages | 145

Lamb & Leek Sausages | 146

Merguez Sausages | 147

Chorizo Patties With Pebre | 149

Classic Backyard Burgers

Enjoy these lightly seasoned basic burgers with any of the suggested toppings on pages 101 and 102, or top them with cheese to make classic cheeseburgers.

1 **egg**

Half **small onion,** grated

1 tbsp **Dijon mustard**

1 tsp **Worcestershire sauce**

1 clove **garlic,** minced

½ tsp each **salt** and **pepper**

½ tsp **dried oregano**

1 lb (450 g) regular or lean **ground beef**

4 **buns**

Whisk together 2 tbsp water, egg, onion, mustard, Worcestershire sauce, garlic, salt, pepper and oregano; mix in beef. Shape into four ¾-inch (2 cm) thick patties.

Grill, covered, on greased grill over medium heat, turning once, until no longer pink inside or instant-read thermometer registers 160°F (71°C), about 15 minutes. Serve in buns.

Makes 4 burgers.

Keeping a stash of homemade burgers in the freezer makes large-crowd or impromptu barbecues easy. Just layer the uncooked patties between waxed paper in an airtight container and freeze for up to 1 month. Thaw in refrigerator.

PER BURGER: about 392 cal, 28 g pro, 16 g total fat (6 g sat. fat), 32 g carb, 2 g fibre, 107 mg chol, 749 mg sodium. % RDI: 10% calcium, 30% iron, 2% vit A, 2% vit C, 32% folate.

Brandy Dijon Beef Burgers

This quintessential burger, with a touch of extra class, is especially good topped with Cherry Tomato Salsa (page 521).

2 tbsp **butter**

¾ cup finely chopped **onion**

1 clove **garlic,** minced

¾ tsp chopped **fresh thyme**
    (or ¼ tsp dried)

2 tbsp **brandy**

1 **egg**

1 tbsp **Dijon mustard**

½ tsp each **salt** and **pepper**

1 lb (450 g) **lean ground beef**

In skillet, melt butter over medium heat; fry onion, garlic and thyme until golden, about 8 minutes. Add brandy; cook until evaporated, about 1 minute. Scrape into bowl; let cool slightly. Stir in egg, mustard, salt and pepper; mix in beef. Shape into four ¾-inch (2 cm) thick patties.

Grill, covered, on greased grill over medium heat, turning once, until no longer pink inside or instant-read thermometer registers 160°F (71°C), about 15 minutes.

Makes 4 burgers.

PER BURGER (WITHOUT BUN): about 267 cal, 23 g pro, 18 g total fat (8 g sat. fat), 3 g carb, 1 g fibre, 124 mg chol, 472 mg sodium. % RDI: 3% calcium, 18% iron, 8% vit A, 3% vit C, 9% folate.

Steak Burgers

For medium-rare burgers, you should ideally grind your own meat or have your butcher grind a steak. If you're using store-bought ground beef, make sure to cook the burgers until they're no longer pink inside. Use large "stuffing" mushrooms.

1 lb (450 g) **ground sirloin**

2 tsp **Worcestershire sauce**

¾ tsp **salt**

½ tsp **pepper**

2 thick slices **sweet onion**

4 **extra-large white mushrooms**
  or cremini mushrooms, cut into
  ½-inch (1 cm) thick slices

1 tbsp **olive oil**

4 **buns**

4 **lettuce leaves**

4 thick slices **tomato**

Lightly mix together beef, Worcestershire sauce, ½ tsp of the salt and ¼ tsp of the pepper. Shape into four ¾-inch (2 cm) thick patties, handling meat as little as possible.

Skewer onions through edges to keep rings intact. Toss together onions, mushrooms, oil, and remaining salt and pepper.

Grill mushrooms (in grill basket if grill rack has wide spaces) and onions over medium-high heat until golden, 4 to 5 minutes. Remove skewers from onions and separate into rings.

Grill burgers, covered, on greased grill over high heat, turning once, until medium-rare, 3 to 5 minutes. Serve in buns with onions and mushrooms, lettuce and tomato.

Makes 4 burgers.

Overworking the meat mixture for burgers can make them shrink during cooking. To prevent this, shape into balls then gently press into ¾-inch (2 cm) thick patties.

PER BURGER: about 423 cal, 28 g pro, 18 g total fat (5 g sat. fat), 36 g carb, 3 g fibre, 60 mg chol, 862 mg sodium, 582 mg potassium. % RDI: 10% calcium, 38% iron, 5% vit A, 15% vit C, 36% folate.

Puttanesca Burgers

The flavours of fragrant puttanesca pasta sauce permeate these spicy, garlicky patties. Serve on toasted ciabatta buns or with a green salad.

1 **egg**

¼ cup **fresh bread crumbs**

¼ cup chopped **fresh parsley**

¼ cup finely chopped **Kalamata olives**

¼ cup **bottled strained tomatoes** (passata)

1 **onion,** grated

2 cloves **garlic,** minced

1 tbsp **anchovy paste**

1 tsp **hot pepper flakes**

½ tsp each **salt** and **pepper**

8 oz (225 g) **lean ground pork**

8 oz (225 g) **lean ground beef**

Whisk together egg, bread crumbs, parsley, olives, tomatoes, onion, garlic, anchovy paste, hot pepper flakes, salt and pepper; mix in pork and beef. Shape into four ¾-inch (2 cm) thick patties.

Grill, covered, on greased grill over medium heat, turning once, until no longer pink inside or instant-read thermometer registers 160°F (71°C), about 15 minutes. Let rest for 5 minutes before serving.

Makes 4 burgers.

PER BURGER (WITHOUT BUN): about 266 cal, 25 g pro, 16 g total fat (6 g sat. fat), 7 g carb, 1 g fibre, 114 mg chol, 655 mg sodium, 434 mg potassium. % RDI: 4% calcium, 19% iron, 7% vit A, 10% vit C, 11% folate.

Stuffed Cheddar Burgers

*These cheese-stuffed burgers are even more delicious — and indulgent —
when topped with crisp bacon.*

1 **egg**

¼ cup **dry bread crumbs**

1 **small onion,** grated

2 tsp **Dijon mustard**

½ tsp **dried thyme**

½ tsp **salt**

¼ tsp **pepper**

1 lb (450 g) **lean ground beef**

½ cup shredded **extra-old
Cheddar cheese**

4 **buns**

Whisk together 2 tbsp water, egg, bread crumbs, onion,
mustard, thyme, salt and pepper; mix in beef.

Shape into 4 balls; make well in each. Fill each with one-
quarter of the cheese; press meat over to enclose. Shape
into four ¾-inch (2 cm) thick patties.

Grill, covered, on greased grill over medium heat,
turning once, until no longer pink inside or instant-read
thermometer registers 160°F (71°C), about 15 minutes.
Serve in buns.

Makes 4 burgers.

VARIATION
Stuffed Feta Burgers
Replace thyme with oregano, beef with ground pork or
lamb, and Cheddar with crumbled feta. Top burgers
with sliced tomato and cucumber.

PER BURGER: about 464 cal, 32 g pro, 20 g total fat (8 g sat. fat), 37 g carb, 2 g fibre, 121 mg chol,
867 mg sodium. % RDI: 20% calcium, 34% iron, 6% vit A, 2% vit C, 38% folate.

Shiitake Beef Burgers

These delectable burgers are infused with Chinese flavours. Serve them with hot mustard to spread on the buns.

12 **dried shiitake mushrooms**

1 tbsp **peanut oil** or vegetable oil

2 tbsp **Chinese rice wine**
  or dry sherry

2 tsp grated **fresh ginger**

¼ tsp **salt**

Pinch **granulated sugar**

1 **egg**

2 tbsp **soy sauce**

2 tsp **sesame oil**

½ tsp **pepper**

1 lb (450 g) **ground beef**

4 **green onions,** thinly sliced

HOISIN GARLIC SAUCE:

2 tsp **sesame oil**

3 cloves **garlic,** minced

2 tbsp **hoisin sauce**

¼ tsp **granulated sugar**

Hoisin Garlic Sauce: In small saucepan, heat oil over medium-low heat; fry garlic until soft and fragrant, 2 to 3 minutes. Stir in hoisin sauce, sugar and 1 tbsp water; cook, stirring, for 30 seconds. Scrape into bowl; let cool.

Soak dried shiitake mushrooms in 1½ cups warm water until soft, about 30 minutes. Reserving soaking liquid, drain. Remove stems (save for stockpot); dice caps.

In small nonstick skillet, heat peanut oil over medium-high heat; fry mushrooms until golden, about 4 minutes. Add wine, ginger, salt and sugar; sauté for 30 seconds. Add reserved mushroom liquid; cook until liquid is reduced to about 2 tbsp. Scrape into bowl; let cool.

Whisk in egg, soy sauce, sesame oil and pepper; mix in beef and green onions. Shape into four ¾-inch (2 cm) thick patties.

Grill, covered, on greased grill over medium heat, turning once, until no longer pink inside or instant-read thermometer registers 160°F (71°C), about 15 minutes. Spread one-quarter of the hoisin garlic sauce over top of each burger.

Makes 4 burgers.

PER BURGER (WITHOUT BUN): about 334 cal, 25 g pro, 20 g total fat (6 g sat. fat), 14 g carb, 2 g fibre, 107 mg chol, 868 mg sodium. % RDI: 4% calcium, 21% iron, 3% vit A, 5% vit C, 15% folate.

Argentine Burgers

These fresh-tasting burgers borrow flavours from Argentine chimichurri – parsley, hot pepper and vinegar. Top with ripe tomato slices.

1 cup packed **fresh parsley**

¼ cup **dry bread crumbs**

2 tbsp packed **fresh oregano** (or 1½ tsp dried)

2 tbsp **olive oil**

Half to 1 **jalapeño pepper,** seeded and chopped

1 tbsp **red wine vinegar**

¼ tsp each **salt** and **pepper**

4 cloves **garlic,** minced

1 **egg yolk**

1 lb (450 g) **lean ground beef** or veal

4 **buns**

In food processor, finely chop together parsley, bread crumbs, oregano, oil, jalapeño, vinegar, 1 tbsp water, salt and pepper; pulse in garlic and egg yolk. Scrape into large bowl; mix in beef. Shape into four ¾-inch (2 cm) thick patties.

Grill, covered, on greased grill over medium heat, turning once, until no longer pink inside or instant-read thermometer registers 160°F (71°C), about 15 minutes. Serve in buns.

Makes 4 burgers.

PER BURGER: about 508 cal, 30 g pro, 23 g total fat (7 g sat. fat), 45 g carb, 2 g fibre, 115 mg chol, 652 mg sodium. % RDI: 7% calcium, 36% iron, 11% vit A, 20% vit C, 42% folate.

Rosemary Beef Burgers With Jalapeño Mayo

There's just enough jalapeño in the mayo to give it a pleasant kick. If you're a heat lover, feel free to increase the amount to taste.

1 **egg**

¼ cup **sodium-reduced beef broth**

1 **small onion,** grated

¼ cup **dry bread crumbs**

2 tsp finely chopped **fresh rosemary**

½ tsp each **salt** and **pepper**

1 lb (450 g) **lean ground beef**

4 **kaiser rolls,** halved, or hamburger buns

JALAPEÑO MAYO:

¼ cup **light mayonnaise**

2 tbsp chopped **fresh parsley**

1 tbsp minced **jalapeño pepper**

1 clove **garlic,** minced

Beat egg with beef broth. Stir in onion, bread crumbs, rosemary, salt and pepper; mix in beef. Shape into four ¾-inch (2 cm) thick patties.

Grill, covered, on greased grill over medium-high heat, turning once, until no longer pink inside or instant-read thermometer registers 160°F (71°C), about 15 minutes.

Jalapeño Mayo: Meanwhile, stir together mayonnaise, parsley, jalapeño and garlic.

Toast rolls on grill. Spread jalapeño mayo on rolls; sandwich burgers in rolls.

Makes 4 burgers.

PER BURGER: about 534 cal, 30 g pro, 27 g total fat (9 g sat. fat), 41 g carb, 2 g fibre, 130 mg chol, 897 mg sodium, 419 mg potassium. % RDI: 10% calcium, 32% iron, 4% vit A, 8% vit C, 39% folate.

Jalapeño Cheeseburgers With Tomato Salad

Stuffing a burger with cheese takes it to another level of excellence. This version is inspired by the fried stuffed jalapeños found on so many pub menus.

1 **egg**

1 **small onion,** grated and drained

¼ cup **dry bread crumbs**

½ tsp + pinch **salt**

¼ tsp + pinch **pepper**

1 lb (450 g) **lean ground beef**

Three-quarters **sweet onion,** cut into 4 thick rounds

2 tsp **olive oil**

4 **hamburger buns**

CHEESE FILLING:

1 cup shredded **old Cheddar cheese,** about 3 oz (85 g)

¼ cup **cream cheese,** softened

¼ cup chopped drained **pickled jalapeño peppers**

2 tbsp chopped **fresh parsley**

TOMATO SALAD:

One-quarter **sweet onion**

1 lb (450 g) **tomatoes**

2 tbsp chopped **fresh parsley**

2 tbsp **extra-virgin olive oil**

1 tbsp **lemon juice**

2 tsp chopped **fresh oregano**

Half small clove **garlic,** minced

Pinch each **salt** and **pepper**

Cheese Filling: Mix together Cheddar, cream cheese, jalapeños and parsley. Shape into four 2½-inch (6 cm) circles. Freeze on baking sheet for 15 minutes.

Meanwhile, whisk together egg, onion, bread crumbs, ½ tsp of the salt and ¼ tsp of the pepper; mix in beef. Shape into eight 5-inch (12 cm) wide patties. Sandwich cheese circles between patties, gently pinching edges to seal. Refrigerate for 30 minutes.

Tomato Salad: Meanwhile, thinly slice onion; soak in cold water for 10 minutes. Drain well. Cut tomatoes into wedges. Whisk together parsley, oil, lemon juice, oregano, garlic, salt and pepper; toss with onion and tomatoes until coated.

Grill patties, covered, on greased grill over medium heat, turning once, until no longer pink inside or instant-read thermometer registers 160°F (71°C), about 15 minutes.

Meanwhile, brush onion rounds with oil; sprinkle with remaining salt and pepper. Grill, covered, over medium heat, turning once, until softened and caramelized, 8 to 10 minutes.

Sandwich burgers and onion rounds in buns. Serve with tomato salad.

Makes 4 burgers.

PER BURGER: about 697 cal, 39 g pro, 41 g total fat (17 g sat. fat), 44 g carb, 4 g fibre, 156 mg chol, 962 mg sodium, 827 mg potassium. % RDI: 32% calcium, 40% iron, 30% vit A, 63% vit C, 57% folate.

Smoky Beef Burgers With Chipotle Ketchup

For a smoky cheeseburger, melt some aged Cheddar on top – or go overboard and use smoked Cheddar.

1 tbsp **butter**

3 oz (85 g) **double-smoked bacon,** finely chopped

1 **onion,** finely chopped

2 cloves **garlic,** minced

1 **egg**

3 tbsp **dry red wine**

½ tsp each **salt** and **pepper**

1 lb (450 g) **ground beef** or bison

CHIPOTLE KETCHUP:

⅓ cup **ketchup**

1 **canned chipotle pepper in adobo sauce,** minced

1 tbsp **adobo sauce** from canned chipotles

Chipotle Ketchup: Mix together ketchup, chipotle pepper and adobo sauce.

In small skillet, cook butter with bacon over medium-high heat until bacon fat is rendered. Add onion and garlic; sauté until golden, about 3 minutes. Scrape into bowl; let cool. Whisk in egg, wine, salt and pepper; mix in beef. Shape into four ¾-inch (2 cm) thick patties.

Grill, covered, on greased grill over medium heat, turning once, until no longer pink inside or instant-read thermometer registers 160°F (71°C), about 15 minutes. Serve with chipotle ketchup.

Makes 4 burgers.

PER BURGER (WITHOUT BUN): about 371 cal, 26 g pro, 24 g total fat (12 g sat. fat), 11 g carb, 1 g fibre, 130 mg chol, 849 mg sodium. % RDI: 3% calcium, 19% iron, 11% vit A, 10% vit C, 10% folate.

Hamburger Buns

Step aside, store-bought buns — here are the finest hamburger buns you'll ever taste. For a grainier bun, use multigrain flour or replace up to 2 cups of the all-purpose flour with whole wheat or whole spelt flour.

2 tbsp **granulated sugar**

1 cup **warm water**

1 pkg **active dry yeast**
(2¼ tsp)

1 cup **milk**

2 tbsp **butter**

1½ tsp **salt**

5 cups **all-purpose flour**
(approx)

1 **egg yolk**

Sesame seeds (optional)

In large bowl, dissolve 1 tsp of the sugar in the warm water. Sprinkle in yeast; let stand until frothy, 10 minutes.

Meanwhile, heat milk, remaining sugar, butter and salt over low heat just until butter is melted; let cool to lukewarm. Add to yeast mixture.

In stand mixer with paddle attachment or using wooden spoon, beat in 3 cups of the flour, 1 cup at a time, until smooth. Stir in enough of the remaining flour to make stiff dough.

Turn out onto lightly floured surface. Knead, adding more flour if necessary to prevent sticking, until smooth and elastic, 10 minutes. Place in greased bowl, turning to grease all over. Cover and let rise in warm draft-free place until doubled in bulk, 1 to 1½ hours.

Lightly push down dough; turn out onto lightly floured surface. Roll into log and divide into 16 pieces; shape each into ball, stretching and pinching dough underneath to smooth tops. Place, 2 inches (5 cm) apart, on greased baking sheet; flatten slightly. Cover and let rise in warm draft-free place until doubled in bulk, 30 to 60 minutes.

Whisk egg yolk with 1 tbsp water; brush gently over tops. Sprinkle with sesame seeds (if using). Bake in 400°F (200°C) oven until golden and buns sound hollow when tapped on bottoms, 20 to 25 minutes. Transfer to rack; let cool. (*Make-ahead: Freeze in airtight container for up to 2 months.*)

Makes 16 buns.

PER BUN: about 174 cal, 5 g pro, 2 g total fat (1 g sat. fat), 32 g carb, 1 g fibre, 18 mg chol, 239 mg sodium. % RDI: 2% calcium, 12% iron, 3% vit A, 25% folate.

Stuffed Meatball Sliders

You won't need a fork for these meatballs, which are filled with a gooey melted-cheese surprise. Look for slider or mini hamburger buns in the grocery store's bakery section.

¼ cup **fresh bread crumbs**

¼ cup **milk**

1 **egg,** lightly beaten

1 lb (450 g) **ground veal**

1 cup grated **onion**

¼ cup grated **Parmesan cheese**

¼ cup chopped **fresh parsley**

½ tsp **salt**

¼ tsp **hot pepper flakes**

8 **mini bocconcini cheese balls**

½ cup **bottled strained tomatoes** (passata)

8 **large fresh basil leaves**

8 **slider buns**

Mix together bread crumbs, milk and egg; let stand for 5 minutes. Mix in veal, onion, Parmesan cheese, parsley, salt and hot pepper flakes just until combined. Shape into 8 balls; make well in centre of each. Fill each with 1 bocconcini ball; press meat over to enclose. Shape into eight ½-inch (1 cm) thick patties.

Grill, covered, on greased grill over medium-high heat, turning once, until meat is no longer pink inside and cheese is melted, or instant-read thermometer registers 160°F (71°C), about 15 minutes.

Sandwich burgers, tomatoes and basil in buns.

Makes 8 sliders.

PER SLIDER: about 236 cal, 18 g pro, 10 g total fat (5 g sat. fat), 20 g carb, 1 g fibre, 91 mg chol, 398 mg sodium, 256 mg potassium. % RDI: 11% calcium, 14% iron, 7% vit A, 5% vit C, 8% folate.

From left: Bocconcini Chicken
Burger (page 125), Feta & Lamb
Burger Pita (page 119), Glazed
Cheddar Pork Burger (page 110)
and Veal Patty Melt (page 104)

Bison Burgers

Farmer's markets and specialty butchers are good sources for homegrown bison. Try these burgers with grainy mustard on whole wheat buns.

1 tbsp **vegetable oil**

¾ cup finely chopped **onion**

1 **egg**

¼ cup **dry bread crumbs**

2 tbsp **beer** or water

2 tbsp **grainy mustard**

½ tsp crumbled **dried thyme**

½ tsp each **salt** and **pepper**

1 lb (450 g) **ground bison**

4 **buns**

In nonstick skillet, heat oil over medium heat; fry onion, stirring often, until softened, about 10 minutes.

Whisk together egg, bread crumbs, beer, mustard, thyme, salt and pepper; mix in onion. Mix in bison. Shape into four ¾-inch (2 cm) thick patties.

Grill, covered, on greased grill over medium heat, turning once, until no longer pink inside or instant-read thermometer registers 160°F (71°C), about 15 minutes. Serve in buns.

Makes 4 burgers.

PER BURGER: about 499 cal, 29 g pro, 24 g total fat (8 g sat. fat), 39 g carb, 3 g fibre, 123 mg chol, 859 mg sodium. % RDI: 12% calcium, 40% iron, 2% vit A, 3% vit C, 39% folate.

Veal & Gorgonzola Burgers With Onions

Serve these burgers in focaccia buns, or focaccia bread cut in half horizontally.

1 **egg**

1 clove **garlic,** minced

¼ cup minced **fresh parsley**

3 tbsp **canned ground tomatoes**

½ tsp **salt**

¼ tsp **pepper**

1 lb (450 g) **ground veal**

4 oz (115 g) **Gorgonzola cheese**

SAUTÉED ONION:

2 tbsp **extra-virgin olive oil**

12 **fresh sage leaves**

1 **large white onion,** cut into rings

¼ cup **white vermouth** or dry white wine

Pinch **salt**

Sautéed Onion: In skillet, heat oil over medium-high heat; fry sage until fragrant, about 20 seconds. Add onion; sauté until golden (lowering heat if browning unevenly), about 20 minutes. Add vermouth and salt; cook until no liquid remains, 2 to 3 minutes.

Whisk together egg, garlic, parsley, tomatoes, salt and pepper; mix in veal. Shape into 4 balls; make well in each. Fill each with one-quarter of the cheese; press meat over to enclose. Shape into four ¾-inch (2 cm) thick patties.

Grill, covered, on greased grill over medium heat, turning once, until meat is no longer pink inside or instant-read thermometer registers 160°F (71°C), about 15 minutes. Serve topped with sautéed onion.

Makes 4 burgers.

PER BURGER (WITHOUT BUN): about 389 cal, 31 g pro, 25 g total fat (10 g sat. fat), 9 g carb, 2 g fibre, 168 mg chol, 866 mg sodium. % RDI: 21% calcium, 14% iron, 14% vit A, 15% vit C, 20% folate.

Italian Stuffed Veal Burgers

These mouthwatering burgers are adapted from the meat loaf (polpettone) *recipe of Rosa Paris of Toronto. Rosa is from the small town of Modugno in Puglia, southern Italy, and this burger reflects the rich flavours of her native cuisine.*

Half bunch **spinach,** blanched, or half pkg (300 g pkg) frozen whole-leaf spinach, thawed

2 cloves **garlic,** minced

½ tsp each **salt** and **pepper**

1 **egg**

¼ cup **dry Italian bread crumbs**

¼ cup grated **Parmesan cheese**

1 tbsp chopped **fresh parsley**

1 lb (450 g) **ground veal**

2 slices **prosciutto cotto** (Italian cooked ham) or Black Forest ham

2 slices **provolone cheese**

Mix together spinach and half each of the garlic, salt and pepper.

Whisk together egg, bread crumbs, Parmesan cheese, parsley and remaining garlic, salt and pepper; mix in veal.

Place prosciutto cotto on cutting board; top each slice with 1 slice cheese, then half of the spinach mixture. Roll up; cut each roll-up in half. Shape veal mixture into 4 balls; make well in each. Fill each with 1 of the roll-ups; press meat over to enclose. Shape into four ¾-inch (2 cm) thick patties.

Grill, covered, on greased grill over medium heat, turning once, until no longer pink inside or instant-read thermometer registers 160°F (71°C), about 15 minutes.

Makes 4 burgers.

PER BURGER (WITHOUT BUN): about 293 cal, 33 g pro, 14 g total fat (7 g sat. fat), 7 g carb, 1 g fibre, 157 mg chol, 856 mg sodium. % RDI: 20% calcium, 14% iron, 25% vit A, 8% vit C, 20% folate.

Quick-Fix Burger Toppings

Tart-Sweet Cucumber Slices

Toss together 1 cup thinly sliced cucumber, ⅓ cup thinly sliced red or sweet onion, 2 tbsp white wine vinegar and 2 tsp granulated sugar; let stand for 30 minutes. Drain.

Makes about 1⅓ cups.

PER 1 TBSP: about 3 cal, 0 g pro, 0 g total fat (0 g sat. fat), 6 g carb, 0 g fibre, 0 mg chol, 0 mg sodium.

Grilled Marinated Peppers

Grill 4 sweet red peppers, turning, until charred; let cool. Peel and seed; cut into 1-inch (2.5 cm) wide strips. Whisk together 3 tbsp extra-virgin olive oil; 1 tbsp sherry vinegar; and ¼ tsp each salt, pepper and granulated sugar. Toss with red peppers.

Makes about 2 cups.

PER 1 TBSP: about 15 cal, trace pro, 1 g total fat (trace sat. fat), 1 g carb, trace fibre, 0 mg chol, 18 mg sodium. % RDI: 1% iron, 5% vit A, 40% vit C, 1% folate.

Minty Mayonnaise

Whisk together ½ cup mayonnaise; 2 tbsp each chopped fresh mint and cilantro; half jalapeño pepper, seeded and minced; 2 tsp lemon juice; and pinch each salt and pepper.

Makes about ½ cup.

PER 1 TBSP: about 100 cal, trace pro, 11 g total fat (2 g sat. fat), 1 g carb, trace fibre, 5 mg chol, 79 mg sodium. % RDI: 1% calcium, 1% iron, 2% vit A, 2% vit C, 1% folate.

Tahini Sauce

Whisk together ¼ cup Balkan-style plain yogurt; ¼ cup tahini; 2 tbsp each extra-virgin olive oil and water; 1 tbsp lemon juice; 1 clove garlic, minced; and ¼ tsp each sweet paprika and salt.

Makes about ¾ cup.

PER 1 TBSP: about 50 cal, 1 g pro, 5 g total fat (1 g sat. fat), 2 g carb, trace fibre, 1 mg chol, 70 mg sodium. % RDI: 3% calcium, 4% iron, 1% vit A, 3% folate.

Brandied Mushrooms

In small nonstick skillet, heat 1 tbsp olive oil or butter over medium heat; fry 1 shallot or small onion and 1 clove garlic, minced, until softened, about 2 minutes. Add 2 cups sliced mushrooms, 2 tbsp each minced fresh parsley and brandy, and ¼ tsp each salt and dried thyme. Fry, stirring occasionally, until mushrooms are lightly browned, about 8 minutes. If desired, stir in ½ tsp truffle oil.

Makes 1 cup.

PER ¼ CUP (WITHOUT TRUFFLE OIL): about 33 cal, 1 g pro, 2 g total fat (trace sat. fat), 1 g carb, trace fibre, 0 mg chol, 73 mg sodium. % RDI: 1% calcium, 2% iron, 1% vit A, 2% vit C, 2% folate.

»

«

Golden Onions

In skillet, heat 2 tbsp olive oil over medium-low heat. Fry 2 onions, thinly sliced; 1 clove garlic, sliced; and 1 bay leaf, stirring occasionally, until golden, about 15 minutes. Stir in ¼ cup dry white wine (or water and 2 tsp wine vinegar), ¼ tsp each salt and black pepper, and pinch ground allspice or cloves. Cook until no liquid remains; discard bay leaf. Stir in 2 tbsp minced fresh parsley.

Makes 1 cup.

PER ¼ CUP: about 30 cal, trace pro, 2 g total fat (trace sat. fat), 3 g carb, trace fibre, 0 mg chol, 74 mg sodium. % RDI: 1% calcium, 1% iron, 1% vit A, 4% vit C, 3% folate.

Blue Cheese and Horseradish Sauce

Mix together 2 tbsp each crumbled blue cheese and light sour cream; 1 tbsp each minced fresh chives, prepared horseradish and mayonnaise; ¼ tsp pepper; and pinch salt.

Makes ⅓ cup.

PER 1½ TBSP: about 37 cal, 2 g pro, 3 g total fat (1 g sat. fat), 2 g carb, trace fibre, 5 mg chol, 96 mg sodium. % RDI: 4% calcium, 1% iron, 2% vit A, 2% folate.

Fresh Tomato and Onion Relish

Mix together half each tomato and dill pickle, finely diced; 1 tbsp each minced red onion, minced fresh parsley, chopped capers and extra-virgin olive oil; ½ tsp red wine vinegar; ¼ tsp dried oregano; and dash hot pepper sauce.

Makes ½ cup.

PER 2 TBSP: about 37 cal, trace pro, 3 g total fat (trace sat. fat), 1 g carb, trace fibre, 0 mg chol, 171 mg sodium. % RDI: 1% iron, 2% vit A, 8% vit C, 2% folate.

Why Do Ground Meats Need to Be Cooked Well?

Bacteria is introduced to meat through its air-exposed surface. Since ground meat has significantly more surface area than a simple cut of meat, it is particularly susceptible to bacterial contamination. Searing a steak kills the surface bacteria, allowing you to serve the meat rare, but burgers must be cooked through to a specific temperature to be safe.

Different ground meats are fully cooked at slightly different temperatures. To test, take one burger off the grill and insert an instant-read thermometer horizontally; leave for 30 seconds before reading the temperature.

GROUND MEAT	SAFE INTERNAL TEMPERATURE
Chicken, Turkey	165°F (74°C)
Beef, Bison, Veal, Venison	160°F (71°C)
Lamb	160°F (71°C)
Pork	160°F (71°C)
Fish	158°F (70°C)

From top: Brandied
Mushrooms, Minty
Mayonnaise, Tart-
Sweet Cucumber
Slices, Golden
Onions, Grilled
Marinated Peppers
and Tahini Sauce
(pages 101 and 102)

Veal Patty Melts

An old-fashioned diner favourite, the patty melt gets a delicious flavour update with veal.

2 tbsp **vegetable oil**

2 **onions,** sliced

Pinch each **salt** and **pepper**

2 tsp **Russian mustard** or sweet mustard

8 slices **dark rye bread**

4 oz (115 g) **Swiss cheese,** thinly sliced

PATTIES:

1 **egg**

1 clove **garlic,** minced

¼ cup chopped **fresh parsley**

1 tbsp **Dijon mustard**

½ tsp **salt**

¼ tsp **caraway seeds**

¼ tsp **pepper**

1 lb (450 g) **ground veal**

In large skillet, heat oil over medium heat; fry onions, salt and pepper, stirring occasionally, until golden, about 10 minutes.

Patties: Whisk together 1 tbsp water, egg, garlic, parsley, mustard, salt, caraway seeds and pepper; mix in veal. Shape into four ¾-inch (2 cm) thick patties.

Grill, covered, on greased grill over medium heat, turning once, until no longer pink inside or instant-read thermometer registers 160°F (71°C), about 15 minutes.

Spread mustard over 4 of the bread slices; top with patties, cheese and fried onions. Sandwich with remaining bread. Grill, covered, on greased grill over medium-low heat, turning once, until bread is toasted and cheese is melted, about 6 minutes.

Makes 4 burgers.

Photo, page 97

PER BURGER: about 513 cal, 38 g pro, 26 g total fat (9 g sat. fat), 31 g carb, 4 g fibre, 171 mg chol, 846 mg sodium, 535 mg potassium. % RDI: 33% calcium, 21% iron, 13% vit A, 12% vit C, 35% folate.

Flank Steak Sandwiches With Pepper Sauce

A savoury red pepper sauce and fresh arugula are ideal partners for juicy slices of grilled steak.

1 lb (450 g) **beef flank marinating steak,** 1 inch (2.5 cm) thick

¼ tsp each **salt, cayenne pepper** and **pepper**

1 bunch **arugula,** trimmed

4 **oval buns,** halved lengthwise

PEPPER SAUCE:

1 **sweet red pepper**

¼ cup **blanched almonds,** toasted

¼ cup chopped seeded **tomato**

1 clove **garlic,** sliced

2 tbsp minced **fresh parsley**

1 tbsp each **tomato paste, olive oil** and **red wine vinegar**

½ tsp each **salt** and **sweet paprika**

Pepper Sauce: Grill red pepper, covered, on greased grill over medium-high heat, turning occasionally, until charred, 15 to 20 minutes. Let cool. Peel and seed. In food processor, purée together red pepper, almonds, tomato, garlic, parsley, tomato paste, oil, vinegar, salt and paprika.

Meanwhile, sprinkle steak with salt, cayenne and pepper. Grill, covered, on greased grill over medium-high heat, turning once, until medium-rare, 8 to 10 minutes. Transfer to cutting board and tent with foil; let stand for 10 minutes before thinly slicing across the grain.

Sandwich arugula, steak and pepper sauce in buns.

Makes 4 sandwiches.

PER SANDWICH: about 434 cal, 33 g pro, 16 g total fat (4 g sat. fat), 39 g carb, 4 g fibre, 48 mg chol, 828 mg sodium, 597 mg potassium. % RDI: 13% calcium, 38% iron, 25% vit A, 100% vit C, 50% folate.

Cheesesteak Sandwiches for Two

Here's a homestyle version of Philadelphia's signature sandwich. It's ideal for a small family, but you can double or triple the recipe for more people.

1 tbsp **extra-virgin olive oil**

1 **large sweet onion,** sliced

2 cloves **garlic,** sliced

½ tsp each **salt** and **pepper**

½ tsp **white wine vinegar**

¼ tsp **dried thyme**

8 oz (225 g) **beef strip loin grilling steak**

2 **soft oval buns,** halved

4 slices **provolone cheese**

Pickled peppers (optional)

In skillet, heat oil over medium-low heat; cook onion, garlic, half each of the salt and pepper, the vinegar and thyme until very soft and slightly caramelized, about 20 minutes.

Meanwhile, sprinkle steak with remaining salt and pepper. Grill, covered, on greased grill over medium-high heat, turning once, until desired doneness, about 8 minutes for medium-rare. Transfer to cutting board and tent with foil; let stand for 10 minutes before slicing thinly.

Meanwhile, top cut sides of buns with cheese and grill until melted. Sandwich steak, onions, and peppers (if using) in buns.

Makes 2 sandwiches.

PER SANDWICH: about 651 cal, 41 g pro, 23 g total fat (7 g sat. fat), 68 g carb, 5 g fibre, 69 mg chol, 1,371 mg sodium, 687 mg potassium. % RDI: 32% calcium, 46% iron, 5% vit A, 15% vit C, 64% folate.

Green Onion Pork Burgers

Serve these Chinese-inspired burgers topped with Napa Slaw (below) on sesame buns.

1 **egg**

1 cup finely chopped **green onions**

⅓ cup **dry bread crumbs**

1 **green hot pepper,** seeded and minced (optional)

1 clove **garlic,** minced

1 tbsp **soy sauce**

1 tbsp **fish sauce** or soy sauce

1 tbsp **Chinese rice wine** or dry sherry (or 1 tsp balsamic vinegar)

2 tsp grated **fresh ginger**

2 tsp **sesame oil**

½ tsp **white pepper**

¼ tsp **hot pepper sauce**

1 lb (450 g) **lean ground pork**

Whisk together egg, onions, bread crumbs, hot pepper (if using), garlic, soy sauce, fish sauce, wine, ginger, sesame oil, white pepper and hot pepper sauce; mix in pork. Shape into four ¾-inch (2 cm) thick patties.

Grill, covered, on greased grill over medium heat, turning once, until no longer pink inside or instant-read thermometer registers 160°F (71°C), about 15 minutes.

Makes 4 burgers.

Napa Slaw

Whisk together 2 tbsp unseasoned rice vinegar, 2 tsp granulated sugar, 1 tsp sesame oil, ½ tsp salt and pinch hot pepper flakes. Toss in 3 cups shredded napa cabbage; 1 small carrot, shredded; and ½ cup thinly sliced sweet red pepper until coated. Let stand for 15 minutes before serving.

Makes 1½ cups, enough for 4 servings.

PER BURGER (WITHOUT BUN OR SLAW): about 309 cal, 25 g pro, 18 g total fat (6 g sat. fat), 10 g carb, 1 g fibre, 116 mg chol, 763 mg sodium. % RDI: 6% calcium, 16% iron, 6% vit A, 15% vit C, 13% folate.

Glazed Cheddar Pork Burgers

Skewering the onions keeps the slices together while grilling. The maple, mustard and vinegar glaze gives the burgers a delicious tang.

2 tbsp **Dijon mustard**

2 tbsp **maple syrup**

1 tsp **cider vinegar**

1 **small red onion,** cut into 4 thick slices

1 tbsp **vegetable oil**

Pinch each **salt** and **pepper**

4 **buns**

PATTIES:

1 **egg,** beaten

¾ cup shredded **extra-old Cheddar cheese**

¼ cup **dry bread crumbs**

1 clove **garlic,** minced

½ tsp crumbled **dried sage**

½ tsp **salt**

¼ tsp **pepper**

1 lb (450 g) **lean ground pork**

Patties: Stir together 1 tbsp water, egg, cheese, bread crumbs, garlic, sage, salt and pepper; mix in pork. Shape into four ¾-inch (2 cm) thick patties.

Whisk together Dijon mustard, maple syrup and cider vinegar; set aside.

Skewer onion slices through edges to keep rings intact. Brush both sides with oil; sprinkle with salt and pepper. Grill, covered, on greased grill over medium heat, turning once, until tender, about 10 minutes. Remove skewers and separate into rings.

Meanwhile, grill patties, covered, on greased grill over medium heat for 5 minutes. Turn and brush with half of the mustard mixture; grill for 5 minutes. Turn again; brush with remaining mustard mixture. Grill until no longer pink inside or instant-read thermometer registers 160°F (71°C), about 5 minutes. Serve in buns with onions.

Makes 4 burgers.

Photo, page 97

PER BURGER: about 586 cal, 34 g pro, 28 g total fat (10 g sat. fat), 47 g carb, 3 g fibre, 140 mg chol, 979 mg sodium, 536 mg potassium. % RDI: 27% calcium, 28% iron, 8% vit A, 2% vit C, 39% folate.

Grilled Cubanos

Spicy brown mustard adds a nice, sharp contrast to this meaty Latin American sandwich; look for it in the condiment aisle. This sandwich is a high-sodium treat, so try to include less-salty foods in the rest of your day's meals.

6 large cloves **garlic**

¼ tsp **coarse sea salt**

1 tbsp **vegetable oil**

½ tsp **pepper**

1 lb (450 g) **pork tenderloin** (about 2 tenderloins)

1 **large red onion,** cut into ½-inch thick (1 cm) rounds

¼ cup **spicy brown mustard**

4 **kaiser rolls,** halved

4 thin slices **deli baked ham**

2 **dill pickles,** thinly sliced lengthwise

4 slices **provolone cheese** or Swiss cheese

On cutting board, coarsely chop garlic; sprinkle with salt. With flat side of knife or fork, mash into paste. Transfer to small bowl; mix in oil and pepper until combined. Rub all over pork.

Grill, covered, on greased grill over medium-high heat, turning often, until just a hint of pink remains in centre and instant-read thermometer registers 160°F (71°C), about 20 minutes. Transfer to cutting board; let rest for 10 minutes before thinly slicing across the grain.

Meanwhile, skewer onion slices through edges to keep rings intact. Grill onion slices, covered, on greased grill over medium heat, turning once, until tender and beginning to brown, about 6 minutes.

Spread mustard over bottom halves of rolls; sandwich ham, pork, pickle, grilled onions and cheese in rolls.

Place sandwiches on greased grill over medium-low heat; top with heavy baking sheet and weight. Grill, covered and turning once, until rolls are toasted and cheese is melted, about 6 minutes. Cut in half before serving.

Makes 4 sandwiches.

TIP
Use a foil-wrapped brick or heavy cast-iron skillet as the weight on the barbecue – don't use canned goods, as the heat can cook the contents.

PER SANDWICH: about 479 cal, 41 g pro, 15 g total fat (5 g sat. fat), 45 g carb, 4 g fibre, 81 mg chol, 1,451 mg sodium, 709 mg potassium. % RDI: 22% calcium, 30% iron, 5% vit A, 11% vit C, 32% folate.

Curried Pork Burgers

Fragrant with Indian curry paste and just a little spicy from the jalapeño, this burger is a perennial favourite with Canadian Living readers.

½ cup chopped **fresh cilantro**

⅓ cup crumbled **feta cheese**

2 tbsp **curry paste**

2 cloves **garlic,** minced

2 tsp minced **fresh ginger**

1 **jalapeño pepper,** seeded and minced

¾ tsp **ground cumin**

¼ tsp each **salt** and **pepper**

1 lb (450 g) **lean ground pork**

4 leaves **Boston lettuce**

4 **soft buns**

GRILLED RED ONIONS:

Half **large red onion,** cut into ½-inch (1 cm) thick rounds

1 tsp **vegetable oil**

Pinch each **salt** and **pepper**

Mix together cilantro, feta cheese, curry paste, garlic, ginger, jalapeño, cumin, salt and pepper; mix in pork. Shape into four ¾-inch (2 cm) thick patties. Cover and refrigerate for 10 minutes or up to 4 hours.

Grill, covered, on greased grill over medium-high heat, turning once, until no longer pink inside or instant-read thermometer registers 160°F (71°C), about 15 minutes.

Grilled Red Onions: Meanwhile, skewer onion rounds through edges to keep rings intact. Brush both sides with oil; sprinkle with salt and pepper. Grill, covered, on greased grill over medium-high heat, turning once, until softened, about 10 minutes. Remove skewers and separate into rings.

Sandwich burgers, onions and lettuce in buns.

Makes 4 burgers.

PER BURGER: about 472 cal, 29 g pro, 22 g total fat (7 g sat. fat), 38 g carb, 3 g fibre, 84 mg chol, 889 mg sodium, 516 mg potassium. % RDI: 17% calcium, 25% iron, 4% vit A, 10% vit C, 36% folate.

Juicy Pork Burgers

Pork makes for a succulent and flavourful burger. Yogurt, mustard and Worcestershire sauce add extra moisture so the patties don't dry out.

½ cup minced **sweet green pepper**

½ cup minced **sweet onion**

¼ cup **plain yogurt**

1 tbsp minced **fresh sage** (or 1 tsp crumbled dried)

2 tsp **hot mustard**

1 tsp **Worcestershire sauce**

¾ tsp **salt**

¼ tsp **pepper**

1 lb (450 g) **lean ground pork**

Mix together green pepper, onion, yogurt, sage, mustard, Worcestershire sauce, salt and pepper; mix in pork. Shape into four ¾-inch (2 cm) thick patties.

Grill, covered, on greased grill over medium heat, turning once, until no longer pink inside or instant-read thermometer registers 160°F (71°C), about 15 minutes.

Makes 4 burgers.

PER BURGER (WITHOUT BUN): about 215 cal, 22 g pro, 12 g total fat (5 g sat. fat), 4 g carb, 1 g fibre, 74 mg chol, 543 mg sodium, 393 mg potassium. % RDI: 5% calcium, 9% iron, 1% vit A, 25% vit C, 6% folate.

Lamb Burgers

Minty Mayonnaise (page 101) is a tasty partner to these straightforward lamb burgers.

1 **egg**

¼ cup **dry bread crumbs**

1 **onion,** grated

2 tbsp **wine vinegar**

2 tsp **Dijon mustard**

1 tsp **dried marjoram**

1 clove **garlic,** minced

½ tsp each **salt** and **pepper**

1 lb (450 g) **ground lamb**

4 **buns**

Whisk together 2 tbsp water, egg, bread crumbs, onion, vinegar, mustard, marjoram, garlic, salt and pepper; mix in lamb. Shape into four ¾-inch (2 cm) thick patties.

Grill, covered, on greased grill over medium heat, turning once, until no longer pink inside or instant-read thermometer registers 160°F (71°C), about 15 minutes. Serve in buns.

Makes 4 burgers.

PER BURGER: about 503 cal, 27 g pro, 26 g total fat (10 g sat. fat), 38 g carb, 3 g fibre, 126 mg chol, 786 mg sodium. % RDI: 12% calcium, 30% iron, 2% vit A, 3% vit C, 40% folate.

Lamb Burgers With Grilled Vegetables

Top these Middle Eastern–spiced burgers with yogurt or hummus and pickled peppers.

1 **egg**

1 cup minced **red onion**

¼ cup **fresh bread crumbs**

¼ cup chopped **fresh dill**

¼ cup chopped **fresh parsley**

4 cloves **garlic,** minced

1 tbsp **pine nuts** (optional)

1 tbsp **ketchup**

½ tsp each **salt** and **pepper**

¼ tsp **sweet paprika**

¼ tsp **cayenne pepper**

1 lb (450 g) **lean ground lamb** or lean ground beef

GRILLED VEGETABLES:

4 thick slices peeled **large eggplant** or 12 thick slices Asian eggplant (unpeeled)

4 thick slices **tomato**

2 tbsp **extra-virgin olive oil**

¼ tsp each **salt** and **pepper**

Whisk together egg, onion, bread crumbs, dill, parsley, garlic, pine nuts (if using), ketchup, salt, pepper, paprika and cayenne; mix in lamb. Shape into four ¾-inch (2 cm) thick patties.

Grill, covered, on greased grill over medium heat, turning once, until no longer pink inside or instant-read thermometer registers 160°F (71°C), about 15 minutes.

Grilled Vegetables: Meanwhile, brush eggplant and tomato with oil; sprinkle with salt and pepper. Grill, covered and turning once, until tender, about 5 minutes for eggplant and 1 minute for tomato. Serve on burgers.

Makes 4 burgers.

PER BURGER (WITHOUT BUN): about 336 cal, 24 g pro, 21 g total fat (7 g sat. fat), 13 g carb, 3 g fibre, 126 mg chol, 567 mg sodium. % RDI: 4% calcium, 21% iron, 9% vit A, 27% vit C, 19% folate.

Herb & Spice Lamb Burgers

Serve these lively and sophisticated burgers topped with sliced tomato, sliced cucumber and Tahini Sauce (page 101), or with Grilled Marinated Peppers (page 101).

1 **egg**

1 **small onion,** finely chopped

⅓ cup minced **fresh mint**

⅓ cup minced **fresh parsley**

2 tbsp **lemon juice**

1 tbsp minced seeded **green hot pepper**

2 cloves **garlic,** minced

2 tsp **ground coriander**

1 tsp **dried marjoram** or oregano

¾ tsp **salt**

½ tsp **ground cumin**

½ tsp **pepper**

¼ tsp **ground allspice**

1 lb (450 g) **lean ground lamb**

Whisk together egg, onion, mint, parsley, lemon juice, hot pepper, garlic, coriander, marjoram, salt, cumin, pepper and allspice; mix in lamb. Shape into four ¾-inch (2 cm) thick patties.

Grill, covered, on greased grill over medium heat, turning once, until no longer pink inside or instant-read thermometer registers 160°F (71°C), about 15 minutes.

Makes 4 burgers.

PER BURGER (WITHOUT BUN): about 251 cal, 21 g pro, 16 g total fat (7 g sat. fat), 4 g carb, 1 g fibre, 120 mg chol, 371 mg sodium. % RDI: 5% calcium, 20% iron, 8% vit A, 25% vit C, 15% folate.

Feta & Lamb Burger Pitas

Serve with leaf lettuce, sliced cucumbers and chopped tomatoes to add to the pita.

¼ cup **plain yogurt**

1 tbsp chopped **fresh mint**

4 **pitas (with pockets)**

½ cup crumbled **feta cheese**

2 tbsp sliced **Kalamata olives**

PATTIES:

1 **egg**

¼ cup **dried bread crumbs**

Half **onion,** grated

2 cloves **garlic,** minced

2 tbsp **wine vinegar**

2 tsp **Dijon mustard**

½ tsp **salt**

½ tsp **dried oregano**

¼ tsp **pepper**

1 lb (450 g) **ground lamb**

Patties: Whisk together 1 tbsp water, egg, bread crumbs, onion, garlic, vinegar, mustard, salt, oregano and pepper; mix in lamb. Shape into four ¾-inch (2 cm) thick patties.

Grill, covered, on greased grill over medium heat, turning once, until no longer pink inside or instant-read thermometer registers 160°F (71°C), about 15 minutes.

Mix yogurt with mint. Serve burgers in pitas with yogurt mixture, feta cheese and olives.

Makes 4 burgers.

Photo, page 96

PER BURGER: about 544 cal, 31 g pro, 27 g total fat (12 g sat. fat), 43 g carb, 2 g fibre, 143 mg chol, 1,129 mg sodium, 454 mg potassium. % RDI: 20% calcium, 30% iron, 5% vit A, 2% vit C, 48% folate.

Venison Burgers With Red Wine Mushrooms

Fabulously tasty but very lean, venison benefits from the addition of a little animal fat, such as lard or butter; egg yolks add extra richness.

3 tbsp **lard** or butter

1 **onion,** finely chopped

¾ tsp **salt**

1 tsp **sweet paprika**

¼ tsp **chipotle chili powder**
   or pinch cayenne pepper

¼ tsp **ground cumin**

¼ tsp **pepper**

2 **egg yolks**

1 tsp **Worcestershire sauce**

1 lb (450 g) **ground venison**

RED WINE MUSHROOMS:

8 oz (225 g) **white mushrooms** or
   cremini mushrooms

2 tbsp **butter**

1 clove **garlic,** minced

⅓ cup **dry red wine**

¼ tsp **salt**

¼ tsp **dried oregano,** crumbled

1 tsp **sherry vinegar** or
   red wine vinegar

2 tbsp chopped **fresh parsley**

Red Wine Mushrooms: With mandoline or sharp knife, slice mushrooms as thinly as possible. In skillet, melt butter over medium-high heat; sauté mushrooms and garlic until mushrooms are browned, 3 to 5 minutes. Add wine, salt and oregano; cook until no liquid remains. Stir in vinegar. Remove from heat; stir in parsley.

In skillet, melt lard over medium-high heat; fry onion and ¼ tsp of the salt, stirring often, until golden, 6 to 8 minutes. Reduce heat to low; stir in paprika, chipotle chili powder, cumin and pepper. Cook, stirring, for 1 minute. Scrape into bowl; let cool slightly. Whisk in egg yolks, Worcestershire sauce and remaining salt; mix in venison. Shape into four ¾-inch (2 cm) thick patties.

Grill, covered, on greased grill over medium heat, turning once, until no longer pink inside or instant-read thermometer registers 160°F (71°C), about 15 minutes. Top with red wine mushrooms.

Makes 4 burgers.

PER BURGER (WITHOUT BUN): about 382 cal, 28 g pro, 26 g total fat (12 g sat. fat), 6 g carb, 2 g fibre, 218 mg chol, 710 mg sodium, 598 mg potassium. % RDI: 4% calcium, 34% iron, 14% vit A, 10% vit C, 16% folate.

Grilled Prosciutto & Fig Sandwiches

Look for fig spread in the cheese section of your grocery store. The brand we used, Dalmatia Fig Spread, comes from Korcula, Croatia. Prosciutto and cheese are both naturally high in sodium, so watch your portion size and choose lower-sodium foods to balance out your day.

¼ cup **prepared fig spread**

8 slices **crusty Italian bread**

8 thin slices **prosciutto**
(about 4 oz/115 g)

8 thin slices **Asiago cheese**
(about 4 oz/115 g)

2 cups lightly packed **baby arugula**

2 tbsp **olive oil**

Spread fig spread over 4 of the bread slices; top with prosciutto, Asiago cheese, arugula and remaining bread. Brush both sides of each sandwich with olive oil.

Grill, covered, on greased grill over medium heat, turning once and pressing occasionally with spatula, until bread is toasted and cheese is melted, about 12 minutes. Cut in half before serving.

Makes 4 sandwiches.

PER SANDWICH: about 501 cal, 23 g pro, 22 g total fat (9 g sat. fat), 51 g carb, 4 g fibre, 55 mg chol, 1,388 mg sodium, 348 mg potassium. % RDI: 33% calcium, 21% iron, 12% vit A, 5% vit C, 51% folate.

Gourmet Teriyaki Chicken Sandwiches

If you're doing some casual entertaining, why not serve these flavourful open-faced sandwiches? Add a simple green salad, and dinner practically serves itself.

4 **boneless skinless chicken breasts**

2 tsp **vegetable oil**

⅓ cup **Teriyaki Sauce** (page 531)

4 thick slices **crusty bread**

4 leaves **leaf lettuce** or frisée

4 tsp toasted **sesame seeds**

CAPER MAYONNAISE:

½ cup light or regular **mayonnaise**

2 tbsp **extra-virgin olive oil**

1 tbsp minced drained **capers**

2 tsp **Dijon mustard**

2 tsp **lemon juice**

¼ tsp **white pepper**

Caper Mayonnaise: Mix together mayonnaise, oil, capers, mustard, lemon juice and pepper.

Brush chicken all over with oil. Grill, covered, on greased grill over medium-high heat, turning once, for 8 minutes. Brush both sides with some of the teriyaki sauce. Grill, covered, turning and brushing with remaining sauce, until no longer pink inside, about 2 minutes. Let stand for 3 minutes before slicing.

Spread caper mayonnaise on bread; top with lettuce and chicken. Sprinkle with sesame seeds.

Makes 4 sandwiches.

PER SANDWICH: about 447 cal, 35 g pro, 23 g total fat (4 g sat. fat), 23 g carb, 1 g fibre, 88 mg chol, 1,299 mg sodium. % RDI: 4% calcium, 16% iron, 3% vit A, 5% vit C, 20% folate.

Grilled Chicken Banh Mi

If you can't find chicken cutlets for these Vietnamese subs, slice 2 boneless skinless chicken breasts in half horizontally. Sandwich each piece between plastic wrap and pound with meat mallet or heavy skillet to ¼-inch (5 mm) thickness.

2 tbsp **Asian sweet chili sauce**

1 tbsp **soy sauce**

1 **green onion,** minced

4 **chicken cutlets**

½ cup **boiling water**

¼ cup **unseasoned rice vinegar**

3 tbsp **granulated sugar**

½ tsp **salt**

1 **carrot,** cut into 2-inch (5 cm) julienne

1 cup **daikon radish** julienne (2 inch/5 cm)

4 **small submarine rolls,** halved

¼ cup **mayonnaise**

1 tsp **sriracha**

12 sprigs **fresh cilantro**

In resealable plastic bag or shallow dish, whisk sweet chili sauce, soy sauce and green onion; add chicken, turning to coat. Marinate for 30 minutes or, covered and refrigerated, up to 1 day, turning occasionally.

Meanwhile, whisk together boiling water, rice vinegar, sugar and salt until sugar is dissolved. Let cool. Add carrot and daikon; cover and refrigerate for 1 hour or up to 1 week. Drain.

Discarding marinade, grill chicken, covered, on greased grill over medium heat, turning once, until no longer pink inside, about 11 minutes. Transfer chicken to cutting board; let stand for 5 minutes before slicing lengthwise to fit rolls.

Meanwhile, toast rolls on grill.

Mix mayonnaise with sriracha; spread on rolls. Sandwich chicken, carrot mixture and cilantro in rolls.

Makes 4 sandwiches.

Asian sweet chili sauce is a thick, translucent sauce. It's very sweet – a bit like plum sauce – and usually served with chicken. Sriracha is a spicy Vietnamese chili sauce. It's sold in a distinctive squeeze bottle emblazoned with a picture of a rooster.

PER SANDWICH: about 392 cal, 23 g pro, 14 g total fat (3 g sat. fat), 42 g carb, 2 g fibre, 51 mg chol, 964 mg sodium, 424 mg potassium. % RDI: 9% calcium, 17% iron, 38% vit A, 13% vit C, 34% folate.

Bocconcini Chicken Burgers

Grinding chicken thighs in your food processor for this burger, rather than using already-ground chicken, gives the best flavour and texture. A Caprese salad topping of bocconcini cheese, tomatoes and basil adds a fresh kick.

4 **buns**

4 slices **bocconcini cheese** (one 4-oz/115 g ball)

1 **plum tomato,** sliced

4 **large fresh basil leaves**

PATTIES:

1 lb (450 g) **boneless skinless chicken thighs**

1 **egg**

Half **onion,** grated

2 cloves **garlic,** minced

⅓ cup grated **Parmesan cheese**

¼ cup **dry bread crumbs**

2 tbsp chopped **fresh basil**

2 tbsp chopped drained **oil-packed sun-dried tomatoes**

¼ tsp each **salt** and **pepper**

Patties: In food processor, pulse chicken until coarsely ground; set aside. Whisk together 1 tbsp water, egg, onion, garlic, cheese, bread crumbs, basil, sun-dried tomatoes, salt and pepper; mix in chicken. Shape into four ¾-inch (2 cm) thick patties.

Grill, covered, on greased grill over medium heat, turning once, until no longer pink inside or instant-read thermometer registers 165°F (74°C), about 15 minutes.

Serve burgers in buns with bocconcini, tomato and basil leaves.

Makes 4 burgers.

Photo, page 96

PER BURGER: about 499 cal, 39 g pro, 20 g total fat (8 g sat. fat), 40 g carb, 3 g fibre, 170 mg chol, 904 mg sodium, 534 mg potassium. % RDI: 35% calcium, 29% iron, 12% vit A, 15% vit C, 40% folate.

Thai-Style Grilled Chicken Wraps

For an extra hit of fresh flavour, tuck a few more sprigs of fresh cilantro and mint into the wrap before rolling it up.

¼ cup **lime juice**

¼ cup each chopped **fresh cilantro** and **fresh mint**

2 tbsp **fish sauce**

1 tbsp **vegetable oil**

1 **Thai bird's-eye pepper** or jalapeño pepper, seeded

1 clove **garlic,** minced

8 **boneless skinless chicken thighs**

4 tsp **light mayonnaise**

1 tsp packed **brown sugar**

4 **large flour tortillas**

1 **green onion,** thinly sliced

8 leaves **romaine lettuce,** trimmed

Whisk together 2 tbsp of the lime juice; 1 tbsp each of the cilantro, mint and fish sauce; the oil; Thai pepper; and garlic. Add chicken, turning to coat. Marinate for 10 minutes.

Reserving any remaining marinade, place chicken on greased grill over medium heat; brush with marinade. Grill, covered and turning once, until juices run clear when chicken is pierced, about 10 minutes. Let cool before slicing thinly.

Whisk together remaining lime juice, cilantro, mint and fish sauce; the mayonnaise; and sugar. Toss with chicken to coat.

Divide among tortillas; sprinkle with onion and top with lettuce. Fold in sides and bottom; roll up. Grill, turning once, until slightly crisp and grill marked, about 3 minutes.

Makes 4 wraps.

PER WRAP: about 469 cal, 32 g pro, 17 g total fat (4 g sat. fat), 45 g carb, 3 g fibre, 97 mg chol, 1,166 mg sodium, 479 mg potassium. % RDI: 6% calcium, 32% iron, 9% vit A, 15% vit C, 56% folate.

Grilled Salmon Patties

These patties are quite wet when they are first made, but they firm up in the freezer. If you can't get skinless fillets, simply remove the skin from the fillets with a sharp boning knife.

1 **egg,** lightly beaten

1 **green onion,** minced

¼ cup chopped **fresh cilantro**

2 tbsp grated **fresh ginger**

1 tsp **pepper**

½ tsp **coarse sea salt**

¼ tsp **hot pepper flakes**

1 lb (450 g) **skinless salmon fillets,** finely chopped

3 tbsp **light mayonnaise**

Lime wedges

Whisk together egg, green onion, cilantro, ginger, pepper, salt and hot pepper flakes; gently mix in salmon. Shape into eight 1-inch (2.5 cm) thick patties. Freeze in single layer on baking sheet just until firm, 30 minutes.

Grill, covered, on greased grill over medium heat, turning once, until no longer translucent in centre, about 12 minutes. Serve with mayonnaise and lime wedges.

Makes 4 servings.

PER SERVING: about 245 cal, 22 g pro, 16 g total fat (3 g sat. fat), 3 g carb, trace fibre, 106 mg chol, 340 mg sodium, 409 mg potassium. % RDI: 2% calcium, 5% iron, 5% vit A, 7% vit C, 18% folate.

Grilled Whitefish BLTs

Whitefish is one of the special pleasures of central Canadian waters. Its delicate white flesh is versatile, as in this sandwich inspired by Ontario chef Paul Johnston.

2 **skin-on whitefish fillets,** each about 12 oz (340 g)

2 tbsp **extra-virgin olive oil**

1 tbsp chopped **fresh tarragon,** thyme or coriander

1 tsp grated **lime zest**

1 tsp **lime juice**

¼ tsp each **salt** and **pepper**

4 pieces **focaccia,** each 4 inches (10 cm) square

4 **lettuce leaves**

4 slices **prosciutto**

1 **yellow tomato** or red tomato, sliced

DILL PICKLE AIOLI:

2 cloves **garlic,** minced

Pinch **salt**

½ cup light or regular **mayonnaise**

2 tbsp finely chopped **dill pickle**

2 tsp **lemon juice**

Pinch each **turmeric** and **cayenne pepper**

Dill Pickle Aioli: On cutting board, coarsely chop garlic; sprinkle with salt. With flat side of knife or fork, mash into paste. Transfer to bowl; whisk in mayonnaise, pickle, lemon juice, turmeric and cayenne.

Cut each fillet in half diagonally. Whisk together oil, tarragon, lime zest and juice, salt and pepper; rub all over fish. Let stand for 30 minutes.

Grill, covered and skin side down, on greased grill over medium-high heat, turning once, until fish flakes easily when tested, about 8 minutes.

Cut each piece of focaccia in half horizontally; serve fish sandwiched in focaccia with dill pickle aioli, lettuce, prosciutto and tomato.

Makes 4 sandwiches.

PER SANDWICH: about 731 cal, 42 g pro, 31 g total fat (4 g sat. fat), 69 g carb, 4 g fibre, 100 mg chol, 1,626 mg sodium. % RDI: 13% calcium, 32% iron, 12% vit A, 17% vit C, 85% folate.

Grilled Salmon Sandwiches With Bok Choy Slaw

Bok choy gives the slaw on this tender salmon sandwich a bit of Asian flair.

4 **skinless salmon fillets,** each 6 oz (170 g)

½ tsp **salt**

¼ tsp **white pepper**

4 tsp **sesame oil**

4 **sesame buns**

BOK CHOY SLAW:

2 cups shredded **bok choy** or napa cabbage

1 tsp **salt**

½ cup grated **carrot**

¼ cup minced **fresh cilantro**

4 tsp **unseasoned rice vinegar**

GREEN ONION MAYONNAISE:

½ cup thinly sliced **green onions**

⅓ cup **mayonnaise**

4 tsp **sesame oil**

4 tsp **unseasoned rice vinegar**

1 tsp **granulated sugar**

Generous pinch **white pepper**

Bok Choy Slaw: Toss bok choy with salt; let stand for 15 minutes. Using hands, squeeze out moisture; toss together bok choy, carrot, cilantro and vinegar.

Green Onion Mayonnaise: Mix together onions, mayonnaise, sesame oil, vinegar, sugar and pepper.

Sprinkle fish all over with salt and pepper; brush with oil. Grill, covered, on greased grill over medium-high heat, turning once, until just slightly pink in centre and fish flakes easily, 6 to 8 minutes. Serve in buns with green onion mayonnaise and bok choy slaw.

Makes 4 sandwiches.

PER SANDWICH: about 681 cal, 36 g pro, 43 g total fat (7 g sat. fat), 36 g carb, 3 g fibre, 91 mg chol, 1,128 mg sodium, 777 mg potassium. % RDI: 14% calcium, 21% iron, 38% vit A, 40% vit C, 63% folate.

Spiced Tilapia Sandwiches With Onion Salad

Aromatic spices and a creamy tahini sauce turn tilapia into a Middle Eastern delight.

1 tsp **sweet paprika**

1 tsp **ground coriander**

1 tsp **ground cumin**

1 tsp each **salt** and **pepper**

½ tsp **cayenne pepper**

4 **tilapia fillets** or catfish fillets,
    each 6 oz (170 g)

4 tsp **olive oil**

8 thick slices **bread**

ONION SALAD:

1 cup thinly sliced **white onion**
    or sweet onion

1 tsp + pinch **salt**

¼ cup chopped **fresh parsley**

4 tsp **lemon juice**

2 tsp **extra-virgin olive oil**

½ tsp **sweet paprika**

TAHINI YOGURT SAUCE:

¼ cup **plain yogurt**

3 tbsp **tahini**

2 tbsp **lemon juice**

¼ tsp **ground cumin**

½ tsp **hot pepper sauce**

Onion Salad: Toss onion with 1 tsp of the salt; let stand for 20 minutes. Using hands, squeeze out liquid; rinse under cold water and drain, pressing to remove excess moisture. Toss together onions, parsley, lemon juice, oil, paprika and remaining salt.

Tahini Yogurt Sauce: Mix together yogurt, tahini, lemon juice, cumin and hot pepper sauce.

Mix together paprika, coriander, cumin, salt, pepper and cayenne; sprinkle all over fish. Brush with oil. Grill, covered, on greased grill over medium-high heat, turning once, until fish flakes easily when tested, about 6 minutes. Sandwich in bread with tahini yogurt sauce and onion salad.

Makes 4 sandwiches.

PER SANDWICH: about 481 cal, 43 g pro, 19 g total fat (4 g sat. fat), 37 g carb, 4 g fibre, 78 mg chol, 1,125 mg sodium, 777 mg potassium. % RDI: 16% calcium, 35% iron, 9% vit A, 18% vit C, 40% folate.

Grilled Eggplant & Pepper Panini

Warm and melty, this cheese-topped Italian-style sandwich will please vegetarians as well as omnivores.

1 **eggplant,** cut into ¼-inch (5 mm) thick slices

2 **sweet red peppers,** quartered

2 tbsp **extra-virgin olive oil**

2 cloves **garlic,** minced

¼ tsp each **salt** and **pepper**

4 **panini buns**

2 tsp **hot mustard** or Dijon mustard

12 **fresh basil leaves**

4 oz (115 g) thinly sliced **provolone cheese**

Toss together eggplant, peppers, oil, garlic, salt and pepper until coated. Grill, covered, on greased grill over medium-high heat, turning once, until tender, about 10 minutes.

Cut buns in half horizontally; spread with mustard. Sandwich eggplant, peppers, basil and cheese in buns.

Grill, covered, on greased grill over medium heat, pressing often with spatula to flatten and turning once, until buns are crusty and cheese is melted, 5 minutes.

Makes 4 sandwiches.

PER SANDWICH: about 393 cal, 15 g pro, 18 g total fat (6 g sat. fat), 45 g carb, 5 g fibre, 20 mg chol, 770 mg sodium. % RDI: 27% calcium, 21% iron, 30% vit A, 167% vit C, 40% folate.

Bulgur & Mushroom Burgers

Serve these burgers on whole wheat kaiser rolls with lettuce and sliced tomato.

1 cup **boiling water**

¾ cup **bulgur**

1 **egg,** beaten

1 cup **fresh whole wheat bread crumbs**

¼ cup minced **fresh parsley**

8 oz (225 g) **mushrooms**

2 tbsp **extra-virgin olive oil**

1 **small onion,** finely chopped

2 cloves **garlic,** minced

¼ cup **dry white wine** or vegetable broth

½ tsp **salt**

¼ tsp **pepper**

¼ tsp **dried thyme**

In heatproof bowl, pour boiling water over bulgur; let stand until doubled in bulk, about 20 minutes. Mix in egg, bread crumbs and parsley.

Meanwhile, roughly break mushrooms into pieces; in food processor, pulse until finely chopped. In skillet, heat oil over medium heat; fry onion and garlic until softened, about 3 minutes. Stir in mushrooms, wine, salt, pepper and thyme; cook over medium-high heat, stirring occasionally, until liquid is evaporated and mushrooms begin to brown, about 8 minutes.

Mix into bulgur mixture. Shape into four ¾-inch (2 cm) thick patties.

Grill, covered, on greased grill over medium heat, turning once, until heated through and crispy, about 15 minutes.

Makes 4 burgers.

PER BURGER (WITHOUT BUN): about 220 cal, 7 g pro, 9 g total fat (1 g sat. fat), 30 g carb, 5 g fibre, 47 mg chol, 370 mg sodium. % RDI: 4% calcium, 19% iron, 4% vit A, 12% vit C, 20% folate.

Grilled Portobello & Cheese Burgers

Meaty, dense portobello mushrooms are a delicious substitute for hamburgers – even for meat lovers.

4 **large portobello mushrooms**

4 thick slices **red onion**

3 tbsp **olive oil**

¼ tsp each **salt** and **pepper**

4 slices **provolone cheese**

4 **whole wheat hamburger buns**

⅓ cup **prepared roasted red pepper spread** or mayonnaise

4 leaves **lettuce**

8 slices **tomato**

8 **fresh basil leaves**

Remove stems and gills from mushrooms; wipe caps clean. Skewer onion slices through edges to keep rings intact. Brush mushrooms and onion with oil; sprinkle with salt and pepper.

Grill, covered, on greased grill over medium-high heat, turning once, until tender and grill marked, about 10 minutes. Remove onions to plate.

Top each mushroom cap with 1 slice cheese; grill, covered, just until cheese is melted, 2 minutes.

Meanwhile, spread buns with red pepper spread. Sandwich lettuce, tomato, mushrooms, onion and basil in buns.

Makes 4 burgers.

PER BURGER: about 414 cal, 16 g pro, 25 g total fat (7 g sat. fat), 37 g carb, 7 g fibre, 23 mg chol, 704 mg sodium, 704 mg potassium. % RDI: 26% calcium, 15% iron, 21% vit A, 22% vit C, 22% folate.

Grilled Eggplant & Tomato Sandwiches

Focaccia makes this sandwich delightfully soft and delicious. Try the romano mayo on cold-cut sandwiches, too.

1 **large eggplant,** about 1 lb (450 g)

½ tsp **salt**

¼ cup **extra-virgin olive oil**

1 tbsp **lemon juice**

½ tsp **dried thyme**

Pinch **pepper**

1 **focaccia**

2 **tomatoes,** sliced

6 **large fresh basil leaves**

ROMANO MAYO:

¼ cup **light mayonnaise**

2 tbsp grated **Romano cheese**

1 tsp **lemon juice**

¼ tsp **pepper**

Peel eggplant; cut into ½-inch (1 cm) thick slices. Sprinkle with salt. Let stand in colander until moisture seeps out, about 10 minutes. Pat dry with paper towel. Whisk together oil, lemon juice, thyme and pepper; brush half over eggplant.

Grill eggplant, covered, on greased grill over medium heat, turning once and brushing with remaining oil mixture, until tender, about 10 minutes.

Romano Mayo: Meanwhile, whisk together mayonnaise, cheese, lemon juice and pepper.

Cut focaccia into quarters; cut each quarter in half horizontally. Sandwich eggplant, romano mayo, tomatoes and basil in focaccia.

Makes 4 sandwiches.

PER SANDWICH: about 490 cal, 11 g pro, 23 g total fat (4 g sat. fat), 64 g carb, 8 g fibre, 9 mg chol, 987 mg sodium, 298 mg potassium. % RDI: 5% calcium, 36% iron, 7% vit A, 17% vit C, 55% folate.

Italian Sausage Spiral

It takes a bit of skill to fill the casing of this sausage spiral evenly, but it is wonderfully easy to grill and makes a stunning presentation.

3 lb (1.35 kg) **boneless pork shoulder,** cut into 1½-inch (4 cm) chunks

2 tbsp chopped **fresh parsley**

2 tbsp chopped drained **oil-packed sun-dried tomatoes**

2 tsp **salt**

1½ tsp **pepper**

1 tsp minced **garlic**

Sausage casings

Using coarse disc on sausage grinder, grind pork. Mix in parsley, sun-dried tomatoes, salt, pepper and garlic. Chill well, in refrigerator for 3 to 4 hours or in freezer for 1½ to 2 hours.

Prepare casings, and grinding and stuffing equipment according to preferred method (see Sausage Tips, page 140).

Grind meat mixture through medium disc, sprinkling with up to ½ cup ice water, if needed, to keep mixture moist. Fill casings, without tying into links; coil together to form flat spiral.

Insert two 12-inch (30 cm) skewers, perpendicular to each other, through sides of spiral to secure. Prick sausage in several places.

Grill, covered, over medium-high heat, turning occasionally, until browned and juices run clear when sausage is pierced, or instant-read thermometer registers 160°F (71°C), 20 to 30 minutes.

Makes one 3-lb (1.35 kg) sausage spiral, about 8 to 10 servings.

VARIATION
Italian Sausage Patties
Omit casings; shape ground meat mixture into 12 patties. Grill, covered, on greased grill over medium-high heat, turning once, until no longer pink inside, about 15 minutes.

PER EACH OF 10 SERVINGS: about 251 cal, 24 g pro, 16 g total fat (6 g sat. fat), 1 g carb, trace fibre, 84 mg chol, 538 mg sodium, 343 mg potassium. % RDI: 1% calcium, 11% iron, 1% vit A, 3% vit C, 3% folate.

Sausage Tips

Preparing Casings

Soak fresh or frozen salted casings in plenty of water to cover for 15 minutes. Rinse under cold water, running water through inside. Keep casings well moistened for stuffing, leaving in water if not using immediately.

Preparing Meat Mixture

The colder the mixture, the easier it is to grind. Cold keeps the fat from softening and making the mixture sticky. Chilled water is often added to the mixture to give it extra moisture – add up to ½ cup ice water per 3 lb (1.35 kg) meat as necessary during last grinding or stuffing.

Stuffing Methods

Grinder With Sausage Stuffing Tube Attachment

With this attachment, you can grind meat directly into casings during the last grinding. For narrow casings or firmer mixtures, this can be difficult. For easier stuffing, grind meat first, then remove the grinding disc; run mixture again, through open tube, into casings.

Attach stuffing tube to grinder. Thread 1 length of casing onto tube, leaving about 3 inches (8 cm) hanging off.

Grind meat mixture directly into casings, being careful not to leave air pockets or overstuff. Prick any small air pockets with needle; press out air. Twist or tie to form links.

Stuffing by Hand With Piping Bag

For this method, it's convenient to have one person squeezing and refilling the bag and another handling the casing.

Place widest round tip in piping bag. Thread casing onto tip, leaving about 3 inches (8 cm) hanging off.

Stuff bag with meat mixture. Squeeze into casing, being careful not to leave air pockets or overstuff. Prick any small air pockets with needle; press out air. Twist or tie to form links.

Stuffing by Hand With Funnel

This method takes some practice, but in no time, you'll be an expert. It's the easiest method for one person to fill sausages without a machine.

Use funnel with ½- to ¾-inch (1 to 2 cm) diameter opening. Thread casing onto opening, leaving about 3 inches (8 cm) hanging off.

Place handful of meat mixture in funnel. With thumb, press mixture into casing, being careful not to leave air pockets or overstuff. Prick any small air pockets with needle; press out air. Twist or tie to form links.

Hot Italian Sausages

Here's a basic and simple sausage that is good for novices. You can play around with the flavourings to taste, of course, adding a little dried oregano or marjoram, for instance. Other common seasonings include ground coriander and paprika.

3 lb (1.35 kg) **boneless pork shoulder,** cut into 1½-inch (4 cm) chunks

1 tbsp **dried red hot peppers**

2 tsp **fennel seeds**

2 tsp **salt**

1 tsp **pepper**

Sausage casings

Using coarse disc on sausage grinder, grind pork. Mix in hot peppers, fennel seeds, salt and pepper. Chill well, in refrigerator for 3 to 4 hours or in freezer for 1½ to 2 hours.

Prepare casings, and grinding and stuffing equipment according to preferred method (see Sausage Tips, opposite).

Grind meat mixture through medium disc, sprinkling with up to ½ cup ice water, if needed, to keep mixture moist. Fill casings; twist into 6-inch (15 cm) links. Prick each in 3 or 4 places.

Grill, covered, over medium-high heat, turning once, until browned and juices run clear when sausage is pierced, or instant-read thermometer registers 160°F (71°C), 20 to 25 minutes.

Makes 8 to ten 6-inch (15 cm) sausages.

VARIATION
Hot Italian Sausage Patties
Omit casings; shape ground meat mixture into 12 patties. Grill, covered, on greased grill over medium-high heat, turning once, until no longer pink inside, about 15 minutes.

PER EACH OF 10 SAUSAGES: about 250 cal, 24 g pro, 16 g total fat (6 g sat. fat), 1 g carb, trace fibre, 84 mg chol, 521 mg sodium, 321 mg potassium. % RDI: 1% calcium, 11% iron, 1% vit A, 2% vit C, 2% folate.

Beef & Pork Bratwurst

These fairly lean, mainly beef bratwurst-type sausages are just touched with garlic and sweet spices, making them exceptionally tasty.

3 lb (1.35 kg) **boneless beef blade roast,** cut into 1-inch (2.5 cm) cubes

2 lb (900 g) **skinless pork belly,** cut into 1-inch (2.5 cm) cubes

3 tbsp **salt**

4 tsp **granulated sugar**

4 cloves **garlic,** pressed or minced

4 tsp **sweet paprika**

1¼ tsp finely ground **caraway seeds**

1 tsp **nutmeg**

¾ tsp **black pepper**

½ tsp **white pepper**

Generous ¼ tsp **ground cloves**

Generous ¼ tsp **saltpeter** (optional)

⅓ cup chilled **beef broth** or pork stock, or ice water

Sausage casings

Toss beef with pork belly. Mix salt, sugar, garlic, paprika, caraway seeds, nutmeg, black and white pepper, cloves, and saltpeter (if using); sprinkle over meat, tossing to coat. Transfer to resealable plastic bag; seal and refrigerate for 2 days, turning once or twice a day.

Mix in broth. Chill in freezer for 2 to 3 hours.

Place large bowl over another bowl of ice. Using coarse disc on sausage grinder, grind meat mixture into chilled bowl. Change to fine disc; grind through again, keeping bowl and meat mixture as chilled as possible.

Prepare casings, and grinding and stuffing equipment according to preferred method (see Sausage Tips, page 140).

Grind meat mixture a second time through fine disc. Fill casings; twist into 5-inch (12 cm) links. Prick each in 3 or 4 places.

Grill, covered, over medium-high heat, turning often, until browned and juices run clear when sausage is pierced, or instant-read thermometer registers 160°F (71°C), 20 to 30 minutes.

Makes about twenty 5-inch (12 cm) sausages.

TIP
Saltpeter (potassium nitrate) is a natural preservative and gives the sausage a pinkish hue, but it isn't necessary for the flavour.

PER SAUSAGE: about 344 cal, 18 g pro, 30 g total fat (11 g sat. fat), 2 g carb, trace fibre, 69 mg chol, 1,098 mg sodium, 204 mg potassium. % RDI: 1% calcium, 12% iron, 2% vit A, 2% vit C, 1% folate.

Pork, Apple, Sage & Stilton Sausages

Cheese isn't a typical sausage filling, but here it adds a creamy tang that's addictive. Be sure to work with a partner and use medium-width pork sausage casings – lamb casings are too narrow.

2 tbsp **olive oil**

2 cups minced **onion**

2 cups chopped peeled **tart apple**

3 lb (1.35 kg) **boneless pork shoulder,** cut into 1½-inch (4 cm) cubes

2 cups crumbled **Stilton cheese** or other crumbly blue cheese

¼ cup **grainy Dijon mustard**

1 tbsp **dried sage leaves,** crumbled

1¼ tsp **salt**

1 tsp **cracked pepper**

Pork sausage casings

In large skillet, heat oil over medium-high heat; sauté onion until golden, about 10 minutes. Stir in apple; cook, stirring, for 5 minutes. Let cool completely.

In large bowl, toss together pork, Stilton, mustard, sage, salt, pepper and onion mixture. Transfer to resealable plastic bag; seal and refrigerate for 1 to 2 days.

Place large bowl over another bowl of ice. Using coarse disc on sausage grinder, grind meat mixture into chilled bowl. Change to fine disc; grind through again, keeping bowl and meat mixture as chilled as possible.

Prepare casings, and grinding and stuffing equipment according to preferred method (see Sausage Tips, page 140).

Grind meat mixture a second time through fine disc. Fill casings; twist into 5-inch (12 cm) links. Prick each in 3 or 4 places.

Grill, covered, over medium-high heat, turning occasionally, until browned and juices run clear when sausage is pierced, or instant-read thermometer registers 160°F (71°C), 20 to 30 minutes.

Makes about thirteen 5-inch (12 cm) sausages.

PER SAUSAGE: about 385 cal, 24 g pro, 30 g total fat (12 g sat. fat), 5 g carb, 1 g fibre, 95 mg chol, 538 mg sodium, 381 mg potassium. % RDI: 8% calcium, 10% iron, 12% vit A, 2% vit C, 11% folate.

Beef, Caramelized Shallot & Thyme Sausages

The beef makes this sausage surprisingly lean, but offers a rich meatiness that's the perfect counterpoint to sweet shallots and fresh thyme.

2 tbsp **olive oil**

1 tbsp **butter**

3 cups sliced **shallots**

6 cloves **garlic,** minced

2 tbsp **red wine vinegar**

1 tbsp **soy sauce**

1¼ tsp **salt**

1 tsp **cracked pepper**

3 lb (1.35 kg) **boneless beef blade roast,** cut into 1½-inch (4 cm) cubes

2 tbsp **fresh thyme**

Pork sausage casings

In large skillet, heat oil with butter over medium-high heat; sauté shallots until deep golden and very tender, about 20 minutes. Stir in garlic, red wine vinegar, soy sauce, salt and pepper; cook, stirring, for 2 minutes. Let cool completely.

In large bowl, toss together beef, shallot mixture and thyme until well combined. Transfer to resealable plastic bag; seal and refrigerate for 1 to 2 days.

Place large bowl over another bowl of ice. Using coarse disc on sausage grinder, grind meat mixture into chilled bowl. Change to fine disc; grind through again, keeping bowl and meat mixture as chilled as possible.

Prepare casings, and grinding and stuffing equipment according to preferred method (see Sausage Tips, page 140.)

Grind meat mixture a second time through fine disc. Fill casings; twist into 5-inch (12 cm) links. Prick each in 3 or 4 places.

Grill, covered, over medium-high heat, turning occasionally, until browned and juices run clear when sausage is pierced, or instant-read thermometer registers 160°F (71°C), 20 to 30 minutes.

Makes about thirteen 5-inch (12 cm) sausages.

PER SAUSAGE: about 200 cal, 21 g pro, 11 g total fat (4 g sat. fat), 4 g carb, 1 g fibre, 58 mg chol, 335 mg sodium, 232 mg potassium. % RDI: 2% calcium, 17% iron, 3% vit A, 2% vit C, 4% folate.

Lamb & Leek Sausages

These fabulous sausages are inspired by memories of those made by a long-closed butcher in Toronto's Greektown on Danforth Avenue. These are mildly spicy, but if you want a sweet sausage, just omit the hot pepper.

4 lb (1.8 kg) **boneless lamb shoulder** or leg, cut into 1-inch (2.5 cm) cubes

1 lb (450 g) **skinless pork belly,** cut into 1-inch (2.5 cm) cubes

2 tbsp **salt**

2½ tsp **dried Greek oregano** or 2 tsp dried marjoram

2 tsp **ground coriander**

2 tsp **ground dried hot peppers**

1½ tsp **pepper**

1¼ tsp **ground allspice**

1 lb (450 g) **leeks** (white and light green parts only), chopped

¾ cup **dry white wine**

Sausage casings

Toss lamb with pork. Mix together salt, oregano, coriander, hot peppers, pepper and allspice; sprinkle over meat, tossing to coat. Mix in leeks and wine. Transfer to resealable plastic bag; seal and refrigerate for 1 day, turning once or twice.

Prepare casings, and grinding and stuffing equipment according to preferred method (see Sausage Tips, page 140).

Grind meat mixture through coarse disc. Fill casings; twist into 5-inch (12 cm) links. Prick each in 3 or 4 places.

Grill, covered, over medium-high heat, turning once, until browned and juices run clear when sausage is pierced, or instant-read thermometer registers 160°F (71°C), 20 to 25 minutes.

Makes about twenty-five 5-inch (12 cm) sausages.

Homemade sausages don't contain preservatives, so you need to cook them within 1 day of making them. If you want to keep them longer, separate into links and freeze in recipe-friendly portions in an airtight container for up to 1 month.

PER SAUSAGE: about 248 cal, 14 g pro, 20 g total fat (8 g sat. fat), 1 g carb, trace fibre, 63 mg chol, 597 mg sodium, 196 mg potassium. % RDI: 2% calcium, 11% iron, 1% vit A, 2% vit C, 7% folate.

Merguez Sausages

These popular North African sausages are flavoured with harissa, a spice paste often available in gourmet and specialty stores. Narrow lamb casings can be harder to fill. If you're using a grinder with a stuffing tube attachment, grind the meat mixture first, then remove the grinding disc before filling the casings using the stuffing tube.

3 lb (1.35 kg) **boneless lamb shoulder,** cut into 2-inch (5 cm) chunks

4 cloves **garlic,** chopped

1 tbsp **harissa**

2 tsp **salt**

1 tsp **pepper**

1 tsp **ground fennel seeds**

½ tsp **ground allspice**

½ tsp **cayenne pepper**

Sausage casings, preferably lamb

Toss together lamb, garlic, harissa, salt, pepper, fennel seeds, allspice and cayenne pepper. Transfer to resealable plastic bag; seal and refrigerate overnight or up to 1 day, turning once or twice.

Using coarse disc on sausage grinder, grind lamb mixture. Chill well, in refrigerator for 3 to 4 hours or in freezer for 1½ to 2 hours.

Prepare casings, and grinding and stuffing equipment according to preferred method (see Sausage Tips, page 140).

Grind meat mixture through medium disc, sprinkling with up to ½ cup ice water, if needed, to keep mixture moist. Fill casings; twist into 6-inch (15 cm) links. Prick each in 3 or 4 places.

Grill, covered, over medium heat, turning once, until browned and juices run clear when sausage is pierced, or instant-read thermometer registers 160°F (71°C), 15 to 20 minutes.

Makes about twenty-four 6-inch (15 cm) sausages.

VARIATION
Merguez Patties
Omit casings; shape ground meat mixture into 12 patties. Grill, covered, on greased grill over medium heat, turning once, until no longer pink inside, 15 minutes.

PER SAUSAGE: about 120 cal, 10 g pro, 9 g total fat (4 g sat. fat), 1 g carb, trace fibre, 39 mg chol, 226 mg sodium, 121 mg potassium. % RDI: 1% calcium, 6% iron, 1% vit A, 4% folate.

Chorizo Patties With Pebre

Many South American feasts, especially in Argentina and Chile, involve a mixed grill that includes chorizo. Here, it is made into a simple patty. Serve with Chilean Pickled Onions (below).

⅓ cup **dry red wine**

2 cloves **garlic,** minced

1 tbsp **sweet paprika**

1 tsp **ground coriander**

¾ tsp **salt**

½ tsp each **nutmeg** and **white pepper**

⅛ tsp each **cayenne pepper** and **ground cloves**

⅓ cup finely diced **salt pork** (cured, not dry salted)

1⅓ lb (600 g) **lean ground pork**

⅔ lb (300 g) **lean ground beef**

Pebre Sauce (page 179)

Whisk together wine, garlic, paprika, coriander, salt, nutmeg, pepper, cayenne and cloves; mix in salt pork. Let stand for 30 to 60 minutes. Mix in pork and beef; cover and refrigerate for 1 to 3 days.

Shape into 8 patties. Grill, covered, on greased grill over medium heat, turning once, until no longer pink inside or instant-read thermometer registers 160°F (71°C), about 15 minutes. Serve with pebre sauce.

Makes 8 patties.

Chilean Pickled Onions

Slice 1 each Spanish onion and red onion into thin rings; place in heatproof bowl. Pour in enough boiling water to cover; let stand for 15 minutes. Drain; chill under cool water. Drain again; return to bowl. Slice 1 or 2 hot peppers into thin rings; mix with onions.

Whisk together ½ cup lime juice, 2 tbsp granulated sugar, 2 tbsp white wine vinegar or cider vinegar, and ½ tsp salt; pour over onions. Cover and refrigerate for 6 hours or up to 1 week.

Makes 4 cups.

PER PATTY (WITHOUT SAUCE OR ONIONS): about 232 cal, 24 g pro, 14 g total fat (5 g sat. fat), 1 g carb, 0 g fibre, 63 mg chol, 348 mg sodium. % RDI: 1% calcium, 12% iron, 6% vit A, 2% vit C, 5% folate.

Steak Tostadas With
Avocado & Radish
Slaw (page 173)

steaks, chops & ribs

Peppercorn-Crusted Steaks | 153

Grilled Steaks With Roquefort
  Cheese Butter | 155

Peppercorn Thyme T-Bones | 156

Mexican-Style Rib Eye Medallions
  With Peppers | 157

Grilled Tenderloin Steaks With
  Mushrooms & Peppers | 159

Rib Eye Steaks With Herb Butter | 160

Rib Steaks With Beer Marinade | 163

Thick-Cut Sirloin Steak | 164

Old-Style Red Wine Marinated
  "London Broil" | 165

Korean Steak Barbecue | 166

Rib Steak With
  Cherry Tomato Salsa | 168

Cumin Flank Steak With
  Avocado Salad | 169

Salt & Pepper Steak
  With Green Sauce | 170

Steak Tostadas With Avocado
  & Radish Slaw | 173

Grilled Steak Diable | 175

Gibson Flatiron Steak | 176

How to Trim a Flatiron Steak | 177

Mustard Garlic Flank Steak | 178

Grilled Flank Steak & Pebre | 179

Soy-Marinated Flank Steak | 180

Arugula & Beefsteak Salad With
  Tomato Vinaigrette | 183

Texas Barbecued Beef Ribs | 184

Devilled Beef Ribs | 185

Korean Beef Short Ribs | 186

How to Cut Traditional Kalbi | 187

Savoury Beef Short Ribs | 188

Hot-Smoked Spiced
  Beef Back Ribs | 189

Steak House Beef Ribs With
  Stout Barbecue Sauce | 191

Chipotle-Glazed Beef Short Ribs | 192

Grilled Venison Chops | 195

Garlic-Marinated Veal Chops With
  Grilled Potato Salad | 196

Deli-Style Spiced Bison Steaks | 197

Grilled Veal Chops With Fines-Herbes
  Butter | 199

Ginger Garlic Pork Chops | 200

Barbecued Peach Pork Chops | 202

Pork Chops With Chimichurri Rojo | 204

Grilled Pork Chops With
  Pineapple Salsa | 207

Grilled Lemon Pork Chops | 208

Slow-Grilled Barbecue Pork Ribs | 210

Barbecue Beer Ribs | 211

Whiskey Sour Ribs | 213

Rosemary Baby Back Ribs | 214

Chinese-Style Grilled Ribs | 216

Indonesian-Style Ribs | 217

Smoked Garlic Ribs With Fresh Tomato
  Barbecue Sauce | 220

Gremolata Rack of Lamb | 221

Lamb Chops With Spinach Biryani | 223

Teriyaki Orange Lamb Chops | 224

Mojito Rack of Lamb | 225

Grilled Lamb Chops With
  French Bean Salad | 226

Lamb Chops With Orzo Salad | 228

Peppered Lamb With Mint Butter | 230

Grilled Liver With Mushrooms
  & Onions | 231

Grilled Calves' Liver With
  Green Onions | 232

Peppercorn-Crusted Steaks

For extra flavour, top the steaks off with a dab of blue cheese, such as Roquefort, Gorgonzola, Borgonzola, Bleu Bénédictin or a creamy Danish blue. Bring the cheese to room temperature before using.

2 tbsp **black peppercorns**

2 cloves **garlic,** minced

2 tbsp **Dijon mustard**

2 tbsp **olive oil**

4 **beef grilling steaks,** about
    8 oz (225 g) each

¼ tsp **salt**

Crush peppercorns until size of sesame seeds; mix with garlic, mustard and oil. Trim fat around edges of steaks to ⅛-inch (3 mm) thickness; slash fat at 1-inch (2.5 cm) intervals to prevent curling. Spread all over with peppercorn mixture; sprinkle with salt.

For rare, grill on greased grill over high heat, or for medium-rare to well-done, grill over medium-high heat, turning once, until desired doneness (see Tip, below).

Makes 4 servings.

Every grill is different, so there are ranges of times and temperatures that will deliver a perfectly done steak. Here are general guidelines for a 1-inch (2.5 cm) thick unmarinated steak. Grill over high heat for rare, 5 to 6 minutes or until instant-read thermometer registers 130°F (55°C). Grill over medium-high heat for medium-rare, 8 to 10 minutes or 140°F (60°C); for medium, 10 to 12 minutes or 150°F (66°C); or for well-done, about 14 minutes or 160°F (71°C). In cool or windy weather, grill with the lid down. Let the grilled steak rest for a few minutes before digging in.

PER SERVING: about 341 cal, 43 g pro, 17 g total fat (5 g sat. fat), 3 g carb, trace fibre, 103 mg chol, 326 mg sodium. % RDI: 5% calcium, 39% iron, 6% folate.

Grilled Steaks With Roquefort Cheese Butter

Pepper-crusted steak with a dab of butter is a classic. Adding creamy Roquefort cheese to the butter takes the combination to a gourmet level.

2 tbsp **mixed peppercorns** or black peppercorns

4 **beef grilling medallions,** about 6 oz (170 g) each

2 tsp **vegetable oil**

½ tsp **salt**

ROQUEFORT CHEESE BUTTER:

½ cup **Roquefort cheese** or other blue cheese

¼ cup **butter,** softened

2 tbsp minced **shallot**

2 tbsp minced **fresh parsley**

Roquefort Cheese Butter: Mash together Roquefort, butter, shallot and parsley; refrigerate until firm.

Crush peppercorns until size of sesame seeds. Brush steaks all over with oil; coat with peppercorns. For rare, grill on greased grill over high heat, or for medium-rare to well-done, grill over medium-high heat, turning once, until desired doneness (see Tip, page 153). Sprinkle with salt; top with dab of Roquefort cheese butter.

Makes 4 servings.

VARIATION
Grilled Steak With Brandy Butter Sauce
Omit Roquefort Cheese Butter. Grill steaks as directed. Meanwhile, in skillet, melt ¼ cup butter over medium heat; fry 2 tbsp minced shallot until softened, about 1 minute. Add ¼ cup brandy and ¼ cup red wine; increase heat to medium-high and cook until reduced by half. Add ½ cup beef broth; cook until reduced by half. Add ¼ cup whipping cream; simmer until thickened. Add any accumulated juices from cooked steaks. Serve over steaks.

PER SERVING: about 453 cal, 41 g pro, 30 g total fat (16 g sat. fat), 4 g carb, 1 g fibre, 137 mg chol, 996 mg sodium, 506 mg potassium. % RDI: 21% calcium, 32% iron, 21% vit A, 7% vit C, 12% folate.

Peppercorn Thyme T-Bones

Pair these tender T-bone steaks with a simple grilled potato side. Check out three tasty options on page 434.

4 **beef T-bone grilling steaks**
   or other grilling steaks, about
   8 oz (225 g) each

1 tbsp **mixed peppercorns**

1 tbsp **mustard seeds**

6 cloves **garlic,** pressed or minced

1 tbsp chopped **fresh thyme**

1 tbsp **olive oil** or vegetable oil

¼ tsp **salt**

Trim fat around edges of steaks to ⅛-inch (3 mm) thickness; slash fat at 1-inch (2.5 cm) intervals to prevent curling.

Coarsely grind peppercorns with mustard seeds; mix in garlic, thyme, oil and salt. Rub all over steaks.

For rare, grill on greased grill over high heat, or for medium-rare to well-done, grill over medium-high heat, turning once, until desired doneness (see Tip, page 153).

Makes 4 servings.

PER SERVING: about 294 cal, 34 g pro, 15 g total fat (4 g sat. fat), 4 g carb, 1 g fibre, 62 mg chol, 231 mg sodium. % RDI: 4% calcium, 34% iron, 3% vit C, 5% folate.

Mexican-Style Rib Eye Medallions With Peppers

Covering the grilled peppers tightly lets the steam loosen their skins for easy peeling.

2 tbsp **extra-virgin olive oil**

2 cloves **garlic,** pressed or minced

1 tsp **pepper**

1 tsp **dried oregano,** crumbled

¾ tsp **salt**

½ tsp **ground cumin**

½ tsp **ground coriander**

4 **beef rib eye grilling medallions,**
   about 6 oz (170 g) each

3 **poblano peppers,** or 1 sweet
   green pepper and 3 jalapeño
   peppers

2 **sweet red peppers**

Mix together 4 tsp of the oil, the garlic, pepper, oregano, salt, cumin and coriander; rub all over steaks. Marinate for 15 minutes.

Meanwhile, grill poblano and red peppers, covered, over high heat, turning often, until charred. Place in bowl and cover tightly; let cool. Peel, core and seed; cut into thick strips. Toss with remaining oil.

For rare, grill steaks on greased grill over high heat, or for medium-rare to well-done, grill over medium-high heat, turning once, until desired doneness (see Tip, page 153). Serve topped with peppers.

Makes 4 servings.

PER SERVING: about 342 cal, 25 g pro, 23 g total fat (8 g sat. fat), 9 g carb, 2 g fibre, 60 mg chol, 481 mg sodium. % RDI: 3% calcium, 29% iron, 23% vit A, 235% vit C, 11% folate.

Grilled Tenderloin Steaks With Mushrooms & Peppers

Choose peppers in different bright colours – yellow, red or orange – for the prettiest presentation.

2 **sweet peppers,** halved

1 lb (450 g) **oyster mushrooms,** trimmed

2 tbsp **extra-virgin olive oil**

4 tsp **sherry vinegar** or wine vinegar

1 clove **garlic,** pressed or minced

1 tsp **fresh thyme**

1¼ tsp **salt**

¾ tsp **pepper**

4 **beef tenderloin grilling steaks,** about 4 oz (115 g) each

Grill peppers over medium-high heat for 3 minutes; turn. Grease grill and add mushrooms. Grill, turning occasionally, until tender and lightly charred, about 5 minutes. Cut peppers into strips. In large bowl, whisk together oil, vinegar, garlic, thyme and ¼ tsp each of the salt and pepper; add hot vegetables and toss to coat.

Sprinkle steaks with remaining salt and pepper. For rare, grill on greased grill over high heat, or for medium-rare to well-done, grill over medium-high heat, turning once, until desired doneness (see Tip, page 153). Serve topped with grilled vegetables.

Makes 4 servings.

PER SERVING: about 273 cal, 24 g pro, 15 g total fat (4 g sat. fat), 10 g carb, 3 g fibre, 53 mg chol, 790 mg sodium. % RDI: 2% calcium, 34% iron, 22% vit A, 163% vit C, 19% folate.

Rib Eye Steaks With Herb Butter

Use fresh-picked garden herbs for this summer staple. The steaks pair well with tender sweet corn and smashed red potatoes.

4 **beef rib eye grilling steaks**
  or medallions, about 6 oz
  (170 g) each

¼ tsp each **salt** and **pepper**

HERB BUTTER:

3 tbsp **butter,** softened

1 small clove **garlic,** minced

1 tbsp each minced **fresh chives**
  and **parsley**

2 tsp minced **fresh tarragon**
  (or ½ tsp dried)

1 tsp **Dijon mustard**

Pinch **pepper**

Herb Butter: Mash together butter, garlic, chives, parsley, tarragon, mustard and pepper. Shape into 1-inch (2.5 cm) diameter log; wrap tightly in plastic wrap. Freeze until firm, about 15 minutes.

Meanwhile, sprinkle steaks with salt and pepper. Grill on greased grill over medium-high heat, turning once, until medium-rare, 5 to 8 minutes. Transfer to platter and tent with foil; let stand for 5 minutes before serving.

Slice butter into rounds; serve on top of steak.

Makes 4 servings.

PER SERVING: about 412 cal, 33 g pro, 30 g total fat (15 g sat. fat), 1 g carb, trace fibre, 105 mg chol, 285 mg sodium, 396 mg potassium. % RDI: 2% calcium, 29% iron, 9% vit A, 3% vit C, 5% folate.

Rib Steaks With Beer Marinade

The flavours of beer and beef meld beautifully. Carve these giant steaks at the table for a dramatic presentation.

⅓ cup **beer**

1 tbsp **extra-virgin olive oil**

2 tsp **coarse salt**

2 tsp **cracked pepper**

4 cloves **garlic,** minced

2 **bone-in beef rib grilling steaks**
    each 1 rib thick, about 3 lb
    (1.35 kg) total

4 tsp **grainy mustard**

In large dish, whisk together beer, oil, salt, pepper and garlic; add steaks, turning to coat and massaging marinade into meat. Cover and marinate, refrigerated, for 4 hours or up to 1 day.

Reserving marinade, remove steak; brush both sides with mustard. Place on greased grill over medium-high heat; drizzle with reserved marinade. Grill, turning once, until desired doneness, 10 to 12 minutes for rare. Transfer to cutting board; let stand for 5 minutes before carving off bone and slicing.

Makes 6 to 8 servings.

PER EACH OF 8 SERVINGS: about 204 cal, 22 g pro, 11 g total fat (4 g sat. fat), 1 g carb, trace fibre, 51 mg chol, 475 mg sodium. % RDI: 2% calcium, 15% iron, 3% folate.

Thick-Cut Sirloin Steak

Ask the butcher to cut the steak 2 inches (5 cm) thick for this party-size entrée.

3 lb (1.35 kg) **beef top sirloin grilling steak,** 1½ to 2 inches (4 to 5 cm) thick

2 tbsp chopped **fresh rosemary** or thyme (or 1 tsp dried)

2 tbsp **olive oil** or vegetable oil

2 tbsp **wine vinegar**

4 cloves **garlic,** smashed

2 tsp **Worcestershire sauce**

¾ tsp each **salt** and **pepper**

Trim fat around edge of steak to ⅛-inch (3 mm) thickness; slash remaining fat at 1-inch (2.5 cm) intervals to prevent curling. In large dish, whisk together rosemary, oil, vinegar, garlic, Worcestershire sauce, salt and pepper; add steak, turning to coat. Marinate for 20 minutes or, covered and refrigerated, up to 1 day.

Reserving marinade, place steak on greased grill over medium-high heat; brush generously with marinade. Grill, covered and turning once, until desired doneness, 18 to 20 minutes for rare or 20 to 24 minutes for medium-rare. Transfer to cutting board; let stand for 5 minutes before slicing thinly across the grain.

Makes 8 to 12 servings.

PER EACH OF 12 SERVINGS: about 207 cal, 22 g pro, 12 g total fat (4 g sat. fat), 1 g carb, 0 g fibre, 69 mg chol, 202 mg sodium. % RDI: 1% calcium, 18% iron, 3% folate.

Old-Style Red Wine Marinated "London Broil"

Long marinating in wine is a time-tested method of flavouring and tenderizing less-expensive cuts of beef. The sauce is divine, but if you don't have time to make it, the steak is wonderful grilled on its own.

3 lb (1.35 kg) **beef top sirloin grilling steak,** 1½ to 2 inches (4 to 5 cm) thick

1 **onion,** thinly sliced

3 cloves **garlic,** smashed

Few sprigs **fresh parsley**

Few sprigs **fresh thyme** or ¾ tsp dried

8 **fresh sage leaves** or ¾ tsp crumbled dried sage

2 **bay leaves**

8 **juniper berries,** crushed, or 2 tbsp gin

5 **whole cloves**

½ tsp **black peppercorns,** crushed

¼ tsp **salt** (approx)

1½ cups **dry red wine** (approx)

1 tsp **granulated sugar**

2 tbsp **butter**

Sea salt

Freshly ground pepper

In resealable plastic bag, combine steak, onion, garlic, parsley, thyme, sage, bay leaves, juniper berries, cloves, peppercorns and ¼ tsp salt; pour in enough wine to cover completely. Seal and marinate, refrigerated, for 2 to 6 days.

Reserving marinade, remove beef. Strain marinade into saucepan, discarding solids; stir in sugar and pinch salt. Bring to boil over high heat; boil, skimming off foam, until syrupy and reduced to about 2 tbsp. Remove from heat; whisk in butter until fully incorporated. Keep warm.

Grill beef, covered, on greased grill over medium-high heat, turning once, until rare to medium (do not overcook), 20 to 30 minutes. Transfer to cutting board; let stand for 5 minutes before slicing across the grain. Season with sea salt and pepper to taste. Drizzle with sauce.

Makes 8 to 10 servings.

TIP

Patience is a virtue: This steak is good after 2 days of marinating, but it's best after 5 or even 6 days. And because the beef is marinated in a plastic bag instead of a dish, it doesn't take up much room in the fridge.

PER EACH OF 10 SERVINGS: about 190 cal, 27 g pro, 8 g total fat (4 g sat. fat), 1 g carb, 0 g fibre, 69 mg chol, 129 mg sodium, 366 mg potassium. % RDI: 1% calcium, 20% iron, 2% vit A, 3% folate.

Korean Steak Barbecue

Koreans usually eat grilled steak cut up and wrapped in lettuce or perilla (Korean shiso) leaves with raw garlic, hot sauce, green onions and rice. It's an appetizing and nutritious way to enjoy a good cut of beef.

1½ lb (675 g) **beef rib eye grilling steak(s),** or strip loin or sirloin grilling steak(s)

¼ cup **Korean Barbecue Sauce** (page 531)

2 tsp toasted **sesame seeds**

2 heads **leaf lettuce,** separated into leaves

4 large cloves **garlic,** sliced

4 **green onions,** cut into 1½-inch (4 cm) lengths

4 **finger hot peppers,** cut into 4 or 5 pieces each

Hot cooked **short-grain rice**

HOT SAUCE FOR STEAK:

⅓ cup **Korean hot pepper paste** (kochujang)

2 tbsp **sesame oil**

2 tbsp **unseasoned rice vinegar**

2 tsp toasted **sesame seeds**

2 tsp **granulated sugar**

2 tsp **soy sauce**

Hot Sauce for Steak: Mix together hot pepper paste, sesame oil, vinegar, sesame seeds, sugar and soy sauce to make smooth paste.

Score both sides of steak, making crisscross pattern about ¼ inch (5 mm) deep. Place steak in dish; add Korean Barbecue Sauce and sesame seeds, turning to coat. Marinate for 15 minutes or, refrigerated, up to 2 hours.

Grill on greased grill over medium-high heat until desired doneness, 10 to 12 minutes for medium-rare.

Slice steak; serve with lettuce, garlic, green onions, hot peppers, rice and hot sauce.

Makes 4 to 6 servings.

TIPS

• To eat this the traditional Korean way, put a spoonful of rice on a leaf, top it with a slice of steak, some garlic dipped in hot sauce to taste, green onion and hot pepper, then wrap it all up in the leaf.

• Look for Korean hot pepper paste, or kochujang, at Korean and larger Chinese grocery stores. Unfortunately, there is no comparable substitute.

PER EACH OF 6 SERVINGS, INCLUDING ½ CUP RICE AND 2 TBSP HOT SAUCE: about 479 cal, 28 g pro, 20 g total fat (7 g sat. fat), 45 g carb, 3 g fibre, 54 mg chol, 857 mg sodium. % RDI: 9% calcium, 42% iron, 28% vit A, 55% vit C, 35% folate.

Rib Steak With Cherry Tomato Salsa

Ask your butcher to cut a thick-cut one-rib roast for this spectacular grill.

1 **one-rib prime rib steak with bone,** about 2 lb (900 g)

3 cloves **garlic,** pressed or minced

1 tbsp **olive oil** or vegetable oil

2 tsp **ancho chili powder**

2 tsp **ground coriander**

1 tsp **ground cumin**

1 tsp **salt**

CHERRY TOMATO SALSA:

2 cups **cherry tomatoes**

Half **white onion** or sweet onion

2 to 4 **jalapeño peppers**

⅓ cup finely chopped **fresh cilantro**

4 tsp **lime juice**

1 tsp **salt**

At ½-inch (1 cm) intervals, diagonally score both sides of steak, making scant ¼-inch (5 mm) deep cuts. Mix together garlic, oil, ancho chili powder, coriander, cumin and salt; rub all over steak, pushing into cuts. Marinate for 30 minutes or, covered and refrigerated, up to 1 day.

Cherry Tomato Salsa: Grill tomatoes, onion and peppers in greased grill basket or wok over high heat until lightly charred; let cool. Skin and seed peppers; finely chop tomatoes, onion and peppers. Toss together vegetables, cilantro, lime juice and salt.

Grill steak on greased grill over medium-high heat, turning once, until desired doneness, about 12 minutes for rare, or 14 to 16 minutes for medium-rare. Transfer to cutting board; let stand for 5 minutes before carving off bone and slicing thinly across the grain. Serve with cherry tomato salsa.

Makes 4 to 6 servings.

PER EACH OF 6 SERVINGS: about 207 cal, 22 g pro, 11 g total fat (4 g sat. fat), 6 g carb, 2 g fibre, 48 mg chol, 830 mg sodium. % RDI: 3% calcium, 18% iron, 7% vit A, 23% vit C, 10% folate.

Cumin Flank Steak With Avocado Salad

Flank steak is usually considered a marinating steak, but if you cook it to no more than medium-rare and slice it thinly across the grain, it doesn't need marinating.

1 tbsp **olive oil** or vegetable oil

1 tsp **ground cumin**

¼ tsp each **salt** and **pepper**

1 lb (450 g) **beef flank marinating steak**

AVOCADO SALAD:

2 tbsp **wine vinegar**

1 tbsp **extra-virgin olive oil**

½ tsp **hot pepper sauce**

¼ tsp **salt**

1 **sweet red pepper,** thinly sliced

½ cup thinly sliced **red onion**

2 **avocados,** peeled, pitted and sliced

½ cup chopped **fresh cilantro**

Avocado Salad: Whisk together vinegar, oil, hot pepper sauce and salt. Add red pepper and onion; toss to coat.

Mix together oil, cumin, salt and pepper; brush over both sides of steak. Let stand for 15 to 30 minutes.

Grill steak on greased grill over medium-high heat, turning once, until medium-rare, 8 to 10 minutes. Transfer to cutting board; let stand for 5 minutes before slicing thinly across the grain.

Meanwhile, add avocados to red pepper mixture. Gently toss with cilantro; serve with steak.

Makes 4 servings.

PER SERVING: about 429 cal, 29 g pro, 31 g total fat (7 g sat. fat), 11 g carb, 6 g fibre, 46 mg chol, 358 mg sodium. % RDI: 3% calcium, 24% iron, 24% vit A, 110% vit C, 35% folate.

Salt & Pepper Steak With Green Sauce

Liven up classic steak with a delectable sauce. Or, better yet, make the variations and offer all three sauces to sample and savour. You can refrigerate them for up to 3 days.

2 lb (900 g) **boneless beef grilling steak,** about 1½ inches (4 cm) thick

1½ tsp each **coarse salt** and **pepper**

GREEN SAUCE:

1 cup chopped **fresh cilantro**

½ cup chopped **green onions**

⅓ cup chopped **fresh parsley**

1 **jalapeño pepper,** seeded and finely chopped

1 clove **garlic,** minced

1 **tomato,** finely diced

⅓ cup **olive oil**

3 tbsp each **red wine vinegar** and **lemon juice**

¼ tsp **salt**

Sprinkle both sides of steak with salt and pepper. Grill, covered, on greased grill over medium-high heat, turning once, until medium-rare, 8 to 10 minutes. Transfer to cutting board and tent with foil; let stand for 5 minutes before slicing thinly across the grain.

Green Sauce: Meanwhile, in food processor, pulse together cilantro, onions, parsley, jalapeño pepper, garlic and 3 tbsp water until finely chopped. Stir in tomato, oil, vinegar, lemon juice and salt. Serve with steak.

Makes 6 to 8 servings.

VARIATIONS

Salt & Pepper Steak With Horseradish Cream

Omit green sauce. Drain ½ cup prepared horseradish in sieve, pressing out liquid; transfer to bowl. Stir in ½ cup mayonnaise, 3 tbsp sour cream and pinch pepper. Serve with steak.

Salt & Pepper Steak With Mustard Cream Sauce

Omit green sauce. In saucepan, cook 1 cup whipping cream over medium heat until reduced by about half, 15 to 18 minutes. Remove from heat; whisk in ¼ cup Dijon mustard and 2 tbsp finely chopped fresh chives. Serve with steak.

PER EACH OF 8 SERVINGS: about 228 cal, 23 g pro, 14 g total fat (3 g sat. fat), 2 g carb, 1 g fibre, 53 mg chol, 413 mg sodium, 367 mg potassium. % RDI: 2% calcium, 19% iron, 6% vit A, 15% vit C, 8% folate.

Steak Tostadas With Avocado & Radish Slaw

Tostadas are simply open-face tacos that you can customize with your favourite toppings. For a hint of creaminess, sprinkle crumbled queso fresco or feta on top.

12 corn or flour **tostadas,** warmed

Lime wedges

STEAK:

4 tsp **vegetable oil**

1 lb (450 g) **beef flank marinating steak**

2 tsp **ground cumin**

½ tsp **coarse salt**

½ tsp **hot pepper flakes**

AVOCADO & RADISH SLAW:

1 tbsp **lime juice**

2 tsp **vegetable oil**

½ tsp each **coarse salt** and **cracked pepper**

1 **avocado,** peeled, pitted and diced

6 **large radishes,** thinly sliced

1 **green onion,** thinly sliced

¼ cup chopped **fresh cilantro**

1 tbsp minced seeded **jalapeño pepper**

Steak: Drizzle oil over steak; sprinkle with cumin, salt and hot pepper flakes. Rub in seasoning; marinate for 15 minutes.

Avocado & Radish Slaw: Meanwhile, whisk together lime juice, oil, salt and pepper; gently toss in avocado, radishes, green onion, cilantro and jalapeño pepper.

Grill steak, covered, on greased grill over medium-high heat, turning once, until medium-rare, 8 to 10 minutes. Transfer to cutting board; let rest for 5 minutes before slicing thinly across the grain.

Serve tostadas topped with steak and slaw; serve with lime wedges to squeeze over top.

Makes 4 to 6 servings.

PER EACH OF 6 SERVINGS: about 314 cal, 18 g pro, 21 g total fat (4 g sat. fat), 17 g carb, 4 g fibre, 32 mg chol, 370 mg sodium, 366 mg potassium. % RDI: 3% calcium, 16% iron, 2% vit A, 12% vit C, 16% folate.

Grilled Steak Diable

It may seem like there's a lot of pepper on this devilishly tasty steak, but inevitably some will fall through the grates. Serve the sliced steak with fresh radishes and a cellar of sea salt on the side.

3 lb (1.35 kg) **beef sirloin steak,** 1½ inches (4 cm) thick

6 sprigs **fresh thyme**

4 cloves **garlic,** crushed

3 **bay leaves,** broken into pieces

¾ cup **dry red wine**

¼ cup **extra-virgin olive oil**

¼ cup **black peppercorns**

¼ cup **Dijon mustard**

Sea salt

In large dish, combine steak, thyme, garlic and bay leaves. Whisk wine with oil; pour over steak, turning to coat. Cover and marinate, refrigerated, overnight or up to 1 day, turning a few times. Bring to room temperature.

Coarsely crush peppercorns. Remove steak from marinade; pat dry. Brush mustard all over steak; sprinkle all over with cracked pepper, pressing to adhere.

Grill, covered, on greased grill over medium-high heat, turning once, until desired doneness, about 10 minutes for rare or 13 minutes for medium-rare. Transfer to cutting board; tent with foil and let stand for 5 minutes before slicing thinly across the grain. Season with sea salt to taste.

Makes 8 to 10 servings.

PER EACH OF 10 SERVINGS: about 243 cal, 31 g pro, 11 g total fat (3 g sat. fat), 3 g carb, 0 g fibre, 73 mg chol, 140 mg sodium. % RDI: 4% calcium, 30% iron, 2% vit C, 5% folate.

Gibson Flatiron Steak

The juniper, herbs and other flavourings in the gin and vermouth, along with the pickled onions typically in a Gibson cocktail, brilliantly spike a marinating steak.

⅔ cup **gin**

⅓ cup **white vermouth**

4 cloves **garlic,** crushed

2 **onions,** thinly sliced

1 wide strip **lemon zest**

½ tsp **pepper**

Sea salt

3 lb (1.35 kg) **beef top blade flatiron grilling steak,** trimmed (see How to Trim a Flatiron Steak, opposite), or top sirloin grilling steak

1 tbsp **vegetable oil**

Pickled cocktail onions

In resealable plastic bag, mix together gin, vermouth, garlic, onions, lemon zest, pepper and pinch salt; add steak. Seal and marinate, refrigerated, overnight or up to 2 days, turning occasionally.

Brush steak with oil. Grill on greased grill over medium-high heat, turning once, until desired doneness, about 10 minutes for rare or 13 minutes for medium-rare. Transfer to cutting board; let stand for 5 minutes before slicing thinly across the grain. Season with more salt to taste; garnish with cocktail onions.

Makes 6 to 8 servings.

PER EACH OF 8 SERVINGS: about 222 cal, 26 g pro, 12 g total fat (4 g sat. fat), 1 g carb, 0 g fibre, 70 mg chol, 53 mg sodium. % RDI: 3% calcium, 19% iron, 2% vit C, 3% folate.

How to Trim a Flatiron Steak

Flatiron steak (see Gibson Flatiron Steak, opposite), also known as top blade steak, is a cut of meat you generally see in restaurants rather than home kitchens. Recently, this flavourful cut has become more widely available. It's actually two steaks with a layer of connective tissue running through the centre. Sometimes you can buy it already trimmed and halved down the middle, but grocery stores usually sell it whole, so you'll have to trim it yourself, which is actually quite simple.

Step 1
Using sharp, preferably flexible, boning knife, trim off exterior connective tissue.

Step 2
Cut steak in half through centre, moving knife along interior connective tissue, butterflying it (as seen here) or cutting into two steaks, if desired.

Step 3
Trim off interior connective tissue.

Mustard Garlic Flank Steak

Serve slices of this juicy steak with grilled mushrooms and a fresh tomato salad.

3 cloves **garlic,** pressed or minced

2 tbsp **Dijon mustard**

1 tbsp **balsamic vinegar**

1 tbsp **vegetable oil**

1½ lb (675 g) **beef flank marinating steak**

4 sprigs **fresh rosemary**

¼ tsp each **salt** and **pepper**

In large dish, whisk together garlic, mustard, vinegar and oil; add steak, turning to coat. Place 2 sprigs of the rosemary on top of and 2 underneath steak. Cover and marinate, refrigerated, for 4 hours or up to 1 day. Discard rosemary.

Grill on greased grill over medium-high heat, turning once, until desired doneness, 8 to 10 minutes for medium-rare. Transfer to cutting board; sprinkle with salt and pepper. Let stand for 5 minutes before slicing thinly across the grain.

Makes 6 to 8 servings.

Flank steaks are best when grilled rare to medium-rare; never grill them more than medium or they will be tough and dry. Slice the cooked steak very thinly on the diagonal across the grain.

PER EACH OF 8 SERVINGS: about 140 cal, 18 g pro, 7 g total fat (2 g sat. fat), 1 g carb, trace fibre, 36 mg chol, 147 mg sodium. % RDI: 1% calcium, 11% iron, 1% folate.

Grilled Flank Steak & Pebre

This piquant Chilean fresh herb salsa, similar to Argentine chimichurri, serves as both marinade and condiment. Serve with Chilean Pickled Onions (page 149) for authentic flavour. If you like your beef well-done, choose a top sirloin grilling steak.

2 lb (900 g) **beef flank marinating steak**

Pebre Sauce (right)

Place steak in large dish; spoon half of the pebre sauce (without tomatoes) over steak, turning to coat. Cover and refrigerate steak and remaining pebre sauce separately for 4 hours or overnight.

Reserving marinade, grill steak on greased grill over medium-high heat, turning and basting with reserved marinade halfway through, until desired doneness, 8 to 10 minutes for medium-rare. Transfer to cutting board; let stand for 2 to 3 minutes before slicing thinly across the grain.

Meanwhile, stir tomatoes into remaining pebre sauce; serve with steak.

Makes 6 to 8 servings.

Pebre Sauce

In food processor, combine 2 green onions, chopped; 1 cup each packed fresh cilantro and parsley; 2 jalapeño peppers, seeded; and ½ cup water. Pulse until finely chopped. Transfer to bowl. Stir in ¼ cup corn oil or olive oil; ¼ cup sherry vinegar or red wine vinegar; 2 cloves garlic, minced; and ¼ tsp salt. Stir in 2 tomatoes, finely diced, just before serving.

PER EACH OF 8 SERVINGS: about 262 cal, 26 g pro, 16 g total fat (4 g sat. fat), 3 g carb, 1 g fibre, 44 mg chol, 135 mg sodium. % RDI: 2% calcium, 17% iron, 9% vit A, 37% vit C, 11% folate.

Soy-Marinated Flank Steak

Serve this steak with refreshing Quick Pickled Cucumbers (below).

¼ cup **sodium-reduced soy sauce**

1 tbsp **mirin** or granulated sugar

5 tsp **sesame oil**

2 tsp minced **fresh ginger**

3 cloves **garlic,** thinly sliced

8 **green onions,** trimmed

2 lb (900 g) **beef flank marinating steak**

In large dish, whisk together soy sauce, mirin, 1 tbsp of the sesame oil, ginger and garlic. Add green onions; add steak, turning to coat. Marinate for 20 minutes or, covered and refrigerated, up to 8 hours.

Remove steak and onions from marinade; in small saucepan, bring marinade to boil over medium-high heat. Reduce heat and simmer for 3 minutes.

Grill steak on greased grill over medium-high heat, turning once and basting with marinade, until desired doneness, 8 to 10 minutes for medium-rare. Transfer to cutting board; let stand for 2 to 3 minutes before slicing thinly across the grain.

Meanwhile, brush onions with remaining sesame oil; grill until tender, about 4 minutes. Serve with steak.

Makes 6 to 8 servings.

Quick Pickled Cucumbers

Toss 2 English cucumbers, very thinly sliced, with ¾ tsp salt; let stand for 15 minutes. Squeeze out excess moisture. Toss together cucumbers; ¼ cup unseasoned rice vinegar; 4 tsp each granulated sugar and sesame oil; 3 cloves garlic, minced; and ¾ tsp hot pepper flakes.

Makes 8 servings.

PER EACH OF 8 SERVINGS (WITHOUT CUCUMBERS): about 215 cal, 25 g pro, 9 g total fat (3 g sat. fat), 6 g carb, 1 g fibre, 48 mg chol, 406 mg sodium, 360 mg potassium. % RDI: 3% calcium, 18% iron, 2% vit A, 7% vit C, 7% folate.

Arugula & Beefsteak Salad With Tomato Vinaigrette

Fresh and grassy, arugula is a fine base for slices of rich grilled steak. Any grilling steak will do, so choose your favourite cut.

8 oz (225 g) **beef grilling steak**

¼ tsp **pepper**

8 cups **arugula leaves**

2 **mini-cucumbers** (or half English cucumber)

⅓ cup thinly sliced **sweet onion**

⅓ cup shaved **Parmesan cheese**

TOMATO VINAIGRETTE:

Half small clove **garlic,** pressed

2 tsp **balsamic vinegar**

2 tsp **red wine vinegar**

¼ tsp **salt**

¼ tsp **anchovy paste**

¼ cup **extra-virgin olive oil**

⅓ cup finely chopped seeded drained **canned tomatoes**

Sprinkle steak with pepper. Grill, covered, on greased grill over high heat for rare or medium-high heat for medium-rare to well-done, turning once, until desired doneness (see Tip, page 153). Transfer to cutting board; let stand for 5 minutes before slicing.

Tomato Vinaigrette: Whisk together garlic, balsamic and wine vinegars, salt and anchovy paste. Whisk in oil; whisk in tomatoes.

Place arugula in salad bowl (or 4 individual plates or bowls). Using mandoline, vegetable peeler or knife, slice cucumbers lengthwise as thinly as possible to form ribbons. Top arugula with cucumbers and onion. Slice steak thinly across the grain; arrange over salad. Spoon vinaigrette over top; garnish with Parmesan cheese.

Makes 4 servings.

PER SERVING: about 294 cal, 18 g pro, 22 g total fat (6 g sat. fat), 8 g carb, 2 g fibre, 41 mg chol, 396 mg sodium. % RDI: 28% calcium, 24% iron, 30% vit A, 37% vit C, 55% folate.

Texas Barbecued Beef Ribs

It's easy to add a smokehouse taste to sweet-and-spicy beef back ribs.

2 tbsp **cracked pepper**

1 tbsp packed **brown sugar**

1 tbsp **dried oregano**

1 tbsp **smoked paprika**

2 tsp **celery salt**

1 tsp **cayenne pepper**

2 racks **beef back ribs** (about 9 lb/ 4 kg total), each with 6 ribs

BARBECUE SAUCE:

2 tsp **vegetable oil**

1 cup finely chopped **onion**

2 cloves **garlic,** minced

½ cup **liquid honey**

½ cup **ketchup**

1 can (4 oz/112 mL) **green chilies,** drained and chopped

1 tbsp **chili powder**

1 tsp **dry mustard**

Mix together pepper, brown sugar, oregano, paprika, celery salt and cayenne; rub all over ribs. Cover and marinate, refrigerated, for 4 to 24 hours.

Barbecue Sauce: Heat oil over medium-high heat; sauté onion until golden, about 10 minutes. Add garlic; cook for 1 minute. Stir in honey, ketchup, chilies, chili powder and mustard; bring to boil. Reduce heat and simmer for 10 minutes.

Soak 4 cups wood chips in water for 1 hour; drain. Place in pan over gas flame or on coals in barbecue (or according to manufacturer's instructions). Grill ribs, covered, over indirect medium-low heat (see Tip, page 189) until fork-tender and meat pulls away from ends of bones, about 1½ hours. Remove to plate.

Remove wood chip pan; grease grill. Brush ribs generously with some of the barbecue sauce; grill over direct medium-high heat, turning once, until glazed, about 15 minutes. Cut ribs into 1-rib portions. Serve with remaining barbecue sauce.

Makes 12 servings.

PER SERVING: about 654 cal, 52 g pro, 39 g total fat (17 g sat. fat), 19 g carb, 1 g fibre, 134 mg chol, 474 mg sodium, 716 mg potassium. % RDI: 5% calcium, 37% iron, 7% vit A, 9% vit C, 10% folate.

Devilled Beef Ribs

In traditional culinary terminology, devilled refers to foods flavoured with mustard. These ribs feature two kinds of mustard plus horseradish for a piquant bite.

1 tbsp **vegetable oil**

1 **onion,** chopped

3 cloves **garlic,** minced

2 tsp **dried thyme**

½ tsp each **salt** and **pepper**

½ cup **Dijon mustard**

½ cup **grainy mustard**

⅓ cup **white wine** or chicken broth

¼ cup **liquid honey**

2 tbsp **prepared horseradish**

1 rack **beef back ribs,** about 3 to 4 lb (1.35 to 1.8 kg)

2 tbsp minced **fresh parsley**

Heat oil over medium heat; fry onion, garlic, thyme, salt and pepper, stirring occasionally, until softened, about 5 minutes. Let cool.

Whisk in Dijon and grainy mustards, wine, honey and horseradish; remove ½ cup and reserve for basting.

Cut ribs into 1-rib portions; arrange in large shallow dish. Spread both sides with remaining mustard mixture. Cover and marinate, refrigerated, for 4 hours or up to 1 day.

Grill ribs, covered and curved side down, on greased grill over medium heat for 5 minutes. Turn; brush with some of the reserved mustard mixture. Grill, brushing with mustard mixture and turning often, until glazed and crusty, about 25 minutes. Sprinkle with parsley.

Makes 3 to 4 servings.

PER EACH OF 4 SERVINGS: about 448 cal, 28 g pro, 26 g total fat (8 g sat. fat), 26 g carb, 1 g fibre, 66 mg chol, 1,158 mg sodium. % RDI: 10% calcium, 28% iron, 2% vit A, 6% vit C, 34% folate.

Korean Beef Short Ribs

Koreans prize short ribs (kalbi) above any other cut of beef for their rich flavour and slight chewiness. See opposite page for a guide to choosing and cutting kalbi.

½ cup **Korean Barbecue Sauce** (page 531)

4 **green onions,** minced

2 tsp toasted **sesame seeds**

2 lb (900 g) **beef short ribs,** prepared (see How to Cut Traditional Kalbi, opposite)

Mix together Korean barbecue sauce, green onions and sesame seeds; add short ribs, tossing to coat. Marinate for 30 minutes or, covered and refrigerated, up to 3 hours.

Grill on greased grill over high heat, reducing heat to medium-high if outside is blackening, just until crusty outside and a hint of pink remains in centre, about 6 minutes.

Makes 4 to 6 servings.

PER EACH OF 6 SERVINGS: about 349 cal, 18 g pro, 26 g total fat (11 g sat. fat), 9 g carb, trace fibre, 56 mg chol, 828 mg sodium. % RDI: 2% calcium, 13% iron, 1% vit A, 2% vit C, 5% folate.

How to Cut Traditional Kalbi

Two cuts of beef short ribs, called *kalbi* or *galbi*, are grilled in Korean cuisine, but it can be confusing trying to find the type you want. In Canada, you can buy both cuts at Korean grocery stores, but some are easy to find under different names in other ethnic or large chain grocery stores.

Traditional kalbi: A single thick piece of short rib is cut into one long, thin piece. You can buy thick chunks of short ribs needed for traditional kalbi at most supermarkets, all Korean food shops and at specialty and Jewish butcher shops, where they are called flanken-style.

L.A.–style kalbi: This refers to thinly cut, multi-boned strips of short ribs first popularized in the large Korean-American community in Los Angeles. Outside of Korean stores, the L.A.–style cut is often called Miami-style short ribs or simply braising short ribs.

Step 1

Place short rib, bone side down, on cutting surface.

Step 2

With knife parallel to cutting surface, cut across rib about ¼ inch (5 mm) from bone, cutting to edge of bone but without cutting off rest of meat.

Step 3

Continue cutting about ¼-inch (5 mm) thick slices through meat, folding out and cutting remaining meat, until a long evenly thick strip extends from bone. Lightly score meat in crisscross pattern.

Savoury Beef Short Ribs

You can't go wrong with this crowd-pleaser. The slow oven roasting frees you up to prepare for your guests; the ribs finish in 10 minutes on the grill.

2½ lb (1.125 kg) thinly sliced (about 1-inch/2.5 cm thick strips) **beef simmering short ribs**

½ tsp each **salt** and **pepper**

1 **large onion,** thickly sliced

4 cloves **garlic**

2 **bay leaves**

1 bottle (340 mL) **dark ale**

½ cup **sodium-reduced beef broth**

2 tbsp **Worcestershire sauce**

1 tbsp **dry mustard**

Sprinkle ribs all over with salt and pepper; place in roasting pan. Mix together onion, garlic, bay leaves, dark ale, beef broth, ½ cup water, Worcestershire sauce and mustard; spoon some of the sauce over ribs and pour the rest into pan.

Cover and roast in 325°F (160°C) oven for 1 hour. Uncover and cook, basting every 30 minutes, until meat is tender enough to fall off bone and sauce clings to ribs, 2 to 2½ hours.

Grill, covered, on greased grill over medium-high heat until crisp outside, about 10 minutes.

Makes 4 to 6 servings.

PER EACH OF 6 SERVINGS: about 513 cal, 21 g pro, 44 g total fat (19 g sat. fat), 7 g carb, trace fibre, 84 mg chol, 368 mg sodium, 451 mg potassium. % RDI: 3% calcium, 14% iron, 3% vit C, 4% folate.

Hot-Smoked Spiced Beef Back Ribs

This spice rub is inspired by Jewish Romanian-style pastrami seasoning. Slow smoke cooking releases most of the fat from the meat, leaving succulent and well-spiced ribs. For the best flavour, grind your own whole spices for this recipe.

6 **dried hot peppers,** seeded and broken into small pieces, or 2 tsp Indian or Mexican ground dried hot peppers

4 tsp **coriander seeds** or 1 tbsp ground coriander

2 tsp **whole allspice** or 1½ tsp ground allspice

1½ tsp **dillseed**

1½ tsp **black peppercorns**

2 tsp **sweet paprika**

1¼ tsp **garlic powder**

1¼ tsp **granulated sugar**

1 tsp **salt**

2 racks **beef back ribs,** 3 to 4 lb (1.35 to 1.8 kg) each

Grind together hot peppers, coriander seeds, allspice, dillseed and peppercorns; mix in paprika, garlic powder, sugar and salt. Rub all over ribs. Marinate for 3 hours or, covered and refrigerated, up to 2 days.

Soak 3 cups wood chips in water for 1 hour; drain. Place in pan over gas flame or on coals in barbecue (or according to manufacturer's instructions). Grill ribs, covered, over indirect medium heat (see Tip, below) until fork-tender and meat pulls away from ends of bones, about 1½ hours.

Makes 6 servings.

To grill over indirect heat on gas grill, set foil drip pan under 1 rack of 2-burner barbecue or under centre rack of 3-burner barbecue. Heat remaining burner(s) to temperature indicated (see Grilling Temperatures, page 8). For charcoal grill, place drip pan in centre and arrange hot charcoal on either side. Set meat on greased grill or on rotisserie and centre over drip pan. Grill as directed.

PER SERVING: about 302 cal, 26 g pro, 20 g total fat (8 g sat. fat), 4 g carb, 1 g fibre, 66 mg chol, 447 mg sodium, 361 mg potassium. % RDI: 3% calcium, 19% iron, 6% vit A, 3% vit C, 3% folate.

Steak House Beef Ribs With Stout Barbecue Sauce

Slow-roasting ribs in the oven before finishing them on the grill makes them fall-off-the-bone tender.

2 racks **beef back ribs,** 3 to 4 lb (1.35 to 1.8 kg) each

3 cloves **garlic,** minced

2 tbsp **sweet paprika**

2 tbsp **chili powder**

1½ tsp **salt**

1 tsp **cayenne pepper**

1 tsp **ground cumin**

1 tsp **dry mustard**

½ tsp **pepper**

Pinch **cinnamon**

STOUT BARBECUE SAUCE:

2 tbsp **vegetable oil**

1 **onion,** diced

2 cloves **garlic,** sliced

1⅓ cups **bottled strained tomatoes** (passata)

1 cup **stout beer**

¼ cup **fancy molasses**

2 tbsp **cider vinegar**

1 tbsp packed **brown sugar**

¼ tsp **salt**

Cut ribs into 1- or 2-rib portions. Mix together garlic, paprika, chili powder, salt, cayenne, cumin, mustard, pepper and cinnamon; rub all over ribs. Marinate for 30 minutes.

Place, meaty side up, in shallow roasting pan. Cover and roast in 325°F (160°C) oven until meat is tender, about 1¼ hours. *(Make-ahead: Refrigerate for up to 1 day.)*

Stout Barbecue Sauce: In saucepan, heat oil over medium heat; fry onion and garlic, stirring occasionally, until softened, about 6 minutes. Stir in tomatoes, stout, molasses, vinegar, sugar and salt; bring to boil. Reduce heat and simmer, stirring occasionally, until reduced to about 2 cups, 35 to 40 minutes. Strain into bowl.

Toss ribs with half of the sauce. Grill, covered, on greased grill over medium heat, turning once and basting with remaining sauce, until glazed and browned, 12 to 15 minutes.

Makes 8 servings.

PER SERVING: about 327 cal, 21 g pro, 18 g total fat (7 g sat. fat), 19 g carb, 2 g fibre, 51 mg chol, 588 mg sodium, 689 mg potassium. % RDI: 5% calcium, 27% iron, 17% vit A, 13% vit C, 6% folate.

Chipotle-Glazed Beef Short Ribs

Look for cans of chipotle peppers in adobo sauce in your grocery store's Mexican food aisle. If you can't find any, replace chipotle peppers with 2 jalapeño peppers, roasted and seeded, and 1 tbsp hot pepper sauce (such as Tabasco).

2 tsp **dried oregano**

1 tsp **ground cumin**

1 tsp **chili powder**

½ tsp **sweet paprika**

½ tsp **salt**

¼ tsp **pepper**

1 clove **garlic**

4 lb (1.8 kg) **beef simmering short ribs,** cut into 2-inch (5 cm) pieces

CHIPOTLE BARBECUE SAUCE:

1 tbsp **vegetable oil** (optional)

1 **onion,** sliced

2 cloves **garlic,** minced

3 **canned chipotle peppers in adobo sauce,** coarsely chopped

¼ cup packed **brown sugar**

¼ cup **lime juice**

2 tbsp **adobo sauce** from canned chipotles

1 tbsp **tomato paste**

¼ tsp **salt**

In resealable plastic bag, combine oregano, cumin, chili powder, paprika, salt, pepper and garlic. Add ribs, tossing to coat. Seal and refrigerate for 8 to 24 hours.

Place ribs in roasting pan; cover and roast in 350°F (180°C) oven until meat is tender enough to fall off bone, 2 to 2½ hours. Transfer to plate. Skim fat from pan juices, reserving 1 tbsp fat for sauce. Set pan juices aside.

Chipotle Barbecue Sauce: In saucepan, heat reserved beef fat (or vegetable oil) over medium-high heat; sauté onion and garlic until softened.

Add reserved pan juices, chipotle peppers, brown sugar, lime juice, adobo sauce, tomato paste and salt; simmer over medium-low heat, stirring occasionally, for 15 minutes. Transfer to blender and purée until smooth.

Grill ribs, covered, on greased grill over medium-high heat, turning and basting often with chipotle barbecue sauce, until heated through and crisp outside, about 10 minutes.

Makes 6 to 8 servings.

PER EACH OF 8 SERVINGS: about 503 cal, 23 g pro, 40 g total fat (18 g sat. fat), 11 g carb, 1 g fibre, 86 mg chol, 367 mg sodium, 514 mg potassium. % RDI: 4% calcium, 17% iron, 7% vit A, 3% vit C, 5% folate.

Grilled Venison Chops (opposite) and
Creamy Potato Salad (page 480)

Grilled Venison Chops

If you're not a hunter or a lucky friend of a hunter with game to spare, venison chops are an expensive but wonderful luxury. This recipe is easily doubled or tripled for more than just two chops. Don't cook venison chops past medium or they'll be dry.

¼ cup grated **onion**

¼ cup **gin**

2 cloves **garlic,** pressed or minced

2 tsp minced **fresh rosemary**

¾ tsp **pepper**

Pinch **salt** (approx)

2 **venison chops,** about 1 lb
   (450 g) total

¾ tsp **Indian ground dried hot
   peppers,** ancho chili powder
   or other chili powder

¼ tsp **ground cumin**

1 tbsp **lard** or butter, melted, or
   olive oil

Mix together onion, gin, garlic, rosemary, ½ tsp of the pepper and pinch salt; add chops, turning to coat. Cover and marinate, refrigerated, for 4 to 8 hours, turning once or twice.

Remove chops from marinade, brushing off onion; sprinkle both sides with ground hot peppers, cumin and remaining pepper.

Grill, covered, on greased grill over medium-high heat, basting with lard and turning once, until desired doneness, about 10 minutes for medium-rare. Season with more salt to taste.

Makes 2 servings.

PER SERVING: about 327 cal, 51 g pro, 11 g total fat (4 g sat. fat), 1 g carb, trace fibre, 139 mg chol, 106 mg sodium, 701 mg potassium. % RDI: 2% calcium, 52% iron, 3% vit A, 2% vit C, 7% folate.

Garlic-Marinated Veal Chops With Grilled Potato Salad

Savour a sophisticated meat-and-potatoes meal with this easy, elegant pairing.

1½ lb (675 g) **mini new red potatoes,** halved or quartered

1 tbsp **olive oil**

4 **veal chops,** about 1 inch (2.5 cm) thick

GARLIC MARINADE:

⅓ cup **olive oil**

2 tbsp **white wine vinegar**

1 tbsp **grainy Dijon mustard**

4 cloves **garlic,** minced

2 tsp **maple syrup**

½ tsp each **coarse salt** and **cracked pepper**

1 tbsp **fresh thyme**

2 tsp finely chopped **fresh tarragon**

Garlic Marinade: Whisk together oil, vinegar, mustard, garlic, maple syrup, salt and pepper. Stir in thyme and tarragon just until combined.

Toss potatoes with oil to coat. Grill in grill basket over medium heat, tossing often, until tender, about 30 minutes. Transfer to bowl; drizzle 2 tbsp of the garlic marinade over top. Let cool to room temperature.

Meanwhile, in shallow dish, arrange veal chops in single layer. Pour remaining marinade over chops, turning to coat. Marinate for 30 minutes.

Reserving any remaining marinade, place chops on greased grill; brush with marinade. Grill, covered and turning once, until medium-rare, 10 to 12 minutes. Transfer to warmed platter; let stand for 5 minutes. Serve with grilled potato salad.

Makes 4 servings.

TIP
Don't have a grill basket? Fold long rectangle of foil in half, then scrunch into bowl shape. Grill potatoes in bowl as directed.

PER SERVING: about 491 cal, 30 g pro, 28 g total fat (5 g sat. fat), 31 g carb, 3 g fibre, 104 mg chol, 334 mg sodium, 1,064 mg potassium. % RDI: 5% calcium, 18% iron, 45% vit C, 18% folate.

Deli-Style Spiced Bison Steaks

Bison (buffalo) is lean, exceptionally tasty meat – like very rich beef – and is suited to this Montreal-style spice mix. Of course, you can substitute beef steaks for the bison.

4 **bison rib eye steaks** or strip loin steaks, about 1 lb (450 g) each

4 tsp **extra-virgin olive oil**

DELI-STYLE STEAK SPICE MIX:

1 tbsp **coriander seeds,** lightly toasted

1 tbsp **black peppercorns**

1 tsp **dillseed**

4 tsp **coarse sea salt** or kosher salt

2 tsp **sweet paprika**

2 tsp **hot pepper flakes**

1½ tsp **granulated garlic** (or 1 tsp garlic powder)

Deli-Style Steak Spice Mix: Coarsely grind together coriander seeds, peppercorns and dillseed; mix in salt, paprika, hot pepper flakes and garlic.

Rub each steak with 1 tsp of the oil; sprinkle each with 2 tsp to 1 tbsp of the spice mix, according to taste. Grill steaks on greased grill over high heat for rare or over medium-high heat for medium-rare to well-done, turning once, until desired doneness (see Tip, page 153). Transfer to cutting board; let stand for 3 minutes before slicing thinly across the grain.

Makes 8 servings.

PER SERVING: about 272 cal, 50 g pro, 6 g total fat (2 g sat. fat), 2 g carb, 1 g fibre, 142 mg chol, 512 mg sodium. % RDI: 2% calcium, 44% iron, 4% vit A.

Grilled Veal Chops With Fines-Herbes Butter

Delectable veal chops deserve simple grilling and lightly seasoned yet tasty sauces. If you wish, gild the lily by sautéing mushrooms and serving them atop the butter.

4 **veal chops**

½ tsp **pepper**

¼ tsp **salt**

2 tsp **olive oil** or vegetable oil

FINES-HERBES BUTTER:

½ cup minced **shallots**

½ cup **dry white wine** or white vermouth

3 **anchovy fillets,** minced, or ¼ tsp salt

2 cloves **garlic,** pressed or minced

⅓ cup **butter,** softened

2 tbsp finely chopped **fresh chervil** (optional)

4 tsp finely chopped **fresh chives**

4 tsp minced **fresh parsley**

2 tsp minced **fresh tarragon**

½ tsp **salt**

Fines-Herbes Butter: In small saucepan over medium-high heat, boil shallots, wine, anchovies and garlic until about 2 tsp liquid remains; transfer to bowl and let cool. Mash in butter, chervil (if using), chives, parsley, tarragon and salt until smooth. Keep cool.

Sprinkle veal with pepper and salt; brush with oil. Grill, covered, on greased grill over medium-high heat until medium-rare, 10 to 12 minutes. Transfer to warmed platter; let stand for 3 minutes. Spoon one-quarter of the fines-herbes butter over each chop.

Makes 4 servings.

PER SERVING: about 505 cal, 49 g pro, 30 g total fat (15 g sat. fat), 4 g carb, 1 g fibre, 233 mg chol, 826 mg sodium. % RDI: 6% calcium, 16% iron, 17% vit A, 5% vit C, 17% folate.

Ginger Garlic Pork Chops

Bone-in chops may require some carving, but the superior flavour from the bones makes the effort more than worthwhile.

2 **bone-in pork loin chops,** about 1 inch (2.5 cm) thick, 1½ lb (675 g) total

1 **green onion,** thinly sliced diagonally

MARINADE:

¼ cup **vegetable oil**

4 cloves **garlic,** minced

2 tbsp grated **fresh ginger**

2 tbsp **soy sauce**

2½ tsp **fish sauce**

2 tsp **white vinegar**

1½ tsp **granulated sugar**

¾ tsp **pepper**

Marinade: Whisk together oil, garlic, ginger, soy sauce, fish sauce, vinegar, sugar and pepper. Reserve 2½ tbsp in refrigerator.

Pour remaining marinade into large shallow dish; add pork chops, turning to coat. Cover and marinate, refrigerated, for 30 minutes or up to 24 hours.

Grill, covered, on greased grill over medium-high heat, turning once, until juices run clear when pork is pierced and just a hint of pink remains inside, 12 to 15 minutes. Transfer to cutting board and tent with foil; let stand for 5 minutes.

To serve, cut sections off either side of bone; slice thinly across the grain. Drizzle with reserved marinade; sprinkle with green onion.

Makes 4 servings.

PER SERVING: about 259 cal, 24 g pro, 16 g total fat (3 g sat. fat), 4 g carb, trace fibre, 66 mg chol, 520 mg sodium, 364 mg potassium. % RDI: 3% calcium, 9% iron, 1% vit A, 5% vit C, 4% folate.

Barbecued Peach Pork Chops

Juicy grilled peaches become an instant chutney for grilled pork.

4 **bone-in pork loin chops,** about ½ inch (1 cm) thick

¼ cup chopped **fresh basil** or mint

¼ cup **red pepper jelly,** melted

2 tbsp **cider vinegar**

1 tbsp **grainy mustard**

3 cloves **garlic,** minced

¼ tsp **salt**

Pinch **pepper**

2 **firm ripe peaches** (unpeeled), sliced

Trim fat around edges of chops to ⅛-inch (3 mm) thickness; slash fat at 1-inch (2.5 cm) intervals to prevent curling.

In large dish, mix together basil, red pepper jelly, vinegar, mustard, garlic, salt and pepper. Transfer 2 tbsp to bowl; toss with peaches until coated. Add chops to remaining basil mixture; turn to coat. Marinate for 20 minutes.

Grill chops and peaches, covered, on greased grill over medium-high heat, turning once, until peaches are browned, about 6 minutes. Remove peaches; keep warm. Grill chops until juices run clear when pork is pierced and just a hint of pink remains inside, about 4 minutes more.

Makes 4 servings.

PER SERVING: about 219 cal, 22 g pro, 6 g total fat (2 g sat. fat), 20 g carb, 1 g fibre, 57 mg chol, 244 mg sodium. % RDI: 4% calcium, 6% iron, 2% vit A, 5% vit C, 3% folate.

Pork Chops With Chimichurri Rojo

Chimichurri rojo is the assertive cousin of the classic green parsley-and-garlic chimichurri verde made famous in Argentine cuisine. It's wonderful on all kinds of grilled meats.

4 **boneless pork loin centre chops,** 1 lb (450 g) total

⅓ cup **Chimichurri Rojo** (page 531)

Trim fat around edges of chops to ⅛-inch (3 mm) thickness; slash fat at 1-inch (2.5 cm) intervals to prevent curling. Place chops in shallow dish; pour chimichurri rojo over top, turning to coat. Cover and marinate, refrigerated, for 4 to 24 hours.

Reserving any remaining marinade, place chops on greased grill over medium-high heat; brush with marinade. Grill, covered and turning once, until juices run clear when pork is pierced and just a hint of pink remains inside, about 8 minutes.

Makes 4 servings.

PER SERVING: about 186 cal, 22 g pro, 10 g total fat (3 g sat. fat), 2 g carb, trace fibre, 60 mg chol, 148 mg sodium. % RDI: 2% calcium, 9% iron, 5% vit A, 5% vit C, 2% folate.

Grilled Pork Chops With Pineapple Salsa

Serve this fresh and zesty dish with rice and green beans or grilled vegetables.

3 tbsp **lime juice**

3 tbsp **soy sauce**

4 tsp finely grated **fresh ginger**

4 tsp **vegetable oil**

2 cloves **garlic,** minced

4 **bone-in pork chops,** about 1¾ lb (790 g)

PINEAPPLE SALSA:

Half **pineapple,** peeled, cored and cubed

1 **green onion,** thinly sliced

¼ cup diced **red onion**

2 tsp **lime juice**

1 **small hot pepper** (such as Thai bird's-eye), thinly sliced (optional)

In shallow dish, whisk together lime juice, soy sauce, ginger, oil and garlic. Add chops, turning to coat. Marinate for 10 minutes.

Pineapple Salsa: Meanwhile, stir together pineapple, green onion, red onion, lime juice, and hot pepper (if using).

Grill chops, covered, on greased grill over medium-high heat, turning once, until juices run clear when pork is pierced and just a hint of pink remains inside, about 8 minutes. Serve with pineapple salsa.

Makes 4 servings.

PER SERVING: about 277 cal, 28 g pro, 13 g total fat (4 g sat. fat), 11 g carb, 1 g fibre, 77 mg chol, 694 mg sodium, 497 mg potassium. % RDI: 4% calcium, 11% iron, 1% vit A, 42% vit C, 9% folate.

Grilled Lemon Pork Chops

Serve these chops with a medley of pretty grilled vegetables, such as mini sweet peppers, sliced fennel bulbs, corn on the cob, whole small onions, wedges of squash and pole beans.

4 **bone-in pork chops,** about 1 inch (2.5 cm) thick

2 tsp **caraway seeds,** cumin seeds or fennel seeds

4 cloves **garlic,** minced

1 tsp grated **lemon zest**

2 tbsp **lemon juice**

2 tbsp **extra-virgin olive oil**

1 tbsp chopped **fresh rosemary** (or 1 tsp dried)

½ tsp **pepper**

¼ tsp **salt**

2 **lemons,** quartered

Trim fat around edges of chops to ⅛-inch (3 mm) thickness; slash fat at 1-inch (2.5 cm) intervals to prevent curling.

Lightly crush caraway seeds. Mix together caraway seeds, garlic, lemon zest and juice, half of the oil, the rosemary, pepper and salt; add chops, turning to coat. Cover and marinate, refrigerated, for 4 hours or up to 1 day, turning occasionally.

Brush lemons with remaining oil. Grill chops and lemons, covered, on greased grill over medium-high heat, turning once, until lemons are slightly charred, and juices run clear when pork is pierced and just a hint of pink remains inside, about 10 minutes. Serve chops with lemons to squeeze over top.

Makes 4 servings.

PER SERVING: about 243 cal, 24 g pro, 14 g total fat (4 g sat. fat), 5 g carb, trace fibre, 66 mg chol, 200 mg sodium. % RDI: 4% calcium, 9% iron, 27% vit C, 3% folate.

Slow-Grilled Barbecue Pork Ribs

Serve with Creamy Potato Salad (page 480) and Tangy Coleslaw (page 475) for the perfect summer dinner.

4 lb (1.8 kg) **pork back ribs** or side ribs

¼ cup packed **brown sugar**

2 tbsp **sweet paprika**

2 tsp **chili powder**

1 tsp **pepper**

1 large clove **garlic,** minced

½ tsp **cayenne pepper**

¼ tsp **salt**

RIB SAUCE:

½ cup **ketchup**

3 tbsp packed **brown sugar**

1 tbsp **sweet paprika**

1 tbsp **chili powder**

1 tbsp **Worcestershire sauce**

2 cloves **garlic,** minced

Dash **hot pepper sauce**

Remove membrane from underside of ribs if attached. Combine brown sugar, paprika, chili powder, pepper, garlic, cayenne pepper and salt; rub all over ribs. Cover and marinate, refrigerated, for 8 to 24 hours.

Rib Sauce: Meanwhile, in saucepan over medium heat, combine ketchup, brown sugar, paprika, chili powder, Worcestershire sauce, garlic and hot pepper sauce; bring to boil. Reduce heat to medium-low; simmer until reduced to about ½ cup, about 15 minutes.

Set foil drip pan under 1 rack of 2-burner barbecue or under centre rack of 3-burner barbecue. Heat remaining burner(s) to medium heat.

Grill ribs, covered and meaty side down, on greased grill over unlit burner, turning once, until meat is tender and pulls away from ends of bones, about 1 hour.

Brush both sides of ribs with about half of the sauce. Increase heat to medium-high; close lid and cook, turning once, until glazed, about 10 minutes. Serve with remaining rib sauce.

Makes 6 to 8 servings.

PER EACH OF 8 SERVINGS: about 410 cal, 27 g pro, 25 g total fat (10 g sat. fat), 19 g carb, 2 g fibre, 103 mg chol, 402 mg sodium, 521 mg potassium. % RDI: 6% calcium, 18% iron, 19% vit A, 10% vit C, 4% folate.

Barbecue Beer Ribs

Any brown ale will do for this marinade, but stout has a wonderful toasty flavour that lends itself well to the grill.

3 racks **pork back ribs,** 5 to 6 lb
   (2.25 to 2.7 kg) total

1½ cups **stout beer** or dark ale

1 **onion,** grated

1 clove **garlic,** minced

1 tsp **Worcestershire sauce**

¼ tsp **salt**

¼ tsp **ground cloves**

¼ tsp **hot pepper sauce**

⅔ cup chopped pitted **dates**

⅓ cup **tomato paste**

2 tbsp packed **brown sugar**

2 tbsp **white wine vinegar**

1 tbsp **Dijon mustard**

1 tbsp **fancy molasses**

Remove membrane from underside of ribs if attached; place ribs in large dish. Mix together stout, onion, garlic, Worcestershire sauce, salt, cloves and hot pepper sauce; pour over ribs. Cover and marinate, refrigerated, for 4 to 24 hours.

Reserving marinade, remove ribs and pat dry. Grill, covered, on greased grill over medium-low heat, turning 4 times, until tender, 1½ to 2 hours.

Meanwhile, in saucepan, combine reserved marinade, dates, tomato paste, brown sugar, vinegar, mustard and molasses; bring to boil. Boil, stirring occasionally, until reduced to 2 cups, about 10 minutes.

Brush both sides of ribs with sauce. Increase heat to medium-high; close lid and cook, turning once, until glazed, about 15 minutes. Cut into 1- to 3-rib portions.

Makes 6 to 8 servings.

PER EACH OF 8 SERVINGS: about 521 cal, 29 g pro, 35 g total fat (13 g sat. fat), 21 g carb, 2 g fibre, 137 mg chol, 235 mg sodium. % RDI: 7% calcium, 17% iron, 3% vit A, 10% vit C, 4% folate.

Whiskey Sour Ribs

The sweet caramel taste of bourbon paired with tart lemon makes these soused ribs irresistible.

2 racks **pork back ribs,** 5 to 6 lb (2.25 to 2.7 kg) total

4 cloves **garlic,** pressed or minced

2 tbsp **bourbon** or Canadian whiskey

1 tbsp grated **fresh ginger**

1 tbsp **lemon juice**

1 tsp **pepper**

¾ tsp **salt**

½ tsp **cayenne pepper**

WHISKEY SOUR BARBECUE SAUCE:

½ cup packed **brown sugar**

¼ cup **bourbon** or Canadian whiskey

¼ cup **lemon juice**

¼ cup **canned crushed tomatoes**

2 tbsp **fancy molasses**

2 cloves **garlic,** pressed or minced

Cut rib racks in half; remove membrane from underside if attached. Mix together garlic, bourbon, ginger, lemon juice, pepper, salt and cayenne; rub all over ribs. Place in resealable plastic bag; seal and marinate, refrigerated, overnight or for up to 2 days.

Place ribs in roasting pan; cover with foil. Roast in 375°F (190°C) oven until tender, about 1½ hours.

Whiskey Sour Barbecue Sauce: Meanwhile, in saucepan over medium heat, mix together sugar, bourbon, lemon juice, tomatoes and molasses; boil until reduced by half, about 12 minutes. Reduce heat and stir in garlic; simmer for 1 minute.

Grill ribs, covered, on greased grill over medium-high heat, turning once, until lightly browned on both sides, about 8 minutes. Brush meaty sides of racks with some of the sauce; grill, covered, for 5 minutes. Turn; continue basting and grilling until both sides are glazed, about 5 minutes. Cut into 1- to 3-rib portions.

Makes 6 to 8 servings.

PER EACH OF 8 SERVINGS: about 467 cal, 29 g pro, 29 g total fat (11 g sat. fat), 19 g carb, 0 g fibre, 70 mg chol, 286 mg sodium. % RDI: 4% calcium, 13% iron, 1% vit A, 5% vit C, 5% folate.

Rosemary Back Ribs

If using a charcoal barbecue, place drip pan in centre and arrange hot charcoal on either side. Set meat on greased grill over drip pan. Grill as directed.

2 lb (900 g) **pork back ribs**

2 cloves **garlic,** minced

2 tbsp chopped **fresh rosemary**

1 tbsp **extra-virgin olive oil**

1 tsp **salt**

½ tsp **hot pepper flakes**

½ tsp **pepper**

1 **lemon,** quartered

Remove membrane from underside of ribs if attached. Cut ribs into 4 sections.

Combine garlic, rosemary, oil, salt, hot pepper flakes and pepper; rub all over ribs. Cover and marinate, refrigerated, for 1 to 24 hours.

Set foil drip pan under 1 rack of 2-burner barbecue or under centre rack of 3-burner barbecue. Heat remaining burner(s) to medium.

Grill ribs, covered and meat side down, on greased grill over unlit burner, turning once, until meat is tender and pulls away from ends of bones, about 1 hour. Serve with lemon to squeeze over ribs.

Makes 4 servings.

PER SERVING: about 370 cal, 26 g pro, 28 g total fat (10 g sat. fat), 2 g carb, trace fibre, 103 mg chol, 696 mg sodium, 339 mg potassium. % RDI: 4% calcium, 9% iron, 2% vit A, 10% vit C, 2% folate.

Chinese-Style Grilled Ribs

Although Chinese cuisine rarely includes grilled meats, there is no reason that Chinese seasonings can't be used to enhance your grilling repertoire.

¾ cup **hoisin sauce**

2 tbsp ground or finely minced **fresh lemongrass,** or 1 tsp finely grated lime or lemon zest

1 tbsp **light soy sauce**

1 tbsp **dark soy sauce**

1 tbsp finely grated **fresh ginger**

2 cloves **garlic,** minced

1 tsp **Sichuan pepper** or ½ tsp white pepper

3 to 4 lb (1.35 to 1.8 kg) **small pork ribs**

2 tsp **sesame oil**

1½ tsp toasted **sesame seeds**

½ to 1½ tsp **hot pepper flakes**

In small saucepan, mix together hoisin sauce, lemongrass, light and dark soy sauces, ginger, garlic and Sichuan pepper; bring to boil. Reduce heat to low and simmer for 5 minutes. Let cool.

Remove membrane from underside of ribs if attached; place ribs in large dish. Pour half of the hoisin mixture over top; refrigerate remaining marinade. Marinate ribs at cool room temperature for 3 hours or, preferably, covered and refrigerated, up to 2 days.

Grill, covered, on greased grill over medium heat, turning constantly to avoid burning, until meat is tender, 20 to 25 minutes. Cut into 1-rib portions; toss with reserved marinade until coated. Grill, turning a few times, until glazed, 2 to 3 minutes. Serve sprinkled with sesame oil, sesame seeds and hot pepper flakes.

Makes 4 to 6 servings.

PER EACH OF 6 SERVINGS: about 403 cal, 27 g pro, 27 g total fat (10 g sat. fat), 11 g carb, 1 g fibre, 103 mg chol, 634 mg sodium, 359 mg potassium. % RDI: 4% calcium, 11% iron, 1% vit A, 2% vit C, 5% folate.

Indonesian-Style Ribs

Although most Indonesians are Muslims and don't eat pork (which is, however, consumed by the large Chinese and smaller Balinese populations), Indonesian flavours complement pork ribs quite well.

3 to 4 lb (1.35 to 1.8 kg) **small pork ribs**

3 cloves **garlic,** minced

2 tbsp ground or finely minced **fresh lemongrass**

2 tbsp **fish sauce**

1½ tbsp minced **fresh cilantro**

2 tsp finely grated **fresh ginger**

2 **kaffir lime leaves,** centre vein removed and minced, or ½ tsp finely grated lime zest

¼ cup coarsely ground **roasted peanuts**

SWEET & SPICY SAUCE:

¼ cup **peanut oil** or vegetable oil

⅓ cup sliced **shallots**

5 cloves **garlic,** sliced

4 tsp minced **Thai bird's-eye peppers** or other hot peppers

½ cup **kecap manis** (sweet soy sauce)

⅓ cup **lime juice**

Remove membrane from underside of ribs if attached. Mix together garlic, lemongrass, fish sauce, cilantro, ginger and lime leaves; rub all over ribs. Marinate for 2 hours or, covered and refrigerated, up to 1 day.

Sweet & Spicy Sauce: In small saucepan, heat oil over medium-high heat; fry shallots until golden. With slotted spoon, transfer shallots to paper towel; let drain. Add garlic to pan; fry until golden. Transfer to paper towel; let drain. In mortar with pestle, pound Thai peppers until paste; add shallots and garlic and pound until almost smooth (or mince together as finely as possible). Transfer to large bowl; mix in sweet soy sauce and lime juice.

Grill ribs, covered, on greased grill over medium heat, turning constantly to avoid burning, until meat is tender, 20 to 25 minutes. Cut into 1-rib portions; toss with sauce until coated. Grill, turning a few times, until glazed, 2 to 3 minutes. Serve sprinkled with peanuts.

Makes 4 to 6 servings.

Photo, page 218

TIP
If you can't find kecap manis for this recipe, boil together ½ cup granulated sugar, ⅓ cup soy sauce and 2 tbsp fancy molasses until sugar is dissolved.

PER EACH OF 6 SERVINGS: about 555 cal, 29 g pro, 36 g total fat (12 g sat. fat), 29 g carb, 1 g fibre, 103 mg chol, 1,410 mg sodium, 577 mg potassium. % RDI: 7% calcium, 16% iron, 2% vit A, 13% vit C, 9% folate.

Indonesian-Style Ribs
(page 217)

Smoked Garlic Ribs With Fresh Tomato Barbecue Sauce

Smoke-grilling the ribs gives them a deep, sweet flavour that makes a nice backdrop for a fresh tomato barbecue sauce with Spanish flavourings.

3 to 4 lb (1.35 to 1.8 kg) **small pork ribs**

6 cloves **garlic**

1 tsp **salt**

1 tbsp minced **fresh rosemary**

2 tsp **sherry vinegar** or red wine vinegar

¾ tsp **ground cumin**

FRESH TOMATO BARBECUE SAUCE:

3 **ripe tomatoes**

2 tbsp **olive oil**

Half **onion,** minced

1 **dried red New Mexico hot pepper,** seeded and coarsely ground, or 2 tsp New Mexico chili powder or ancho chili powder

1 small clove **garlic,** minced

½ tsp **salt**

1 sprig **fresh rosemary**

½ tsp **sherry vinegar**

¼ tsp **granulated sugar**

¼ tsp **smoked paprika**

Remove membrane from underside of ribs if attached.

On cutting board, coarsely chop garlic; sprinkle with salt. With flat side of knife or fork, mash into paste. Transfer to bowl; mix in rosemary, vinegar and cumin. Rub all over ribs. Marinate for 1 hour or, preferably, covered and refrigerated, up to 1 day.

Soak 3 cups wood chips in water for 1 hour; drain. Place in pan over gas flame or on coals in barbecue (or according to manufacturer's instructions). Grill ribs, covered, over indirect medium heat (see Tip, page 189) until fork-tender and meat pulls away from ends of bones, about 1½ hours.

Fresh Tomato Barbecue Sauce: Meanwhile, halve tomatoes crosswise; on coarse side of box grater, grate flesh, reserving juices and discarding skin. In saucepan, heat oil over medium-low heat; fry onion, hot pepper, garlic and salt until onion is softened. Add tomatoes and juices, rosemary, vinegar, sugar and paprika. Increase heat to medium; simmer, uncovered, until thickened, about 15 minutes. Discard rosemary.

Cut ribs into 1-rib portions. Toss with barbecue sauce until coated.

Makes 4 to 6 servings.

PER EACH OF 6 SERVINGS: about 397 cal, 27 g pro, 30 g total fat (10 g sat. fat), 5 g carb, 1 g fibre, 103 mg chol, 706 mg sodium, 493 mg potassium. % RDI: 5% calcium, 12% iron, 8% vit A, 15% vit C, 5% folate.

Gremolata Rack of Lamb

To french chops, scrape the end of each rib bone clean to within 1 inch (2.5 cm) of the eye of the raw meat. This gives the lamb a restaurant-worthy look and feel.

2 **racks of lamb,** frenched, about 1¼ lb (565 g) each

¼ tsp each **salt** and **pepper**

GREMOLATA:

½ cup minced **fresh parsley**

2 tbsp **extra-virgin olive oil**

4 tsp grated **lemon zest**

2 cloves **garlic,** minced

½ tsp **ground coriander**

¼ tsp each **salt** and **pepper**

Gremolata: Mix together parsley, oil, lemon zest, garlic, coriander, salt and pepper.

Trim excess fat from lamb, leaving thin layer over meat; sprinkle with salt and pepper. Press gremolata onto rounded side. Grill, covered and bare side down, on greased grill over medium heat until medium-rare, 20 to 25 minutes.

Transfer to cutting board and tent with foil; let stand for 5 minutes before carving between bones.

Makes 4 servings.

PER SERVING: about 253 cal, 24 g pro, 16 g total fat (5 g sat. fat), 2 g carb, 1 g fibre, 89 mg chol, 337 mg sodium. % RDI: 3% calcium, 17% iron, 4% vit A, 20% vit C, 5% folate.

Lamb Chops With Spinach Biryani

Tender little lamb chops are divine with this traditional Indian rice dish.
This is a beautiful meal for entertaining.

½ tsp **salt**

¼ tsp each **ground cumin** and **ground coriander**

8 **lamb loin chops**

SPINACH BIRYANI:

1 tbsp **vegetable oil**

1 **onion,** diced

2 cloves **garlic,** minced

1 tbsp mild or medium **curry paste**

¼ tsp each **salt** and **pepper**

1 cup **basmati rice**

¼ cup **raisins**

1 cup **sodium-reduced chicken broth**

4 cups chopped **fresh spinach**

¼ cup toasted **sliced almonds**

Spinach Biryani: In large saucepan, heat oil over medium heat; cook onion until deep golden, about 8 minutes. Add garlic, curry paste, salt and pepper; cook until fragrant, about 2 minutes. Stir in rice and raisins until coated.

Add broth and 1 cup water; bring to boil. Reduce heat, cover and simmer until almost no liquid remains, about 20 minutes. Stir in spinach and almonds. Cover and let stand for 5 minutes.

Meanwhile, combine salt, cumin and coriander; rub over chops. Grill on greased grill over medium-high heat, turning once, until medium-rare, 8 to 12 minutes. Serve with spinach biryani.

Makes 4 servings.

PER SERVING: about 504 cal, 35 g pro, 18 g total fat (4 g sat. fat), 50 g carb, 3 g fibre, 87 mg chol, 786 mg sodium, 688 mg potassium. % RDI: 9% calcium, 27% iron, 30% vit A, 7% vit C, 34% folate.

Teriyaki Orange Lamb Chops

Lamb loin chops are cut across the bone, separating the tenderloin from the loin. They are more tender and are usually cut thicker than the longer rib chops. They marry nicely with orange-flavoured teriyaki sauce, which becomes a tasty glaze.

⅓ cup **Teriyaki Sauce** (page 531)

2 tbsp thawed **orange juice concentrate**

1 tbsp minced **fresh ginger**

2 tsp grated **orange zest**

2 cloves **garlic,** minced

¼ tsp **salt**

Pinch **pepper**

12 **lamb loin chops** or rib chops, 2 lb (900 g) total

2 **green onions,** sliced

In shallow dish, mix together teriyaki sauce, orange juice concentrate, ginger, orange zest, garlic, salt and pepper; add lamb, turning to coat. Cover and marinate, refrigerated, for 4 hours or up to 1 day.

Reserving marinade, place chops on greased grill over medium-high heat; brush with marinade. Grill, turning once, until desired doneness, about 8 minutes for medium-rare. Serve sprinkled with green onions.

Makes 4 servings.

PER SERVING: about 183 cal, 24 g pro, 7 g total fat (3 g sat. fat), 5 g carb, trace fibre, 91 mg chol, 486 mg sodium. % RDI: 3% calcium, 16% iron, 12% vit C, 5% folate.

Mojito Rack of Lamb

Mint and rum define the mojito, one of Cuba's famous cocktails. Here, spicy rum-infused lamb is topped with a fragrant mint chutney, echoing the drink's flavours.

2 **racks of lamb,** about 1 lb
   (450 g) each

2 cloves **garlic,** pressed or minced

4 tsp **amber rum** or dark rum

¼ tsp each **salt** and **pepper**

¼ tsp **cayenne pepper**

¼ tsp **ground cumin**

¼ tsp **turmeric**

MINT CHUTNEY:

½ cup packed **fresh mint leaves**

1 **green onion,** chopped

1 **hot green pepper,** seeded and
   chopped

1 tbsp **lime juice**

2 tsp **granulated sugar**

2 tsp **amber rum**

¼ tsp **salt**

Trim excess fat from lamb, leaving thin layer over meat. Mix together garlic, rum, salt, pepper, cayenne, cumin and turmeric; rub all over lamb. Marinate for 1 hour or, covered and refrigerated, up to 1 day.

Mint Chutney: In food processor, pulse together mint, green onion, hot pepper, lime juice, sugar, rum and salt until finely minced.

Grill lamb, covered, on greased grill over medium-high heat, turning once, until medium-rare, about 20 minutes. Transfer to cutting board; tent with foil and let stand for 5 minutes before carving between bones. Spoon dollop of mint chutney over each chop.

Makes 4 servings.

PER SERVING: about 210 cal, 22 g pro, 10 g total fat (4 g sat. fat), 4 g carb, 0 g fibre, 72 mg chol, 358 mg sodium. % RDI: 2% calcium, 20% iron, 4% vit A, 6% vit C, 12% folate.

Grilled Lamb Chops With French Bean Salad

Simply seasoned meat served with a fresh salad is a classic bistro combination. Blanching the green beans preserves their vibrant green colour.

8 **lamb loin chops**

½ tsp **salt**

¼ tsp **pepper**

8 oz (225 g) **green beans,** trimmed

4 tsp **red wine vinegar**

1 tbsp chopped **fresh chives**

1 tsp **Dijon mustard**

¼ cup **olive oil**

1 head **Boston lettuce,** torn

⅓ cup thinly sliced **sweet onion**

Sprinkle lamb with ¼ tsp of the salt and pepper. Grill on greased grill over medium-high heat, turning once, until medium-rare, about 6 minutes, or until medium, about 8 minutes. Transfer to plate; keep warm.

Meanwhile, in saucepan of boiling salted water, cook green beans until tender-crisp, about 5 minutes. Chill in cold water; drain and pat dry. Cut in half.

In large bowl, whisk together vinegar, chives, mustard and remaining salt; slowly drizzle in oil, whisking until emulsified. Add lettuce, onion and green beans; toss to coat. Serve with lamb chops.

Makes 4 servings.

PER SERVING: about 280 cal, 22 g pro, 20 g total fat (5 g sat. fat), 5 g carb, 2 g fibre, 46 mg chol, 486 mg sodium, 415 mg potassium. % RDI: 5% calcium, 16% iron, 17% vit A, 12% vit C, 26% folate.

Lamb Chops With Orzo Salad

Orzo pasta is a nice change from rice or potatoes as a side. For this salad, be careful not to overcook the orzo or it will be too sticky.

1 clove **garlic**

¼ tsp **salt**

½ tsp **dried Italian herb seasoning**

¼ tsp **pepper**

8 **lamb loin chops**

ORZO SALAD:

1 cup **orzo pasta**

1½ cups halved **cherry tomatoes**

⅓ cup crumbled **feta cheese**

¼ cup chopped **fresh cilantro**

¼ cup finely diced **red onion**

2 tbsp **red wine vinegar**

1 tbsp **extra-virgin olive oil**

¼ tsp each **salt** and **pepper**

Orzo Salad: In saucepan of boiling salted water, cook orzo until tender, about 8 minutes. Drain well. Toss together orzo, tomatoes, feta cheese, cilantro, onion, vinegar, oil, salt and pepper.

Meanwhile, on cutting board, coarsely chop garlic; sprinkle with salt. With flat side of knife or fork, mash into paste. Stir in Italian herb seasoning and pepper; rub all over lamb chops.

Grill chops on greased grill over medium-high heat, turning once, until medium-rare, about 8 minutes. Serve with orzo salad.

Makes 4 servings.

PER SERVING: about 358 cal, 26 g pro, 12 g total fat (5 g sat. fat), 36 g carb, 3 g fibre, 80 mg chol, 575 mg sodium, 319 mg potassium. % RDI: 9% calcium, 17% iron, 7% vit A, 13% vit C, 10% folate.

Peppered Lamb With Mint Butter

Cuts such as ¾-inch (2 cm) thick boneless lamb leg steaks or loin chops can be used instead of medallions.

8 **lamb medallions,** 1¼ lb (565 g) total, or 8 lamb loin chops, about 2 lb (900 g) total, trimmed

2 tsp **vegetable oil**

1 tbsp **coarsely cracked pepper**

MINT BUTTER:

¼ cup **butter,** softened

1 tbsp chopped **fresh mint** (or ¾ tsp dried)

2 tsp **white wine vinegar**

1 **shallot,** minced

½ tsp **pepper**

Mint Butter: Mash together butter, mint, vinegar, shallot and pepper. On plastic wrap, shape into 3-inch (8 cm) long log; seal ends. Refrigerate until firm, about 30 minutes.

Rub lamb with oil; sprinkle with pepper. Grill on greased grill over medium-high heat, turning once, until medium-rare, about 8 minutes. Transfer to platter. Cut mint butter into 8 slices; place 1 slice on each medallion.

Makes 4 servings.

PER SERVING: about 330 cal, 30 g pro, 22 g total fat (11 g sat. fat), 2 g carb, trace fibre, 152 mg chol, 174 mg sodium. % RDI: 3% calcium, 22% iron, 11% vit A, 2% vit C, 1% folate.

Grilled Liver With Mushrooms & Onions

You'll be surprised at how good this diner special tastes when grilled at home.

3 cups sliced **mushrooms,** about 8 oz (225 g)

1 **onion,** finely chopped

3 tbsp **balsamic vinegar**

1 tbsp **butter,** melted

½ tsp crumbled **dried sage**

½ tsp each **salt** and **pepper**

1 tsp **Dijon mustard**

1 lb (450 g) **calves' liver** or beef liver, cut into ½-inch (1 cm) thick slices

1 tbsp **vegetable oil**

2 tbsp minced **fresh parsley**

Arrange mushrooms and onion on heavy-duty foil; drizzle with 1 tbsp of the vinegar and butter. Sprinkle with sage and half each of the salt and pepper; seal to form packet. Grill over medium heat, turning once, until tender, about 10 minutes.

Meanwhile, whisk remaining vinegar with mustard. Pat liver dry; brush with oil and sprinkle with remaining salt and pepper.

Grill on greased grill over medium-high heat, turning and brushing twice with vinegar mixture, until glazed, browned on both sides and still slightly pink in centre, about 8 minutes. Sprinkle with parsley; serve with mushrooms and onion.

Makes 3 servings.

TIP

Calves' liver is mild, tender and pricey. Improve the taste and texture of less-expensive beef liver by soaking it in milk in the refrigerator for up to 4 hours. Drain, pat dry and proceed with recipe.

Supermarket liver is often cut too thin to grill, so ask for liver that's sliced ½ inch (1 cm) thick at the butcher counter.

PER SERVING: about 336 cal, 32 g pro, 15 g total fat (5 g sat. fat), 19 g carb, 1 g fibre, 547 mg chol, 557 mg sodium. % RDI: 3% calcium, 83% iron, 1,196% vit A, 53% vit C, 119% folate.

Grilled Calves' Liver With Green Onions

Milk-fed calves' liver is unsurpassed in taste and delicacy. Grain-fed veal liver, baby beef liver, or lamb or pork liver are good, too.

1 lb (450 g) **calves' liver,** cut into ⅓- to ½-inch (8 mm to 1 cm) thick slices

1 tsp **red wine vinegar**

½ tsp **salt** (approx)

¼ tsp **pepper**

¼ tsp **ground sage**

¼ tsp **ground savory**

Pinch **cayenne pepper**

3 tbsp **butter**

1 small clove **garlic,** pressed or minced

¼ tsp **smoked paprika** or sweet paprika

8 **green onions**

Sprinkle liver with vinegar, rubbing to coat evenly; let stand for 5 minutes. Pat dry. Sprinkle both sides with ½ tsp salt, pepper, sage, savory and cayenne.

In small saucepan or in microwave, melt together butter, garlic, paprika and pinch salt.

Brush liver and onions with butter mixture. Grill on greased grill over medium-high heat, turning once, until onions are tender, 2 to 3 minutes, and liver is lightly browned and still slightly pink in centre, 3 to 6 minutes.

Makes 3 servings.

PER SERVING: about 315 cal, 29 g pro, 18 g total fat (10 g sat. fat), 8 g carb, 1 g fibre, 527 mg chol, 558 mg sodium, 488 mg potassium. % RDI: 4% calcium, 49% iron, 2,069% vit A, 10% vit C, 172% folate.

Barbecued Pork
Belly (page 266)

roasts

Rotisserie Prime Rib | 237

Garlicky Prime Rib | 239

Roast Sirloin With Orange
    Barbecue Sauce | 241

Beef Tenderloin Roast With
    Oyster Mushrooms | 242

Honey Garlic Prime Rib Roast | 243

Texas Barbecue Brisket | 244

Tandoori Barbecued Beef | 246

Rolled Veal Roast | 249

Veal Loin Rib Roast | 250

Rotisserie Pork Rib Roast | 251

Herbed Pork Rib Roast | 252

Plum-Glazed Pork Loin | 254

Smoked Pork Loin | 255

Barbecued Char Siu | 256

Pork Tenderloin With
    Romano Cheese | 257

Peach & Leek–Stuffed
    Butterflied Pork Loin | 258

Balsamic Honey Tenderloin | 259

Gorgonzola Pork Tenderloin
    Steaks | 260

Sweet & Sour Pork Tenderloin | 262

Saucy Pulled Pork on a Bun | 263

Lemon Mint Pork Tenderloin | 265

Barbecued Pork Belly | 266

Mexican Pork Shoulder | 268

Smoke-Grilled Lamb Shoulder | 270

Wine-Marinated Leg of Lamb | 271

Armenian Butterflied Leg of Lamb | 272

How to Butterfly a Leg of Lamb | 273

Rotisserie Greek-Style Leg of Lamb | 276

Leg of Lamb With Red Currant
    Mint Sauce | 277

Rotisserie Prime Rib

This simple yet sophisticated recipe is a household favourite of Winnipeg chef Michael Dacquisto.

6 lb (2.7 kg) **beef prime rib roast**

⅓ cup minced **garlic**

⅓ cup **vegetable oil**

¼ cup **coarse sea salt**

¼ cup **cracked pepper**

¼ cup **fresh thyme leaves**

¼ cup **Dijon mustard**

10 sprigs **fresh rosemary**

Trim fat from outside of roast to ¼-inch (5 mm) thickness. Mash together garlic, oil, salt, pepper, thyme and mustard until paste; spread evenly over top of roast. Lay rosemary over top; with kitchen string, tie tightly at 1-inch (2.5 cm) intervals. Cover and refrigerate for 1 to 2 days.

Secure rotisserie prong to 1 end of roast; push spit through centre and secure other end with prong. Grill, covered, on rotisserie over indirect medium-low heat (see Tip, below), 2 to 2½ hours for rare to medium (see Tip, page 239).

Transfer to cutting board; tent with foil. Let stand for 10 minutes. Remove string and rosemary before carving.

Makes 10 to 12 servings.

To grill over indirect heat on gas grill, set foil drip pan under 1 rack of 2-burner barbecue or under centre rack of 3-burner barbecue. Heat remaining burner(s) to temperature indicated (see Grilling Temperatures, page 8). For charcoal grill, place drip pan in centre and arrange hot charcoal on either side. Set meat on greased grill or rotisserie and centre over drip pan. Grill as directed.

PER EACH OF 12 SERVINGS: about 307 cal, 32 g pro, 18 g total fat (5 g sat. fat), 3 g carb, trace fibre, 72 mg chol, 2,447 mg sodium. % RDI: 3% calcium, 24% iron, 5% vit C, 4% folate.

Garlicky Prime Rib

Think big when entertaining: Grill this succulent, crowd-satisfying roast beef.

6 cloves **garlic,** minced

1 tsp **salt**

2 tbsp chopped **fresh thyme**

2 tbsp **coriander seeds**

1 tbsp **black peppercorns**

1 tbsp **dillseed**

1 tbsp **vegetable oil**

8 lb (3.6 kg) **beef prime rib roast**

On cutting board, coarsely chop garlic; sprinkle with salt. With flat side of knife or fork, mash into paste; stir in thyme. Transfer to bowl. Coarsely crush together coriander seeds, peppercorns and dillseed; add to garlic mixture. Mix in oil. Spread over roast. Marinate for 1 hour or, covered and refrigerated, up to 1 day.

Grill, covered and bone side down, on greased grill over indirect medium heat (see Tip, page 237), 2 to 2½ hours for rare or medium-rare (see Tip, below).

Transfer to cutting board; tent with foil and let stand for 10 minutes before carving.

Makes 12 servings.

Use an instant-read thermometer or ovenproof meat thermometer to test the internal temperature of beef roasts: rare (130°F/55°C), medium-rare (140°F/60°C), medium (150°F/66°C), medium-well (155°F/69°C) and well-done (160°F/71°C). This is the temperature at which the roast should come off the grill; as the meat rests, the temperature will rise a few degrees.

PER SERVING: about 334 cal, 42 g pro, 17 g total fat (6 g sat. fat), 2 g carb, 1 g fibre, 97 mg chol, 295 mg sodium. % RDI: 3% calcium, 27% iron, 5% folate.

Roast Sirloin With Orange Barbecue Sauce

This roast, sliced and topped with zesty orange barbecue sauce, is great on crusty rolls, but you could also serve it on its own with potatoes or rice.

3 lb (1.35 kg) **beef top sirloin roast**

1 tbsp **vegetable oil**

¼ tsp each **salt** and **pepper**

8 **kaiser rolls,** halved

ORANGE BARBECUE SAUCE:

1 tbsp **vegetable oil**

1 **small onion,** chopped

2 cloves **garlic,** minced

1 tbsp **sweet paprika**

1 tbsp **chili powder**

¼ tsp each **salt** and **pepper**

1 can (19 oz/540 mL) **stewed tomatoes**

1 can (5½ oz/156 mL) **tomato paste**

⅓ cup packed **brown sugar**

⅓ cup **cider vinegar**

1 tbsp grated **orange zest**

⅓ cup **orange juice**

2 tbsp **Dijon mustard**

Brush roast with oil; sprinkle with salt and pepper. Grill, covered, on greased grill over indirect medium heat (see Tip, page 237), 1½ to 2½ hours for rare to medium (see Tip, page 239).

Orange Barbecue Sauce: Meanwhile, in saucepan, heat oil over medium heat; fry onion, garlic, paprika, chili powder, salt and pepper, stirring occasionally, until onion is softened, about 5 minutes. Mash in tomatoes, tomato paste, sugar, vinegar, orange zest and juice, and mustard; bring to boil. Reduce heat and simmer, stirring occasionally, until thickened and reduced by one-third, about 40 minutes.

Transfer roast to cutting board; tent with foil and let stand for 10 minutes before carving into thin slices. Serve on rolls with orange barbecue sauce.

Makes 8 servings.

PER SERVING: about 503 cal, 40 g pro, 14 g total fat (3 g sat. fat), 55 g carb, 6 g fibre, 77 mg chol, 806 mg sodium. % RDI: 12% calcium, 52% iron, 18% vit A, 43% vit C, 36% folate.

Beef Tenderloin Roast With Oyster Mushrooms

Beef tenderloin roast is so lean that it's best to cook it over direct high heat like a steak. This luxurious, rich roast bastes itself from the inside with porcini-flavoured butter.

½ oz (15 g) **dried porcini mushrooms**

1 tbsp **brandy** or dry sherry

½ cup **butter,** softened

1 clove **garlic,** pressed or minced

2 tbsp minced **fresh parsley**

2 tbsp finely chopped **fresh chives**

1 tsp minced **fresh thyme** or ½ tsp minced fresh rosemary

1¼ tsp **salt** (approx)

¾ tsp **pepper**

3 lb (1.35 kg) **beef tenderloin roast,** tied

1 lb (450 g) **oyster mushrooms**

Banana leaf or heavy-duty foil

TIP

Look for frozen banana leaves at Chinese, South and Southeast Asian, and Latin American stores. Always grill or steam them before wrapping food to make them stronger and more flexible.

In spice grinder, grind porcini mushrooms to fine powder; set aside 2 tsp. Stir brandy into remainder; mash together moistened porcini powder, butter, garlic, parsley, chives, thyme, and ¼ tsp each of the salt and pepper. Set aside ¼ cup of the butter mixture.

With long thin sharp knife, make slit all the way through centre of tenderloin from both ends; stuff remaining butter mixture evenly into slit. Mix together reserved porcini powder, 1 tsp of the remaining salt and the remaining pepper; sprinkle all over roast.

Place oyster mushrooms on banana leaf (see Tip, left); top with reserved butter mixture and pinch salt. Wrap to make package, securing with string if using leaf.

Grill beef, covered, on greased grill over high heat, turning often, until rare to medium (do not cook tenderloin past medium), about 16 minutes for medium-rare (see Tip, page 239).

Transfer to cutting board; tent with foil and let stand for 10 minutes before slicing.

Meanwhile, grill mushroom package over high heat for 10 minutes. Serve mushrooms with juices over sliced roast.

Makes 8 servings.

PER SERVING: about 350 cal, 38 g pro, 19 g total fat (11 g sat. fat), 4 g carb, 1 g fibre, 110 mg chol, 528 mg sodium, 604 mg potassium. % RDI: 2% calcium, 36% iron, 11% vit A, 3% vit C, 11% folate.

Honey Garlic Prime Rib Roast

A flavour-packed roast like this one just needs a simple glaze to yield a crusty exterior around the juicy, tender interior.

2 lb (900 g) **beef prime rib roast**

1 tsp **vegetable oil**

1 tsp each **salt** and **pepper**

HONEY GARLIC SAUCE:

⅓ cup **ketchup**

3 tbsp **liquid honey**

1 tbsp each **vegetable oil** and **sherry vinegar**

1½ tsp **dry mustard**

¼ tsp **salt**

Pinch **cayenne pepper**

Honey Garlic Sauce: In saucepan, whisk together ⅓ cup water, ketchup, honey, oil, vinegar, mustard, salt and cayenne. Bring to boil over medium-high heat; reduce heat and simmer, stirring occasionally, until consistency of corn syrup, about 5 minutes.

Brush roast with oil; sprinkle with salt and pepper. Grill, covered, on greased grill over medium-high heat, turning 3 times, until medium-rare to medium (see Tip, page 239), about 40 minutes. Brush all over with half of the honey garlic sauce; grill, turning once, until slightly crusty, about 6 minutes.

Transfer to cutting board; tent with foil and let stand for 5 minutes before slicing thinly. Serve with remaining honey garlic sauce.

Makes 6 servings.

PER SERVING: about 236 cal, 21 g pro, 11 g total fat (3 g sat. fat), 13 g carb, trace fibre, 48 mg chol, 709 mg sodium. % RDI: 1% calcium, 14% iron, 2% vit A, 3% vit C, 4% folate.

Texas Barbecue Brisket

Starting the brisket in the oven lets you recreate this smokehouse classic at home.

1 tbsp **chili powder**

1 tbsp **smoked paprika**

1 tbsp **kosher salt** or coarse
   sea salt

2 tsp **granulated sugar**

1 tsp **ground cumin**

1 tsp **pepper**

5 to 6 lb (2.25 to 2.7 kg)
   beef brisket

BRISKET SAUCE:

1 tbsp **vegetable oil**

Half **onion,** finely chopped

2 cloves **garlic,** minced

2 cups **dark ale** or sodium-reduced
   beef broth

¼ cup packed **brown sugar**

¼ cup **Worcestershire sauce**

¼ cup **cider vinegar**

1 tbsp **salt**

2 tsp **dry mustard**

2 tbsp **tomato paste**

Mix together chili powder, paprika, salt, sugar, cumin and pepper; rub all over brisket. Marinate for 1 hour or, covered and refrigerated, up to 1 day.

Brisket Sauce: In small saucepan, heat oil over medium heat; fry onion and garlic, stirring, until soft and translucent. Stir in ale, brown sugar, Worcestershire sauce, vinegar, salt and mustard (if using beef broth, reduce salt to 1½ tsp); bring to boil. Reduce heat and simmer for 10 minutes.

Place brisket in roasting pan; loosely cover with foil. Roast in 300°F (150°C) oven, basting with brisket sauce every 30 minutes after first hour, until falling-apart tender, about 3 hours. Transfer to plate. Skim fat off juices in pan; add juices to remaining sauce. *(Make-ahead: Refrigerate brisket and sauce separately overnight.)*

Soak 4 cups wood chips in water for 30 minutes. Prepare barbecue for indirect grilling (see Tip, page 237). For gas barbecue, follow manufacturer's instructions or seal soaked chips in foil to make packet; poke several holes in top. Place over lit burner; close lid. For charcoal barbecue, place soaked chips directly on coals. Grill brisket, covered and basting with some of the remaining sauce every 15 minutes (without allowing too much smoke to escape), until dark brown and crisp, about 1 hour.

Transfer to cutting board; tent with foil and let stand for 15 minutes before slicing thinly across the grain.

Meanwhile, in saucepan over medium-high heat, whisk remaining sauce with tomato paste; simmer until thickened, about 10 minutes. Serve with brisket.

Makes 8 to 10 servings.

PER EACH OF 10 SERVINGS: about 355 cal, 35 g pro, 18 g total fat (6 g sat. fat), 12 g carb, 1 g fibre, 89 mg chol, 1,323 mg sodium, 506 mg potassium. % RDI: 3% calcium, 31% iron, 6% vit A, 5% vit C, 6% folate.

Tandoori Barbecued Beef

Serve with spiced rice and a fresh cucumber-yogurt salad for a delicious alfresco meal.

½ cup **low-fat plain yogurt**

2 cloves **garlic,** minced

1 tbsp **tandoori curry paste**

1 tbsp grated **fresh ginger**

½ tsp each **coarse salt** and **cracked pepper**

3 lb (1.35 kg) **beef eye of round roast**

Mix together yogurt, garlic, curry paste, ginger, salt and pepper; rub all over roast. Cover and marinate, refrigerated, for 1 to 24 hours.

Prepare barbecue for indirect grilling (see Tip, page 237). Grill roast, covered, on greased grill over indirect medium heat, until medium-rare, about 1½ to 1¾ hours (see Tip, page 239).

Transfer to cutting board; tent with foil and let stand for 10 minutes before carving.

Make 8 servings.

PER SERVING: about 226 cal, 36 g pro, 7 g total fat (3 g sat. fat), 1 g carb, trace fibre, 74 mg chol, 157 mg sodium, 386 mg potassium. % RDI: 2% calcium, 16% iron, 4% folate.

Rolled Veal Roast

Delicately flavoured, melt-in-your-mouth veal is always a special dish, but here it is made even more scrumptious with the addition of bacon and Parmesan cheese.

5 lb (2.25 kg) **veal outside round roast**

1 tsp each **salt** and **pepper**

4 oz (115 g) thinly sliced **pancetta** or bacon

¼ cup grated **Parmesan cheese**

¼ cup chopped **fresh parsley**

1 tbsp minced **garlic**

Place roast, fat side down, on cutting board; cut horizontally in half along 1 long side, leaving 3 inches (7.5 cm) attached. Open like book; sprinkle with ½ tsp each of the salt and pepper. Lay pancetta over top; sprinkle with Parmesan cheese, parsley and garlic. Roll up roast, ensuring that fat is on outside; with kitchen string, tie tightly at 2-inch (5 cm) intervals. Sprinkle with remaining salt and pepper.

Secure rotisserie prong to 1 end of roast; push spit through centre and secure other end with prong. Grill, covered, on rotisserie over indirect medium-high heat (see Tip, page 237) until medium (see Tip, page 239), 1 to 1½ hours.

Transfer to cutting board; tent with foil and let stand for 15 minutes. Remove string before carving.

Makes 8 to 10 servings.

TIP
If you don't have a rotisserie, grill over indirect heat, turning roast every 15 minutes.

PER EACH OF 10 SERVINGS: about 328 cal, 52 g pro, 12 g total fat (6 g sat. fat), 1 g carb, trace fibre, 191 mg chol, 459 mg sodium, 726 mg potassium. % RDI: 4% calcium, 13% iron, 2% vit A, 3% vit C, 14% folate.

Veal Loin Rib Roast

A luxurious cut of meat, veal rib roast should be absolutely tender and lusciously rich. Grain-fed "rosé veal" produces a slightly coarser, beefier roast, but it's more ethically raised than white veal and still extremely delicious.

3 cloves **garlic,** smashed

½ tsp **salt**

1 tbsp chopped **fresh sage**

6 **anchovy fillets**

1 tbsp **olive oil**

1 tsp **fennel seeds,** coarsely crushed

½ tsp **coarsely ground pepper**

3 lb (1.35 kg) **veal loin rib roast,** about 3 ribs

¼ cup **dry white wine** or white vermouth

¼ cup **butter,** melted

On cutting board, sprinkle garlic with salt. With flat side of knife or fork, mash into paste. Mash in sage and anchovies; transfer to bowl. Mix in oil, fennel seeds and pepper; rub all over roast. Marinate for 1 hour or, covered and refrigerated, up to 1 day.

Mix wine with butter. Grill roast, covered and bone side down, on greased grill over indirect medium heat (see Tip, page 237), basting often with wine mixture, until medium (see Tip, page 239), 1¼ to 1½ hours.

Transfer to cutting board; tent with foil and let stand for 10 minutes before carving.

Makes 4 or 5 servings.

When cooking frenched rib roasts, wrap the bones in foil to keep them from charring, if desired.

PER EACH OF 5 SERVINGS: about 309 cal, 35 g pro, 18 g total fat (6 g sat. fat), 1 g carb, trace fibre, 165 mg chol, 564 mg sodium, 452 mg potassium. % RDI: 4% calcium, 12% iron, 4% vit A, 2% vit C, 9% folate.

Rotisserie Pork Rib Roast

This roast dazzles the senses with its crisp, browned crust and tender, juicy, smoke-touched flesh. Make sure your butcher hasn't trimmed off too much of the fat cap on the top of the roast; a thin layer will keep the meat moist.

3 lb (1.35 kg) **pork rib roast** (French rack)

3 cloves **garlic,** slivered

1¼ tsp **salt**

½ tsp **pepper**

8 sprigs **fresh rosemary**

1 **onion,** coarsely chopped

3 **anchovy fillets**

1½ cups **dry white wine**

Cut slits all over roast; insert 1 garlic sliver into each. Sprinkle with ¾ tsp of the salt and the pepper. Lay rosemary over top; with kitchen string, tie tightly at 1-inch (2.5 cm) intervals (if roast is already tied, thread rosemary under string).

Place roast in resealable plastic bag. In blender, purée together onion, anchovies and wine; pour over roast. Seal and marinate, refrigerated, for 8 hours or, preferably, 1 to 2 days, turning occasionally.

Reserving marinade, remove roast; let come to room temperature. Secure rotisserie prong to 1 end of roast; push spit through centre and secure other end with prong. Grill, covered, on rotisserie over indirect medium heat (see Tip, page 237), basting with reserved marinade every 10 minutes, for 1 hour. Sprinkle roast with remaining salt; grill, without basting, until just a hint of pink remains in centre or instant-read thermometer registers 160°F (71°C), about 1 hour.

Transfer to cutting board; tent with foil and let stand for 10 to 15 minutes. Remove string and rosemary before carving.

Makes 8 servings.

PER SERVING: about 186 cal, 23 g pro, 9 g total fat (3 g sat. fat), 2 g carb, trace fibre, 56 mg chol, 438 mg sodium, 391 mg potassium. % RDI: 3% calcium, 7% iron, 2% vit C, 2% folate.

Herbed Pork Rib Roast

The spectacular look of this succulent roast belies how simple it is to make. If you can only find smaller short roasts, you can tie two racks together.

¾ tsp **fennel seeds**

3 tbsp **extra-virgin olive oil**

4 cloves **garlic,** minced

2 tbsp minced **fresh rosemary**

1 tbsp minced **fresh sage**

1 tbsp **lemon juice**

½ tsp each **salt** and **pepper**

3½ lb (1.5 kg) **pork rib roast** (French rack)

In dry small skillet over low heat, lightly toast fennel seeds, about 2 minutes. Let cool; gently crush. Mix together crushed fennel seeds, oil, garlic, rosemary, sage, lemon juice, salt and pepper.

With long thin sharp knife, make 2-inch (5 cm) slit all the way through centre of roast from both ends; stuff 1 tbsp of the fennel mixture evenly into slit. Spread remainder over top of roast. Cover and marinate, refrigerated, for 2 hours or up to 1 day.

Prepare barbecue for indirect grilling (see Tip, page 237), adding 1 inch (2.5 cm) water to drip pan. Grill roast, covered and bone side down, on greased grill over indirect medium-high heat, turning every 20 minutes, until just a hint of pink remains in centre or instant-read thermometer registers 160°F (71°C), 1½ to 2 hours.

Transfer to cutting board; tent with foil and let stand for 15 minutes before carving.

Makes 6 to 8 servings.

PER EACH OF 8 SERVINGS: about 250 cal, 26 g pro, 15 g total fat (5 g sat. fat), 1 g carb, trace fibre, 64 mg chol, 187 mg sodium. % RDI: 3% calcium, 7% iron, 2% vit C, 1% folate.

Plum-Glazed Pork Loin

Slices of this lightly sweet pork would be particularly delicious with a side of Cool Wild Rice & Mushrooms (page 501).

2 tbsp **soy sauce**

2 tbsp **lime juice**

2 tsp finely grated or minced **fresh ginger**

2 cloves **garlic,** pressed or minced

½ tsp **pepper**

3 lb (1.35 kg) **boneless pork loin roast**

¼ cup **plum sauce** or apricot jam

Mix soy sauce, lime juice, ginger, garlic and pepper; rub all over roast. Cover and marinate, refrigerated, for 8 hours or up to 1 day, turning occasionally.

Reserving marinade, place roast on greased grill over medium heat; brush with some of the marinade. Grill, covered, turning and basting with remaining marinade occasionally, for 1½ hours. Brush with plum sauce; grill, turning occasionally, until just a hint of pink remains in centre or instant-read thermometer registers 160°F (71°C), about 10 minutes.

Transfer to cutting board; tent with foil and let stand for 10 minutes before carving.

Makes 8 servings.

PER SERVING: about 186 cal, 25 g pro, 7 g total fat (2 g sat. fat), 4 g carb, trace fibre, 68 mg chol, 313 mg sodium. % RDI: 3% calcium, 6% iron, 2% vit C, 3% folate.

Smoked Pork Loin

You can also cook this pork loin without a rotisserie over indirect heat; just stand it bone side down.

½ cup packed **brown sugar**

1 tbsp **sweet paprika**

2 cloves **garlic,** minced

2 tsp **ground cumin**

2 tsp **salt**

1 tsp minced **fresh thyme**

1 tsp **pepper**

4 lb (1.8 kg) **bone-in pork loin roast**

Mix together sugar, paprika, garlic, cumin, salt, thyme and pepper; rub all over roast. Cover and marinate, refrigerated, for 6 hours or up to 1 day.

Soak 6 cups hickory wood chips in water for 1 hour. Secure rotisserie prong to 1 end of roast; push spit through centre and secure other end with prong.

Prepare barbecue for indirect grilling (see Tip, page 237). For gas barbecue, follow manufacturer's instructions or seal soaked chips in foil to make packet; poke several holes in top. Place over lit burner; close lid. For charcoal barbecue, place soaked chips directly on coals.

Grill pork, covered, on rotisserie over indirect medium heat until crisp but just a hint of pink remains in centre or instant-read thermometer registers 160°C (71°C), 1¼ to 1½ hours.

Transfer to cutting board; tent with foil and let stand for 10 minutes before carving.

Makes 6 to 8 servings.

PER EACH OF 8 SERVINGS: about 279 cal, 31 g pro, 10 g total fat (4 g sat. fat), 15 g carb, 1 g fibre, 88 mg chol, 653 mg sodium, 487 mg potassium. % RDI: 4% calcium, 15% iron, 4% vit A, 3% vit C, 3% folate.

Barbecued Char Siu

A honey and hoisin sauce marinade defines this famous Cantonese dish. Leftover slices make a wonderful topping for ramen.

¼ cup **soy sauce**

¼ cup **liquid honey**

2 tbsp **mirin**

2 tbsp **oyster sauce**

2 tbsp **hoisin sauce**

1 tbsp grated **fresh ginger**

2 tsp **five-spice powder**

2 tsp **sesame oil**

2 lb (900 g) **boneless pork butt (shoulder) roast,** cut into 4 pieces

In small saucepan, whisk together soy sauce, honey, mirin, oyster sauce, hoisin sauce, ginger, five-spice powder and sesame oil; cook over medium heat, whisking often, until honey is melted and sauce is slightly thickened, about 10 minutes. Let cool completely. Reserve ¼ cup for basting; cover and refrigerate.

Place roast in resealable plastic bag; pour remaining sauce over roast. Seal and refrigerate for 4 hours or up to 2 days, turning occasionally.

Prepare barbecue for indirect grilling (see Tip, page 237). Grill roast, covered, on greased grill over indirect medium heat, turning often and brushing with reserved marinade, until just a hint of pink remains in centre or instant-read thermometer registers 160°F (71°C), 45 to 55 minutes.

Transfer to greased grill over direct high heat; grill, turning, until outside is browned and sauce is caramelized, about 30 seconds per side. Transfer to cutting board; tent with foil and let stand for 5 minutes before carving.

Makes 8 to 10 servings.

PER EACH OF 10 SERVINGS: about 220 cal, 16 g pro, 12 g total fat (4 g sat. fat), 12 g carb, trace fibre, 56 mg chol, 570 mg sodium, 237 mg potassium. % RDI: 1% calcium, 9% iron, 2% vit C, 3% folate.

Pork Tenderloin With Romano Cheese

Flattening the tenderloin ensures quick cooking and, therefore, juicy meat.

2 **pork tenderloins,** about
  12 oz (340 g) each

2 tbsp **olive oil**

2 tbsp **dry white wine**

2 cloves **garlic,** pressed or pounded
  into paste

1 tsp **fennel seeds,** crushed

¾ tsp **salt**

½ tsp finely grated **lemon zest**

½ tsp **pepper**

½ tsp **hot pepper flakes**

8 **fresh sage leaves,** finely sliced
  into chiffonade, or 1 tsp
  crumbled dried sage

½ cup grated **Romano cheese**

Lemon wedges

Remove any silverskin (connective tissue) from pork. Halve each tenderloin crosswise; cut each horizontally lengthwise almost but not all the way through. Open like book. Between sheets of waxed paper or plastic wrap, pound each to even ½-inch (1 cm) thickness.

Whisk together oil, wine, garlic, fennel seeds, salt, lemon zest, pepper, hot pepper flakes and sage; rub all over pork. Marinate for 30 minutes or, covered and refrigerated, up to 8 hours.

Grill on greased grill over high heat, turning once and sprinkling cheese evenly over top during last minute of grilling, until just a hint of pink remains in centre or instant-read thermometer registers 160°F (71°C), 4 to 6 minutes. Serve with lemon wedges.

Makes 4 servings.

Try to get smaller pork tenderloins, about 12 oz (340 g), for the best flavour and delicate texture. Avoid any that are labelled "seasoned" – they have been injected with brine, which will dilute the marinade and dull its flavour.

PER SERVING (WITHOUT LEMON WEDGES): about 339 cal, 48 g pro, 14 g total fat (5 g sat. fat), 2 g carb, 1 g fibre, 120 mg chol, 671 mg sodium, 660 mg potassium. % RDI: 14% calcium, 17% iron, 3% vit A, 3% vit C, 5% folate.

Peach & Leek–Stuffed Butterflied Pork Loin

This unusual combination of flavourings makes a fantastic sweet-and-savoury roast.

1 tbsp **butter**

1 tbsp **olive oil**

2 **leeks** (white and light green parts only), sliced

1 clove **garlic,** minced

1 **peach** (unpeeled), chopped

½ tsp each **salt** and **cracked pepper**

½ cup **dry white wine**

1 tbsp each chopped **fresh thyme** and **fresh rosemary**

3 lb (1.35 kg) **boneless centre-cut pork loin roast**

6 slices **prosciutto**

In large skillet, melt butter with oil over medium heat; cook leeks, stirring often, until softened, about 4 minutes. Add garlic; cook for 1 minute. Stir in peach, salt and pepper. Add wine; bring to boil. Reduce heat and simmer until no liquid remains, about 3 minutes. Stir in thyme and rosemary. Let cool.

Meanwhile, place roast, fat side up, on cutting board with short end facing. Starting at right side, cut in half horizontally almost but not all the way through; open like book. Starting in centre, cut left side in half horizontally almost but not all the way through; open like book. Repeat on right side. Between sheets of waxed paper or plastic wrap, pound to even ½-inch (1 cm) thickness.

Leaving 1-inch (2.5 cm) border uncovered on 1 short side, spread leek stuffing over meat. Starting at opposite short side, roll up tightly. Lay prosciutto crosswise over roast. With kitchen string, tie at 2-inch (5 cm) intervals.

Prepare barbecue for indirect grilling (see Tip, page 237). Grill, covered, on greased grill over indirect medium heat until just a hint of pink remains in centre or instant-read thermometer registers 160°F (71°C), 1¼ to 1½ hours.

Transfer to cutting board; tent with foil and let stand for 10 minutes before carving.

Makes 8 to 10 servings.

PER EACH OF 10 SERVINGS: about 275 cal, 33 g pro, 14 g total fat (5 g sat. fat), 3 g carb, 1 g fibre, 84 mg chol, 403 mg sodium, 569 mg potassium. % RDI: 2% calcium, 10% iron, 2% vit A, 5% vit C, 5% folate.

Balsamic Honey Tenderloin

Glaze quick-cooking, succulent pork tenderloin with simple standbys —
mustard, honey and vinegar — to create a delicious crust.

2 **pork tenderloins,** about
   12 oz (340 g) each

2 tbsp **liquid honey**

2 tbsp **grainy mustard**

2 tbsp **balsamic vinegar**

1 tbsp **olive oil**

1 clove **garlic,** minced

¼ tsp each **salt** and **pepper**

Remove any silverskin (connective tissue) from pork. Mix together honey, mustard, vinegar, oil, garlic, salt and pepper; add pork, turning to coat. Marinate for 20 minutes or, covered and refrigerated, up to 1 day.

Reserving marinade, place pork on greased grill over medium-high heat; brush with marinade. Grill, covered, turning occasionally, until just a hint of pink remains in centre or instant-read thermometer registers 160°F (71°C), about 18 minutes.

Transfer to cutting board; tent with foil and let stand for 5 minutes before slicing.

Makes 4 to 6 servings.

PER EACH OF 6 SERVINGS: about 182 cal, 27 g pro, 5 g total fat (1 g sat. fat), 5 g carb, 0 g fibre, 61 mg chol, 167 mg sodium. % RDI: 1% calcium, 10% iron, 2% folate.

Gorgonzola Pork Tenderloin Steaks

Pork tenderloin benefits from quick, hot cooking, so pounding it into steaks makes sense. The Gorgonzola melts over the meat for an instant sauce.

2 **pork tenderloins,** about 12 oz (340 g) each

2 tbsp **extra-virgin olive oil**

1 tsp minced **fresh rosemary** or thyme

1 clove **garlic,** pressed or pounded into paste

½ tsp each **salt** and **pepper**

4 oz (115 g) **Gorgonzola cheese,** at room temperature

4 tsp finely chopped **fresh chives**

Remove any silverskin (connective tissue) from pork. Halve each tenderloin crosswise; cut each piece horizontally lengthwise, almost but not all the way through. Open like book. Between sheets of waxed paper or plastic wrap, pound each piece to even ½-inch (1 cm) thickness. Mix together oil, rosemary, garlic, salt and pepper; rub all over pork.

Grill on greased grill over high heat, turning once, until just a hint of pink remains in centre or instant-read thermometer registers 160°F (71°C), 4 to 6 minutes.

Transfer to warmed platter. Cut cheese into 4 slices; lay 1 slice on each tenderloin piece. Sprinkle with chives.

Makes 4 servings.

TIP

For a milder taste, choose sweet (dolce) Gorgonzola.

PER SERVING: about 390 cal, 47 g pro, 21 g total fat (9 g sat. fat), 1 g carb, trace fibre, 119 mg chol, 843 mg sodium. % RDI: 17% calcium, 16% iron, 10% vit A, 2% vit C, 10% folate.

Sweet & Sour Pork Tenderloin

Instead of the usual pineapple, this recipe uses orange marmalade to sweeten vinegar-marinated pork.

2 **pork tenderloins,** about 12 oz (340 g) each

2 tbsp **cider vinegar**

1 tbsp **Dijon mustard**

1 tbsp **vegetable oil**

2 tsp chopped **fresh thyme** (or ½ tsp dried)

¼ tsp each **salt** and **pepper**

2 tbsp **orange marmalade**

Remove any silverskin (connective tissue) from pork. Mix together vinegar, mustard, oil, thyme, salt and pepper; add pork, turning to coat. Cover and marinate, refrigerated, for 2 hours or up to 1 day.

Reserving marinade, place pork on greased grill over medium-high heat; brush with marinade. Grill, covered and turning once, until just a hint of pink remains in centre or instant-read thermometer registers 160°F (71°C), about 20 minutes. Brush both sides of pork with marmalade, turning after 30 seconds.

Transfer to cutting board; tent with foil and let stand for 5 minutes before slicing.

Makes 4 servings.

PER SERVING: about 276 cal, 41 g pro, 9 g total fat (2 g sat. fat), 8 g carb, 0 g fibre, 92 mg chol, 275 mg sodium. % RDI: 2% calcium, 17% iron, 3% vit C, 6% folate.

Saucy Pulled Pork on a Bun

Rubbed with a spicy mixture, this slow-barbecued pork is shredded, tossed with sauce and piled high on crusty rolls.

2 tbsp **sweet paprika**

2 tbsp packed **brown sugar**

1 tbsp **chili powder**

1 tbsp **ground cumin**

1 tbsp **dried thyme**

1 tsp each **salt** and **pepper**

3 lb (1.35 kg) **boneless pork butt (shoulder) roast,** untied if necessary

1 batch **Smoky Barbecue Sauce** (page 529) or 1 bottle (455 mL) hickory barbecue sauce

¼ cup **cider vinegar**

¼ cup packed **brown sugar**

½ tsp **hot pepper sauce**

8 **kaiser rolls,** halved

Mix together paprika, sugar, chili powder, cumin, thyme, salt and pepper; rub all over pork. Cover and marinate, refrigerated, for 4 hours or up to 1 day.

Grill pork, covered and fat side up, on greased grill over indirect medium heat (see Tip, page 237), until meat is fork-tender, about 3 hours.

Transfer to cutting board; tent with foil and let stand for 20 minutes. Using 2 forks or hands, pull into shreds; place in bowl.

Meanwhile, in saucepan, combine smoky barbecue sauce, vinegar, brown sugar and hot pepper sauce; bring to boil. Reduce heat and simmer, stirring occasionally, for 5 minutes.

Pour 1½ cups of the sauce over pork, tossing to coat. Serve on rolls with remaining sauce.

Makes 8 servings.

PER SERVING: about 652 cal, 37 g pro, 30 g total fat (10 g sat. fat), 57 g carb, 3 g fibre, 95 mg chol, 1,262 mg sodium. % RDI: 9% calcium, 40% iron, 19% vit A, 12% vit C, 31% folate.

Lemon Mint Pork Tenderloin

Serve with Mediterranean Barley Rice Salad (page 502) for a fresh, summery supper.

1 tbsp grated **lemon zest**

3 tbsp each **lemon juice, extra-virgin olive oil** and **liquid honey**

1 tbsp chopped **fresh mint**

1 clove **garlic,** minced

2 **pork tenderloins,** about 12 oz (340 g) each

¼ tsp each **salt** and **pepper**

Whisk together lemon zest and juice, oil, honey, mint and garlic. Add pork, turning to coat; marinate for 10 minutes or, covered and refrigerated, up to 8 hours.

Reserving any remaining marinade, place pork on greased grill over medium-high heat; brush with marinade. Grill, covered and turning once, until just a hint of pink remains in centre or instant-read thermometer registers 160°F (71°C), 15 to 20 minutes.

Transfer to cutting board; tent with foil and let stand for 5 minutes before carving into ½-inch (1 cm) thick slices. Sprinkle with salt and pepper.

Makes 4 to 6 servings.

PER EACH OF 6 SERVINGS: about 222 cal, 25 g pro, 9 g total fat (2 g sat. fat), 10 g carb, trace fibre, 61 mg chol, 148 mg sodium, 375 mg potassium. % RDI: 1% calcium, 9% iron, 8% vit C, 3% folate.

Barbecued Pork Belly

To keep the skin beautifully crisp, don't tent the pork with foil when it comes off the barbecue. Slice thickly and enjoy with a light salad to complement the rich meat.

2½ to 3 lb (1.125 to 1.35 kg) **whole raw pork belly**

4 **bay leaves,** crumbled

1 tbsp packed **brown sugar**

1 tbsp **smoked paprika**

1 tbsp **ground cumin**

2 tsp **coarse kosher salt**

1 tsp **ground coriander**

1 tsp **cracked pepper**

1 tsp **hot pepper flakes**

Chopped **fresh cilantro**

Pat pork belly dry with paper towel; cut several vertical slashes just through fat layer, about ½ inch (1 cm) apart.

Mix together bay leaves, brown sugar, paprika, cumin, salt, coriander, pepper and hot pepper flakes; sprinkle over meaty side of pork belly. Cover tightly with plastic wrap; refrigerate for 4 hours or up to 2 days. Let stand at room temperature for 30 minutes before grilling.

Prepare barbecue for indirect grilling (see Tip, page 237). Grill pork belly, covered and skin side up, on greased grill over indirect medium heat until pork is very tender, about 1½ hours. Transfer, skin side down, to greased grill over direct medium-high heat; grill, uncovered and turning once, until skin is golden and crisp.

Transfer to cutting board; let stand for 10 minutes before slicing. Serve garnished with cilantro.

Makes 10 to 12 servings.

TIP

For this recipe, you need a chunk of plain raw pork belly that has not been cured, smoked or brined. This cut is widely available in Chinatown markets and in many Asian grocery stores.

PER EACH OF 12 SERVINGS: about 418 cal, 9 g pro, 41 g total fat (14 g sat. fat), 2 g carb, 1 g fibre, 58 mg chol, 289 mg sodium, 208 mg potassium. % RDI: 2% calcium, 9% iron, 4% vit A, 2% vit C, 1% folate.

Mexican Pork Shoulder

This pork is wonderful on its own, but it makes great tacos, too. Just shred the meat instead of slicing and serve it in corn tortillas with avocado and fresh cilantro.

4 **dried ancho chilies,** stemmed and seeded

2 **dried chipotle peppers**

½ cup chopped **onion**

⅓ cup **cider vinegar**

3 cloves **garlic,** smashed

1 tbsp **dried oregano**

3 to 4 lb (1.35 to 1.8 kg) **pork butt (shoulder) roast**

2 tsp **salt**

¼ cup **butter,** softened

In dry small skillet over medium-low heat, toast anchos and chipotles, turning once, until dark and pliable, 1 to 2 minutes. In small saucepan, combine anchos, chipotles and just enough water to cover; bring to boil. Reduce heat and simmer over medium heat until soft, about 15 minutes. Reserving ½ cup of the cooking liquid, drain.

In blender, purée together anchos, chipotles, onion, vinegar, garlic and oregano, adding some of the reserved cooking liquid to make smooth paste. Sprinkle roast all over with salt; rub all over with butter. Rub chili paste all over roast, pressing into every crevice. Cover and marinate, refrigerated, for 4 hours or up to 1 day.

Soak 6 cups mesquite or other wood chips in water for 1 hour. Prepare barbecue for indirect grilling (see Tip, page 237). For gas barbecue, follow manufacturer's instructions or seal soaked chips in foil to make packet; poke holes in top. Place over lit burner; close lid. For charcoal barbecue, place soaked chips directly on coals. Grill roast, covered, over indirect medium heat until dark brown and crisp and meat is fork-tender, 2 to 2¼ hours.

Transfer to cutting board; tent with foil and let stand for 15 minutes before slicing.

Makes 8 to 10 servings.

PER EACH OF 10 SERVINGS: about 273 cal, 28 g pro, 16 g total fat (7 g sat. fat), 5 g carb, 2 g fibre, 96 mg chol, 576 mg sodium, 515 mg potassium. % RDI: 2% calcium, 17% iron, 19% vit A, 3% vit C, 7% folate.

Smoke-Grilled Lamb Shoulder

Fairly fatty lamb shoulder calls for slow grilling. Highly spiced and lightly smoked, this shoulder cooks undisturbed on the grill for about two hours to produce succulent, flavourful meat.

½ cup chopped **fresh cilantro** (roots, stems and leaves)

2 tbsp chopped **fresh ginger**

4 cloves **garlic,** smashed

1 tbsp **lemon juice**

1¼ tsp **salt**

2 tbsp **ground dried hot peppers** or chili powder of choice

2 tsp **ground coriander**

1 tsp **turmeric**

¾ tsp **ground allspice**

¾ tsp **ground cumin**

½ tsp **pepper**

1 **lamb shoulder,** foreshank attached, about 5 lb (2.25 kg)

In food processor, purée together cilantro, ginger, garlic, lemon juice and salt; mix in hot peppers, coriander, turmeric, allspice, cumin and pepper. With tip of sharp knife, make deep slashes all over lamb; rub spice mixture all over lamb and into slashes. Marinate for 1 hour or, covered and refrigerated, up to 1 day.

Soak 3 cups wood chips in water for 1 hour. Prepare barbecue for indirect grilling (see Tip, page 237). For gas barbecue, follow manufacturer's instructions or seal soaked chips in foil to make packet; poke several holes in top. Place over lit burner; close lid. For charcoal barbecue, place soaked chips directly on coals. Grill lamb, covered, over indirect medium-high heat, until fork-tender and crisp outside, about 2 hours.

Transfer to cutting board; tent with foil and let stand for 10 minutes before carving.

Makes 8 servings.

PER SERVING: about 291 cal, 34 g pro, 15 g total fat (6 g sat. fat), 3 g carb, 1 g fibre, 118 mg chol, 472 mg sodium, 440 mg potassium. % RDI: 4% calcium, 26% iron, 6% vit A, 5% vit C, 17% folate.

Wine-Marinated Leg of Lamb

A simple wine marinade transforms an already beautiful butterflied leg of lamb into something decadently delicious.

4 cloves **garlic,** pressed or pounded into paste

1 tbsp minced **fresh rosemary** or 2 tsp dried oregano

2 tsp **fennel seeds**

2 **bay leaves,** crumbled

¾ tsp **pepper**

¾ tsp **ground allspice**

½ tsp **salt**

1 **butterflied leg of lamb,** 2½ to 3 lb (1.125 to 1.35 kg); see How to Butterfly a Leg of Lamb, page 273

2 tbsp **extra-virgin olive oil**

1 cup **dry red wine** (approx)

Sea salt

Mix together garlic, rosemary, fennel seeds, bay leaves, pepper, allspice and salt; rub all over lamb. In resealable plastic bag, combine lamb and oil; pour in wine, adding up to ½ cup more wine to cover lamb, if necessary. Turn to coat. Seal and marinate at cool room temperature for 4 hours or, refrigerated, up to 2 days.

Reserving marinade, remove lamb with spices still clinging to meat. For best results, thread onto 3 long flat metal skewers to produce as even thickness as possible. Grill, covered, on greased grill over medium-high heat, turning once and basting with reserved marinade in first 10 minutes, until medium-rare or instant-read thermometer registers 140°F (60°C), 20 to 25 minutes, or until desired doneness.

Transfer to cutting board; tent with foil and let stand for 10 minutes before slicing thinly across the grain. Season with sea salt to taste.

Makes 8 to 10 servings.

PER EACH OF 10 SERVINGS: about 167 cal, 24 g pro, 7 g total fat (2 g sat. fat), trace carb, trace fibre, 75 mg chol, 80 mg sodium, 292 mg potassium. % RDI: 1% calcium, 13% iron, 9% folate.

Armenian Butterflied Leg of Lamb

In this dish, adapted from a wonderful Armenian recipe for roasted lamb leg, the perfect combination of seasonings flavours a grilled butterflied leg.

¼ cup chopped **fresh parsley**

1 tsp grated **lemon zest**

¼ cup **lemon juice**

3 tbsp **olive oil**

4 cloves **garlic,** minced

1 tbsp chopped **fresh marjoram**
 (or 1 tsp dried)

2 tsp **caraway seeds,** crushed

¼ tsp each **salt** and **pepper**

1 **butterflied leg of lamb,**
 2½ to 3 lb (1.125 to 1.35 kg);
 see How to Butterfly a Leg
 of Lamb (opposite)

2 slices **bacon,** chopped

Mix together parsley, lemon zest and juice, oil, garlic, marjoram, caraway seeds, salt and pepper.

Trim fat from lamb. Using tip of sharp knife, cut slits all over lamb; insert bacon piece into each. Add lamb to marinade, turning to coat. Cover and marinate, refrigerated, for 8 hours or up to 2 days, turning occasionally. For best results, thread onto 3 long flat metal skewers to produce as even thickness as possible.

Grill, covered, on greased grill over medium-high heat, turning once, until medium-rare or instant-read thermometer registers 140°F (60°C), 20 to 30 minutes, or until desired doneness.

Transfer to cutting board; tent with foil and let stand for 10 minutes before slicing thinly across the grain. Serve with any accumulated juices.

Makes 8 to 10 servings.

PER EACH OF 10 SERVINGS: about 166 cal, 20 g pro, 9 g total fat (4 g sat. fat), 1 g carb, trace fibre, 74 mg chol, 102 mg sodium. % RDI: 1% calcium, 13% iron, 1% vit A, 3% vit C, 1% folate.

How to Butterfly a Leg of Lamb

Step 1

Using boning knife, trim excess fat from lamb, leaving a thin layer of fat and membrane to hold lamb together. Starting at wide end close to bone and using short strokes with tip of knife, cut around flat pelvic bone to loosen.

Step 2

Holding pelvic bone, cut through tendons of ball-and-socket joint connecting pelvic bone to thigh bone.

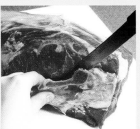

Step 3

Turn lamb fat side up. Cutting right to thigh bone, cut leg open lengthwise. Following close to bone and using short strokes, cut meat and tendons away from bone to reveal another ball-and-socket joint connecting thinner shank bone.

Step 4

Repeat cutting meat away from shank bone; save bones for stock or discard. Lay meat membrane-side down. From inside edge of 1 of 2 thickest lobes and holding knife blade flat, cut in half horizontally almost but not all the way through; repeat on other lobe. Open like book.

Rotisserie Greek-Style Leg
of Lamb (page 276)

Rotisserie Greek-Style Leg of Lamb

A large leg of lamb roasts to perfection on the rotisserie. Serve with rice and a Greek Village Salad (page 505).

1 **large whole leg of lamb,** 6 to 7 lb (2.7 to 3.15 kg)

4 cloves **garlic,** quartered lengthwise

2 tbsp **lemon juice**

1½ tsp **fennel seeds**

1 tsp **salt**

1 tsp **dried (preferably Greek) oregano,** crumbled

¾ tsp **pepper**

½ tsp **ground allspice**

BASTING SAUCE:

¼ cup **butter,** melted

2 tbsp **extra-virgin olive oil**

2 tbsp **lemon juice**

2 tsp **dried (preferably Greek) oregano,** crumbled

¼ tsp **salt**

With tip of knife, make 16 slits all over lamb; insert 1 piece garlic into each. Rub all over with lemon juice. Pound fennel seeds to coarse powder; mix in salt, oregano, pepper and allspice. Sprinkle all over lamb. Marinate for 1 hour or, covered and refrigerated, up to 1 day (bring to room temperature before grilling).

Basting Sauce: Whisk together butter, oil, lemon juice, oregano and salt.

Secure rotisserie prong to haunch end of leg; push spit through leg. Secure shank end with prong; tie tightly with string (prong might not stay stuck into narrow shank end). Grill, covered, on rotisserie over indirect medium heat (see Tip, page 237), basting often with sauce after first 20 minutes, until medium-rare to medium or instant-read thermometer registers 150 to 160°F (65 to 71°C), 1½ to 2 hours, or until desired doneness.

Makes 8 servings.

Photo, page 274

VARIATION
Greek-Style Leg of Lamb for a Crowd
For more than 8 people, use 2 legs and double all other ingredients. Tie legs to rotisserie spit, keeping flatter sides facing in and each haunch facing the other leg's shank. Secure prong on 1 side; push spit through centre. Secure other prong; tie legs together in 2 or 3 places.

PER SERVING: about 360 cal, 47 g pro, 17 g total fat (7 g sat. fat), 2 g carb, trace fibre, 153 mg chol, 456 mg sodium, 582 mg potassium. % RDI: 3% calcium, 27% iron, 3% vit A, 3% vit C, 18% folate.

Leg of Lamb With Red Currant Mint Sauce

This easy marinated lamb makes a quick-cooking and satisfying dinner with friends. This recipe is terrific for using up the overeager mint in your garden.

¼ cup **red wine vinegar**

3 tbsp **extra-virgin olive oil**

3 cloves **garlic,** minced

1 tbsp chopped **fresh thyme**
  (or 1 tsp dried)

1 **butterflied leg of lamb,**
  about 3 lb (1.35 kg);
  see How to Butterfly a Leg
  of Lamb (page 273)

½ tsp each **salt** and **pepper**

RED CURRANT MINT SAUCE:

½ cup **red currant jelly**

⅓ cup packed chopped **fresh mint**

2 tbsp **Port** (optional)

2 tbsp **red wine vinegar**

Pinch each **salt** and **pepper**

Mix together vinegar, oil, garlic and thyme; add lamb, turning to coat. Cover and marinate, refrigerated, for 4 hours or up to 1 day.

Red Currant Mint Sauce: In food processor, purée together red currant jelly, mint, Port (if using), vinegar, salt and pepper.

Remove lamb from marinade; sprinkle with salt and pepper. For best results, thread onto 3 long flat metal skewers to produce as even thickness as possible. Grill, covered, on greased grill over medium-high heat until medium-rare or instant-read thermometer registers 140°C (60°C), 20 to 30 minutes, or until desired doneness.

Transfer to cutting board; tent with foil and let stand for 10 minutes before slicing thinly across the grain. Serve with red currant mint sauce.

Makes 8 to 10 servings.

PER EACH OF 10 SERVINGS: about 191 cal, 23 g pro, 5 g total fat (2 g sat. fat), 11 g carb, trace fibre, 84 mg chol, 157 mg sodium. % RDI: 1% calcium, 16% iron, 1% vit A.

Indian Hot Wings With Mint
Dipping Sauce (page 321)

poultry

Mediterranean Lemon &
    Rosemary Rotisserie Chickens | 281

Beer-Can Chicken With
    Greek Spices | 283

Rotisserie Piri-Piri Chickens | 284

Spiced Spatchcock Chicken | 285

Basic Brined Rotisserie Chicken | 287

Carnival Chicken | 288

Spatchcock Barbecue Chicken | 290

Thai Grilled Chicken | 291

Grilled Chicken With Buttery
    Barbecue Sauce | 292

Chicken With Puerto Rican Adobo
    Seasoning | 293

Coriander Chicken | 294

Oregano Chicken With
    Tomato Salsa | 295

Lime-Grilled Chicken Breasts
    With Avocado Salsa | 296

Crisp & Juicy Barbecued Chicken | 298

Citrus Sesame Chicken | 299

Buttermilk & Spice Grilled
    Drumsticks | 300

Balsamic Peppercorn
    Chicken Legs | 301

Chicken Drumsticks With Apple
    Stout Barbecue Sauce | 302

Quick Korean Chicken | 303

Chicken Cutlets With Cilantro
    Peanut Sauce | 304

Flash-Grilled Chicken Breasts
    With Oyster Mushrooms | 306

Mango Chicken | 307

Grilled Chicken Mozzarella | 309

Chicken With Tabbouleh Salad | 311

Grilled Chicken &
    Charred Corn Salad | 312

Indonesian Chicken Breast Salad | 314

Chinese Chicken Breast Salad | 315

Middle Eastern
    Chicken Breast Salad | 317

Sticky Glazed Grilled Chicken
    With Cucumber Salad | 318

Five-Spice Chicken Wings | 320

Indian Hot Wings With
    Mint Dipping Sauce | 321

Chili Chicken Wings | 324

Three-Pepper Chicken Wings | 325

Paris Wings With Crudités | 327

Mexican Wings & Green Salsa | 328

Tuscan Cornish Hens | 329

Lemon Pepper Cornish Hens | 330

Grilled Brined Whole Turkey | 333

Grilled Turkey Breast
    With Sautéed Banana Peppers | 334

Lemon Sage Barbecued Turkey
    Breast | 336

Mushroom-Stuffed Turkey
    Breast Rolls | 337

Parmesan-Crusted Turkey
    Scaloppine | 338

Last-Minute Turkey Scaloppine | 339

Chipotle-Glazed Turkey Thighs | 340

Cider & Maple Grilled Duck | 341

Grilled Orange Duck | 342

Rosemary Skewered Quails | 345

Grilled Marinated Quails | 346

Korean Grilled Quails | 347

Mediterranean Lemon & Rosemary Rotisserie Chickens

If you don't have a rotisserie, grill whole chickens over indirect heat, giving them a quarter-turn every 15 minutes or so. It's easy to halve this recipe, but roast two chickens no matter how many people you're feeding; they're so good for leftovers.

2 **whole chickens,** about
    4 lb (1.8 kg) each

2 tsp **salt**

1 tsp **pepper**

2 cloves **garlic,** pressed or minced

14 sprigs **fresh rosemary**

BASTING LIQUID:

1 **lemon**

2 cloves **garlic,** smashed

2 tbsp **olive oil**

Pinch **salt**

Sprinkle inside of each chicken with ½ tsp of the salt and ¼ tsp of the pepper; rub garlic all over inside.

Basting Liquid: Reserving rind, halve and juice lemon; stir together lemon juice, garlic, oil and salt.

Place 1 of the squeezed-out lemon halves and 3 sprigs rosemary inside each chicken. With kitchen string, truss together legs and tail to close each cavity. Secure rotisserie prong to 1 end of 1 of the chickens; push spit through centre of both chickens and secure other end with prong. Sprinkle each chicken all over with ½ tsp of the remaining salt and ¼ tsp of the remaining pepper. Lay 2 sprigs rosemary on top and 2 on bottom of each chicken; tie string around each chicken, securing rosemary, wings and legs against body.

Grill, covered, on rotisserie over indirect medium-high heat (see Tip, below). After first 30 minutes, brush chicken every 10 minutes with basting liquid and pan drippings, grilling until juices run clear when thickest part of thigh is pierced, about 1½ hours total.

Makes 6 to 8 servings.

To grill over indirect heat on gas grill, set foil drip pan under 1 rack of 2-burner barbecue or under centre rack of 3-burner barbecue. Heat remaining burner(s) to temperature indicated (see Grilling Temperatures, page 8). For charcoal grill, place drip pan in centre and arrange hot charcoal on either side. Set meat on greased grill or rotisserie and centre over drip pan. Grill as directed.

PER EACH OF 8 SERVINGS: about 517 cal, 48 g pro, 34 g total fat (9 g sat. fat), 1 g carb, trace fibre, 188 mg chol, 460 mg sodium. % RDI: 2% calcium, 18% iron, 8% vit A, 8% vit C, 5% folate.

Beer-Can Chicken With
Italian Herbs (variation)

Beer-Can Chicken With Greek Spices

Popular in the United States, this method yields chicken that's tender and very juicy. The Greek spicing makes it just a bit more special for a backyard or tailgate barbecue.

1 **whole chicken,** about
    3½ lb (1.5 kg)

1 can (355 mL) **beer**

Lemon wedges

GREEK SPICE RUB:

1 tbsp **dried (preferably Greek)
    oregano,** crumbled

2 tsp **dried mint**

1 tsp **ground cumin**

1 tsp **pepper**

¾ tsp **salt**

¾ tsp **cinnamon**

Greek Spice Rub: Mix together oregano, mint, cumin, pepper, salt and cinnamon; sprinkle 2 tsp all over inside of chicken. Rub 1 tbsp all over outside of chicken.

Pour off ⅓ cup of the beer. With can opener, make 5 holes in top of can; spoon in remaining spice rub. Holding chicken upright, push cavity down onto can.

Prepare barbecue for indirect grilling (see Tip, page 281). Stand chicken on grill over drip pan. Grill, covered, over indirect medium heat until juices run clear when thickest part of thigh is pierced, 1 to 1¼ hours. Serve with lemon wedges.

Makes 6 servings.

VARIATION
Beer-Can Chicken With Italian Herbs
Prepare as above, replacing the Greek spice rub with 2 tbsp dried Italian herb seasoning, 1 tbsp grated lemon zest and ¾ tsp each salt and pepper.

PER SERVING (WITHOUT LEMON WEDGES): about 169 cal, 25 g pro, 7 g total fat (2 g sat. fat), 1 g carb, trace fibre, 75 mg chol, 244 mg sodium. % RDI: 2% calcium, 11% iron, 2% vit A, 3% folate.

Rotisserie Piri-Piri Chickens

Piri-piri is a pan-African word for hot peppers. African small red hot peppers are similar in heat and flavour to Thai bird's-eye peppers, but even with the 18 hot peppers here, the chicken is just mildly hot. Because of the lemon, the skin will not roast as crisply as it would on other grilled chickens, but it is every bit as delicious.

2 **whole chickens,** about 3 lb (1.35 kg) each

PIRI-PIRI MARINADE:

18 **Thai bird's-eye peppers** or other small red hot peppers, finely chopped

4 cloves **garlic,** smashed

¼ cup **lemon juice**

2 tbsp **red wine vinegar**

½ cup **extra-virgin olive oil**

2½ tsp **sweet paprika**

2 tsp **salt**

½ tsp **ground cumin**

Piri-Piri Marinade: In blender, purée together Thai peppers, garlic, lemon juice and vinegar until smooth (pepper seeds are no longer visible) and liquefied. (Or, in mortar with pestle, pound Thai peppers with garlic until seeds are crushed and mixture is paste; blend in lemon juice and vinegar.) Blend in oil, paprika, salt and cumin.

Rub chicken inside and out with piri-piri marinade. Cover and marinate, refrigerated, for 4 hours or up to 1 day.

Reserving marinade, remove chicken. With kitchen string, truss together legs and tail to close each cavity. Secure rotisserie prong to 1 end of 1 of the chickens; push spit through centre of both chickens and secure other end with prong. Tie string around each chicken, securing wings and legs against body.

Grill, covered, on rotisserie over indirect medium-high heat (see Tip, page 281), uncovering for final 10 to 15 minutes of grilling. After first 20 minutes and until 10 minutes before chicken is finished, brush about every 10 minutes with reserved marinade. Grill until juices run clear when thickest part of thigh is pierced, about 1½ hours total.

Makes 6 to 8 servings.

PER EACH OF 8 SERVINGS: about 438 cal, 33 g pro, 32 g total fat (7 g sat. fat), 3 g carb, 1 g fibre, 119 mg chol, 677 mg sodium, 445 mg potassium. % RDI: 2% calcium, 11% iron, 21% vit A, 52% vit C, 5% folate.

Spiced Spatchcock Chicken

Spatchcocking a chicken means flattening it after removing the backbone. This decreases cooking time and, along with the tasty basting sauce, helps keep the meat moist and juicy.

1 **whole chicken,** 3 lb (1.35 kg)

2 tbsp **extra-virgin olive oil**

1½ tsp **turmeric**

1 tsp **pepper**

¾ tsp **ground allspice**

½ tsp each **ground cinnamon** and **salt**

¼ tsp **cayenne pepper**

Lime wedges

Using kitchen shears, cut chicken down each side of backbone; remove backbone. Turn chicken breast side up; press firmly on breastbone to flatten.

Mix together oil, turmeric, pepper, allspice, cinnamon, salt and cayenne pepper; rub all over chicken.

Grill, covered and bone side down, on greased grill over indirect medium heat (see Tip, page 281), turning once, until juices run clear when thickest part of thigh is pierced, about 45 minutes.

Transfer to cutting board; let stand for 10 minutes before carving. Serve with lime wedges.

Makes 4 servings.

PER SERVING: about 373 cal, 32 g pro, 26 g total fat (6 g sat. fat), 1 g carb, 1 g fibre, 119 mg chol, 390 mg sodium, 401 mg potassium. % RDI: 2% calcium, 12% iron, 6% vit A, 2% vit C, 4% folate.

Basic Brined Rotisserie Chicken

Brining is one way to ensure juicy meat and shiny, golden skin when cooking a whole chicken on the grill. Use these basic proportions for salt, sweetener and water as a guideline, then have fun creating your own brines with different herbs or citrus fruit instead of apple.

1 **whole chicken,** 3 lb (1.35 kg)

2 cups **boiling water**

¼ cup **coarse sea salt**

2 tbsp **maple syrup** or packed brown sugar

6 cups **cold water**

1 **red apple,** sliced

Half **onion,** sliced

1 tsp **peppercorns**

6 to 8 sprigs **fresh sage**

4 **bay leaves**

Pat chicken dry inside and out. In very large heatproof bowl or container large enough to hold 20 cups, combine boiling water, salt and maple syrup, stirring until salt is dissolved. Add cold water, apple, onion, peppercorns, sage and bay leaves; add chicken, breast side down. Cover and refrigerate for 12 to 24 hours.

Remove chicken from brine; pat dry. Place on rack on baking sheet; refrigerate, uncovered, until skin is dry and tacky, about 3 hours. Secure rotisserie prong to 1 end of chicken; push spit through centre of chicken and secure other end with prong. Tie kitchen string around chicken, securing wings and legs against body.

Grill, covered, on rotisserie over indirect medium heat (see Tip, page 281), until juices run clear when thickest part of thigh is pierced, about 1 hour.

Transfer to cutting board; let stand for 10 minutes before carving.

Makes 4 to 6 servings.

If you don't have a rotisserie, you can grill the whole chicken on the grate over indirect medium heat, turning every 15 minutes.

PER EACH OF 6 SERVINGS: about 207 cal, 22 g pro, 13 g total fat (4 g sat. fat), 1 g carb, 0 g fibre, 79 mg chol, 302 mg sodium, 246 mg potassium. % RDI: 1% calcium, 5% iron, 4% vit A, 2% folate.

Carnival Chicken

Celebrate the sunny Caribbean with this hot and spicy chicken, inspired by the flavours of the islands.

1 **whole chicken,** 3 lb (1.35 kg), cut into serving-size portions, or 3 lb (1.35 kg) chicken pieces

3 **green onions,** minced

3 **Scotch bonnet peppers** or habanero peppers, seeded and minced (or 1 tbsp Caribbean hot sauce)

3 cloves **garlic,** pressed or minced

½ tsp grated **orange zest**

½ tsp grated **lime zest**

3 tbsp **orange juice**

2 tbsp **lime juice**

2 tbsp **vegetable oil**

2 tsp grated **fresh ginger**

1 tsp crumbled **dried oregano**

1 tsp **salt**

¾ tsp **ground allspice**

¾ tsp **ground cumin**

¼ tsp **nutmeg**

¼ tsp **pepper**

Toss together chicken, onions, hot peppers, garlic, orange and lime zests, orange and lime juices, oil, ginger, oregano, salt, allspice, cumin, nutmeg and pepper until coated. Cover and marinate, refrigerated, for 3 hours or, preferably, up to 1 day, turning occasionally. Bring to room temperature.

Grill, covered, on greased grill over medium heat, turning often, until juices run clear when thickest part of thigh is pierced, about 30 minutes.

Makes 4 to 6 servings.

Scotch bonnet or habanero hot peppers are essential to Caribbean cuisine, but they should be handled with caution. If you're not used to handling hot peppers, wear kitchen gloves when you seed and chop them, and avoid touching your face or eyes.

PER EACH OF 6 SERVINGS: about 254 cal, 22 g pro, 17 g total fat (4 g sat. fat), 3 g carb, 1 g fibre, 79 mg chol, 451 mg sodium. % RDI: 2% calcium, 9% iron, 5% vit A, 13% vit C, 6% folate.

Spatchcock Barbecue Chicken

Fragrant herbs and orange zest give this quick-cooking whole chicken a sunny flavour.

1 **whole chicken,** 3 lb (1.35 kg)

2 tbsp **olive oil**

2 cloves **garlic,** minced

1 tbsp each chopped
   **fresh tarragon, marjoram,
   rosemary** and **thyme**

1 tbsp grated **orange zest**

2 **fresh bay leaves**

½ tsp **salt**

¼ tsp **pepper**

Using kitchen shears, cut chicken down each side of backbone; remove backbone. Turn chicken breast side up; press firmly on breastbone to flatten.

In food processor, pulse together oil, garlic, tarragon, marjoram, rosemary, thyme, orange zest, bay leaves, salt and pepper until paste. Rub all over chicken. Cover and marinate, refrigerated, for 1 hour.

Grill, covered and bone side down, on greased grill over indirect medium heat (see Tip, page 281), turning once, until juices run clear when thickest part of thigh is pierced, about 45 minutes.

Transfer to cutting board; let stand for 10 minutes before carving.

Makes 4 to 6 servings.

PER EACH OF 6 SERVINGS: about 249 cal, 22 g pro, 17 g total fat (4 g sat. fat), 1 g carb, trace fibre, 79 mg chol, 259 mg sodium, 260 mg potassium. % RDI: 2% calcium, 8% iron, 5% vit A, 3% vit C, 3% folate.

Thai Grilled Chicken

All over Southeast Asia, chicken is marinated with aromatics, such as garlic, ginger, cilantro and lime, then grilled and served with a dipping sauce.

½ cup chopped **fresh cilantro** (leaves, stems and roots)

4 cloves **garlic,** chopped

2 tbsp **fish sauce**

2 tbsp **lime juice**

1½ tsp chopped **fresh ginger**

2 tsp grated **lime zest**

1½ tsp **coriander seeds**

1 tsp packed **brown sugar**

½ tsp **pepper**

¼ tsp **cayenne pepper**

4 lb (1.8 kg) **chicken pieces**

Fresh cilantro sprigs

THAI DIPPING SAUCE:

¼ cup **lime juice**

2 tbsp **fish sauce**

1 clove **garlic,** minced

1½ tsp **granulated sugar**

½ to 1½ tsp finely chopped **Thai bird's-eye peppers** (or 1 jalapeño or other hot pepper, finely chopped)

In food processor, purée together chopped cilantro, garlic, fish sauce, lime juice and ginger. Add lime zest, coriander seeds, brown sugar, pepper and cayenne; purée until smooth, scraping down side of bowl often. Place chicken in large bowl; add cilantro mixture, turning to coat. Cover and marinate, refrigerated, for 8 hours or up to 1 day, turning often.

Thai Dipping Sauce: Mix together lime juice, fish sauce, garlic, sugar and Thai peppers.

Reserving any marinade, place chicken, bone side down, on greased grill over medium heat. Grill, covered and basting once with marinade, for 15 minutes. Turn; grill until juices run clear when thickest part is pierced, about 30 minutes. Garnish with cilantro sprigs; serve with Thai dipping sauce.

Makes 6 to 8 servings.

PER EACH OF 8 SERVINGS: about 206 cal, 30 g pro, 8 g total fat (2 g sat. fat), 4 g carb, trace fibre, 89 mg chol, 785 mg sodium. % RDI: 3% calcium, 11% iron, 3% vit A, 5% vit C, 5% folate.

Grilled Chicken With Buttery Barbecue Sauce

The flavour-packed basting sauce keeps this chicken moist and juicy.

1 **whole chicken,** 3 lb (1.35 kg)

1 tbsp **butter,** melted

½ tsp each **salt** and **pepper**

BUTTERY BARBECUE SAUCE:

¼ cup **butter**

2 cups finely diced **onion**

¼ cup **cider vinegar**

1 clove **garlic,** minced

⅔ cup **ketchup**

¼ cup **liquid honey**

2 tbsp packed **brown sugar**

2 tsp **dry mustard**

1 tsp **smoked paprika**

¼ tsp **cayenne pepper**

Buttery Barbecue Sauce: In saucepan, heat 1 tbsp of the butter over medium heat; fry onion, stirring often, until golden, about 8 minutes. Add vinegar and garlic; cook until no liquid remains. Stir in ketchup, honey, sugar, mustard, paprika and cayenne pepper; bring to boil. Reduce heat and simmer, stirring occasionally, until as thick as ketchup, about 25 minutes. Remove from heat. Stir in remaining butter.

Meanwhile, using kitchen shears, cut chicken down each side of backbone; remove backbone. Turn chicken breast side up; press firmly on breastbone to flatten.

Brush chicken with butter; sprinkle with salt and pepper. Grill, covered and bone side down, on greased grill over medium heat, turning once, for 35 minutes. Continue grilling, brushing twice with ½ cup of the barbecue sauce total, until juices run clear when thickest part of thigh is pierced, 10 to 15 minutes. Serve with remaining barbecue sauce.

Makes 4 to 6 servings.

PER EACH OF 6 SERVINGS: about 297 cal, 22 g pro, 18 g total fat (7 g sat. fat), 12 g carb, 1 g fibre, 93 mg chol, 417 mg sodium, 340 mg potassium. % RDI: 2% calcium, 7% iron, 10% vit A, 3% vit C, 4% folate.

Chicken With Puerto Rican Adobo Seasoning

Puerto Rican adobo seasoning is a favourite among the island's cooks and always includes garlic, onion, oregano and other spices. Here's our tasty version.

⅓ cup **tomato paste**

3 tbsp **orange juice**

2 tbsp **lime juice**

2 tbsp **olive oil**

3 cloves **garlic,** pressed

1 tsp **salt**

1 tsp **sweet paprika**

½ tsp **onion powder**

½ tsp **dried oregano,** crumbled

¼ tsp **cayenne pepper**

¼ tsp **pepper**

¼ tsp **ground cumin**

1 **whole chicken,** 3 lb (1.35 kg),
   cut into serving-size portions,
   or 3 lb (1.35 kg) chicken pieces

Mix together tomato paste, orange and lime juices, oil, garlic, salt, paprika, onion powder, oregano, cayenne, pepper and cumin; set aside half of the spice mixture. Toss remainder with chicken until coated.

Grill chicken, covered, on greased grill over medium heat, turning occasionally, for 20 minutes. Grill, brushing with reserved spice mixture, until juices run clear when thickest part of thigh is pierced, 10 to 15 minutes.

Makes 4 to 6 servings.

PER EACH OF 6 SERVINGS: about 207 cal, 20 g pro, 12 g total fat (3 g sat. fat), 5 g carb, 1 g fibre, 68 mg chol, 452 mg sodium. % RDI: 2% calcium, 10% iron, 9% vit A, 17% vit C, 5% folate.

Coriander Chicken

This chicken combines the slightly citrusy taste of ground coriander seeds with the complementary flavour of the fresh leaves, called cilantro.

¾ cup **Balkan-style plain yogurt**

4 cloves **garlic,** minced

3 tbsp **lemon juice**

1 tbsp **sweet paprika**

1 tbsp **ground coriander**

1 tbsp **olive oil** or vegetable oil

1 tsp **ground cumin**

½ tsp each **salt** and **cayenne pepper**

8 **chicken thighs,** about 2 lb (900 g), or 4 legs, skinned

¼ cup **fresh cilantro leaves**

Mix together yogurt, garlic, lemon juice, paprika, coriander, oil, cumin, salt and cayenne; add chicken, tossing to coat. Cover and marinate, refrigerated, for 8 hours or up to 1 day.

Reserving marinade, place chicken, bone side down, on greased grill over medium heat; brush with marinade. Grill, covered and turning once, until juices run clear when chicken is pierced, 20 to 30 minutes for thighs, 45 minutes for legs. Serve sprinkled with cilantro.

Makes 4 servings.

PER SERVING: about 247 cal, 29 g pro, 12 g total fat (3 g sat. fat), 4 g carb, trace fibre, 126 mg chol, 347 mg sodium. % RDI: 7% calcium, 16% iron, 11% vit A, 13% vit C, 6% folate.

Oregano Chicken With Tomato Salsa

Smashing garlic with the side of a knife instead of mincing allows it to flavour the marinade without little bits of it burning on the grill.

3 tbsp **wine vinegar**

2 tbsp chopped **fresh oregano**
  (or ½ tsp dried)

2 tbsp **extra-virgin olive oil**

4 cloves **garlic,** smashed

½ tsp each **salt** and **pepper**

4 **bone-in chicken breasts**

TOMATO SALSA:

2 cups **cherry tomatoes,** quartered

⅓ cup diced **red onion**

2 tbsp chopped **fresh mint**

8 **olives,** halved and pitted

1 tbsp **wine vinegar**

1 tbsp **extra-virgin olive oil**

¼ tsp each **salt** and **pepper**

Mix together vinegar, oregano, oil, garlic, salt and pepper; add chicken, turning to coat. Marinate for 20 minutes or, covered and refrigerated, up to 1 day.

Reserving marinade, place chicken, bone side down, on greased grill over medium heat; brush with half of the marinade. Grill, covered, for 25 minutes. Turn; brush with remaining marinade. Grill, covered, until no longer pink inside, about 20 minutes.

Tomato Salsa: Meanwhile, toss together tomatoes, onion, mint, olives, vinegar, oil, salt and pepper; serve over chicken.

Makes 4 servings.

PER SERVING: about 301 cal, 30 g pro, 17 g total fat (3 g sat. fat), 7 g carb, 1 g fibre, 93 mg chol, 579 mg sodium. % RDI: 3% calcium, 11% iron, 7% vit A, 23% vit C, 8% folate.

Lime-Grilled Chicken Breasts With Avocado Salsa

Marinating and quick-cooking the chicken breasts keeps the meat juicy.

4 **boneless skinless chicken breasts**

⅓ cup **lime juice**

¼ cup **fresh cilantro,** minced

¼ cup **extra-virgin olive oil**

2 cloves **garlic**

1 tsp **salt**

¼ tsp **pepper**

2 **tomatoes,** chopped

Half **red onion,** finely chopped

2 **jalapeño peppers,** seeded and finely chopped

1 tbsp **red wine vinegar**

1 **avocado**

Lime wedges

Cut each chicken breast in half horizontally. Between sheets of waxed paper or plastic wrap, pound each to even ¼-inch (5 mm) thickness.

In glass bowl, combine ¼ cup of the lime juice, 3 tbsp of the cilantro, 2 tbsp of the olive oil, the garlic and half each of the salt and pepper. Add chicken, tossing to coat. Cover and marinate, refrigerated, for 30 minutes.

Meanwhile, combine tomatoes, onion, jalapeños, vinegar and remaining lime juice, cilantro, oil, salt and pepper. Peel, pit and cut avocado into large dice; gently toss with salsa, without breaking up.

Grill chicken, covered, on greased grill over medium-high heat, turning once, until no longer pink inside, about 6 minutes. Transfer to plates; top with salsa. Serve with lime wedges.

Makes 4 servings.

PER SERVING: about 380 cal, 33 g pro, 23 g total fat (4 g sat. fat), 12 g carb, 5 g fibre, 79 mg chol, 655 mg sodium, 851 mg potassium. % RDI: 3% calcium, 9% iron, 8% vit A, 32% vit C, 31% folate.

Crisp & Juicy Barbecued Chicken

Grilling chicken pieces over indirect heat, then moving them over direct heat to crisp and colour, makes for perfectly cooked chicken with deliciously crispy skin.

4 **green onions,** chopped

4 cloves **garlic**

2 **jalapeño peppers,** seeded and c hopped

½ cup packed **fresh basil leaves**

¼ cup **extra-virgin olive oil**

2 tbsp **wine vinegar**

1 tsp **salt**

1 tsp **smoked paprika** or sweet paprika

½ tsp **hot pepper flakes**

3½ lb (1.5 kg) **chicken pieces**

In food processor, purée together onions, garlic, jalapeños, basil, oil, vinegar, salt, paprika and hot pepper flakes until loose paste forms. Transfer to bowl; toss with chicken until coated. Cover and marinate, refrigerated, for 6 hours or up to 1 day, turning occasionally.

Grill, covered and bone side down, on greased grill over indirect medium heat (see Tip, page 281) until bottom is grill marked, about 25 minutes. Turn; grill until juices run clear when thickest part is pierced, about 20 minutes. If skin is not crisp, move over direct heat for a few minutes.

Makes 6 servings.

PER SERVING: about 363 cal, 32 g pro, 24 g total fat (6 g sat. fat), 2 g carb, 1 g fibre, 120 mg chol, 389 mg sodium, 443 mg potassium. % RDI: 2% calcium, 9% iron, 10% vit A, 5% vit C, 6% folate.

Citrus Sesame Chicken

Bone-in chicken is economical and has superior flavour and juiciness. Pair this sunny main dish with saffron rice and blanched snow peas.

1 each **orange, lemon** and **lime**

2 tbsp **soy sauce**

2 tbsp **sesame oil**

½ tsp **hot pepper sauce**

3 lb (1.35 kg) **bone-in chicken breasts** or legs, skinned

1 tbsp **sesame seeds**

1 tbsp **liquid honey**

Finely grate orange, lemon and lime zests into large bowl; squeeze out juices and add to bowl. Mix in soy sauce, half of the sesame oil and the hot pepper sauce; add chicken, turning to coat. Marinate for 30 minutes or, covered and refrigerated, up to 1 day.

Reserving marinade, place chicken, bone side down, on greased grill over medium heat; brush generously with some of the marinade. Grill, covered, for 25 minutes. Turn; brush with remaining marinade. Grill for 10 minutes.

Meanwhile, combine sesame seeds, remaining sesame oil and honey; brush over both sides of chicken. Grill, turning once, until no longer pink inside for breasts or juices run clear when legs are pierced, about 10 minutes.

Makes 6 servings.

PER SERVING: about 249 cal, 39 g pro, 7 g total fat (1 g sat. fat), 6 g carb, trace fibre, 99 mg chol, 302 mg sodium. % RDI: 1% calcium, 6% iron, 1% vit A, 17% vit C, 4% folate.

Buttermilk & Spice Grilled Drumsticks

A long soak in a buttermilk mixture tenderizes and adds moisture to these lightly spiced chicken drumsticks.

2 lb (900 g) **chicken drumsticks**

2 tsp **sweet paprika**

1 tsp **dried thyme,** crumbled

¾ tsp **salt**

½ tsp **pepper**

½ tsp grated **lemon zest**

¼ tsp **cayenne pepper**

BUTTERMILK MARINADE:

1 cup **buttermilk**

2 tbsp **lemon juice**

2 cloves **garlic,** pressed or minced

Buttermilk Marinade: Mix together buttermilk, lemon juice and garlic; add drumsticks, rolling to coat. Cover and marinate, refrigerated, for 3 to 12 hours, turning occasionally. Drain well; discard marinade.

In large bowl, whisk together paprika, thyme, salt, pepper, lemon zest and cayenne; add chicken, tossing to coat. Marinate for 10 minutes.

Grill, covered, on greased grill over medium heat, turning often, until juices run clear when thickest part is pierced, 20 to 25 minutes.

Makes 4 to 6 servings.

PER EACH OF 6 SERVINGS: about 178 cal, 17 g pro, 11 g total fat (3 g sat. fat), 3 g carb, trace fibre, 69 mg chol, 377 mg sodium. % RDI: 5% calcium, 11% iron, 7% vit A, 5% vit C, 4% folate.

Balsamic Peppercorn Chicken Legs

Cooking tames the tang of vinegar and blends the robust flavours of mustard, peppercorns and garlic on these juicy legs.

8 **chicken legs**

¾ cup **balsamic vinegar** or red wine vinegar

3 tbsp **extra-virgin olive oil**

2 tbsp **Dijon mustard**

6 cloves **garlic,** minced

1 tbsp **coarsely cracked pepper**

2 tsp **dried thyme**

2 tsp **dried oregano**

½ tsp **salt**

Place chicken in large shallow glass dish. Whisk together vinegar, oil, mustard, garlic, pepper, thyme, oregano and salt; pour over chicken. Cover and marinate, refrigerated, for 2 to 8 hours, turning once.

Reserving marinade, place chicken on greased grill over medium heat; brush with marinade. Discard any remaining marinade. Grill, covered and turning once, until juices run clear when thickest part of thigh is pierced, about 40 minutes.

Makes 8 servings.

PER SERVING: about 196 cal, 20 g pro, 12 g total fat (3 g sat. fat), 1 g carb, 0 g fibre, 92 mg chol, 119 mg sodium. % RDI: 1% calcium, 9% iron, 3% vit A, 4% folate.

Chicken Drumsticks With Apple Stout Barbecue Sauce

This recipe makes double the sauce you need. Refrigerate the remainder for up to one month and brush over your favourite grilled meats or fish before grilling.

2 lb (900 g) **chicken drumsticks**

APPLE STOUT BARBECUE SAUCE:

1 tbsp **vegetable oil**

1 **onion,** chopped

2 cloves **garlic,** minced

1½ cups **stout beer,** porter or other dark beer

1 cup **unsweetened applesauce**

½ cup each **maple syrup** and **cooking molasses**

½ cup **cider vinegar**

1 can (5½ oz/156 mL) **tomato paste**

½ tsp **salt**

Apple Stout Barbecue Sauce: In saucepan, heat oil over medium-high heat; sauté onion and garlic until softened. Add stout, applesauce, maple syrup, molasses, vinegar, tomato paste and salt. In blender, purée until smooth. Press through fine-mesh sieve into clean saucepan. Bring to simmer over medium heat; cook until thickened and reduced to about 3 cups, 15 to 20 minutes.

Meanwhile, grill chicken, covered, on greased grill over medium heat, turning every 10 minutes, until juices run clear when thickest part is pierced, about 30 minutes.

Brush chicken with half of the barbecue sauce; grill, uncovered and turning often, until glazed, 5 minutes.

Makes 4 to 6 servings.

PER EACH OF 6 SERVINGS: about 277 cal, 17 g pro, 11 g total fat (3 g sat. fat), 27 g carb, 1 g fibre, 67 mg chol, 185 mg sodium, 601 mg potassium. % RDI: 5% calcium, 17% iron, 4% vit A, 8% vit C, 4% folate.

Quick Korean Chicken

This is an instant Korean-style barbecued chicken – great for last-minute dinners.

8 **boneless skinless chicken thighs,** about 1½ lb (675 g) total

¼ cup **sodium-reduced soy sauce**

2 tbsp **sesame oil**

4 tsp **granulated sugar**

2 tsp minced **fresh ginger**

2 tsp **sesame seeds**

½ tsp **pepper**

4 cloves **garlic,** thinly sliced

4 **green onions,** trimmed

Trim any fat from thighs. Between 2 sheets of waxed paper or plastic wrap, pound to even scant ½-inch (1 cm) thickness. Mix soy sauce, oil, sugar, ginger, sesame seeds, pepper and garlic; add chicken and onions, turning to coat. Marinate for 15 minutes, turning occasionally.

Brush garlic off chicken and onions. Grill chicken, covered, on greased grill over medium-high heat, turning once, for 6 minutes. Add onions; grill, covered, until juices run clear when thickest part of chicken is pierced and onions are slightly charred, about 2 minutes. Cut onions into bite-size pieces.

Makes 4 servings.

PER SERVING: about 250 cal, 33 g pro, 12 g total fat (3 g sat. fat), 2 g carb, trace fibre, 123 mg chol, 167 mg sodium. % RDI: 3% calcium, 14% iron, 3% vit A, 3% vit C, 8% folate.

Chicken Cutlets With Cilantro Peanut Sauce

This green sauce is like an Asian-style pesto. It's equally nice on grilled fish.

1½ cups packed **fresh parsley**

½ cup packed **fresh cilantro**

⅓ cup chopped **roasted peanuts**

¼ cup **peanut oil** or vegetable oil

2½ tbsp **white wine vinegar**

½ tsp each **salt** and **pepper**

4 **boneless skinless chicken breasts**

Finely chop parsley and cilantro. Mix together parsley, cilantro, peanuts, all but 2 tsp of the oil, the vinegar and half each of the salt and pepper.

Cut each chicken breast in half horizontally, almost but not all the way through; open like book. Between sheets of waxed paper or plastic wrap, pound each to even ¼-inch (5 mm) thickness. Brush with remaining oil; sprinkle with remaining salt and pepper.

Grill chicken, covered, on greased grill over medium-high heat, turning once, until no longer pink inside, 5 minutes. Serve topped with cilantro peanut sauce.

Makes 4 servings.

PER SERVING: about 347 cal, 34 g pro, 22 g total fat (4 g sat. fat), 4 g carb, 2 g fibre, 79 mg chol, 422 mg sodium, 597 mg potassium. % RDI: 5% calcium, 16% iron, 21% vit A, 52% vit C, 25% folate.

Flash-Grilled Chicken Breasts With Oyster Mushrooms

Splitting and flattening the breasts lets them quickly absorb the simple Spanish-style marinade, so they grill fast and stay moist. The mushrooms make an elegant topping.

4 **boneless skinless chicken breasts**

2 tbsp **extra-virgin olive oil**

2 cloves **garlic,** pressed or minced

1 tsp minced **fresh thyme** or scant ½ tsp dried

½ tsp **salt**

Generous ¼ tsp **smoked paprika**

OYSTER MUSHROOM PACKET:

12 oz (340 g) **oyster mushrooms**

⅓ cup chopped **fresh parsley**

1 tbsp **extra-virgin olive oil**

1 tsp **sherry vinegar**

1 **small shallot,** thinly sliced

¼ tsp **salt**

Cut each chicken breast in half horizontally, almost but not all the way through; open like book. Between sheets of waxed paper or plastic wrap, pound each to even ¼-inch (5 mm) thickness.

Mix together oil, garlic, thyme, salt and paprika; add chicken, turning to coat. Marinate for 20 minutes or, covered and refrigerated, up to 12 hours.

Oyster Mushroom Packet: Trim off and discard tough stem ends from mushrooms; tear large mushrooms into smaller pieces. Place on heavy-duty foil; sprinkle with parsley, oil, vinegar, shallot and salt. Toss until coated; seal to form packet. Prick 2 or 3 steam vents in top. Grill over high heat until tender, about 8 minutes. Keep warm.

Grill chicken on greased grill over high heat, turning once, until no longer pink inside, 3 to 4 minutes. Serve topped with mushroom mixture.

Makes 4 servings.

PER SERVING: about 272 cal, 33 g pro, 12 g total fat (2 g sat. fat), 7 g carb, 2 g fibre, 79 mg chol, 516 mg sodium. % RDI: 2% calcium, 15% iron, 6% vit A, 10% vit C, 12% folate.

Mango Chicken

Combining fresh mango with mango chutney in the sauce brings the fruit's flavour front and centre.

1 tbsp **vegetable oil**

1 **small onion,** chopped

1 clove **garlic,** minced

1 tbsp **chili powder**

Half **mango,** peeled and chopped

¼ cup **mango chutney**

1 tsp grated **lime zest**

3 tbsp **lime juice**

2 tbsp **granulated sugar**

½ tsp **salt**

¼ tsp **pepper**

4 **bone-in chicken breasts,** skinned

Lime wedges

In saucepan, heat oil over medium heat; fry onion, garlic and chili powder, stirring occasionally, until onion is softened, about 5 minutes. Stir in mango, chutney, lime zest and juice, sugar, salt and pepper; bring to boil. Reduce heat and simmer, stirring occasionally, until mango is very tender, about 8 minutes. Let cool.

In blender or food processor, purée mango mixture until smooth. Transfer to large bowl; add chicken, turning to coat. Cover and marinate, refrigerated, for 4 hours or up to 1 day, turning occasionally.

Reserving any remaining marinade, place chicken on greased grill over medium heat; brush with marinade. Grill, covered and turning once, until no longer pink inside, 30 to 45 minutes. Serve with lime wedges.

Makes 4 servings.

PER SERVING: about 281 cal, 33 g pro, 6 g total fat (1 g sat. fat), 24 g carb, 1 g fibre, 84 mg chol, 721 mg sodium. % RDI: 2% calcium, 7% iron, 16% vit A, 18% vit C, 4% folate.

Grilled Chicken Mozzarella

Basil, tomato and mozzarella – the taste of summer in every mouthful!

4 **large boneless skinless chicken breasts,** about 2 lb (900 g) total

3 tbsp **olive oil**

2 cloves **garlic,** minced

1 tbsp **lemon juice**

¾ tsp **dried oregano**

½ tsp each **salt** and **pepper**

8 thick slices **tomato**

8 slices **mozzarella cheese**

8 **fresh basil leaves**

Cut each chicken breast in half horizontally. Between sheets of waxed paper or plastic wrap, pound each to even ¼-inch (5 mm) thickness.

Whisk together oil, garlic, lemon juice, oregano, salt and pepper; remove one-quarter and set aside. Add chicken to remaining oil mixture, turning to coat; marinate for 10 minutes. Discard marinade.

Grill chicken and tomato, covered, on greased grill over medium-high heat for 4 minutes. Turn chicken and tomato; top chicken with mozzarella. Grill until chicken is no longer pink inside and tomato is softened and slightly charred, about 2 minutes.

To serve, top each chicken breast with 1 slice of tomato; drizzle with reserved oil mixture. Top with basil leaf.

Makes 8 servings.

PER SERVING: about 221 cal, 31 g pro, 10 g total fat (4 g sat. fat), 2 g carb, trace fibre, 86 mg chol, 220 mg sodium, 402 mg potassium. % RDI: 12% calcium, 4% iron, 7% vit A, 7% vit C, 4% folate.

Chicken With Tabbouleh Salad

Bulgur, or cracked wheat, is available in most supermarkets, usually near the rice, pasta or couscous. It makes a tasty base for simple Middle Eastern–style salads.

2 tbsp **extra-virgin olive oil**

2 cloves **garlic,** minced

1 tsp **dried mint**

½ tsp each **ground coriander** and **salt**

Pinch each **ground cloves** and **cinnamon**

4 **boneless skinless chicken breasts**

TABBOULEH SALAD:

3 cups **boiling water**

1½ cups **bulgur**

1 cup chopped **fresh parsley**

1 **green onion,** minced

¼ cup **lemon juice**

2 tbsp **extra-virgin olive oil**

¼ tsp each **salt** and **pepper**

Tabbouleh Salad: In heatproof bowl, pour boiling water over bulgur; cover and let stand until tender, about 15 minutes. Drain, squeezing out as much water as possible. Stir in parsley, onion, lemon juice, oil, salt and pepper.

Meanwhile, mix together oil, garlic, mint, coriander, salt, cloves and cinnamon; brush all over chicken. Marinate for 10 minutes.

Grill chicken, covered, on greased grill over medium-high heat, turning once, until no longer pink inside, about 10 minutes. Serve with tabbouleh salad.

Makes 4 servings.

PER SERVING: about 458 cal, 38 g pro, 16 g total fat (3 g sat. fat), 43 g carb, 7 g fibre, 79 mg chol, 522 mg sodium, 642 mg potassium. % RDI: 5% calcium, 28% iron, 14% vit A, 42% vit C, 31% folate.

Grilled Chicken & Charred Corn Salad

This grilled salad is a great excuse to eat – and cook – alfresco. The smoked paprika adds to the grilled flavour, but you can use regular sweet or hot paprika in its place.

2 **boneless skinless chicken breasts**

½ tsp each **salt** and **pepper**

2 **cobs of corn,** husked

1 bunch **asparagus,** trimmed

¼ cup **olive oil**

4 tsp **white wine vinegar**

¼ tsp **Dijon mustard**

1 clove **garlic,** minced

¼ tsp **smoked paprika**

8 cups torn **romaine lettuce**

2 **large tomatoes,** chopped

1 **green onion,** sliced

Sprinkle chicken with half each of the salt and pepper. Brush corn and asparagus with 1 tbsp of the oil.

Grill chicken and corn, covered, on greased grill over medium-high heat, turning chicken once and corn as needed, until chicken is no longer pink inside and corn is slightly charred and tender, 10 minutes for chicken, 15 minutes for corn. Transfer to plate; keep warm.

Grill asparagus, covered and turning often, until tender-crisp, 6 to 8 minutes.

Diagonally slice chicken. Cut corn from cobs. Cut asparagus into 1-inch (2.5 cm) pieces.

In large bowl, whisk together vinegar, mustard, garlic, paprika and remaining oil, salt and pepper. Toss in corn, asparagus, lettuce, tomatoes and green onion; serve topped with chicken.

Makes 4 servings.

PER SERVING: about 364 cal, 32 g pro, 17 g total fat (3 g sat. fat), 26 g carb, 7 g fibre, 67 mg chol, 384 mg sodium, 1,113 mg potassium. % RDI: 6% calcium, 21% iron, 101% vit A, 75% vit C, 133% folate.

Indonesian Chicken Breast Salad

Indonesian salads often include a mix of raw and cooked vegetables and fruit. Raid your refrigerator and use your imagination for the salad ingredients.

1 tsp grated **lime zest**

1 tbsp **lime juice**

1 tbsp **peanut oil** or vegetable oil

2 tsp grated **fresh ginger**

½ tsp **salt**

¼ tsp **turmeric**

¼ tsp **cayenne pepper**

4 **boneless skinless chicken breasts**

Indonesian Peanut Dressing (right)

SALAD:

1 small head **iceberg lettuce,** shredded

8 oz (225 g) **green beans,** cooked

1 **sweet pepper,** sliced

1 **star fruit** or half small pineapple, sliced

Half **English cucumber,** sliced

Half **jicama,** sliced

2 cups cubed **medium tofu,** blanched and drained

Mix together lime zest and juice, oil, ginger, salt, turmeric and cayenne; add chicken, turning to coat. Marinate for 30 minutes or, covered and refrigerated, up to 1 day.

Grill, covered, on greased grill over medium-high heat, turning once, until no longer pink inside, about 12 minutes. Transfer to cutting board; let stand for 5 minutes before slicing.

Salad: Meanwhile, arrange lettuce, beans, pepper, star fruit, cucumber, jicama and tofu on 4 plates.

Top each salad plate with chicken; spoon Indonesian peanut dressing over top.

Makes 4 servings.

Indonesian Peanut Dressing

In small skillet, heat 2 tbsp peanut oil or vegetable oil over medium-high heat; sauté 2 shallots, thinly sliced, and 3 cloves garlic, thinly sliced, until golden. Drain oil through sieve into heatproof bowl; mince shallots and garlic and add to bowl with oil. Stir in ⅓ cup natural peanut butter, 3 tbsp soy sauce, 1 to 2 tbsp minced hot pepper, 1 tbsp fancy molasses, 1 tbsp lime juice and ¼ tsp five-spice powder. Stir in enough cold water (3 to 4 tbsp) to make smooth and pourable.

Makes about 1 cup.

PER SERVING: about 558 cal, 49 g pro, 28 g total fat (5 g sat. fat), 34 g carb, 11 g fibre, 79 mg chol, 980 mg sodium. % RDI: 23% calcium, 38% iron, 13% vit A, 100% vit C, 73% folate.

Chinese Chicken Breast Salad

Savoury Chinese sesame dressing makes this salad irresistible. You can use homemade Teriyaki Sauce (page 531) or bottled – it's up to you.

2 tbsp **teriyaki sauce**

1 tbsp **sesame oil**

½ tsp **hot pepper flakes**

¼ tsp **white pepper**

4 **boneless skinless chicken breasts**

SESAME DRESSING:

¼ cup **Asian sesame paste** or tahini

1 tbsp **sesame oil**

1 tbsp **soy sauce**

2 tsp **unseasoned rice vinegar** or cider vinegar

2 tsp **hot mustard**

2 cloves **garlic,** pressed or minced

1 tsp **granulated sugar**

¼ tsp **salt**

Pinch **white pepper**

SALAD:

4 ribs **celery**

4 cups shredded **napa cabbage** or Chinese lettuce

1 bunch **radishes,** sliced

Half **English cucumber,** sliced

2 **green onions,** thinly sliced

Mix together teriyaki sauce, oil, hot pepper flakes and pepper; add chicken, turning to coat. Marinate for 30 minutes or, covered and refrigerated, up to 1 day.

Sesame Dressing: With fork, whisk together sesame paste, sesame oil, soy sauce, rice vinegar, mustard, garlic, sugar, salt and pepper; whisk in enough cold water (¼ to ⅓ cup) to make smooth and pourable.

Grill chicken, covered, on greased grill over medium-high heat, turning once, until no longer pink inside, about 12 minutes. Transfer to cutting board; let stand for 5 minutes before slicing.

Salad: Meanwhile, in pot of boiling salted water, blanch celery until tender-crisp, 20 to 30 seconds; drain. Chill under cold water; drain. Cut into bite-size pieces. Arrange cabbage on 4 plates; top with celery, radishes and cucumber.

Top each salad plate with chicken; spoon sesame dressing over top. Sprinkle with green onions.

Makes 4 servings.

PER SERVING: about 343 cal, 36 g pro, 17 g total fat (3 g sat. fat), 15 g carb, 5 g fibre, 79 mg chol, 822 mg sodium. % RDI: 17% calcium, 21% iron, 9% vit A, 55% vit C, 58% folate.

Middle Eastern Chicken Breast Salad

This summery grilled Middle Eastern–inspired salad gets its delicious nuttiness from the tahini and pistachios.

¼ cup chopped **fresh dill**

2 tbsp **extra-virgin olive oil**

1 **shallot** (or half small onion), minced

1 tbsp grated **lemon zest**

¼ tsp each **salt** and **pepper**

4 **boneless skinless chicken breasts**

TAHINI DRESSING:

¼ cup **Balkan-style plain yogurt**

¼ cup **tahini**

3 tbsp **lemon juice**

2 tbsp **warm water**

½ tsp **ground cumin**

¼ tsp each **salt** and **pepper**

SALAD:

2 heads **Belgian endive,** chopped

1 bunch **watercress** (tough stems removed), coarsely chopped

Half head **radicchio,** chopped

1 each rib **celery** and **green onion,** thinly sliced

1 cup halved **cherry tomatoes**

¼ cup hulled **pistachios** or slivered almonds

2 tbsp chopped **fresh mint** or parsley

Mix together dill, oil, shallot, lemon zest, salt and pepper; add chicken, turning to coat. Cover and marinate, refrigerated, for 4 to 12 hours, turning occasionally.

Tahini Dressing: Whisk together yogurt, tahini, lemon juice, water, cumin, salt and pepper until smooth.

Grill chicken, covered, on greased grill over medium-high heat, turning once, until no longer pink inside, about 12 minutes. Transfer to cutting board; let stand for 5 minutes before slicing.

Salad: Meanwhile, toss together endive, watercress, radicchio, celery, onion, tomatoes, half of the pistachios and the mint; toss with all but 2 tbsp of the tahini dressing.

Divide salad among 4 plates; top with chicken. Spoon remaining dressing over top; sprinkle with remaining pistachios.

Makes 4 servings.

PER SERVING: about 338 cal, 36 g pro, 18 g total fat (3 g sat. fat), 11 g carb, 5 g fibre, 81 mg chol, 405 mg sodium. % RDI: 15% calcium, 21% iron, 20% vit A, 45% vit C, 29% folate.

Sticky Glazed Grilled Chicken With Cucumber Salad

Round out this meal with lightly dressed cold cooked somen or soba noodles.

¼ cup **liquid honey**

2 tbsp **lime juice**

2 tbsp **sodium-reduced tamari**

1 tbsp **sesame oil**

2 cloves **garlic,** minced

2 tsp grated **fresh ginger**

8 **boneless skinless chicken thighs**

1 tbsp toasted **sesame seeds**

CUCUMBER SALAD:

⅓ cup **unseasoned rice vinegar**

2 tsp **liquid honey**

1 tsp **sesame oil**

¼ tsp each **hot pepper flakes** and **salt**

1 **English cucumber,** thinly sliced diagonally

2 **green onions,** thinly sliced

In large bowl, combine honey, lime juice, tamari, sesame oil, garlic and ginger; remove 3 tbsp and set aside. Add chicken to bowl, turning to coat; marinate for 10 minutes.

Cucumber Salad: Meanwhile, whisk together vinegar, honey, sesame oil, hot pepper flakes and salt. Add cucumber and mix until coated; set aside in refrigerator.

Grill chicken, covered, on greased grill over medium heat, turning once and brushing with reserved honey mixture in final 2 minutes, until juices run clear when chicken is pierced, about 10 minutes.

Stir green onions into salad. Serve salad and chicken sprinkled with sesame seeds.

Makes 4 servings.

PER SERVING: about 313 cal, 27 g pro, 12 g total fat (3 g sat. fat), 24 g carb, 1 g fibre, 95 mg chol, 531 mg sodium, 438 mg potassium. % RDI: 4% calcium, 16% iron, 4% vit A, 8% vit C, 10% folate.

Five-Spice Chicken Wings

Aromatic five-spice powder makes sticky chicken wings irresistibly fragrant.

2 tbsp **soy sauce**

2 tbsp **hoisin sauce**

2 tbsp **unseasoned rice vinegar**

1 tbsp **five-spice powder**

1 tbsp **sesame oil** or vegetable oil

½ tsp each **salt** and **pepper**

2 cloves **garlic,** minced

2½ lb (1.125 kg) **chicken wing drumettes** and **winglets** (midsections)

3 tbsp **liquid honey**

Mix together soy sauce, hoisin sauce, vinegar, five-spice powder, oil, salt, pepper and garlic; add wings, tossing to coat. Cover and marinate, refrigerated, for 2 hours or up to 1 day.

Grill, covered, on greased grill or in greased grill basket over medium heat, turning occasionally, until crisp and no longer pink at joints, 20 to 25 minutes.

Brush all over with honey; grill, covered and turning once, until glazed, about 3 minutes.

Makes about 30 pieces.

PER PIECE: about 56 cal, 4 g pro, 3 g total fat (1 g sat. fat), 2 g carb, 0 g fibre, 13 mg chol, 119 mg sodium. % RDI: 2% iron, 1% vit A.

Indian Hot Wings With Mint Dipping Sauce

The cool mint sauce perfectly balances the spicy wings.

¼ cup minced **fresh cilantro**

2 tbsp **Madras curry paste** or other Indian curry paste

2 tbsp **lemon juice**

1 tbsp **vegetable oil**

1½ tsp **ground ginger**

¾ tsp **turmeric**

¾ tsp **ground coriander**

¼ tsp **salt**

2 lb (900 g) **chicken wing drumettes** and **winglets** (midsections)

MINT DIPPING SAUCE:

⅓ cup **Balkan-style plain yogurt**

¼ cup minced **fresh mint** (or 1 tbsp dried)

1 tbsp minced seeded **jalapeño pepper**

2 tsp **lemon juice**

¼ tsp **ground cumin**

¼ tsp **pepper**

Pinch **granulated sugar**

Pinch **salt**

Mix together cilantro, curry paste, lemon juice, oil, ginger, turmeric, coriander and salt; add wings, tossing to coat. Cover and marinate, refrigerated, for 2 hours or up to 1 day.

Mint Dipping Sauce: Mix together yogurt, mint, jalapeño, lemon juice, cumin, pepper, sugar and salt.

Grill wings, covered, on greased grill or in greased grill basket over medium heat, turning occasionally, until crisp and no longer pink at joints, 15 to 25 minutes. Serve with mint dipping sauce.

Makes about 25 pieces.

Photo, page 323

PER PIECE (WITHOUT SAUCE): about 45 cal, 3 g pro, 3 g total fat (1 g sat. fat), 1 g carb, 0 g fibre, 10 mg chol, 31 mg sodium. % RDI: 1% calcium, 2% iron, 1% vit A, 2% vit C.

From left: Chili Chicken Wings (page 324) and Indian Hot Wings With Mint Dipping Sauce (page 321)

Chili Chicken Wings

Skewered lengthwise, these spicy wings stay flat and are easy to handle on the grill.

3 lb (1.35 kg) **chicken wings**

¼ cup **Chili Spice Mix** (page 526)

ANCHO CHILI TOMATO SAUCE:

1 tbsp **vegetable oil**

¼ cup minced **onion**

2 cloves **garlic,** minced

¾ cup **ketchup** or tomato-based
  chili sauce

2 tbsp **fancy molasses**

1 tbsp **cider vinegar**

2 tsp **ancho chili powder**

1 tsp **dry mustard**

1 tsp **hot pepper sauce**

Straighten each chicken wing; push skewer through length from base to tip. Rub all over with chili spice mix. Marinate for 30 minutes or, covered and refrigerated, up to 1 day, turning occasionally.

Ancho Chili Tomato Sauce: Meanwhile, in saucepan, heat oil over medium heat; fry onion and garlic, stirring occasionally, until softened, about 3 minutes. Stir in ketchup, molasses, vinegar, ancho chili powder, mustard and hot pepper sauce; reduce heat and simmer, stirring occasionally, until bubbly, about 5 minutes. Let cool.

Grill wings, covered, on greased grill or in greased grill basket over medium heat, turning once, for 10 minutes. Baste with sauce; grill, basting and turning occasionally, until crisp and no longer pink at joints, 15 to 25 minutes.

Makes about 30 pieces.

Photo, page 322

PER PIECE: about 93 cal, 7 g pro, 5 g total fat (1 g sat. fat), 4 g carb, trace fibre, 21 mg chol, 137 mg sodium. % RDI: 1% calcium, 5% iron, 6% vit A, 3% vit C, 1% folate.

Three-Pepper Chicken Wings

Black, white and cayenne peppers combine to make an intensely flavoured wing marinade that's equally appealing on chicken pieces.

5 cloves **garlic,** pressed or minced

1 tbsp grated **fresh ginger**

1 tsp **black pepper**

1 tsp **white pepper**

1 tsp **cayenne pepper**

¾ tsp **salt**

¼ cup **sesame oil**

2 tbsp **Chinese black vinegar** or balsamic vinegar

2 lb (900 g) **chicken wing drumettes** and **winglets** (midsections)

In large heatproof bowl, mix together garlic; ginger; black, white and cayenne peppers; and salt. In small skillet or saucepan, heat sesame oil over medium-high heat until haze forms over surface but oil is not smoking; pour over garlic mixture. Add vinegar to skillet; bring to boil (this will happen almost immediately) and pour into bowl. Add wings, tossing to coat. Marinate for 30 minutes or, covered and refrigerated, up to 1 day.

Reserving any remaining marinade, place wings on greased grill or in greased grill basket over medium heat; brush with marinade. Grill, covered, turning occasionally, until crisp and no longer pink at joints, 15 to 25 minutes.

Makes about 25 pieces.

PER PIECE: about 57 cal, 4 g pro, 4 g total fat (1 g sat. fat), 1 g carb, trace fibre, 11 mg chol, 80 mg sodium, 33 mg potassium. % RDI: 1% iron, 1% vit A.

Paris Wings
With Crudités

Serve these classy wings with French-style crudités, such as haricots verts, Belgian endive, baby carrots and French breakfast radishes to dip in the cheese sauce.

3 lb (1.35 kg) **chicken wing drumettes** and **winglets** (midsections)

¼ cup **white vermouth**

3 tbsp **Dijon mustard**

2 cloves **garlic,** pressed or minced

1 tbsp minced **fresh thyme** or 1 tsp dried

2 tsp minced **fresh tarragon** or ¾ tsp crumbled dried tarragon

¾ tsp **salt**

¼ tsp **pepper**

1 tbsp **olive oil** or vegetable oil

Hot pepper sauce

Vegetable crudités

ROQUEFORT DIPPING SAUCE:

3 oz (85 g) **Roquefort cheese**

3 tbsp **buttermilk** or milk

2 tsp **sherry vinegar** or cider vinegar

Pinch **salt**

Pinch **pepper**

2 tbsp finely chopped **fresh chives**

Milk (optional)

Toss together wings, vermouth, mustard, garlic, thyme, tarragon, salt and pepper until wings are coated. Cover and marinate, refrigerated, for 2 hours or up to 1 day. Bring to room temperature; toss with oil until coated.

Roquefort Dipping Sauce: With fork, mash together Roquefort cheese, buttermilk, vinegar, salt and pepper until almost smooth. Stir in chives; add a little milk to thin, if desired.

Grill wings, covered, on greased grill or in greased grill basket over medium heat until crisp and no longer pink at joints, 15 to 25 minutes. Serve with Roquefort dipping sauce, hot pepper sauce and crudités.

Makes about 35 pieces.

PER PIECE WITH 1 TSP ROQUEFORT DIPPING SAUCE (WITHOUT HOT PEPPER SAUCE OR CRUDITÉS): about 95 cal, 7 g pro, 7 g total fat (2 g sat. fat), 1 g carb, trace fibre, 24 mg chol, 172 mg sodium. % RDI: 2% calcium, 3% iron, 2% vit A.

Mexican Wings & Green Salsa

Tomatillos, sometimes called Spanish or Mexican green tomatoes, have a delicate, lightly acidic flavour that's nice with the rich, smoky chipotles. The green salsa is also good with tortilla chips.

2 cloves **garlic,** minced

2 **canned chipotles in adobo sauce**

2 tbsp **adobo sauce** from canned chipotles

2 tbsp **lime juice**

1 tbsp **vegetable oil**

1 tsp **dried oregano**

¼ tsp **cinnamon**

¼ tsp **salt**

2 lb (900 g) **chicken wing drumettes** and **winglets** (midsections)

Green Salsa (right)

Mash together garlic, chipotle peppers, adobo sauce, lime juice, oil, oregano, cinnamon and salt until smooth; add wings, tossing to coat. Cover and marinate, refrigerated, for 2 hours or up to 1 day.

Grill wings, covered, on greased grill or in greased grill basket over medium heat, turning occasionally, until crisp and no longer pink at joints, 20 to 25 minutes. Serve with green salsa.

Makes about 25 pieces.

Green Salsa

Mix together ⅓ cup chopped grilled fresh tomatillos, chopped drained canned tomatillos or chopped green tomatoes; 1 or 2 jalapeño or serrano pepper(s), seeded and minced; 2 tbsp minced green onions (white part only); 4 tsp chopped fresh cilantro or parsley; 2 tsp lime juice; and pinch each granulated sugar and salt.

Makes about ¾ cup.

PER PIECE: about 40 cal, 3 g pro, 3 g total fat (1 g sat. fat), 1 g carb, trace fibre, 9 mg chol, 46 mg sodium. % RDI: 1% iron, 2% vit A.

Tuscan Cornish Hens

Cornish hens are tender, juicy and delicate-tasting. They're perfect candidates for the grill — simple enough for family meals and special enough for entertaining.

4 **small Cornish hens,** about 1 lb (450 g) each

⅓ cup **lemon juice**

¼ cup **extra-virgin olive oil**

4 cloves **garlic,** minced

1 tbsp chopped **fresh rosemary**

2 tsp **fennel seeds,** crushed

½ tsp each **salt** and **pepper**

Using kitchen shears, cut each hen down each side of backbone; remove backbone (save for stockpot). Turn hens breast side up; press firmly on breastbones to flatten. Tuck wings behind backs.

Mix together lemon juice, oil, garlic, rosemary, fennel seeds, salt and pepper; add hens, turning to coat. Cover and marinate, refrigerated, for 4 hours or up to 1 day, turning occasionally.

Grill hens, covered and bone side down, on greased grill over medium heat, turning occasionally, until juices run clear when thickest part of thigh is pierced and skin is crisp, 25 to 30 minutes.

Makes 4 servings.

PER SERVING: about 586 cal, 45 g pro, 43 g total fat (11 g sat. fat), 2 g carb, trace fibre, 262 mg chol, 274 mg sodium. % RDI: 3% calcium, 15% iron, 7% vit A, 5% vit C, 2% folate.

Lemon Pepper Cornish Hens

This recipe gives a Mediterranean twist to tender, succulent Cornish hens.

2 **large Cornish hens,** about
    1½ lb (675 g) each

1½ tsp grated **lemon zest**

¼ cup **lemon juice**

3 cloves **garlic,** pressed

1 tbsp **pepper**

2 tsp packed **brown sugar**

2 tsp grated **fresh ginger**

1½ tsp **dried oregano,** crumbled

1 tsp **salt**

½ tsp **ground cumin**

¼ tsp **ground cloves**

Extra-virgin olive oil

Using kitchen shears, cut each hen down each side of backbone; remove backbone (save for stockpot). Snip through breastbone to separate each hen into halves.

Mix together lemon zest and juice, garlic, pepper, sugar, ginger, oregano, salt, cumin and cloves; add hens, turning to coat. Cover and marinate, refrigerated, for 2 hours or up to 1 day. Bring to room temperature.

Brush hens lightly with oil; grill, covered and bone side down, on greased grill over medium heat, turning occasionally and basting with a little more oil, until juices run clear when thickest part of thigh is pierced and skin is crisp, 25 to 30 minutes.

Makes 4 servings.

PER SERVING: about 454 cal, 32 g pro, 33 g total fat (8 g sat. fat), 6 g carb, 1 g fibre, 186 mg chol, 668 mg sodium. % RDI: 4% calcium, 16% iron, 5% vit A, 17% vit C, 3% folate.

Grilled Brined Whole Turkey

Cooking the turkey in a pan makes it easy to move around and cook on the barbecue. The brining adds flavour and guarantees a moist and juicy bird.

1 **whole turkey,** about 10 lb (4.5 kg)

¼ tsp **pepper**

4 sprigs **fresh thyme**

3 sprigs **fresh parsley**

2 cloves **garlic**

1 **onion,** halved

BRINE:

12 cups **cold water**

1 cup **pickling salt**

¼ cup packed **brown sugar**

1 tbsp **black peppercorns**

3 **bay leaves**

MAPLE BEER GLAZE:

¼ cup **maple syrup**

¼ cup **beer**

3 tbsp **grainy mustard**

2 tbsp **vegetable oil**

1 tbsp chopped **fresh thyme**
    (or 1 tsp dried)

Brine: In container large enough to submerge turkey, combine water, salt and sugar; stir until dissolved. Add peppercorns and bay leaves.

Remove neck and giblets from turkey (save for stockpot); add turkey to brine. Cover container; set on tray. Refrigerate for 12 hours or up to 1 day.

Maple Beer Glaze: Mix together maple syrup, beer, mustard, oil and thyme.

Remove turkey from brine; rinse under cold water and pat dry. Sprinkle pepper in cavity; stuff with thyme, parsley, garlic and onion. Skewer neck skin to back to close. Place on greased rack in large disposable foil roasting pan; pour in 2 cups water.

Grill turkey, covered, in pan on grill over indirect medium heat (see Tip, page 281), brushing with maple beer glaze every 45 minutes and maintaining level of water in pan, until instant-read thermometer inserted in thickest part of thigh registers 180°F (82°C), 2¼ to 2½ hours. Let stand for 15 minutes before carving.

Makes 8 to 10 servings.

TIP
When you brine a turkey, the pan drippings are too salty for gravy, so don't use them. If you want gravy, make a simple one from the neck, gizzard and heart.

PER EACH OF 10 SERVINGS: about 536 cal, 65 g pro, 26 g total fat (7 g sat. fat), 7 g carb, trace fibre, 190 mg chol, 1,137 mg sodium. % RDI: 7% calcium, 32% iron, 3% vit C, 8% folate.

Grilled Turkey Breast With Sautéed Banana Peppers

A turkey breast is excellent for smaller gatherings – you'll have much less left over than you would from a whole bird – and it cooks much more quickly.

6 long sprigs **fresh rosemary**
    or thyme

4 **bay leaves**

1 **skin-on boneless turkey breast,**
    2 to 2½ lb (900 g to 1.125 kg)

½ tsp **salt**

¼ tsp **pepper**

2 tbsp **olive oil**

SAUTÉED BANANA PEPPERS:

4 **hot banana peppers**

4 **sweet banana peppers**
    (or 3 Cubanelle peppers
    or 2 sweet green peppers)

3 tbsp **olive oil**

3 **anchovy fillets** (optional),
    chopped

½ cup minced **white onion**

2 cloves **garlic,** minced

½ tsp **white wine vinegar**

¼ tsp **ground cumin**

¼ tsp **smoked paprika**

Generous ¼ tsp **salt**

3 tbsp finely chopped **fresh parsley**

Sautéed Banana Peppers: Grill hot and sweet banana peppers, covered, on greased grill over high heat, turning often, until charred all over. Transfer to bowl; cover and let cool. Peel, seed and julienne peppers. In skillet, heat oil over medium-high heat; fry anchovies (if using) until beginning to break down, about 1 minute. Reduce heat to medium; add onion and garlic and sauté until softened, reducing heat if beginning to colour. Stir in peppers, vinegar, cumin, paprika and salt (increase to ½ tsp if not using anchovies); cook over medium-low heat for 5 minutes. Stir in parsley; cook for 30 seconds. Remove from heat.

Lay rosemary sprigs and bay leaves over turkey breast. Tie tightly with kitchen string at 2-inch (5 cm) intervals, slightly flattening breast. Sprinkle all over with salt and pepper.

Grill, covered and skin side up, on greased grill over medium-high heat, basting with oil and turning occasionally, until instant-read thermometer registers 165°F (74°C), turkey is no longer pink inside and skin is crisp, about 45 minutes. Transfer to cutting board; let stand for 5 minutes before removing string and herbs and slicing.

Meanwhile, reheat sautéed banana peppers (if desired). Spoon over turkey slices.

Makes 8 servings.

PER SERVING: about 257 cal, 26 g pro, 15 g total fat (3 g sat. fat), 4 g carb, 2 g fibre, 64 mg chol, 349 mg sodium. % RDI: 3% calcium, 12% iron, 3% vit A, 58% vit C, 8% folate.

Lemon Sage Barbecued Turkey Breast

Toss some potatoes (see One Potato, Two Potato, page 434) on the side of the grill toward the end of cooking.

1 **skin-on boneless turkey breast,**
about 3 lb (1.35 kg)

4 oz (115 g) thinly sliced **prosciutto**
or ham

10 **fresh sage leaves**

LEMON SAGE BASTING SAUCE:

1 tbsp grated **lemon zest**

3 tbsp **lemon juice**

2 tbsp **extra-virgin olive oil**

1 tbsp chopped **fresh sage**

¼ tsp **pepper**

Lemon Sage Basting Sauce: Mix together lemon zest and juice, oil, sage and pepper.

Place turkey, skin side down, on work surface with tapered end facing; cut horizontally between filet and breast almost but not all the way through. Open like book. Brush with 2 tbsp of the basting sauce. Lay prosciutto over 1 half of turkey breast; top with sage leaves. Fold uncovered side over; tie tightly with kitchen string at 2-inch (5 cm) intervals.

Place turkey, skin side down, on greased grill over indirect medium heat (see Tip, page 281); baste with 2 tbsp of the remaining basting sauce. Grill, covered, for 1½ hours. Turn; brush with half of the remaining basting sauce. Grill, basting occasionally, until instant-read thermometer registers 165°F (74°C), turkey is no longer pink inside and skin is crisp, about 1 hour.

Makes 8 servings.

PER SERVING: about 229 cal, 36 g pro, 8 g total fat (2 g sat. fat), 1 g carb, trace fibre, 84 mg chol, 252 mg sodium. % RDI: 2% calcium, 12% iron, 5% vit C, 4% folate.

Mushroom-Stuffed Turkey Breast Rolls

Turkey scaloppine rolled around a moist stuffing makes a fast, lean main. Try this dish with veal or pork scaloppine when you need a change of pace.

2 tbsp **olive oil**

⅓ cup minced **shallots**

2 tbsp chopped **fresh sage**

8 oz (225 g) **mushrooms,** finely chopped

¾ tsp **salt**

¼ tsp **pepper** (approx)

¼ cup **dry sherry,** white vermouth or dry white wine

⅓ cup **fresh bread crumbs**

2 tsp **lemon juice**

4 pieces **turkey breast scaloppine,** about 1 lb (450 g) total

¼ tsp **sweet paprika**

In nonstick skillet, heat half of the oil over medium-high heat; fry shallots until softened, about 2 minutes. Stir in sage; fry for 1 minute. Add mushrooms, ½ tsp of the salt and pinch of the pepper; sauté until mushrooms are softened, 2 to 3 minutes. Stir in sherry; cook until liquid no longer pools on bottom of pan, about 2 minutes. Remove from heat; mix in bread crumbs and lemon juice.

Spread each turkey slice with one-quarter of the mushroom mixture; starting at 1 short end, roll up around filling. Thread all 4 rolls crosswise onto 2 skewers, about 1 inch (2.5 cm) in from each end, leaving a little space between rolls. Brush with remaining oil; sprinkle with paprika, remaining salt and ¼ tsp pepper.

Grill, covered, on greased grill over medium-high heat until turkey is no longer pink inside, 10 to 12 minutes.

Makes 4 servings.

Check your turkey scaloppine to make sure they are cut across the grain – not with it – or they will be chewy.

PER SERVING: about 227 cal, 28 g pro, 8 g total fat (1 g sat. fat), 8 g carb, 1 g fibre, 74 mg chol, 500 mg sodium. % RDI: 3% calcium, 18% iron, 2% vit A, 3% vit C, 9% folate.

Parmesan-Crusted Turkey Scaloppine

You can vary these savoury cutlets a number of ways, depending on what's available in your local market. Try red veal or chicken scaloppine instead of the turkey, swap in Romano cheese for the Parmesan, or use fresh basil instead of the sage.

2 tbsp **extra-virgin olive oil**

8 **fresh sage leaves,** minced

¼ tsp each **salt, pepper** and **hot pepper flakes**

1 lb (450 g) **turkey breast scaloppine**

1 cup grated **Parmesan cheese**

¼ cup **all-purpose flour**

Lemon wedges

Mix together oil, sage, salt, pepper and hot pepper flakes; rub all over turkey. Marinate for 5 minutes.

On plate, mix cheese with flour. Coat scaloppine in cheese mixture, turning and pressing to adhere.

Grill, covered, on greased grill over medium-high heat, turning once, until golden and no longer pink inside, 3 to 5 minutes. Serve with lemon wedges.

Makes 4 to 6 servings.

PER EACH OF 6 SERVINGS: about 207 cal, 23 g pro, 10 g total fat (4 g sat. fat), 4 g carb, trace fibre, 52 mg chol, 376 mg sodium, 266 mg potassium. % RDI: 16% calcium, 9% iron, 2% vit A, 7% folate.

Last-Minute Turkey Scaloppine

Quick low-calorie cooking that's tasty and fresh – what more could you want?

2 **tomatoes,** diced

⅓ cup shredded **fresh basil**
 (or ½ tsp dried)

1 clove **garlic,** minced

2 tbsp **extra-virgin olive oil**

1 tbsp **wine vinegar**

½ tsp **salt**

¼ tsp **pepper**

1 lb (450 g) **turkey breast
 scaloppine**

Toss together tomatoes, basil, garlic, half of the oil, the vinegar and half each of the salt and pepper.

Brush remaining oil all over turkey; sprinkle with remaining salt and pepper. Grill, covered, on greased grill over medium-high heat, turning once, until no longer pink inside, about 6 minutes. Serve topped with tomato-basil mixture.

Makes 4 servings.

PER SERVING: about 214 cal, 27 g pro, 10 g total fat (2 g sat. fat), 4 g carb, 1 g fibre, 61 mg chol, 349 mg sodium. % RDI: 3% calcium, 12% iron, 5% vit A, 22% vit C, 8% folate.

Chipotle-Glazed Turkey Thighs

No need to make a complicated barbecue sauce to coat these moist turkey thighs – the chipotle mixture is a simple, ready-in-an-instant sauce.

4 **turkey thighs**

1½ tsp **ground cumin**

½ tsp each **salt** and **pepper**

1 tbsp **vegetable oil**

2 **canned chipotles in adobo sauce**

2 tbsp **adobo sauce** from canned chipotles

3 cloves **garlic,** minced

2 tbsp **lime juice**

1 tbsp **liquid honey**

Sprinkle turkey with cumin, salt and pepper; brush with oil. Grill, covered, on greased grill over medium heat, turning once, until juices run clear when thickest part is pierced, about 45 minutes.

Meanwhile, seed and mince chipotles. Mix together chipotles, adobo sauce, garlic, lime juice and honey; brush over turkey during last 2 minutes of cooking.

Makes 4 servings.

VARIATION
Chipotle-Glazed Turkey Brochettes
Instead of thighs, cut 1½ lb (675 g) turkey breast into 1½-inch (4 cm) cubes. Thread onto skewers; grill until no longer pink inside, 10 to 12 minutes, brushing with chipotle sauce during last 2 minutes of cooking.

PER SERVING: about 446 cal, 48 g pro, 24 g total fat (6 g sat. fat), 9 g carb, 1 g fibre, 151 mg chol, 835 mg sodium. % RDI: 7% calcium, 34% iron, 10% vit A, 5% vit C, 7% folate.

Cider & Maple Grilled Duck

This innovative recipe moves duck out of the roasting pan and onto the barbecue, with equally crispy results.

1 **whole duck,** about 4 lb (1.8 kg)

2 tbsp **coarse salt**

5 **bay leaves,** broken into pieces

5 cloves **garlic,** minced

4 tsp minced **fresh thyme**
  (or 1½ tsp dried)

2 tsp **coarsely ground pepper**

⅓ cup **maple syrup**

3 cups **dry hard cider** or
  sweet (nonalcoholic) cider

1 tbsp **cider vinegar**

2 **red apples,** cored and cut
  crosswise into ½-inch
  (1 cm) slices

Cut off tailbone, excess neck skin and fat in duck cavity. With kitchen shears, cut out backbone and wing tips. Cut legs off breast; separate wings from breast. Cut breast in half. Mix together salt, bay leaves, garlic, thyme and pepper; rub all over duck pieces. Cover and marinate, refrigerated, for 1 to 2 days, turning once.

Rinse duck well; pat dry. Using skewer, prick skin all over, being careful not to prick into meat under fat. Brush with 2 tbsp of the maple syrup.

In wok or large pot, bring cider to boil. Place duck pieces, close together and skin side up, in steamer or on rack above cider. Cover and steam over medium heat for 1 hour, adding water to wok to maintain level, if necessary.

Remove duck from steamer; skim fat off cider. Bring to boil; boil until reduced to ½ cup, about 12 minutes. Add vinegar and remaining maple syrup. (*Make-ahead: Let cool. Refrigerate duck and cider separately for up to 1 day.*)

Grill duck, covered and bone side down, on greased grill over medium heat, turning and basting with cider mixture every 5 minutes, until skin is crisp and golden, about 25 minutes.

Meanwhile, grill apples, basting with cider mixture and turning once, until slightly softened and grill marked, 6 minutes. Serve apples with duck and any remaining cider mixture.

Makes 4 servings.

PER SERVING: about 737 cal, 29 g pro, 46 g total fat (15 g sat. fat), 55 g carb, 2 g fibre, 128 mg chol, 1,241 mg sodium. % RDI: 6% calcium, 41% iron, 10% vit A, 10% vit C, 5% folate.

Grilled Orange Duck

Because of its high fat content, a raw duck causes huge flare-ups on the grill, making it inconvenient to cook that way. Here, we steam it first to flavour and precook it.

1 **whole young duck,** 4 to 5 lb
   (1.8 to 2.25 kg)

1 tsp **salt**

½ tsp **pepper**

¼ tsp **cinnamon**

¼ tsp **ground cloves**

¼ tsp **nutmeg**

4 **bay leaves**

12 thin slices **fresh ginger**

1 **orange,** thinly sliced

1 strip **orange zest**

½ cup **orange juice**

2 tbsp **liquid honey**

1 tbsp **soy sauce**

2 cloves **garlic,** pressed or minced

If not grilling whole, using kitchen shears, cut duck down each side of backbone; remove backbone. Snip through breastbone to separate duck into halves.

Using skewer, prick duck skin all over, being careful not to prick into meat under fat. Sprinkle all over with salt, pepper, cinnamon, cloves and nutmeg. Place duck, skin side up, on heatproof plate. Lay bay leaves and ginger over top; cover with orange slices.

Bring wok or large pot of water to boil. Place plate in steamer or on rack above boiling water. Cover and steam over medium-high heat, adding more boiling water if necessary to maintain level, until meat feels tender when pierced and leg joints are slightly loose, about 1¼ hours. Discarding bay leaves, ginger, orange slices, fat and juices, transfer duck to rack and let dry, 30 minutes. *(Make-ahead: Refrigerate for up to 1 day.)*

Meanwhile, in small saucepan over high heat, stir together orange zest and juice, honey, soy sauce and garlic; bring to boil. Reduce heat to medium; boil until thin syrupy consistency and reduced by about half. Strain through fine sieve, discarding solids.

Grill duck, bone side down, on greased grill over medium heat, turning occasionally and basting with orange mixture for last 5 minutes, until skin is crisp and meat is heated through, 15 to 20 minutes.

Makes 4 servings.

PER SERVING: about 716 cal, 38 g pro, 56 g total fat (19 g sat. fat), 13 g carb, trace fibre, 165 mg chol, 917 mg sodium. % RDI: 3% calcium, 41% iron, 13% vit A, 20% vit C, 8% folate.

Rosemary Skewered Quails

Quails are a special treat on the grill, and whole quails are the only way to go for best flavour and juiciness.

6 **whole quails**

¼ cup **red wine**

2 tbsp chopped **fresh rosemary**

2 tbsp **liquid honey**

2 tbsp **balsamic vinegar**

2 tbsp **olive oil**

1 tsp **salt**

½ tsp **pepper**

3 cloves **garlic,** halved

Rinse quails; pat dry. Mix together red wine, rosemary, honey, vinegar, oil, salt and pepper; add quails, turning to coat. Cover and marinate, refrigerated, for 4 hours or up to 1 day.

Place 1 piece garlic in cavity of each quail. Line up quails on work surface, alternating breast and leg ends. Insert long metal skewer into first quail, through breast just above wing and out other side; repeat with next quail through legs, pushing close together. Continue skewering remaining quails in same manner. Repeat on other side with second skewer.

Grill, covered and breast side down, on greased grill over medium heat, turning once, until dark golden outside and no longer pink inside at joint where thigh meets body, 20 to 25 minutes.

Makes 6 servings.

If you can't find quails in your local supermarket, buy them from specialty butchers or Chinese grocery stores. Be careful not to overcook them or they will dry out.

PER SERVING: about 276 cal, 25 g pro, 17 g total fat (4 g sat. fat), 5 g carb, trace fibre, 86 mg chol, 272 mg sodium, 237 mg potassium. % RDI: 2% calcium, 33% iron, 7% vit A, 5% vit C, 3% folate.

Grilled Marinated Quails

Quail is especially delicious with Chimichurri Rojo (page 531), while grilled chicken breasts (recipe below) are nicely accented by fresh-tasting Chimichurri Verde (page 531). Basting poultry with an oil mixture is a great way to keep it moist.

6 **whole quails**

¼ cup **lime juice**

¼ cup **extra-virgin olive oil**

2 tbsp each minced **fresh parsley** and **fresh oregano**

3 cloves **garlic,** minced

3 **bay leaves,** torn

¼ tsp each **salt** and **coarsely ground pepper**

¼ tsp **dried thyme**

Using kitchen shears, cut each quail down each side of backbone; remove backbone (save for stockpot). Turn quails breast side up; press on breastbones to flatten.

In large glass bowl, combine 3 tbsp each of the lime juice and oil; add parsley, oregano, garlic, bay leaves, salt, pepper and thyme. Add quails, turning to coat. Cover and marinate, refrigerated, for 4 hours. Discard marinade.

In small bowl, combine remaining lime juice and oil. Grill quails, covered and skin side down, on greased grill over medium-high heat, turning once and basting occasionally with lime-oil mixture, until skin is crisp and no longer pink inside at joint where thigh meets body, 12 to 15 minutes.

Makes 4 to 6 servings.

VARIATION

Grilled Marinated Chicken Breasts

Replace quails with 1½ lb (675 g) boneless skinless chicken breasts. Sprinkle with additional salt and pepper before grilling, if desired.

PER EACH OF 6 SERVINGS: about 267 cal, 20 g pro, 20 g total fat (4 g sat. fat), 2 g carb, 1 g fibre, 66 mg chol, 140 mg sodium, 198 mg potassium. % RDI: 3% calcium, 29% iron, 7% vit A, 7% vit C, 4% folate.

Korean Grilled Quails

Leftover Korean Barbecue Sauce (page 531) will keep for months in the fridge. Keep it on hand for making these quails – some of the easiest, tastiest meats you can make on your grill.

6 **whole quails**

¼ cup **Korean Barbecue Sauce** (page 531)

2 **green onions,** minced

2 tsp **Korean ground hot pepper**

2 tsp toasted **sesame seeds**

2 tsp **sesame oil**

Using kitchen shears, cut each quail down each side of backbone; remove backbone (save for stockpot). Turn quails breast side up; press on breastbones to flatten.

Mix together Korean barbecue sauce, onions, hot pepper, sesame seeds and sesame oil. Add quails, turning to coat. Marinate for 30 minutes or, covered and refrigerated, up to 3 hours.

Grill, covered and skin side down, on greased grill over medium-high heat, turning once, until skin is crisp and meat is no longer pink inside at joint where thigh meets body, 12 to 15 minutes.

Makes 6 servings.

PER SERVING: about 268 cal, 26 g pro, 16 g total fat (4 g sat. fat), 4 g carb, trace fibre, 86 mg chol, 385 mg sodium. % RDI: 2% calcium, 34% iron, 9% vit A, 5% vit C, 5% folate.

Grilled Cilantro Halibut
(page 390)

fish & seafood

Whole Lake Trout With
    Fennel Salad | 351

Whole Trout With Lemon
    Parsley Butter | 353

Trout With Tomato Tomatillo Salsa | 354

Grilled Lemon Herb Trout for Two | 357

Trout With Pink Peppercorn
    & Tarragon Butter | 359

Trout With Herb Stuffing | 360

Grilled Arctic Char With
    Tahini Sauce | 361

Whole Arctic Char With
    Green Onion Butter Sauce | 363

Fishing for Facts | 364

Cedar-Planked Salmon | 365

Salmon & Scallop Grill | 366

Salmon With Lemon
    & Onion Relish | 369

Lemon Dill Salmon Steaks | 370

Masala Salmon | 373

Glazed Salmon Steaks | 374

Pickerel With Cherry Tomato
    Relish | 375

Pickerel & Potato Packets | 377

Grilled Pickerel With Ginger
    & Green Onions | 378

Tilapia Tacos | 379

Grilled Fish Burritos | 381

Fish Tikka | 383

Tilapia With Tomatoes
    & Lemon Relish | 384

Blackened Catfish | 385

Spiced Catfish Fillets With
    Thai Mango Relish | 386

Grilled Halibut With
    Oyster Mushrooms | 388

Lemongrass Barbecued
    Halibut Fillets | 389

Grilled Cilantro Halibut | 390

Portuguese Grilled Sardines With
    Potatoes & Peppers | 392

Grilled Marinated Sardines | 394

Tuna With Grilled Jalapeño Salsa | 395

Tuna Steaks With Mediterranean
    Tomato Relish | 397

Cod in Grape Leaf Packets | 398

Misoyaki | 400

Whitefish With Grilled
    Ratatouille Salad | 402

Chili Barbecued Shrimp | 403

Seafood Caesar Salad | 405

Grilled Curry Shrimp Soft Tacos | 406

"Shrimp on the Barbi" With
    Chinese Dipping Sauce | 409

Kerala Grilled Shrimp | 410

Grilled Shrimp With
    Corn & Black Bean Salad | 412

Rosemary Grilled Scallops | 413

Grilled Stuffed Squid | 414

Greek Grilled Squid | 417

Vietnamese Squid Salad | 418

Grilled Octopus | 419

Baby Octopus With
    Cherry Tomatoes | 420

Grilled Oysters With
    Black Bean Sauce | 424

Buttered Clams on the Grill | 425

Whole Lake Trout With Fennel Salad

Any fish suitable for grilling whole can be made this way. Or use skin-on fillets instead; just sprinkle tops with fennel fronds and grill skin side down.

1 **whole lake trout,** 2 lb (900 g), cleaned

½ tsp **salt**

¼ tsp **pepper**

FENNEL SALAD:

1 **small fennel bulb**

3 tbsp chopped **fresh parsley**

2 tbsp **extra-virgin olive oil**

1 tbsp **wine vinegar**

1 clove **garlic,** minced

½ tsp **salt**

¼ tsp **pepper**

TARRAGON MAYONNAISE:

½ cup **mayonnaise**

2 tbsp chopped **fresh tarragon**

2 tbsp **extra-virgin olive oil** (optional)

1 tsp **Dijon mustard**

½ tsp **wine vinegar**

Fennel Salad: Reserving tops and fronds, slice fennel paper-thin. Whisk together parsley, oil, vinegar, garlic, salt and pepper; toss with fennel until coated. Let stand for 30 minutes or, covered and refrigerated, up to 1 day.

Tarragon Mayonnaise: Mix together mayonnaise, tarragon, oil (if using), mustard and vinegar.

Sprinkle fish inside and out with salt and pepper; stuff cavity with reserved fennel tops and fronds. Grill, covered, in greased fish basket or on greased grill over medium-high heat, turning once, until fish flakes easily, 25 to 30 minutes. Serve with fennel salad and tarragon mayonnaise.

Makes 4 to 6 servings.

Adding a little fragrant extra-virgin olive oil to store-bought mayonnaise will boost the flavour and make it taste more like homemade.

PER EACH OF 6 SERVINGS: about 295 cal, 27 g pro, 18 g total fat (4 g sat. fat), 4 g carb, 1 g fibre, 79 mg chol, 601 mg sodium. % RDI: 10% calcium, 6% iron, 11% vit A, 17% vit C, 17% folate.

Whole Trout With Lemon Parsley Butter

When grilling a whole fish, remember to grease the grill well so the skin doesn't stick to it.

2 **whole trout,** about 1 lb (450 g) each, cleaned

1½ tsp **sea salt** or salt

½ tsp **pepper**

1 **lemon,** sliced

Half bunch **fresh parsley**

1 bunch **fresh thyme** (optional)

LEMON PARSLEY BUTTER:

¼ cup **unsalted butter,** softened

1 tbsp chopped **fresh parsley**

2 tsp grated **lemon zest**

1 tsp **lemon juice**

Pinch each **salt** and **pepper**

Lemon Parsley Butter: Mash together butter, parsley, lemon zest and juice, salt and pepper. Scrape into shallow serving dish, smoothing top; refrigerate until firm, about 1 hour. (Or scrape onto plastic wrap, shape into 1-inch/2.5 cm diameter log and wrap tightly; cut chilled butter into ½-inch/1 cm rounds.)

Sprinkle trout cavities with half each of the salt and pepper. Stuff cavities with lemon slices, parsley, and thyme (if using); skewer closed. Sprinkle outside of fish with remaining salt and pepper.

Grill, covered, on greased grill over medium-high heat, turning once, until fish flakes easily, about 10 minutes per inch (2.5 cm) of thickness. Transfer to platter. Serve with lemon parsley butter.

Makes 6 servings.

To serve whole fish, run thin filleting knife along spine just below head to release flesh. Cut crosswise into portions if large. Using thin, firm, flexible spatula or fish slice and starting at thicker (head) end of fish, gently lift flesh away from bones. Flip fish over and repeat or, using fingers, gently pull away spine and bones, cut flesh into portions.

PER SERVING: about 210 cal, 20 g pro, 14 g total fat (7 g sat. fat), 3 g carb, 1 g fibre, 75 mg chol, 425 mg sodium. % RDI: 8% calcium, 6% iron, 18% vit A, 40% vit C, 13% folate.

Trout With Tomato Tomatillo Salsa

Buy tomatillos fresh during late summer or canned year-round.
Or substitute two small green tomatoes.

1 tbsp **olive oil** or vegetable oil

½ tsp **ground coriander**

½ tsp **ground cumin**

¼ tsp each **salt** and **pepper**

4 **trout fillets,** 8 oz (225 g) each

TOMATO TOMATILLO SALSA:

2 **tomatoes,** peeled, seeded and diced

2 **tomatillos** (see Tip, right), diced

Half **small red onion,** diced

1 or 2 **jalapeño pepper(s),** seeded and minced

1 clove **garlic,** minced

⅓ cup chopped **fresh cilantro**

2 tbsp **orange juice**

2 tbsp **extra-virgin olive oil**

Pinch each **salt** and **pepper**

Tomato Tomatillo Salsa: Toss together tomatoes, tomatillos, onion, jalapeño(s), garlic, cilantro, orange juice, oil, salt and pepper.

Stir together oil, coriander, cumin, salt and pepper; brush over fish. Grill, covered and skin side down, on greased grill over medium-high heat, turning once, until fish flakes easily, about 8 minutes. Serve with tomato tomatillo salsa.

Makes 4 servings.

TIP

Fresh tomatillos should be quickly blanched in boiling water or lightly grilled before using; this intensifies their flavour and removes any mouth-puckering resins that occur naturally in the fruit. Canned tomatillos can be used as is.

PER SERVING: about 418 cal, 44 g pro, 23 g total fat (5 g sat. fat), 6 g carb, 1 g fibre, 120 mg chol, 224 mg sodium. % RDI: 15% calcium, 9% iron, 20% vit A, 33% vit C, 27% folate.

Grilled Lemon Herb Trout for Two

Farmed rainbow trout is an eco-friendly choice you can enjoy without guilt. It's full of healthy fats and has a wonderful rich flavour.

1 **whole trout,** about 2 lb (900 g), cleaned

½ tsp each **salt** and **pepper**

1 **lemon**

2 **bay leaves**

10 sprigs **fresh parsley**

2 sprigs **fresh thyme**

1 tbsp **extra-virgin olive oil**

Sprinkle fish cavity with half each of the salt and pepper. Slice half of the lemon; stuff lemon slices, bay leaves, parsley and thyme into fish cavity.

Rub half of the oil over outside of fish; sprinkle with remaining salt and pepper.

Grill fish and remaining lemon half, covered, on greased grill over medium-high heat, turning once, until fish flakes easily, about 10 minutes per side.

Transfer to platter. Squeeze grilled lemon over top; drizzle with remaining oil.

Makes 2 servings.

PER SERVING: about 488 cal, 61 g pro, 25 g total fat (6 g sat. fat), 2 g carb, trace fibre, 170 mg chol, 679 mg sodium, 1,134 mg potassium. % RDI: 20% calcium, 7% iron, 22% vit A, 32% vit C, 29% folate.

Trout With Pink Peppercorn & Tarragon Butter

Herbed butters are traditional accompaniments to grilled fish, and the tarragon in this one goes especially well with trout or salmon.

2 tsp **pink peppercorns** or mixed peppercorns

¼ cup **butter,** softened

2 tbsp chopped **fresh tarragon** (or 1 tsp dried)

1 tbsp **lemon juice**

½ tsp **salt**

2 **whole trout,** 1¼ lb (565 g) each, cleaned

¼ tsp **pepper**

Place peppercorns in resealable plastic bag. Using bottom of heavy pot, lightly crush peppercorns. Mix together crushed peppercorns, butter, tarragon, lemon juice and ¼ tsp of the salt until smooth. Cover and refrigerate until firm.

Sprinkle fish inside and out with pepper and remaining salt. Grill, covered, in greased fish basket or on greased grill over medium-high heat, turning once, until fish flakes easily, about 15 minutes. Serve with peppercorn and tarragon butter.

Makes 4 servings.

PER SERVING: about 336 cal, 40 g pro, 18 g total fat (8 g sat. fat), 1 g carb, trace fibre, 142 mg chol, 456 mg sodium. % RDI: 13% calcium, 29% iron, 14% vit A, 12% vit C, 8% folate.

Trout With Herb Stuffing

Boning whole trout is actually quite easy, and you don't need to worry about the flesh of the fish getting a bit nicked — you won't be able to tell after it's stuffed. Other types of trout, Arctic char, pickerel and whitefish are other tasty options.

1 **large whole trout,** about 1½ lb (675 g), cleaned

½ tsp **salt** (approx)

¼ tsp **white pepper**

1½ cups **fresh bread crumbs**

2 tbsp **butter**

¼ cup finely chopped **shallots**

¼ cup finely diced **celery**

1 clove **garlic,** minced

3 tbsp finely chopped **fresh chives**

2 tbsp finely chopped **fresh parsley**

1 tbsp finely chopped **celery leaves**

1 tbsp finely chopped **fresh tarragon**

¼ tsp finely grated **lemon zest**

1½ tsp **lemon juice**

Pinch **nutmeg**

1 **egg yolk**

2 tsp **butter,** melted

Pinch **black pepper**

From inside of fish, cut through spine to break at head and tail. Starting at head, slide sharp, fine knife under ribs down each side of fish, then, holding head end of spine, pull out spine along with attached rib bones. Cut out remaining row of bones that run straight down centre from head to tail; trim edges of belly, removing any bones. Feel for and remove any missed bones. Open and flatten fish, skin side down, on work surface; sprinkle with ¼ tsp of the salt and half of the white pepper.

Place bread crumbs in large bowl. In skillet, melt butter over medium heat; fry shallots, diced celery, garlic and pinch of the remaining salt until softened, 4 minutes. Scrape over bread crumbs; toss in chives, parsley, celery leaves, tarragon, lemon zest and juice, nutmeg and remaining white pepper until thoroughly mixed. Stir in egg yolk; spoon over fish. Close around mixture; with soaked toothpicks, fasten edges together at 1½-inch (4 cm) intervals. Lace kitchen string around toothpicks to secure. Brush butter all over skin; sprinkle with generous pinch of the remaining salt and the black pepper.

Grill, covered, on greased grill over medium-high heat, turning once, until instant-read thermometer inserted in centre of stuffing registers 155°F (68°C), about 20 minutes.

Makes 4 servings.

PER SERVING: about 316 cal, 28 g pro, 17 g total fat (8 g sat. fat), 11 g carb, 1 g fibre, 143 mg chol, 483 mg sodium. % RDI: 12% calcium, 10% iron, 22% vit A, 13% vit C, 25% folate.

Grilled Arctic Char With Tahini Sauce

If you like, replace the cumin with ¼ tsp zahtar, a spice mixture available in Middle Eastern stores. Or make your own: mix 1 tbsp toasted sesame seeds, 1½ tsp each ground sumac and dried thyme, and ½ tsp ground cumin.

1½ lb (675 g) skinless **Arctic char fillets**

1 tbsp **vegetable oil**

½ tsp **salt**

¼ tsp **ground cumin**

2 tbsp chopped **fresh parsley**

1 **lemon,** cut into wedges

TAHINI SAUCE:

¼ cup **plain yogurt**

2 tbsp each **tahini** and **light mayonnaise**

2 tsp **lemon juice**

1 clove **garlic,** minced

¼ tsp **sweet paprika**

Pinch **salt**

Tahini Sauce: Whisk together yogurt, tahini, mayonnaise, lemon juice, garlic, paprika and salt.

Brush fish with oil; sprinkle with salt and cumin. Grill, covered, on greased grill over medium-high heat, turning once, until fish flakes easily, 6 to 8 minutes.

Transfer to platter; sprinkle with parsley. Serve with tahini sauce and lemon wedges alongside.

Makes 4 to 6 servings.

PER EACH OF 6 SERVINGS: about 255 cal, 24 g pro, 16 g total fat (1 g sat. fat), 3 g carb, 1 g fibre, 3 mg chol, 293 mg sodium. % RDI: 3% calcium, 5% iron, 2% vit A, 10% vit C, 4% folate.

Whole Arctic Char With Green Onion Butter Sauce

Arctic char (farmed is eco-friendly) is really special. Its delicate pink flesh tastes somewhat like speckled or brook trout with a hint of wild salmon, so it only requires a light touch of flavouring.

1 **whole Arctic char,** 2½ to 3 lb
(1.125 to 1.35 kg), cleaned

2 tsp **coarse sea salt**

2 tsp **coarsely ground pepper**

GREEN ONION BUTTER SAUCE:

1½ cups thinly sliced **green onions**

3 cloves **garlic,** minced

⅓ cup **butter**

3 tbsp **lemon juice**

½ tsp **smoked paprika** or
1 tsp sweet paprika

½ tsp **salt**

¼ tsp **white pepper**

Sprinkle fish inside and out with salt and pepper. Place on greased grill over medium heat (keep some water on hand to sprinkle over burner or coals at beginning when fish oils cause flare-ups). Grill, covered and turning once, until fish flakes easily, 20 to 25 minutes.

Green Onion Butter Sauce: Meanwhile, place onions on heavy-duty foil; top with garlic, butter, lemon juice, paprika, salt and white pepper. Seal to form packet; place on grill during last 5 minutes of fish grilling time.

To serve, lift crispy skin from belly of fish and roll up to back; spoon some of the green onion butter sauce over fish. Serve remainder on side.

Makes 4 to 6 servings.

PER EACH OF 6 SERVINGS: about 220 cal, 23 g pro, 13 g total fat (7 g sat. fat), 4 g carb, 1 g fibre, 93 mg chol, 854 mg sodium, 448 mg potassium. % RDI: 4% calcium, 9% iron, 15% vit A, 10% vit C, 6% folate.

Fishing for Facts

Buying

Buy fish from a supermarket or fish market with rapid turnover; ask what is freshest and adjust your menu.

Fresh fish should have a pleasant (not fishy) smell. Whole fish should be firm, with bright red gills, clear eyes and scales that adhere tightly. Have the fishmonger scale it, clean it and remove the gills.

Fish fillets and steaks should be moist and elastic throughout, with no dry or discoloured edges.

The best fish for grilling whole are those with firm or flaky (not soft) flesh and skin that will crisp nicely, such as pickerel, whitefish, salmon, trout or Arctic char. For fillets and steaks, use any type except soft-fleshed fish, such as cod or sablefish, which can be cooked successfully in packets.

Storing

It is best to use fish the same day it's purchased. Wrap lightly in plastic wrap and place in the coldest part of the refrigerator, preferably on ice or an ice pack. If storing for a day or more, wrap fish in paper towels then plastic; change after 24 hours.

Prepping

Before cooking whole fish, remove any remaining scales by scraping from tail to head with knife. From cavity, pull out any innards and walls of air bladder. Run knife point down spine inside cavity; rinse out any blood with cold water. Cut out gills if still attached. Pat dry.

Grilling

When grilling fish, use tongs and 2 wide spatulas. They're great at getting under and supporting fish when turning.

A fish basket (page 9) makes grilling whole fish a snap. When cooking fillets, steaks or whole fish directly on the grill, make sure to grease the grates liberally to prevent sticking.

Always clean the grill thoroughly with a wire brush and preheat well.

Cedar-Planked Salmon

Grilling salmon on water-soaked cedar planks infuses it with a delightfully woody and smoky taste.

1½ lb (675 g) **salmon fillet,** cut into 2 to 6 pieces

2 tbsp **olive oil**

½ tsp grated **lemon zest**

2 tbsp **lemon juice**

1 tbsp chopped **fresh chives** or green onions

2 tsp **Dijon mustard**

Pinch each **salt** and **pepper**

DILL SAUCE:

½ cup **light sour cream**

2 tbsp finely chopped **cucumber**

1 tbsp chopped **fresh dill** (or 1 tsp dried dillweed)

2 tsp minced **fresh chives** or green onions

Pinch each **salt** and **pepper**

Soak two 12- x 7-inch (30 x 18 cm) untreated cedar planks in water for 30 minutes or up to 1 day.

Place fish on planks. Whisk together oil, lemon zest and juice, chives, mustard, salt and pepper; brush half over fish. Grill, covered, over medium-high heat, brushing once with remaining lemon mixture, until fish flakes easily, 20 to 25 minutes.

Dill Sauce: Meanwhile, stir together sour cream, cucumber, dill, chives, salt and pepper; serve with fish.

Makes 6 servings.

PER SERVING: about 248 cal, 21 g pro, 17 g total fat (3 g sat. fat), 3 g carb, trace fibre, 59 mg chol, 94 mg sodium. % RDI: 5% calcium, 3% iron, 3% vit A, 10% vit C, 14% folate.

Salmon & Scallop Grill

Eco-friendly farmed scallops from the East Coast and wild salmon from the West Coast are graced with a lively Chinese-style relish.

16 **large sea scallops**

1½ lb (675 g) **wild salmon fillet**

GINGER GREEN ONION RELISH:

12 **green onions,** minced

2 sprigs **fresh cilantro,** minced

¼ cup grated **fresh ginger**

1 tbsp minced seeded
    red hot pepper

2 tsp **salt**

Scant ½ tsp **white pepper**

½ cup **peanut oil**

2 tbsp **sesame oil**

Ginger Green Onion Relish: In heatproof bowl, stir onions with cilantro; top with ginger, hot pepper, salt and pepper. Heat peanut oil until light haze appears on surface but oil is not smoking; remove from heat and add sesame oil. Immediately pour over green onion mixture; mix well. Let cool. Reserving oil, strain off most of it, leaving enough to keep relish quite moist.

Brush scallops and flesh side of salmon lightly with reserved oil. Grill fish, covered and skin side down, on greased grill over medium-high heat until skin is crisp. Turn; grill until centre of thickest part just begins to turn opaque, 10 to 15 minutes total. Meanwhile, grill scallops, turning once, just until centres begin to turn opaque, about 5 minutes. Serve scallops and salmon topped with ginger green onion relish.

Makes 8 servings.

PER SERVING: about 276 cal, 28 g pro, 16 g total fat (2 g sat. fat), 6 g carb, 1 g fibre, 66 mg chol, 1,008 mg sodium. % RDI: 6% calcium, 10% iron, 6% vit A, 16% vit C, 18% folate.

Salmon With Lemon & Onion Relish

Loaded with chunks of juicy lemon, the relish is powerfully tangy, so you only need a small amount.

2 **large lemons**

½ cup finely diced **red onion**

2 tbsp minced **fresh dill**

2 tbsp **extra-virgin olive oil**

1 tbsp minced **fresh parsley**

1 tbsp drained **capers,** chopped

1 large clove **garlic,** minced

½ tsp **salt**

¼ tsp **cayenne pepper**

4 **salmon steaks** or fillets, or 2 whole trout, about 1¼ lb (565 g) each, cleaned

Peel and remove pith from lemons; seed and dice flesh. Transfer lemons and any juices to bowl; stir in onion, dill, oil, parsley, capers, garlic, half of the salt, and the cayenne pepper.

Sprinkle fish all over with remaining salt. Grill, covered, on greased grill over medium-high heat, turning once, until fish flakes easily, about 15 minutes. Serve with lemon and onion relish.

Makes 4 servings.

PER SERVING: about 350 cal, 39 g pro, 18 g total fat (4 g sat. fat), 6 g carb, 1 g fibre, 108 mg chol, 420 mg sodium. % RDI: 14% calcium, 7% iron, 15% vit A, 52% vit C, 22% folate.

Lemon Dill Salmon Steaks

This simple, classic flavour combination works with any fish but is best with salmon. Grill lemon halves alongside to squeeze over the steaks.

2 tbsp chopped **fresh dill**

2 tbsp **olive oil**

½ tsp grated **lemon zest**

2 tbsp **lemon juice**

¼ tsp each **salt** and **pepper**

6 **salmon steaks,** 6 oz (170 g) each

Mix together dill, oil, lemon zest and juice, salt and pepper; brush half over 1 side of each salmon steak.

Place salmon, oiled side down, on greased grill over medium-high heat; brush with remaining oil mixture. Grill, covered and turning once, until fish flakes easily, about 10 minutes per inch (2.5 cm) of thickness.

Makes 6 servings.

PER SERVING: about 315 cal, 29 g pro, 21 g total fat (4 g sat. fat), 1 g carb, 0 g fibre, 84 mg chol, 178 mg sodium. % RDI: 2% calcium, 4% iron, 2% vit A, 12% vit C, 21% folate.

Masala Salmon

This dish is better than any restaurant fish tikka. If your curry powder is more than 18 months old, toss it and buy fresh to ensure the most vibrant flavour.

¼ cup **peanut oil** or vegetable oil

1½ cups sliced **onions**

¼ cup **plain yogurt**

¼ cup minced **fresh cilantro**

1 tbsp **lemon juice**

2 **green hot peppers,** minced

2 cloves **garlic,** minced

2 tsp grated **fresh ginger**

2 tsp **curry powder** or paste

1 tsp **salt**

4 **skinless salmon fillets** or steaks, about 6 oz (170 g) each

Fresh cilantro sprigs

In skillet, heat oil over medium-high heat; sauté onions, reducing heat if blackening, until browned and slightly crispy, about 10 minutes. Reserving oil, drain through sieve over heatproof bowl; let cool.

In food processor, purée together onions, yogurt, minced cilantro, lemon juice, hot peppers, garlic, ginger, curry powder, salt and 1 tbsp of the reserved oil. Scrape into large bowl; add fish, turning to coat. Marinate for 15 minutes.

Reserving any leftover marinade, place fish on greased grill over medium-high heat. Grill, covered, turning once and topping with reserved marinade, until fish flakes easily, 10 to 12 minutes. Garnish with cilantro sprigs.

Makes 4 servings.

PER SERVING: about 398 cal, 28 g pro, 29 g total fat (6 g sat. fat), 7 g carb, 1 g fibre, 75 mg chol, 658 mg sodium. % RDI: 5% calcium, 6% iron, 3% vit A, 17% vit C, 24% folate.

Glazed Salmon Steaks

Wild Pacific salmon is a delicious, sustainable option for these big meaty steaks. Its rich flesh is complemented by the sweet Asian-style glaze.

4 **salmon steaks,** about
    1 inch (2.5 cm) thick,
    8 oz (225 g) each

3 tbsp **hoisin sauce**

1 tbsp **orange juice**

2 tsp **maple syrup** or liquid honey

1 tsp **sesame oil**

½ tsp each **coarse salt** and
    cracked pepper

1 tbsp toasted **sesame seeds**

1 **green onion,** thinly sliced

Pat fish dry with paper towels; arrange in shallow baking dish. Whisk together hoisin sauce, orange juice, maple syrup and sesame oil; pour ¼ cup over fish, turning to coat. Set remaining marinade aside. Sprinkle fish with salt and pepper. Marinate for 15 minutes.

Grill, covered, on greased grill over medium heat, turning once and basting with reserved hoisin mixture, until fish flakes easily, about 12 minutes. Serve sprinkled with sesame seeds and green onion.

Makes 4 servings.

PER SERVING: about 385 cal, 36 g pro, 22 g total fat (4 g sat. fat), 9 g carb, 1 g fibre, 99 mg chol, 577 mg sodium, 653 mg potassium. % RDI: 3% calcium, 7% iron, 3% vit A, 13% vit C, 28% folate.

Pickerel With Cherry Tomato Relish

A freshwater fish common in Canada, pickerel is a delicately flavoured base for this zesty tomato relish.

1 **whole pickerel** or whitefish, about 2 lb (900 g), cleaned

½ tsp each **salt** and **pepper**

CHERRY TOMATO RELISH:

2 cups quartered **cherry tomatoes**

½ cup chopped **fresh cilantro**

1 **jalapeño pepper,** seeded and minced

2 tbsp finely chopped **onion**

2 tbsp **extra-virgin olive oil**

½ tsp grated **lime zest**

2 tbsp **lime juice**

1½ tsp grated or minced **fresh ginger**

½ tsp **salt**

2 tsp **ground coriander**

½ tsp **pepper**

Cherry Tomato Relish: Toss together cherry tomatoes, cilantro, jalapeño, onion, oil, lime zest and juice, ginger and salt. In dry small skillet over medium-low heat, lightly toast coriander and pepper until fragrant, about 2 minutes; stir into relish.

Cut 2 diagonal slashes into each side of fish; sprinkle inside and out with salt and pepper. Grill, covered, in greased fish basket or on greased grill over medium-high heat, turning once, until fish flakes easily, about 20 to 25 minutes. Serve with cherry tomato relish.

Makes 4 servings.

PER SERVING: about 203 cal, 26 g pro, 9 g total fat (1 g sat. fat), 5 g carb, 1 g fibre, 111 mg chol, 574 mg sodium. % RDI: 14% calcium, 17% iron, 10% vit A, 35% vit C, 13% folate.

Pickerel & Potato Packets

Cooking in a foil packet on the grill makes cleanup so simple. Use a mandoline to cut thin, even potato slices. If you don't have one, use cooked potatoes cut into thicker slices.

3 tbsp **extra-virgin olive oil**

2 tbsp **lemon juice**

1 tbsp chopped **fresh parsley**

2 tsp chopped **fresh dill**

½ tsp each **salt** and **pepper**

12 oz (340 g) **yellow-fleshed potatoes** (unpeeled), sliced paper-thin crosswise

1 **small onion,** thinly sliced

1½ lb (675 g) **skinless pickerel fillets,** cut in 4 pieces

Whisk together 2 tbsp of the oil, the lemon juice, parsley, dill and half each of the salt and pepper.

Toss together potatoes, onion and remaining oil, salt and pepper. Divide among 4 large squares of double-thickness foil. Top each with 1 piece of the fish; drizzle with lemon mixture. Seal packets, leaving small steam vent in top of each.

Grill packets, covered, over medium-high heat until potatoes are tender, 12 to 15 minutes.

Makes 4 servings.

PER SERVING: about 320 cal, 35 g pro, 12 g total fat (2 g sat. fat), 17 g carb, 2 g fibre, 146 mg chol, 383 mg sodium, 1,138 mg potassium. % RDI: 19% calcium, 26% iron, 4% vit A, 27% vit C, 11% folate.

Grilled Pickerel With Ginger & Green Onions

Fragrant ginger and green onions make this aromatic dish a feast for the senses.

3 tbsp **unseasoned rice vinegar**

2 tbsp finely grated **fresh ginger**

2 tbsp **soy sauce**

1 tbsp **mirin**

4 **pickerel fillets,** about 6 oz (170 g) each

¼ tsp each **coarse salt** and **cracked pepper**

2 **green onions,** cut into 3-inch (7.5 cm) long julienne

In shallow dish large enough to hold fish in single layer, whisk together vinegar, ginger, soy sauce and mirin. Add fish, turning to coat. Marinate for 15 minutes.

Remove fish; transfer marinade to small saucepan. Cook over medium-high heat until slightly reduced, about 5 minutes. Strain; discard ginger.

Meanwhile, sprinkle fish with salt and pepper. Grill, covered and skin side down, on greased grill over medium-high heat until fish flakes easily, 8 to 10 minutes. Serve sprinkled with green onions and drizzled with hot marinade.

Makes 4 servings.

PER SERVING: about 158 cal, 30 g pro, 2 g total fat (trace sat. fat), 4 g carb, trace fibre, 129 mg chol, 651 mg sodium, 627 mg potassium. % RDI: 16% calcium, 16% iron, 4% vit A, 2% vit C, 12% folate.

Tilapia Tacos

Farmed tilapia is common and affordable. Choose American over Asian when possible, as American fish farms are more environmentally conscious.

2 **tilapia fillets,** about 8 oz (225 g) each

1 tsp **smoked paprika**

¾ tsp **salt**

½ tsp **ground cumin**

¼ tsp **pepper**

1 tbsp **vegetable oil**

8 **corn tortillas,** warmed

1 **avocado,** peeled, pitted and sliced

4 **lime wedges**

RED ONION & JALAPEÑO PICKLE:

1 **red onion,** thinly sliced

2 **jalapeño peppers,** thinly sliced

2 tbsp **lime juice**

2 tbsp **cider vinegar**

½ tsp **salt**

½ tsp **granulated sugar**

Red Onion & Jalapeño Pickle: Mix together onion, jalapeños, lime juice, vinegar, salt and sugar; let stand for 20 minutes or, covered and refrigerated, up to 8 hours.

Cut each fillet in half crosswise. Mix together paprika, salt, cumin and pepper; sprinkle over both sides of fish. Brush with oil. Grill, covered and flat side down, over medium-high heat, turning once, until fish flakes easily, 6 to 8 minutes.

For each serving, divide each portion of fish in half; place in warm tortillas. Top with onion and jalapeño pickle and avocado slices; garnish with lime wedge.

Makes 4 servings.

PER SERVING: about 342 cal, 27 g pro, 14 g total fat (2 g sat. fat), 30 g carb, 7 g fibre, 50 mg chol, 794 mg sodium, 798 mg potassium. % RDI: 7% calcium, 14% iron, 4% vit A, 28% vit C, 32% folate.

Grilled Fish Burritos

Prepare the veggies the night before so you can whip up these zesty burritos in minutes for a quick, healthy dinner.

1 cup shredded **red cabbage**

1 cup shredded **green cabbage**

1 cup shredded **carrot**

2 **green onions,** thinly sliced

1 or 2 **jalapeño peppers,** seeded and minced

1 lb (450 g) **tilapia fillets**

1 tbsp **vegetable oil**

½ tsp each **salt** and **cracked pepper**

4 large (10-inch/25 cm) **flour tortillas**

½ cup chopped **fresh cilantro**

LIME SAUCE:

¼ cup **sour cream**

2 tbsp **lime juice**

¼ tsp each **salt** and **cracked pepper**

Lime Sauce: Stir together sour cream, lime juice, salt and pepper.

Toss together red and green cabbage, carrot, green onions, jalapeños and half of the lime sauce.

Brush both sides of fish with oil; sprinkle with salt and pepper. Grill, covered and flat side down, on greased grill over medium-high heat, turning once, until fish flakes easily, 6 to 8 minutes.

Break fish up into large chunks; divide among tortillas. Top with cabbage mixture and cilantro; drizzle with remaining lime sauce. Fold in sides of tortilla over filling; roll up. Return to greased grill over medium-high heat; grill, turning once, just until both sides are browned, about 1 minute.

Makes 4 servings.

PER SERVING: about 342 cal, 29 g pro, 12 g total fat (3 g sat. fat), 33 g carb, 3 g fibre, 56 mg chol, 903 mg sodium, 652 mg potassium. % RDI: 6% calcium, 19% iron, 38% vit A, 35% vit C, 40% folate.

Fish Tikka

This is an extremely popular way to eat fish throughout India and Pakistan and wherever South Asians have settled. Fish tikka is often cooked in a tandoor oven, but at home it's a breeze on the grill. Use fish that's at least ¾ inch (2 cm) thick; you can cut it into large chunks as it is here, or marinate and cook whole fish steaks.

1½ lb (675 g) thick firm **fish fillets**

¾ cup **1% to full-fat plain yogurt**

4 cloves **garlic,** pressed, grated or pounded into paste

2 tbsp **lime juice** or lemon juice

5 tsp **Indian red chili powder** or ground dried hot peppers, or 2 tsp cayenne pepper

2 tsp **sweet paprika**

1½ tsp finely grated **fresh ginger**

1½ tsp **ground coriander**

1 tsp each **ground cumin** and **salt**

¾ tsp **turmeric**

½ tsp **ground mace** or nutmeg

½ tsp **ground ajwain seeds** (see Tip, right)

¼ tsp each **pepper** and **cinnamon**

Pinch **ground cloves**

1 **large Cubanelle pepper** or other sweet pepper, cut into 2-inch (5 cm) chunks

1 **white onion** or sweet onion, cut into ½-inch (1 cm) wide wedges

2 tbsp **peanut oil** or vegetable oil, or butter, melted

Lime halves or wedges

Cut fish into about 2-inch (5 cm) chunks; place in large nonreactive bowl. In separate bowl, stir together yogurt, garlic, lime juice, chili powder, paprika, ginger, coriander, cumin, salt, turmeric, mace, ajwain, pepper, cinnamon and cloves. Scrape over fish; mix well. Cover and marinate, refrigerated, for 2 to 4 hours.

Add pepper and onion; toss until lightly coated. Let stand for 15 minutes. Alternately thread fish, pepper and onion onto long skewers. Drizzle with oil.

Grill, covered, on greased grill over indirect high heat (see Tip, page 281), turning once or twice, until fish flakes easily, about 15 minutes. Serve with lime.

Makes 6 servings.

TIP

Look for ajwain seeds at Indian grocery stores or in the spice aisle of supermarkets. Ajwain seeds contain thymol, the same substance that gives thyme much of its distinctive flavour, so crumbled dried thyme is an acceptable substitute.

PER SERVING: about 205 cal, 25 g pro, 8 g total fat (1 g sat. fat), 8 g carb, 2 g fibre, 37 mg chol, 277 mg sodium, 685 mg potassium. % RDI: 9% calcium, 11% iron, 10% vit A, 12% vit C, 11% folate.

Tilapia With Tomatoes & Lemon Relish

This colourful and fresh summer meal is ideal for outdoor dining.

4 **tilapia fillets,** about 6 oz (170 g) each

1 tbsp **olive oil**

½ tsp each **salt** and **cracked pepper**

4 cups lightly packed **baby arugula** (about 3 oz/85 g)

1 cup **cherry tomatoes,** halved

LEMON RELISH:

⅓ cup **boiling water**

¼ cup **golden raisins**

2 tbsp slivered **lemon zest**

¼ cup toasted **pine nuts** or chopped walnuts

¼ cup chopped **fresh parsley**

3 tbsp **olive oil**

2 tbsp **lemon juice**

1 tbsp finely chopped drained **capers**

Pinch **salt**

Lemon Relish: Stir together boiling water, raisins and lemon zest. Let stand for 10 minutes; drain. Stir in pine nuts, parsley, oil, lemon juice, capers and salt.

Meanwhile, brush both sides of fish with oil; sprinkle with salt and pepper. Grill, covered and flat side down, on greased grill over medium-high heat, turning once, until fish flakes easily, 6 to 8 minutes.

Divide arugula and tomatoes among 4 plates. Top with fish; spoon relish over fish.

Makes 4 servings.

PER SERVING: about 391 cal, 37 g pro, 23 g total fat (4 g sat. fat), 12 g carb, 2 g fibre, 76 mg chol, 438 mg sodium, 834 mg potassium. % RDI: 7% calcium, 17% iron, 12% vit A, 35% vit C, 21% folate.

Blackened Catfish

Butter and a mix of dried spices are the keys to the classic blackened look of this fish. Farmed catfish is an easy-to-find, sustainable choice.

2 tsp **sweet paprika**

1 tsp **ground cumin**

½ tsp **dried oregano**

½ tsp **dried thyme**

½ tsp **cayenne pepper**

½ tsp **garlic powder**

½ tsp **granulated sugar**

½ tsp **salt**

¼ tsp **cracked pepper**

2 **catfish fillets,** 4 to 5 oz (115 to 140 g) each, halved

2 tbsp **butter,** melted

Lime wedges

In shallow dish, mix together paprika, cumin, oregano, thyme, cayenne, garlic powder, sugar, salt and pepper. Brush fish with butter; roll in spice blend to coat.

Grill, covered, on greased grill over medium-high heat, until fish flakes easily, 6 to 8 minutes. Serve with lime wedges.

Makes 4 servings.

PER SERVING: about 209 cal, 18 g pro, 14 g total fat (6 g sat. fat), 2 g carb, 1 g fibre, 72 mg chol, 397 mg sodium, 373 mg potassium. % RDI: 2% calcium, 11% iron, 13% vit A, 3% vit C, 5% folate.

Spiced Catfish Fillets With Thai Mango Relish

Catfish takes to highly spiced preparations exceedingly well. To keep the fillets from breaking up, be sure your fish is fully grilled on one side before flipping it.

4 cloves **garlic,** pressed or minced

1 tbsp **lime juice**

1 tbsp **peanut oil** or vegetable oil

2 tsp finely grated **fresh ginger**

1½ tsp **pepper**

½ tsp each **ground cumin, turmeric** and **salt**

¼ tsp **cayenne pepper**

¼ tsp **granulated sugar**

4 **catfish fillets,** 6 to 8 oz (170 to 225 g) each

THAI MANGO RELISH:

1 **hard half-ripe mango**

¼ cup minced **red onion**

2 to 4 **Thai bird's-eye peppers,** finely chopped

1 tbsp chopped **fresh cilantro**

1 tbsp **palm sugar** or packed light brown sugar

1 tbsp **palm vinegar** or unseasoned rice vinegar

1 tbsp **fish sauce**

1½ tsp each finely chopped **fresh Thai basil** and **mint**

Mix together garlic, lime juice, oil, ginger, pepper, cumin, turmeric, salt, cayenne and sugar; rub all over fish. Marinate for 20 minutes or, covered and refrigerated, up to 2 hours.

Thai Mango Relish: Peel and pit mango; cut flesh into fine julienne or shred on coarse side of box grater to make about 2 cups. Toss together mango, onion, Thai peppers, cilantro, sugar, vinegar, fish sauce, basil and mint.

Grill fish, covered, on greased grill over medium heat until bottom is golden, about 7 minutes. Turn; grill until fish flakes easily, 3 to 5 minutes. Serve topped with some of the Thai mango relish; serve remainder on side.

Makes 4 servings.

PER SERVING: about 382 cal, 36 g pro, 19 g total fat (4 g sat. fat), 17 g carb, 2 g fibre, 120 mg chol, 792 mg sodium, 791 mg potassium. % RDI: 4% calcium, 18% iron, 25% vit A, 35% vit C, 14% folate.

Grilled Halibut With Oyster Mushrooms

You can use other mushrooms, such as wild chanterelles or black trumpets, or sliced cultivated mushrooms, such as king oyster, button or cremini.

8 oz (225 g) **oyster mushrooms**

2 cloves **garlic,** minced

2 tbsp chopped **fresh parsley**

2 tbsp chopped **fresh basil**

2 tbsp chopped **fresh chives**

2 tbsp **butter**

¼ cup **fish stock,** or chicken or vegetable broth

1 tbsp **soy sauce**

2 tsp **lemon juice**

4 **halibut steaks,** about 6 oz (170 g) each

2 tsp **vegetable oil**

¼ tsp each **salt** and **pepper**

Pull mushrooms apart into wide shreds; place on heavy-duty foil. Scatter garlic, parsley, basil and chives over top; dot with butter. Sprinkle with stock, soy sauce and lemon juice; seal to form packet.

Brush fish with oil; sprinkle with salt and pepper. Grill mushroom packet and fish, covered, on greased grill over medium-high heat, turning fish once, until fish flakes easily, 8 to 10 minutes. To serve, spoon mushroom mixture over fish.

Makes 4 servings.

PER SERVING: about 276 cal, 37 g pro, 12 g total fat (4 g sat. fat), 3 g carb, 1 g fibre, 70 mg chol, 603 mg sodium. % RDI: 9% calcium, 17% iron, 15% vit A, 8% vit C, 14% folate.

Lemongrass Barbecued Halibut Fillets

Baby bok choy grills alongside the fish to make a complete light supper. Look for sustainably caught Pacific halibut where there's a choice.

1 cup **coconut milk**

2 tbsp chopped **fresh lemongrass**

1 tbsp chopped **fresh cilantro**

1 **shallot,** chopped

1 tbsp packed **brown sugar**

1 tbsp **lime juice**

1 tbsp **fish sauce**

¼ tsp **salt**

4 **halibut fillets,** about 5 oz (140 g) each

8 heads **baby bok choy**

1 tbsp **vegetable oil**

In blender, purée together coconut milk, lemongrass, cilantro, shallot, sugar, lime juice, fish sauce and salt; rub half over fish. Cover and marinate, refrigerated, for 30 minutes or up to 2 hours.

Cut each head of bok choy in half lengthwise; toss with oil.

Grill halibut and bok choy, covered, on greased grill over medium heat, basting bok choy often with remaining coconut mixture and turning both once, until fish flakes easily and bok choy is wilted, about 8 minutes. Transfer to platter; spoon any remaining coconut mixture over fish and bok choy.

Make 4 servings.

PER SERVING: about 322 cal, 33 g pro, 18 g total fat (10 g sat. fat), 9 g carb, 2 g fibre, 45 mg chol, 972 mg sodium, 1,389 mg potassium. % RDI: 21% calcium, 34% iron, 74% vit A, 70% vit C, 41% folate.

Grilled Cilantro Halibut

Sometimes the simplest dress-up can improve an already good dish. Here is a case in point, in which a light marinade of only a few ingredients enhances grilled fresh fish.

4 **halibut steaks,** about 6 oz
    (170 g) each

Fresh cilantro sprigs

Lemon wedges

MARINADE:

2 tbsp finely chopped **shallots**
    or onion

2 tbsp finely chopped **fresh
    cilantro**

2 tbsp **olive oil** or vegetable oil

1 tbsp **lemon juice**

½ tsp **salt**

¼ tsp **pepper**

Marinade: In shallow glass dish, stir together shallots, cilantro, oil, lemon juice, salt and pepper. Add fish, turning to coat; marinate for 30 minutes.

Grill fish, covered, on greased grill over medium-high heat, turning once, until fish flakes easily, about 6 minutes. Garnish with cilantro sprigs; serve with lemon wedges.

Makes 4 servings.

PER SERVING: about 249 cal, 36 g pro, 11 g total fat (1 g sat. fat), 1 g carb, trace fibre, 380 mg sodium. % RDI: 8% calcium, 11% iron, 7% vit A, 2% vit C, 9% folate.

Portuguese Grilled Sardines With Potatoes & Peppers

Grilled sardines like these are especially emblematic of Portuguese cuisine.

1⅔ lb (755 g) fresh or thawed frozen **sardines,** cleaned

¾ tsp **salt**

½ tsp **pepper**

1½ lb (675 g) **potatoes,** peeled

2 **sweet green peppers**

Half **sweet onion,** cut into rings

⅓ cup **olives**

2 tbsp chopped **fresh parsley**

¼ cup **extra-virgin olive oil**

1 tbsp **red wine vinegar**

Lemon wedges

Sprinkle fish inside and out with pinch each of the salt and pepper. Let stand for 30 minutes.

Meanwhile, in pot of boiling salted water, cook potatoes until tender, about 20 minutes. Drain; keep warm.

Meanwhile, grill green peppers, covered, over high heat, turning often, until charred all over. Let cool enough to handle. Peel, seed and cut into ¾-inch (2 cm) wide strips.

Grill fish, covered, in greased fish basket or on greased grill over high heat, turning once, until skin is golden and crisp, 6 to 12 minutes, depending on size.

Cut warm potatoes into chunks (or leave whole, if desired); mix with peppers, onion, olives and parsley. Whisk together oil, vinegar and remaining salt and pepper; toss with potato mixture until coated. Serve with fish; garnish with lemon wedges.

Makes 4 servings.

Pacific sardines are the ecologically friendly choice for this dish, but fresh ones can be hard to come by in Canada. Stock up and freeze them if they're on special in your local market. Mediterranean sardines are not considered a sustainable choice. However, individually quick frozen (IQF) ones, usually from Portugal, are easy to find in inexpensive 800-gram packages if you simply must have your sardine fix. Look for them in grocery stores in or near Portuguese, Greek or Italian neighbourhoods.

PER SERVING: about 428 cal, 21 g pro, 24 g total fat (5 g sat. fat), 35 g carb, 4 g fibre, 103 mg chol, 1,058 mg sodium, 923 mg potassium. % RDI: 10% calcium, 17% iron, 4% vit A, 93% vit C, 16% folate.

Grilled Marinated Sardines

Boned and marinated, sardines can make an elegant starter or main course.

1⅔ lb (755 g) fresh or thawed
   frozen **sardines**

3 cloves **garlic,** pressed or minced

2 tbsp minced **fresh parsley**

2 tbsp **extra-virgin olive oil**

1 tbsp **lemon juice**

½ tsp **salt**

¼ tsp **pepper**

Pinch **cayenne pepper**

Under cold running water, scale sardines by running fingers up body from tail to head. With scissors, trim off top fin. Slit belly from tail to head; remove gills and innards. Slide finger down both sides of backbone to loosen; pull out backbone. With scissors, cut off tail and head; trim sides, removing any missed bones.

Lay pieces flat, skin side down, on plate; sprinkle with garlic, parsley, oil, lemon juice, salt, pepper and cayenne. Cover and marinate, refrigerated, for 30 minutes or up to 4 hours.

Grill, covered and skin side down, on greased grill over high heat until skin is browned on bottom and fish just begins to flake, 5 to 7 minutes.

Makes 8 to 12 pieces.

PER EACH OF 12 PIECES: about 73 cal, 7 g pro, 5 g total fat (1 g sat. fat), trace carb, trace fibre, 37 mg chol, 134 mg sodium. % RDI: 3% calcium, 4% iron, 1% vit A, 2% vit C, 1% folate.

Tuna With Grilled Jalapeño Salsa

For milder salsa, mix in ½ cup finely chopped grilled fresh or canned tomatillos (see Tip, page 354).

6 **tuna steaks,** about 6 oz (170 g) each

¾ tsp **salt**

Generous ¼ tsp **pepper**

4 tsp **extra-virgin olive oil**

GRILLED JALAPEÑO SALSA:

1 **white onion,** halved

4 cloves **garlic** (unpeeled)

6 **jalapeño peppers**

⅓ cup finely chopped **fresh cilantro**

3 tbsp **lime juice**

2 tbsp **extra-virgin olive oil**

½ tsp **salt**

½ tsp **ground cumin**

Grilled Jalapeño Salsa: Grill onion, garlic and jalapeños, turning often, over medium-high heat until peppers are charred and onion and garlic are tender. Place peppers in bowl; cover and let cool. Let onion and garlic cool. Peel off and discard blackened outside layer of onion; finely chop onion and place in clean bowl. Peel and seed peppers; chop and add to onion. Peel garlic; with fork or side of knife, mash into paste and add to onion mixture. Mix in cilantro, lime juice, oil, salt and cumin.

Sprinkle fish all over with salt and pepper; brush with oil. Grill on greased grill over high heat, turning once, until centre is still rare to medium-rare, 5 to 7 minutes, respectively, for 1-inch (2.5 cm) thick steak. Serve with dollop of grilled jalapeño salsa on top; serve remainder on side.

Makes 6 servings.

PER SERVING: about 338 cal, 40 g pro, 16 g total fat (3 g sat. fat), 6 g carb, 1 g fibre, 65 mg chol, 551 mg sodium. % RDI: 3% calcium, 16% iron, 102% vit A, 15% vit C, 9% folate.

Tuna Steaks With Mediterranean Tomato Relish

Grilled tuna should be eaten rare to medium, like a good steak – if it's cooked all the way through, it can be dry. Choose the freshest possible pole-caught albacore or skipjack tuna from the West Coast.

4 **tuna steaks,** 6 oz (170 g) each

1½ tbsp **extra-virgin olive oil**

¾ tsp each **salt** and **pepper**

MEDITERRANEAN TOMATO RELISH:

¾ cup chopped **ripe tomatoes**

3 tbsp finely chopped **red onion**

2 tbsp chopped **olives**

2 tbsp thinly sliced **caper berries** or 1½ tbsp chopped drained capers

2 tbsp finely chopped **fresh parsley**

2 tbsp **extra-virgin olive oil**

1 clove **garlic,** minced

1½ tbsp **lemon juice**

1 tsp **red wine vinegar**

½ tsp **dried oregano,** crumbled

¼ tsp **hot pepper flakes**

¼ tsp **salt**

Pinch **pepper**

Mediterranean Tomato Relish: Mix together tomatoes, onion, olives, caper berries, parsley, oil, garlic, lemon juice, vinegar, oregano, hot pepper flakes, salt and pepper; let stand for 15 minutes.

Brush both sides of fish with oil; sprinkle with salt and pepper. Grill on greased grill over high heat, turning once, until centre is still rare to medium-rare, about 5 to 7 minutes, respectively, for 1-inch (2.5 cm) thick steak. Serve topped with some of the Mediterranean tomato relish; serve remainder on side.

Makes 4 servings.

PER SERVING: about 367 cal, 40 g pro, 21 g total fat (4 g sat. fat), 4 g carb, 1 g fibre, 65 mg chol, 774 mg sodium, 549 mg potassium. % RDI: 3% calcium, 18% iron, 105% vit A, 15% vit C, 7% folate.

Cod in Grape Leaf Packets

Grape leaves add distinctive flavour and hold delicate fish together on the grill. You can make these packets, which are also perfect as hors d'oeuvres, with many other kinds of fish, such as haddock, pollock, Pacific halibut or sablefish (black cod).

12 **brined grape leaves**

1 lb (450 g) **cod fillets**

⅓ cup chopped **fresh parsley**

⅓ cup chopped **fresh mint**

⅓ cup chopped **green onions**

⅓ cup **extra-virgin olive oil**

3 tbsp **lemon juice**

½ tsp **salt**

¼ tsp **pepper**

8 thin **lemon wedges**

Rinse grape leaves; soak in large bowl of cold water for 1 hour. Rinse; pat dry.

Cut fish into twelve 2½- x 1- x 1-inch (6 x 2.5 x 2.5 cm) pieces. Mix together parsley, mint, onions, all but 2 tbsp of the oil, the lemon juice, salt and pepper.

For each packet, place grape leaf, vein side up and stem closest, on work surface. Spoon 1 tsp of the herb mixture onto bottom of leaf; cover with 1 piece of the fish, then another 1 tsp of the herb mixture. Fold leaf sides over and roll into secure package.

Alternately with 2 lemon wedges, thread 3 packets crosswise onto 2 parallel skewers to hold firmly. Repeat with remaining packets and lemon wedges. Brush with remaining oil. Grill, covered, on greased grill over medium-high heat, turning once, for 15 minutes.

Makes 4 servings.

PER SERVING: about 265 cal, 22 g pro, 19 g total fat (3 g sat. fat), 4 g carb, 2 g fibre, 49 mg chol, 1,018 mg sodium. % RDI: 14% calcium, 58% iron, 14% vit A, 20% vit C, 10% folate.

Misoyaki

Misoyaki means "miso-grilled" and is a favourite Japanese method of grilling fish. The marinade gives the fish flavour and a lovely glazed exterior. This recipe is easiest with thick firm-fleshed fillets or steaks, such as Pacific halibut or wild salmon.

⅔ cup **white miso** or red miso

¼ cup **sake,** dry sherry or
   Chinese rice wine

2 tender small inner ribs **celery**
   with leaves, finely chopped

1 tsp grated **fresh ginger** or
   fresh ginger julienne

4 **green onions**

4 **fish fillets** or steaks, about
   6 oz (170 g) each

Lemon wedges

In blender, purée together miso, sake, celery, ginger and 1 tbsp water, adding up to 1 tbsp more water if necessary to keep ingredients moving.

Place onions in glass or ceramic dish. Spread miso mixture over fish fillets; place over onions. Cover and marinate, refrigerated, for 6 to 12 hours.

Scrape marinade and onions off fish and discard. Grill fish, covered, on greased grill over medium-high heat, turning once, until golden, 12 to 14 minutes. Serve with lemon wedges.

Makes 4 servings.

TIPS

• For authentic Japanese-style grilling, thread 2 pieces fish crosswise onto 2 long metal skewers; repeat with remaining 2 pieces. Place 2 bricks on grill, 10 to 12 inches (25 to 30 cm) apart; place skewers on bricks so fish is suspended over grill. Grill over high heat, turning once, until golden, 12 to 14 minutes.

• Misoyaki is also excellent with softer, fattier fish, especially sablefish (black cod). Grill all softer fish on skewers.

PER SERVING: about 198 cal, 36 g pro, 4 g total fat (1 g sat. fat), 2 g carb, 0 g fibre, 54 mg chol, 260 mg sodium. % RDI: 8% calcium, 11% iron, 7% vit A, 5% vit C, 10% folate.

Whitefish With Grilled Ratatouille Salad

Here, ratatouille, a stew of late-summer vegetables, turns into a perfect grilled salad. Skewering the vegetables by type ensures that they all cook through in the same time.

1 **small eggplant,** peeled and cut into 1-inch (2.5 cm) chunks

1 **zucchini,** cut into 1-inch (2.5 cm) chunks

Half each **sweet red pepper** and **sweet green pepper,** cut into 1-inch (2.5 cm) chunks

1 **small red onion,** cut into 1-inch (2.5 cm) chunks

1½ cups **cherry tomatoes**

⅓ cup **extra-virgin olive oil**

¼ cup chopped **fresh oregano**

3 tbsp **wine vinegar**

2 tsp **Dijon mustard**

2 cloves **garlic,** minced

1 tsp each **salt** and **pepper**

1½ lb (675 g) **skin-on whitefish fillets** or pickerel fillets

In large bowl, combine eggplant, zucchini, red and green peppers, onion and cherry tomatoes. Drizzle with 2 tbsp of the oil; toss until coated. Thread onto long skewers, grouping same vegetables together.

Grill, covered, on greased grill over medium-high heat, turning occasionally, until browned and tender, about 12 minutes. Remove from skewers and return to bowl. Whisk together remaining oil, oregano, vinegar, mustard, garlic and half each of the salt and pepper; toss ¼ cup with vegetables until coated.

Sprinkle fish with remaining salt and pepper; brush both sides with remaining oil mixture. Grill, covered and skin side down, on greased grill over medium-high heat until fish flakes easily, 8 to 10 minutes. Serve with ratatouille salad.

Makes 4 to 6 servings.

PER EACH OF 6 SERVINGS: about 296 cal, 21 g pro, 18 g total fat (3 g sat. fat), 12 g carb, 3 g fibre, 62 mg chol, 486 mg sodium. % RDI: 5% calcium, 10% iron, 12% vit A, 53% vit C, 17% folate.

Chili Barbecued Shrimp

Think of these juicy shrimp as shrimp cocktail on the grill.

2 lb (900 g) **raw extra jumbo shrimp** (size 16 to 20), about 32

½ cup **tomato-based chili sauce**

1 tbsp packed **brown sugar**

2 tsp **cider vinegar**

1 tsp **hot pepper sauce**

¾ tsp **sweet paprika**

1 clove **garlic,** minced

Lemon wedges

Peel and devein shrimp, leaving tails intact. Thread lengthwise onto skewers, 1 shrimp per skewer.

Mix together chili sauce, sugar, vinegar, hot pepper sauce, paprika and garlic; brush half over shrimp.

Grill on greased grill over medium-high heat, turning once, for 5 minutes. Brush with remaining sauce; grill, turning once, until opaque and glazed, 2 to 3 minutes. Serve with lemon wedges.

Makes 8 servings.

PER SERVING (WITHOUT LEMON WEDGES): about 116 cal, 18 g pro, 2 g total fat (trace sat. fat), 6 g carb, 1 g fibre, 129 mg chol, 358 mg sodium. % RDI: 5% calcium, 16% iron, 6% vit A, 7% vit C, 4% folate.

Seafood Caesar Salad

Brine-kissed seafood pairs perfectly with creamy, slightly salty Caesar salad. And this version is a meal in itself.

1 pkg (340 g) **raw large shrimp** (size 31 to 35), peeled and deveined (tails left on)

2 **whole squid,** cleaned

1 tbsp each **lemon juice** and **extra-virgin olive oil**

¼ tsp each **dried Italian herb seasoning** and **pepper**

1 head **romaine lettuce,** torn

2 cups **croutons**

DRESSING:

3 tbsp grated **Parmesan cheese**

2 tbsp **extra-virgin olive oil**

1 tbsp **lemon juice**

1 tsp each **Dijon mustard** and **anchovy paste**

1 clove **garlic,** minced

Pinch each **salt** and **pepper**

Dash **Worcestershire sauce**

2 tbsp **light mayonnaise**

Toss together shrimp, squid, lemon juice, oil, Italian herb seasoning and pepper. Grill, covered, on greased grill over medium heat, turning once, until shrimp are pink and squid is opaque, about 4 minutes. Slice squid into rings; set aside.

Dressing: Meanwhile, in large bowl, whisk together Parmesan cheese, oil, lemon juice, mustard, anchovy paste, garlic, salt, pepper and Worcestershire sauce; whisk in mayonnaise.

Add lettuce and croutons to dressing; toss to coat. Top with shrimp and squid.

Makes 4 servings.

PER SERVING: about 376 cal, 33 g pro, 18 g total fat (3 g sat. fat), 21 g carb, 4 g fibre, 282 mg chol, 447 mg sodium, 745 mg potassium. % RDI: 17% calcium, 35% iron, 96% vit A, 72% vit C, 110% folate.

Grilled Curry Shrimp Soft Tacos

Garnish these Caribbean-inspired tacos with baked tortilla chips and low-fat sour cream. Serve any extra salsa on the side.

⅓ cup **olive oil**

¼ cup **lime juice**

1 tbsp **ketchup**

2 tsp **sodium-reduced soy sauce**

1 tsp **curry powder**

2 cloves **garlic,** minced

¼ tsp each **salt** and **pepper**

Pinch **allspice**

1 lb (450 g) **raw jumbo shrimp** (size 21 to 25), peeled and deveined

2 each **sweet red peppers** and **sweet yellow peppers,** quartered

1 **onion,** cut into ½-inch (1 cm) thick rings

1 **jalapeño pepper,** seeded

¼ cup chopped **fresh cilantro**

8 **whole grain flour tortillas,** each 6 inches (15 cm)

In large bowl, whisk together 3 tbsp of the oil, 2 tbsp of the lime juice, the ketchup, soy sauce, curry powder, garlic, half each of the salt and pepper, and the allspice. Add shrimp; toss to coat.

Brush red and yellow peppers and onion with 1 tbsp of the remaining oil. Grill, covered, on greased grill over medium-high heat, turning once, until charred and tender, 10 to 12 minutes. Cut into chunks.

In food processor, coarsely chop grilled vegetables with jalapeño; transfer to bowl. Toss in cilantro and remaining olive oil, lime juice, salt and pepper.

Grill shrimp, covered, on greased grill over medium-high heat, turning once, until pink and opaque, 4 to 5 minutes. Divide shrimp and salsa among tortillas.

Makes 4 servings.

PER SERVING: about 445 cal, 25 g pro, 18 g total fat (3 g sat. fat), 50 g carb, 6 g fibre, 129 mg chol, 664 mg sodium, 615 mg potassium. % RDI: 8% calcium, 31% iron, 28% vit A, 318% vit C, 23% folate.

"Shrimp on the Barbi" With Chinese Dipping Sauce

The quintessential Australian grill dish, fresh shell-on shrimp are served plain, or with a squeeze of citrus, plain or flavoured butter, or a dipping sauce like this one.

1 lb (450 g) **shell-on raw jumbo shrimp** (size 21 to 25), preferably head-on, deveined (see Tip, below)

¼ tsp each **salt** and **pepper**

CHINESE HOT PEPPER & SOY DIPPING SAUCE:

4 tsp **peanut oil** or vegetable oil

2 **red finger hot peppers,** thinly sliced diagonally

2 **green onions,** cut into julienne

Pinch **salt**

2 tbsp **soy sauce**

2 tsp **sesame oil**

1 tsp **unseasoned rice vinegar**

1 tbsp chopped **fresh cilantro**

Chinese Hot Pepper & Soy Dipping Sauce: In small skillet, heat peanut oil over medium-high heat; fry hot peppers, green onions and salt until wilted and fragrant, about 30 seconds. Scrape into heatproof bowl. Add soy sauce to skillet; bring to simmer. Stir into bowl along with sesame oil and vinegar; top with cilantro.

Sprinkle shrimp with salt and pepper. Grill on greased grill over high heat until pink and opaque, 3 to 5 minutes. Serve with dipping sauce.

Makes 4 servings.

It's easy to devein shell-on shrimp. Bend shrimp into circle; into gap between shell pieces, one or two sections back from head, insert toothpick under vein. Pull out vein between shell pieces.

PER SERVING: about 135 cal, 18 g pro, 6 g total fat (1 g sat. fat), 2 g carb, trace fibre, 129 mg chol, 428 mg sodium, 190 mg potassium. % RDI: 4% calcium, 16% iron, 6% vit A, 10% vit C, 5% folate.

Kerala Grilled Shrimp

Kerala, the tropical southwestern province of India known for its lavishly spiced coconut-based cuisine, is the origin of these extremely tasty grilled shrimp.

1½ tsp **coriander seeds**

¾ tsp **black peppercorns**

4 **whole cloves**

1 tsp **aniseeds** or fennel seeds

¼ tsp **fenugreek seeds** (optional)

1 tsp **turmeric**

½ to 1 tsp **cayenne pepper**

¼ tsp **cinnamon**

Half **onion,** chopped

¼ cup finely grated **fresh coconut** (or unsweetened desiccated coconut)

3 cloves **garlic,** chopped

2 tsp chopped **fresh ginger**

½ tsp **salt**

1 lb (450 g) **raw large shrimp** (size 31 to 35), peeled and deveined

2 tbsp **butter,** melted

Lime wedges

In dry small skillet over medium heat, toast coriander seeds for 1 minute. Add peppercorns and cloves; toast for 30 seconds. Add aniseeds, and fenugreek seeds (if using); toast for 30 seconds. Grind spices to fine powder; mix in turmeric, cayenne and cinnamon.

In food processor, purée together onion, coconut, garlic, ginger and salt, adding up to 2 tbsp water if necessary to form paste; transfer to bowl. Mix in spice mixture; toss with shrimp until coated. Marinate for 30 minutes or, covered and refrigerated, up to 6 hours.

Thread shrimp onto skewers; brush with butter. Grill on greased grill over medium heat, turning once, until pink and opaque, about 12 minutes. Serve with lime wedges.

Makes 6 servings.

PER SERVING: about 138 cal, 16 g pro, 7 g total fat (4 g sat. fat), 4 g carb, 1 g fibre, 125 mg chol, 345 mg sodium. % RDI: 3% calcium, 14% iron, 8% vit A, 5% vit C, 3% folate.

Grilled Shrimp With Corn & Black Bean Salad

The zippy flavours and brilliant colours of this salad complement tender, perfectly grilled shrimp. Grilling the corn concentrates the kernels' sweetness and adds a smoky accent.

1 lb (450 g) **raw jumbo shrimp** (size 21 to 25), peeled and deveined

1 tbsp **peanut oil** or vegetable oil

1 tbsp **lime juice**

1 tsp **soy sauce**

1 tsp **sesame oil**

½ tsp **pepper**

2 cloves **garlic,** minced

1 head **Boston lettuce,** separated into leaves

CORN & BLACK BEAN SALAD:

3 **cobs of corn,** husked

1 can (19 oz/540 mL) **black beans,** drained and rinsed

1 **sweet red pepper,** diced

½ cup chopped **red onion**

½ cup **fresh cilantro leaves,** coarsely chopped

3 tbsp **peanut oil** or vegetable oil

3 tbsp **lime juice**

½ tsp **salt**

½ tsp **ground cumin**

¼ tsp **pepper**

Toss together shrimp, oil, lime juice, soy sauce, sesame oil, pepper and garlic. Cover and marinate, refrigerated, for 1 hour.

Corn & Black Bean Salad: Meanwhile, grill corn on greased grill over medium-high heat, turning occasionally, until kernels are tender, about 15 minutes. Slice kernels off cobs; toss together corn, black beans, red pepper, onion and cilantro. Whisk together oil, lime juice, salt, cumin and pepper; toss with corn mixture until coated.

Grill shrimp on greased grill over medium-high heat, turning once, until pink and opaque, about 6 minutes. Divide lettuce leaves among plates; top with salad then shrimp.

Makes 4 servings.

PER SERVING: about 438 cal, 29 g pro, 18 g total fat (2 g sat. fat), 45 g carb, 9 g fibre, 129 mg chol, 736 mg sodium. % RDI: 7% calcium, 33% iron, 21% vit A, 100% vit C, 95% folate.

Rosemary Grilled Scallops

Farmed scallops are a more sustainable choice than wild, since wild scallops can only be caught by dredging the ocean floor.

4 thick sprigs **fresh rosemary**

12 **sea scallops,** about 1 lb (450 g)

¼ cup **extra-virgin olive oil**

2 tbsp **lemon juice**

1 clove **garlic**

¼ tsp **salt**

¼ tsp **pepper**

6 oz (170 g) **small potatoes**

2 **small Italian eggplants,** about 8 oz (225 g) total

3 **hot banana peppers**

¼ cup **fresh parsley,** chopped

Remove leaves from rosemary, leaving about 1 inch (2.5 cm) intact at tops of stems; chop enough of the removed leaves to make 1 tbsp. Thread 3 scallops, through sides, onto each rosemary stem. Mix together chopped rosemary, oil, lemon juice, garlic, salt and pepper; reserving remainder, brush 2 tbsp over scallops. Cover and marinate, refrigerated, for 30 minutes.

Meanwhile, slice larger or halve smaller potatoes. Cut eggplant into ¾-inch (2 cm) thick slices. Toss together potatoes, eggplant, whole peppers and 2 tbsp of the reserved oil mixture. Grill, covered, over medium heat, turning occasionally, until tender, 8 to 10 minutes for peppers and eggplant, 15 minutes for potatoes.

Seed and cut peppers into ½-inch (1 cm) thick slices; toss together peppers, potatoes, eggplant, remaining oil mixture and parsley.

Grill scallops on greased grill over high heat, turning once, until just turning opaque in centre, 3 to 4 minutes. Serve on grilled vegetables.

Makes 4 servings.

PER SERVING: about 276 cal, 21 g pro, 15 g total fat (2 g sat. fat), 15 g carb, 4 g fibre, 43 mg chol, 373 mg sodium, 765 mg potassium. % RDI: 11% calcium, 25% iron, 7% vit A, 57% vit C, 18% folate.

Grilled Stuffed Squid

Inspired by Spanish and Portuguese flavours, these grilled squid make an elegant first course or part of a seafood grill. If you prefer a bit of heat, use the hot banana pepper.

1 **sweet green pepper** or large Cubanelle pepper

1 **hot banana pepper** (optional)

6 **large whole squid,** 1½ to 1¾ lb (675 to 790 g) total

¼ cup **olive oil**

3 cups finely sliced **sweet onion** or white onion

1 **bay leaf**

¾ tsp (approx) **salt**

⅓ cup chopped **green olives**

1 clove **garlic,** minced

⅓ cup **dry white wine**

¼ cup chopped **fresh parsley**

¼ tsp **pepper**

Lemon wedges

Grill green pepper, and banana pepper (if using), covered, over high heat until charred all over. Place in bowl; cover and let cool. Peel and seed peppers; cut into thin strips.

To clean each squid, pull tentacle section off body. Remove plastic-like quill from body; rinse inside and out. Cut off innards, beak and eyes from base of tentacle portion; cut tentacle portions into 3 or 4 pieces each. (Pull off purplish skin from body if desired; it adds extra flavour if left on.) Set aside in refrigerator.

In skillet, heat 2 tbsp of the oil over medium heat; fry onion, bay leaf and pinch of the salt, stirring often, until onions are golden, 20 to 25 minutes. Add olives, garlic, squid tentacles, peppers and ½ tsp of the remaining salt; fry until garlic is softened, about 2 minutes. Stir in wine; increase heat to high and cook until liquid is evaporated. Stir in half of the parsley. Let cool.

Stuff each squid body half-full of onion mixture; secure open end with short skewer or soaked toothpick. Mix together 1 tbsp of the remaining oil, the pepper and remaining ¼ tsp salt; add squid, turning to coat.

Grill on greased grill over high heat, turning once, until firm but tender, 3 to 5 minutes. Transfer to platter; sprinkle with remaining parsley and oil. Serve with lemon wedges.

Makes 6 servings.

PER SERVING: about 203 cal, 15 g pro, 12 g total fat (2 g sat. fat), 9 g carb, 1 g fibre, 206 mg chol, 447 mg sodium, 349 mg potassium. % RDI: 5% calcium, 9% iron, 4% vit A, 38% vit C, 10% folate.

Greek Grilled Squid

Who doesn't go to a good Greek restaurant and order grilled calamari? Why not enjoy it more often at home? It's easy – and inexpensive to boot.

4 **large whole squid,** 1 to 1¼ lb (450 to 565 g) total

5 tbsp **extra-virgin olive oil**

2 cloves **garlic,** minced

1 tsp **dried oregano** (preferably Greek)

½ tsp **hot pepper flakes**

½ tsp **salt** (approx)

¼ tsp **pepper** (approx)

2 **hot banana peppers**

1 or 2 **ripe tomatoes,** sliced

Half **field cucumber** or quarter English cucumber, sliced

12 **black olives**

2 tbsp **lemon juice**

2 tbsp chopped **fresh parsley**

To clean each squid, pull tentacle section off body. Remove plastic-like quill from body; rinse inside and out. Cut off innards, beak and eyes from base of tentacle portion. (Pull off purplish skin from body if desired; it adds extra flavour if left on.)

At scant ½-inch (1 cm) intervals, slice squid bodies crosswise three-quarters of the way through. Toss together squid bodies and tentacles, 3 tbsp of the oil, the garlic, oregano, hot pepper flakes, ½ tsp of the salt and ¼ tsp of the pepper until coated. Let stand for 30 to 60 minutes.

Meanwhile, grill peppers, covered, on greased grill over high heat, turning often, until charred all over. Place in bowl; cover and let cool. Peel peppers; arrange on platter along with tomatoes and cucumbers.

Grill squid over high heat, turning often, until opaque and lightly browned, 5 minutes. Transfer to platter; top with olives. Sprinkle with pinch each salt and pepper. Drizzle with lemon juice and remaining oil; sprinkle with parsley.

Makes 4 servings.

VARIATION

Buffet-Style Grilled Squid Salad

Prepare as directed, but dice grilled peppers, tomatoes and cucumber; slice grilled squid into rings. In bowl, toss with other ingredients, then transfer to serving plate.

Makes 8 servings.

PER EACH OF 4 SERVINGS: about 270 cal, 15 g pro, 20 g total fat (3 g sat. fat), 9 g carb, 2 g fibre, 206 mg chol, 450 mg sodium, 443 mg potassium. % RDI: 6% calcium, 13% iron, 8% vit A, 50% vit C, 9% folate.

Vietnamese Squid Salad

Heady seafood salads full of fresh herbs and piqued with chilies, tart citrus and fish sauce are a hallmark of Vietnamese and other Southeast Asian cuisines. Cut all the salad ingredients into very fine julienne for the best result.

1 lb (450 g) cleaned **squid** (tubes and tentacles)

1 clove **garlic,** minced

1 **Thai bird's-eye pepper,** minced

1 tbsp **fish sauce**

2 tsp minced **fresh lemongrass**

1 tsp finely grated **fresh ginger**

¼ tsp **pepper**

Dressing for Squid Salad (right)

¼ cup chopped **fresh cilantro**

¼ cup chopped **fresh mint** and/or **Thai basil**

1 tbsp ground **roasted peanuts**

1 tbsp **crispy fried shallots** (see Tip, right)

1 tsp **crispy fried sliced garlic** (see Tip, right)

SALAD:

¼ cup each **cucumber** and **hard semi-ripe mango** fine julienne

¼ cup finely sliced **sweet onion**

2 tbsp each **sweet red, yellow** and **green pepper** fine julienne

2 tbsp **carrot** fine julienne

2 or 3 **Thai bird's-eye peppers,** thinly sliced

Mix together squid tubes and tentacles, minced garlic, Thai pepper, fish sauce, lemongrass, ginger and pepper. Let stand for 10 to 20 minutes.

Salad: Meanwhile, toss together cucumber; mango; onion; red, yellow and green peppers; carrot; and Thai peppers.

Grill squid on greased grill over high heat, turning often, until opaque and lightly browned, about 5 minutes. Cut tubes into rings; cut tentacles into 2 or 3 pieces each. Add to salad; toss with dressing. Toss in cilantro and mint. Serve sprinkled with peanuts, fried shallots and fried garlic.

Makes 6 servings.

Dressing for Squid Salad

Combine 3 tbsp lime juice, 1 tbsp fish sauce, 2 tsp palm vinegar or unseasoned rice vinegar, and 1½ tsp palm sugar or granulated sugar; mix until sugar is dissolved.

TIP

You can buy crispy fried shallots and garlic in Asian markets or make them yourself: fry thinly sliced shallots or garlic in hot oil until golden. Drain on paper towels.

PER SERVING: about 88 cal, 10 g pro, 2 g total fat (trace sat. fat), 8 g carb, 1 g fibre, 137 mg chol, 502 mg sodium, 271 mg potassium. % RDI: 4% calcium, 9% iron, 11% vit A, 42% vit C, 8% folate.

Grilled Octopus

From Portugal to the Philippines, octopus is considered a delicacy. Its meat is tender and sweet when cooked, with a taste somewhere between those of lobster and squid.

1 **onion,** quartered

1¾ tsp **salt**

1 tsp **black peppercorns**

2 **bay leaves**

3 lb (1.35 kg) fresh or thawed frozen **octopus**

3 tbsp **extra-virgin olive oil**

½ tsp **dried oregano**

Pinch **pepper**

1 tbsp finely chopped **fresh parsley**

Sliced **tomato** and/or **cucumber** (optional)

Olives

Lemon wedges

In large saucepan, bring 6 cups water, onion, 1½ tsp of the salt, peppercorns and bay leaves to boil; add octopus and return to boil. Reduce heat; simmer, covered, over low heat until tender, 1½ to 2 hours for fresh, 1 to 1¼ hours for thawed. Drain; let cool. *(Make-ahead: Refrigerate for up to 1 day.)*

Separate head from tentacles; cut off and discard beak in centre where tentacles join. Cut octopus into large pieces. Toss together octopus, 1 tbsp of the oil, oregano, pepper and remaining salt.

Grill on greased grill over high heat, turning once, until hot and edges are crispy, 4 to 6 minutes. Transfer to platter; drizzle with remaining oil and sprinkle with parsley. Serve with tomatoes and/or cucumber (if using), olives and lemon wedges.

Makes 6 servings.

Imported fresh octopus is occasionally available from fishmongers (particularly in Portuguese, Italian or Greek neighbourhoods). Frozen is also good and considerably lower in price; look for it in large grocery stores and Mediterranean and Asian markets. The most eco-friendly choices are Spanish- or Hawaiian-caught.

PER SERVING: about 246 cal, 34 g pro, 9 g total fat (1 g sat. fat), 5 g carb, trace fibre, 109 mg chol, 618 mg sodium, 720 mg potassium. % RDI: 11% calcium, 79% iron, 10% vit A, 17% vit C, 13% folate.

Baby Octopus With Cherry Tomatoes

This spectacular-looking dish is quick and easy — baby octopus is tender enough that it can be grilled directly without boiling first.

1 lb (450 g) **baby octopus**
   (4 to 8, depending on size)

3 tbsp **extra-virgin olive oil**

2 cups **cherry tomatoes,** halved

3 tbsp torn **fresh basil leaves**

2 tbsp pitted **black olives,** sliced

1 tbsp drained **capers,** chopped

1 clove **garlic,** minced

1 tsp **hot pepper flakes**

½ tsp **salt**

¼ tsp **pepper**

If octopus are large, cut in half; toss octopus with 1 tbsp of the oil.

Toss together cherry tomatoes, 2 tbsp of the basil, the olives, capers, garlic, hot pepper flakes, salt, pepper and remaining oil. Place tomato mixture on heavy-duty foil; seal to form packet.

Grill tomato packet over medium-high heat for 10 minutes. Meanwhile, grill octopus, turning often, until tentacles curl and become crispy, about 6 minutes. Serve octopus over tomatoes; top with remaining basil.

Makes 4 servings.

PER SERVING: about 205 cal, 18 g pro, 12 g total fat (2 g sat. fat), 7 g carb, 1 g fibre, 54 mg chol, 653 mg sodium, 558 mg potassium. % RDI: 7% calcium, 43% iron, 14% vit A, 23% vit C, 10% folate.

From top: Buttered Clams on the Grill (page 425) and Grilled Oysters With Black Bean Sauce (page 424)

Grilled Oysters With Black Bean Sauce

A favourite Cantonese dish is oysters steamed with a dollop of garlicky black bean sauce on top, but we think these spicy grilled oysters might even be better. Farmed oysters are your most sustainable pick.

1 tbsp **sesame oil**

2 tbsp minced **shallots**

1 clove **garlic,** minced

2 tbsp **chili black bean sauce**
    or black bean and garlic sauce

1 tsp **Chinese rice wine** or
    dry sherry

½ tsp **granulated sugar**

½ tsp **Chinese black vinegar** or
    balsamic vinegar

2 tbsp chopped **fresh cilantro**

1 **green onion,** thinly sliced

12 **fresh oysters**

In small saucepan, heat sesame oil over medium-low heat; fry shallots and garlic until softened and fragrant, 2 to 3 minutes. Stir in black bean sauce, wine, sugar and vinegar; simmer for 2 minutes. Let cool. Stir in cilantro and green onion.

Shuck oysters, discarding top shell and keeping as much liquid in bottom shell as possible; spoon about ½ tsp bean sauce onto each. Grill over high heat until juices are bubbling.

Makes 12 oysters.

Photo, page 423

PER OYSTER: about 27 cal, 1 g pro, 1 g total fat (trace sat. fat), 3 g carb, trace fibre, 3 mg chol, 56 mg sodium, 38 mg potassium. % RDI: 1% calcium, 7% iron, 2% vit C, 1% folate.

Buttered Clams on the Grill

Serve these simply delicious clams with some sliced baguette to soak up the juices. Go green by choosing farmed or hand-harvested wild clams.

¼ cup **butter**

2 tbsp **lemon juice**

1 clove **garlic,** pressed or minced

2 tbsp chopped **fresh parsley**

1 lb (450 g) **littleneck clams** or small cherrystone clams (about 12)

Mix together butter, lemon juice and garlic; microwave on high until butter is melted (or melt in small skillet). Stir in parsley.

Grill clams, covered, over high heat until they open, about 8 minutes. Carefully, without spilling clam liquor in bottom shells, transfer to platter. Spoon some of the butter mixture into each.

Makes 4 servings.

Photo, page 422

PER SERVING: about 97 cal, 2 g pro, 9 g total fat (6 g sat. fat), 1 g carb, trace fibre, 30 mg chol, 77 mg sodium, 73 mg potassium. % RDI: 1% calcium, 18% iron, 11% vit A, 8% vit C, 2% folate.

Cheese-Stuffed
Banana Peppers
(page 437)

grilled vegetables, cheeses & breads

Grilled Corn on the Cob
   With Ancho Chili Glaze | 429

Corn Butters & Sauces | 431

Chat Masala for Grilled Corn | 432

Grilled Potato Salad Kabobs | 433

One Potato, Two Potato | 434

Cider-Glazed Apples & Onion | 435

Cheese-Stuffed Banana Peppers | 437

Grilling Vegetables | 438

Balsamic Grilled Vegetables | 439

Grilled Radicchio | 440

Oyster Mushrooms & Peppers | 442

Grilled Asparagus With
   Curry Yogurt Sauce | 443

Pattypan Skewers | 444

Grilled Eggplant With Provolone | 447

Grilled Tofu & Vegetable
   Antipasto | 448

Grilled Pineapple | 449

Grilled Halloumi & Tomato Kabobs | 450

Grilled Mozzarella Skewers
   With Anchovy Sauce | 452

Provoleta | 454

Halloumi With Fresh Chilies | 455

Garlic Flatbread | 456

Garlic Bread on the Grill | 459

Rapini & Garlic Pizza
   With Asiago Cheese | 460

Swiss Chard Pizza | 461

Grilled Pizza Mexicana | 462

Grilled Corn Pizza | 463

Smoked Salmon Pizza
   With Marinated Onion | 465

Zucchini Pizza With Fresh
   Tomato Sauce | 466

Barbecued Chicken Pizza | 467

Grilled Steak & Gorgonzola Pizza | 468

Caprese Pizza With Bacon | 470

Sausage & Grilled Pepper Pizza | 471

Grilled Corn on the Cob With Ancho Chili Glaze

Precooked corn grilled with a piquant barbecue sauce (enough for a dozen cobs) is a delicious way to spice up outdoor dining.

Steamed or boiled **cobs of corn**

Peanut oil or vegetable oil

ANCHO CHILI SAUCE:

2 tbsp **ancho chili powder**

1½ tbsp **peanut oil** or vegetable oil

3 cloves **garlic,** pressed or minced

½ tsp **ground cumin**

2 tbsp packed **dark brown sugar**

2 tbsp **dark soy sauce**

2 tbsp **ketchup**

1½ tbsp **cider vinegar**

Ancho Chili Sauce: Mix chili powder with 3 tbsp water to make paste; let stand for 10 minutes. In small saucepan over medium heat, cook chili paste, oil, garlic and cumin until fragrant, 2 to 3 minutes. Stir in ⅓ cup water, sugar, soy sauce, ketchup and vinegar; bring to boil. Reduce heat and simmer until very thick, about 10 minutes. Let cool.

Lightly brush corn with oil; grill, covered, on greased grill over medium-high heat until hot and grill marked, 3 to 4 minutes. Brush with ancho chili sauce; grill, turning, for 1 minute.

Makes about ½ cup sauce, enough for 12 cobs of corn.

PER COB WITH 2 TSP SAUCE: about 159 cal, 4 g pro, 3 g total fat (trace sat. fat), 34 g carb, 3 g fibre, 0 mg chol, 239 mg sodium, 299 mg potassium. % RDI: 1% calcium, 3% iron, 8% vit A, 14% vit C, 26% folate.

From left: Spiced Olive Oil & Butter and Basil Butter

Corn Butters & Sauces

Instead of plain butter and salt, dress up grilled cobs of corn with one of these butter, mayonnaise or olive oil toppings, then salt to taste.

Basil Butter: ¼ cup butter, softened; 2 tbsp grated Parmesan cheese; 1 clove garlic, minced; and 1 tbsp minced fresh basil

Spiced Olive Oil & Butter: 2 tbsp extra-virgin olive oil; 2 tbsp butter, softened; 1 tbsp minced fresh cilantro; 1 tsp curry paste; and ½ tsp lemon juice

Provençal Butter: ¼ cup butter, softened; 1 tbsp Dijon mustard; and ¾ tsp herbes de Provence

Lemon Butter: ¼ cup butter, softened; ½ tsp grated lemon zest; 1 tbsp lemon juice; and ½ tsp pepper

Smoky Orange Mayonnaise: ¼ cup mayonnaise; 2 tsp barbecue sauce; and 1 tsp each chopped canned chipotle pepper and grated orange zest

Lemon Pepper Mayonnaise: ¼ cup mayonnaise; 1 tsp each grated lemon zest and lemon juice; ½ tsp black pepper; and ¼ tsp white pepper

Mediterranean Olive Oil: 3 tbsp extra-virgin olive oil; 4 tsp minced drained oil-packed sun-dried tomatoes; ½ tsp dried thyme; and pinch pepper

Each makes enough for about 6 cobs of corn.

TIP

Grill husked cobs over medium heat for 15 to 20 minutes. Or soak unhusked cobs in water for 20 minutes, then grill for 15 to 20 minutes.

Chat Masala for Grilled Corn

Anyone who has walked through a South Asian shopping district in summertime has experienced the wonderful fragrance (and flavour) of Indian-style grilled corn on the cob, seasoned with the distinctive spice mix chat (or chaat) masala. *Make a jar and keep it all summer for parties or any time you grill sweet local corn.*

1½ tbsp **coarse salt**

3 tbsp **coriander seeds**

5 tsp **cumin seeds**

2 tsp **fennel seeds**

1 tsp **black peppercorns**

8 **whole cloves**

4 tsp **amchur** (green mango powder)

1 tbsp **black salt** (or table salt)

1 tbsp **sweet paprika**

1½ tsp **cayenne pepper**

½ tsp **ground ginger**

¼ tsp **nutmeg**

¼ tsp **asafetida** (or 1 tsp garlic powder)

In skillet over medium heat, toast coarse salt until sand-coloured; transfer to bowl and let cool. One at a time, in dry skillet over medium-low heat, toast coriander, cumin, fennel, peppercorns and cloves until fragrant and slightly darkened, 1 to 3 minutes; add to bowl and let cool. Grind until fine powder; stir in amchur, black salt, paprika, cayenne, ginger, nutmeg and asafetida.

To use, rub cut side of lime half all over corn to moisten; sprinkle with chat masala to taste.

Makes enough for about 50 cobs of corn.

TIP

It's worth the jaunt to the Indian grocery store to pick up a few specialized spices, such as the distinctive, slightly sulfurous black salt; dried green mango powder, or *amchur* (also spelled *amchor* or *amchoor*), for tartness; and asafetida (*hing*) for this ground resin's distinctive garlic-like flavour. You also can buy prepared chat masala at Indian grocers, but it won't be as fresh and fragrant as your own. It's used for sprinkling over corn, fruit, nuts and many other snack foods.

Grilled Potato Salad Kabobs

Potato salad on a stick? Why not? You can use red, white or yellow-fleshed mini potatoes to make these tasty kabobs.

24 **mini new potatoes,** scrubbed

1 **small red onion,** cut into 16 pieces

1 **dill pickle,** cut into 16 pieces

1 clove **garlic,** minced

¼ cup **olive oil**

2 tbsp **white wine vinegar**

1 tbsp **grainy mustard**

2 tsp **maple syrup**

½ tsp each **salt** and **pepper**

In saucepan of boiling lightly salted water, cover and cook potatoes just until tender, about 15 minutes. Chill under cold water until cool.

Onto each of 8 skewers, alternately thread 3 potatoes, 2 pieces red onion and 2 pieces dill pickle. Whisk together garlic, oil, vinegar, mustard, maple syrup, salt and pepper until smooth; brush generously over skewers. Reserve any remaining marinade.

Grill, covered, on greased grill over medium-high heat, turning often, until onions are tender and potatoes are golden, about 12 minutes. Brush with any remaining marinade.

Makes 4 servings.

PER SERVING: about 251 cal, 3 g pro, 14 g total fat (2 g sat. fat), 29 g carb, 3 g fibre, 0 mg chol, 682 mg sodium, 647 mg potassium. % RDI: 3% calcium, 10% iron, 1% vit A, 34% vit C, 11% folate.

One Potato, Two Potato

Lemon Grilled Potatoes

4 **large red potatoes,** scrubbed and cut into 8 wedges each

2 tbsp **olive oil**

2 tsp grated **lemon zest**

½ tsp **salt**

¼ tsp **pepper**

Toss together potatoes, oil, lemon zest, salt and pepper until coated.

Reserving oil mixture, grill potatoes, covered, on greased grill over medium-high heat, turning halfway through and brushing with oil mixture, until golden and tender, about 25 minutes.

Makes 4 servings.

PER SERVING: about 190 cal, 3 g pro, 7 g total fat (1 g sat. fat), 30 g carb, 3 g fibre, 0 mg chol, 296 mg sodium. % RDI: 1% calcium, 12% iron, 28% vit C, 6% folate.

Olive Oil Potatoes

24 **small new potatoes**

2 tbsp **olive oil**

¼ tsp **smoked paprika** or sweet paprika

¼ tsp **salt**

In saucepan of boiling salted water, cover and cook potatoes until almost tender, about 15 minutes. Drain; let cool. Thread onto skewers.

Place on greased grill over medium-high heat; brush with some of the oil. Grill, covered and brushing often with remaining oil, until hot and skins are crisp, 10 to 15 minutes. Sprinkle with paprika and salt.

Makes 6 to 8 servings.

PER EACH OF 8 SERVINGS: about 111 cal, 2 g pro, 3 g total fat (trace sat. fat), 19 g carb, 2 g fibre, 0 mg chol, 298 mg sodium. % RDI: 1% calcium, 6% iron, 20% vit C, 4% folate.

Salt & Pepper Potato Packets

3 lb (1.35 kg) **small potatoes,** peeled (optional) and halved

2 tbsp **olive oil,** or butter, diced

½ tsp **salt**

¼ tsp **pepper**

Place potatoes on heavy-duty foil; sprinkle with oil (increase to 3 tbsp if using peeled potatoes), salt and pepper. Seal to form packet. Grill, covered, over medium-high heat for 10 minutes; turn and cut 1 or 2 vents in top. Grill until tender, about 8 minutes.

Makes 8 servings.

PER SERVING: about 158 cal, 3 g pro, 4 g total fat (trace sat. fat), 29 g carb, 3 g fibre, 0 mg chol, 157 mg sodium. % RDI: 2% calcium, 11% iron, 22% vit C, 18% folate.

Cider-Glazed Apples & Onion

Grilling fruits and vegetables caramelizes their natural sugars. These tangy-sweet apples and onions are a natural accompaniment to grilled pork.

2 tbsp **cider vinegar**

2 tsp packed **brown sugar**

2 tsp **Dijon mustard**

¼ tsp each **salt** and **pepper**

2 **apples,** cored and cut into
   ½-inch (1 cm) thick slices

1 **sweet onion,** cut into
   ½-inch (1 cm) thick slices

Whisk together vinegar, sugar, mustard, salt and pepper; brush half over tops of apple and onion slices.

Place, mustard side down, on greased grill over medium-high heat; brush with remaining mustard mixture. Grill, covered and turning once, until golden and tender, about 10 minutes.

Makes 4 servings.

PER SERVING: about 91 cal, 1 g pro, 1 g total fat (trace sat. fat), 22 g carb, 3 g fibre, 0 mg chol, 180 mg sodium. % RDI: 3% calcium, 4% iron, 12% vit C, 6% folate.

Cheese-Stuffed Banana Peppers

To turn these peppers into a light meal, serve with crusty bread and a tossed salad.

6 **hot banana peppers**

⅔ cup finely diced **mozzarella cheese**

¼ cup diced **sweet onion**

2 tbsp grated **Parmesan cheese**

2 tbsp minced **fresh parsley**

4 tsp drained **capers**

Pinch **pepper**

2 slices **bread,** crusts removed

Pinch **salt**

Extra-virgin olive oil

Cut tops off banana peppers as close to stems as possible. With paring knife, remove cores; with small spoon, scoop out seeds and membranes. Rinse insides to remove any remaining seeds; shake out water.

Mix together mozzarella, onion, Parmesan, parsley, capers and pepper; stuff into each pepper until 1 inch (2.5 cm) below top. Tear bread; stuff into space to seal.

Grill, covered, on greased grill over medium-high heat, turning often, until tender, lightly charred and cheese is melted, 6 to 8 minutes.

Transfer to serving dish; sprinkle with salt. Drizzle with oil to taste.

Makes 6 servings.

PER SERVING: about 90 cal, 5 g pro, 5 g total fat (3 g sat. fat), 7 g carb, 2 g fibre, 15 mg chol, 195 mg sodium, 155 mg potassium. % RDI: 11% calcium, 4% iron, 6% vit A, 57% vit C, 10% folate.

Grilling Vegetables

Brush vegetables with olive or vegetable oil; sprinkle with salt and pepper. Grill on greased grill, on skewers or in greased grill basket or wok. Grill, covered if desired, over medium heat for time specified in chart or until lightly browned and tender-crisp to tender.

Vegetable	Prep/Size	Cooking Time
Asparagus	Snap off tough woody ends	10 minutes, turning often
Belgian endive	Halve lengthwise	15 to 20 minutes, turning once
Carrots	Lengthwise ¼-inch (5 mm) strips	15 minutes, turning once
Corn on the cob	Husk; or leave in husk and soak in water (do not oil)	15 to 20 minutes, turning often
Eggplant	¼-inch (5 mm) thick slices	10 minutes, turning once
Fennel bulb	Lengthwise ¼-inch (5 mm) slices	15 minutes, turning once
Green onions	Trim	5 minutes, turning often
Mushrooms	Whole, 1½ inches (4 cm) or larger	10 minutes, turning once
New potatoes	Whole small or ¼-inch (5 mm) slices	15 to 20 minutes, turning once
Onions	Crosswise ½-inch (1 cm) slices	15 minutes, turning once
Portobello mushrooms	Remove stems	10 minutes, turning once
Radicchio	Halve or quarter if large	10 minutes, turning once
Squash	Crosswise ¼-inch (5 mm) slices	15 minutes, turning once
Sweet peppers	Quarter	10 minutes, turning once
Sweet potatoes	¼-inch (5 mm) slices	15 minutes, turning once
Tomatoes	Halves or ½-inch (1 cm) slices	5 minutes, turning once
Tomatoes, cherry	Skewer	5 minutes, turning often
Zucchini	1½-inch (4 cm) chunks or lengthwise ¼-inch (5 mm) strips	10 minutes, turning once

Balsamic Grilled Vegetables

Grilled and lightly dressed summer vegetables like these are equally delicious served warm or at room temperature.

1 **small red onion,** cut into ½-inch (1 cm) thick slices

4 **sweet peppers,** cut into 1-inch (2.5 cm) wide strips

2 **zucchini,** cut lengthwise into ¼-inch (5 mm) thick strips

BALSAMIC DRESSING:

⅓ cup **extra-virgin olive oil**

3 tbsp **white balsamic vinegar** or balsamic vinegar

1 tsp minced **fresh oregano,** or ½ tsp dried, crumbled

½ tsp each **salt** and **pepper**

Balsamic Dressing: Whisk together oil, vinegar, oregano, salt and pepper.

Skewer onion slices through edges to keep rings intact. Toss together half of the balsamic dressing, the peppers and zucchini; brush some of the remaining dressing over onions. Let stand for 10 minutes.

Grill, covered, on greased grill over medium-high heat, turning once, until tender and grill marked, 10 to 15 minutes. Transfer to platter, peeling skins off peppers, if desired; drizzle with remaining dressing.

Makes 6 servings.

PER SERVING: about 154 cal, 1 g pro, 12 g total fat (2 g sat. fat), 11 g carb, 2 g fibre, 0 mg chol, 197 mg sodium. % RDI: 2% calcium, 6% iron, 21% vit A, 210% vit C, 12% folate.

Grilled Radicchio

Grilling radicchio brings out its sweetness. The bitter-sweet contrast is excellent in Grilled Radicchio Salad (below).

2 heads **radicchio**

3 tbsp **extra-virgin olive oil**

½ tsp **coarse sea salt**

¼ tsp **pepper**

1 tbsp **balsamic vinegar**

Leaving core intact, cut radicchio in half (cut large heads into quarters); thread onto skewers. Brush with half of the oil; sprinkle with half each of the salt and pepper.

Grill, covered, on greased grill over medium-high heat, turning often, until wilted and lightly browned and centre is softened, about 10 minutes. Transfer to platter. Drizzle with vinegar and remaining oil; sprinkle with remaining salt and pepper.

Makes 4 servings.

VARIATION

Grilled Radicchio Salad

Cut, skewer and grill radicchio as directed. Brush with 4 tsp olive oil; grill as directed. Cut out and discard core; thinly slice radicchio. In serving bowl, whisk together 2 tbsp extra-virgin olive oil; 1 tbsp sherry vinegar or wine vinegar; 1 clove garlic, minced; ½ tsp Dijon mustard; and pinch granulated sugar. Add sliced radicchio; toss until coated. Sprinkle with 2 tbsp shaved Parmesan cheese.

PER SERVING: about 113 cal, 1 g pro, 10 g total fat (1 g sat. fat), 5 g carb, 1 g fibre, 0 mg chol, 307 mg sodium. % RDI: 2% calcium, 5% iron, 10% vit C, 16% folate.

Oyster Mushrooms & Peppers

Grilling oyster mushrooms crisps their edges and intensifies their woodsy flavour. Try this recipe with portobellos, shiitake caps or halved large button mushrooms, too.

1 lb (450 g) **oyster mushrooms**

3 **sweet red peppers,** quartered

⅓ cup **extra-virgin olive oil**

⅓ cup chopped **fresh basil**

2 tbsp **balsamic vinegar**

1 clove **garlic,** minced

½ tsp **salt**

¼ tsp **pepper**

Toss together mushrooms, peppers and ¼ cup of the oil. Grill, covered, on greased grill over medium-high heat, turning once, until tender and browned, about 8 minutes for mushrooms, 12 minutes for peppers. Transfer to platter.

Mix together remaining oil, basil, vinegar, garlic, salt and pepper; drizzle over vegetables.

Makes 6 servings.

PER SERVING: about 143 cal, 2 g pro, 12 g total fat (2 g sat. fat), 8 g carb, 2 g fibre, 0 mg chol, 194 mg sodium. % RDI: 1% calcium, 9% iron, 22% vit A, 167% vit C, 9% folate.

Grilled Asparagus With Curry Yogurt Sauce

This fabulous take on classic grilled asparagus is party-worthy indeed.

2 lb (900 g) **asparagus,** trimmed

1 tbsp **vegetable oil**

¼ tsp each **salt** and **pepper**

2 tbsp chopped toasted **cashews** (optional)

CURRY YOGURT SAUCE:

1 tbsp **butter**

¼ cup finely chopped **onion**

1 clove **garlic,** minced

1 tsp grated **fresh ginger**

½ tsp **curry powder**

Pinch each **salt, pepper** and **ground cumin**

2 tbsp finely chopped **green onion** (green part only)

½ cup **Balkan-style plain yogurt**

2 tbsp chopped **fresh mint**

2 tsp **lemon juice**

Curry Yogurt Sauce: In small saucepan, melt butter over medium-low heat; stir in onion and cook until dark golden, about 4 minutes. Stir in garlic, ginger, curry powder, salt, pepper and cumin; cook, stirring, for 30 seconds. Remove from heat; stir in green onion. Let cool slightly. Stir in yogurt, mint and lemon juice.

Toss together asparagus, oil, salt and pepper. Grill, covered, on greased grill over medium-high heat, turning often, until tender and slightly charred, about 7 minutes.

Transfer asparagus to serving platter. Top with curry yogurt sauce; sprinkle with cashews (if using).

Makes 8 servings.

PER SERVING: about 66 cal, 3 g pro, 4 g total fat (2 g sat. fat), 6 g carb, 2 g fibre, 7 mg chol, 103 mg sodium, 235 mg potassium. % RDI: 4% calcium, 7% iron, 11% vit A, 12% vit C, 55% folate.

Pattypan Skewers

Look for pattypan squashes that are no more than 2 inches (5 cm) wide to ensure tenderness.

3 tbsp **extra-virgin olive oil**

1 tbsp **balsamic vinegar**

1 clove **garlic,** minced

¼ tsp each **salt** and **pepper**

18 mini **pattypan squashes,** about 1 lb (450 g)

4 tsp finely chopped drained **oil-packed sun-dried tomatoes**

1 tbsp minced **fresh parsley**

Whisk together oil, vinegar, garlic, salt and pepper; add squashes, tossing to coat. Reserving remaining marinade, thread onto skewers.

Grill, covered, on greased grill over medium-high heat, turning occasionally, until tender, 8 to 10 minutes. Transfer to platter.

Add tomatoes and parsley to reserved marinade; drizzle over squashes.

Makes 4 to 6 servings.

PER EACH OF 6 SERVINGS: about 17 cal, trace pro, 7 g total fat (1 g sat. fat), 4 g carb, 1 g fibre, 0 mg chol, 102 mg sodium. % RDI: 2% calcium, 4% iron, 3% vit A, 12% vit C, 8% folate.

Grilled Eggplant With Provolone

Earthy roasted tomatoes spice up buttery eggplant and savoury provolone cheese.

1 **large eggplant,** about 1½ lb (675 g)

1 tsp **salt**

3 tbsp **olive oil**

5 oz (140 g) shredded **provolone cheese** (about 1½ cups)

CHERRY TOMATO SAUCE:

2 cups **cherry tomatoes** or grape tomatoes

4 **anchovy fillets,** minced

2 cloves **garlic,** minced

2 tbsp **extra-virgin olive oil**

2 tsp **red wine vinegar**

12 **fresh basil leaves,** torn

¼ tsp each **salt** and **pepper**

Peel off strips of eggplant skin lengthwise to create stripes; cut eggplant crosswise into ¾-inch (2 cm) thick rounds. Sprinkle all over with salt; let stand for 30 minutes. Between tea towels, press out liquid.

Cherry Tomato Sauce: Mix together tomatoes, anchovies, garlic, oil, vinegar, basil, salt and pepper; scrape onto heavy-duty foil. Seal to form packet. Grill, covered, over medium-high heat until saucy, 10 to 15 minutes.

Meanwhile, brush both sides of eggplant slices with oil. Grill, covered, on greased grill over medium-high heat until bottoms are golden, about 5 minutes. Turn and cover with cheese; grill until eggplant is tender, bottoms are golden and cheese is melted, 4 to 5 minutes. Transfer to platter; top with cherry tomato sauce.

Makes 4 to 6 servings.

PER EACH OF 6 SERVINGS: about 233 cal, 8 g pro, 18 g total fat (6 g sat. fat), 11 g carb, 3 g fibre, 19 mg chol, 595 mg sodium, 293 mg potassium. % RDI: 18% calcium, 6% iron, 11% vit A, 13% vit C, 10% folate.

Grilled Tofu & Vegetable Antipasto

Garlic plays a key role in this company-ready, vegetarian-friendly antipasto platter.

1 pkg (425 g) **firm tofu**

4 **portobello mushrooms**

4 **green onions,** trimmed

2 **zucchini,** cut in half lengthwise

1 each **sweet red pepper** and
    sweet yellow pepper, quartered

3 tbsp **extra-virgin olive oil**

1 tbsp chopped **fresh basil**

½ tsp each **salt** and **pepper**

BALSAMIC VINAIGRETTE:

3 tbsp **extra-virgin olive oil**

2 tbsp **balsamic vinegar**

1 clove **garlic,** minced

¼ tsp each **salt** and **pepper**

Balsamic Vinaigrette: Mix together oil, vinegar, garlic, salt and pepper.

Drain tofu on paper towels; cut in half lengthwise. Trim stems off mushrooms; place caps in large bowl along with onions, zucchini and red and yellow peppers.

Whisk together oil, basil, salt and pepper; brush 1 tbsp over tofu. Add remainder to vegetables; toss to coat.

Grill zucchini, red and yellow peppers, onions and tofu, covered, on greased grill over medium-high heat for 5 minutes. Turn vegetables and tofu; add mushrooms to grill. Grill, covered, turning mushrooms once, until vegetables are tender-crisp and tofu and mushrooms are browned, about 5 minutes.

Cut tofu into bite-size pieces. Cut zucchini diagonally into ½-inch (1 cm) thick slices. Thinly slice mushrooms. Arrange tofu and vegetables on platter; drizzle with balsamic vinaigrette.

Makes 4 servings.

PER SERVING: about 320 cal, 11 g pro, 25 g total fat (3 g sat. fat), 17 g carb, 4 g fibre, 0 mg chol, 448 mg sodium. % RDI: 19% calcium, 21% iron, 14% vit A, 163% vit C, 34% folate.

Grilled Pineapple

Don't worry about coring the pineapple for this recipe – just eat around it. Grilled pineapple is good with highly spiced or tart grills, especially chicken, pork or fish.

2 tbsp **vegetable oil**

¼ tsp each **salt** and **pepper**

¼ tsp **hot pepper sauce**

1 **pineapple,** peeled and cut into ½-inch (1 cm) thick slices

2 tbsp chopped **fresh cilantro**

Mix together oil, salt, pepper and hot pepper sauce; brush half over 1 side of each pineapple slice. Place, oiled side down, on greased grill over medium heat; brush with remaining oil mixture. Grill, covered and turning once, until browned, about 4 minutes.

Transfer to platter; sprinkle with cilantro.

Makes 8 servings.

PER SERVING: about 79 cal, trace pro, 3 g total fat (trace sat. fat), 13 g carb, 1 g fibre, 0 mg chol, 66 mg sodium. % RDI: 1% calcium, 3% iron, 20% vit C, 3% folate.

Grilled Halloumi & Tomato Kabobs

Halloumi, a tasty, salty cheese from Cypress, stands up well to grilling or frying because it softens but doesn't melt. You can find it in the cheese section of supermarkets or in specialty cheese shops.

24 **cherry tomatoes**

8 oz (225 g) **halloumi cheese,** cut into 16 pieces

1 cup packed **fresh basil leaves**

1 clove **garlic,** smashed

½ cup **olive oil**

½ tsp **pepper**

4 thick slices **oval rustic Italian bread**

Onto each of 8 skewers, alternately thread 3 cherry tomatoes and 2 pieces halloumi cheese. In blender, purée together basil, garlic, olive oil and pepper until smooth, about 30 seconds. Brush generously over kabobs, reserving remaining purée.

Grill kabobs on greased grill over medium heat, turning often, until tomatoes are softened and cheese starts to brown, about 8 minutes.

Meanwhile, grill bread, turning once, until golden, about 5 minutes. Remove from grill; brush with remaining purée. Serve kabobs on bread.

Makes 4 servings.

PER SERVING: about 575 cal, 17 g pro, 44 g total fat (14 g sat. fat), 30 g carb, 3 g fibre, 57 mg chol, 966 mg sodium, 276 mg potassium. % RDI: 34% calcium, 16% iron, 30% vit A, 17% vit C, 35% folate.

Grilled Mozzarella Skewers With Anchovy Sauce

Fresh mozzarella grilled to a perfect, barely oozing consistency between slices of crispy grilled bread – heavenly!

Ten ½-inch (1 cm) thick slices **baguette**

4 balls **bocconcini cheese,** about 4 oz (115 g) total, halved

ANCHOVY SAUCE:

2 tbsp **butter**

2 tbsp **olive oil**

2 **anchovy fillets,** finely chopped

1 tbsp finely chopped **fresh parsley**

1 tbsp drained **capers,** finely chopped

2 tsp **lemon juice**

Anchovy Sauce: In small saucepan over medium heat, cook butter, oil, anchovies, parsley, capers and lemon juice until butter is melted, about 2 minutes.

Beginning and ending with bread, alternately thread bread and cheese onto 2 long skewers.

Grill on greased grill over high heat, turning often, until bread is toasted and cheese is just beginning to melt, 4 to 5 minutes. Transfer to serving plate; drizzle with anchovy sauce.

Makes 2 servings.

PER SERVING: about 505 cal, 19 g pro, 40 g total fat (18 g sat. fat), 19 g carb, 1 g fibre, 83 mg chol, 830 mg sodium, 127 mg potassium. % RDI: 38% calcium, 10% iron, 23% vit A, 5% vit C, 15% folate.

Provoleta

Grilled cheese with chimichurri sauce is an Argentine specialty. Provolone comes in large, long cylinders, so have one thick slice cut to order at the cheese counter.

8 oz (225 g) **provolone cheese,** in 1 thick slice

1 tsp **olive oil**

1 tsp **dried oregano**

CHIMICHURRI SAUCE:

½ cup chopped **fresh parsley**

⅓ cup **olive oil**

2 cloves **garlic,** chopped

2 **shallots,** coarsely chopped

2 tbsp chopped **fresh oregano**

2 tbsp **lemon juice**

2 tbsp **sherry vinegar**

½ tsp each **salt** and **pepper**

Chimichurri Sauce: In food processor, pulse together parsley, oil, garlic, shallots, oregano, lemon juice, vinegar, salt and pepper until finely chopped.

Brush cheese all over with oil; sprinkle with oregano. Grill over medium heat, turning once, until cheese is hot, soft and not quite melting, about 4 minutes. Transfer to plate; drizzle with chimichurri sauce.

Makes 4 servings.

PER SERVING: about 404 cal, 17 g pro, 36 g total fat (13 g sat. fat), 5 g carb, 1 g fibre, 43 mg chol, 842 mg sodium, 183 mg potassium. % RDI: 46% calcium, 11% iron, 23% vit A, 22% vit C, 10% folate.

Halloumi With Fresh Chilies

Anointed with fragrant oil and flavourings, halloumi cheese makes a piquant eastern Mediterranean appetizer.

8 oz (225 g) **halloumi cheese,** cut into 8 scant ¼-inch (5 mm) thick slices

2 tbsp **olive oil**

1 tbsp thinly sliced **red hot pepper**

1 tsp minced **fresh cilantro**

1 tsp minced **fresh mint**

Grill cheese on greased grill over medium-high heat, turning once, until hot and grill marked, about 2 minutes.

Transfer to plate. Drizzle with oil; sprinkle with hot pepper, cilantro and mint.

Makes 4 servings.

PER SERVING: about 269 cal, 13 g pro, 23 g total fat (11 g sat. fat), 2 g carb, trace fibre, 63 mg chol, 751 mg sodium, 10 mg potassium. % RDI: 31% calcium, 1% iron, 21% vit A, 5% vit C.

Garlic Flatbread

Add Middle Eastern flair to any party with this soft-crusted golden flatbread, which is great for scooping dips or salsas (pages 517 to 525).

Pinch **granulated sugar**

¾ cup **warm water**

1 tsp **active dry yeast** or quick-rising (instant) yeast

3 tbsp **extra-virgin olive oil**

1¾ cups **all-purpose flour**

¾ tsp **salt**

1 clove **garlic,** minced

¼ tsp **dried mint** or oregano

In large bowl, dissolve sugar in warm water. Sprinkle in yeast; let stand until frothy, about 10 minutes. Whisk in 2 tbsp of the oil. Stir in flour, about ¼ cup at a time, and salt to form sticky dough.

Turn out dough onto lightly floured surface; knead until smooth, 5 minutes. Place in greased bowl, turning to grease all over; cover and let rise in warm draft-free place until doubled in bulk, about 1½ hours.

Turn out onto lightly floured surface; press fingertips into dough to create dimples. Gently stretch into 15- x 6-inch (38 x 15 cm) rectangle. Place on greased rimless baking sheet. Cover and let rise in warm draft-free place until nearly doubled in bulk, about 45 minutes.

Mix together remaining oil, garlic and mint; brush over flatbread. Grill, oiled side down, on greased grill over medium heat until bubbles form on top and grill marked underneath without charring, 3 to 6 minutes. Turn; grill, covered, just until surface is cooked but not browned, about 1 minute.

Makes 4 to 6 servings.

PER EACH OF 6 SERVINGS: about 195 cal, 4 g pro, 7 g total fat (1 g sat. fat), 28 g carb, 1 g fibre, 0 mg chol, 289 mg sodium. % RDI: 1% calcium, 14% iron, 41% folate.

Garlic Bread on the Grill

For a quick, easy and universally popular side, try this buttery garlic bread.

1 **baguette**

⅓ cup **butter**

3 cloves **garlic,** pressed or minced

Pinch **salt**

Scant ½ tsp **smoked paprika** or sweet paprika

Slice baguette crosswise almost but not all the way through at ¾-inch (2 cm) intervals; place on heavy-duty foil.

In small saucepan over low heat, melt butter; stir in garlic and salt. Simmer very gently until garlic infuses butter (do not let garlic brown), 3 to 4 minutes. Stir in paprika; cook for 30 seconds. Brush over both sides of each slice of baguette; brush any remaining butter mixture over top. Seal foil to make packet.

Grill, covered, over high heat, turning once, until crusty and hot, 10 to 12 minutes.

Makes 6 to 8 servings.

PER EACH OF 8 SERVINGS: about 166 cal, 3 g pro, 9 g total fat (5 g sat. fat), 19 g carb, 1 g fibre, 20 mg chol, 268 mg sodium, 49 mg potassium. % RDI: 3% calcium, 6% iron, 7% vit A, 12% folate.

Rapini & Garlic Pizza With Asiago Cheese

Rapini has a robust taste that pairs well with garlic. Italian Asiago is milder and creamier than Canadian or, especially, American Asiago, which tend to be sharp. You can tone it down by substituting Fontina or mozzarella for part of it.

1 bunch **rapini,** about 1¼ lb (565 g)

½ cup **bottled strained tomatoes** (passata) or canned crushed tomatoes

¼ cup + 1 tbsp **olive oil**

4 **anchovy fillets,** minced

3 cloves **garlic,** pressed or minced

¼ tsp **salt**

Pinch **hot pepper flakes**

1 to 1⅓ lb (450 to 600 g) **pizza dough**

2 cups shredded **Asiago cheese,** about 6 oz (170 g)

In large pot of boiling salted water, blanch rapini just until tender, about 2 minutes. Chill under cold water; drain, squeezing out excess moisture. Chop finely. Mix together rapini, tomatoes, ¼ cup of the oil, anchovies, garlic, salt and hot pepper flakes.

On lightly floured surface, stretch dough to roughly 16- x 12-inch (40 x 30 cm) rectangle. Brush with remaining oil. Grill, oiled side down, on greased grill over medium heat until bubbles form on top and grill marked underneath without charring, 3 to 6 minutes. Turn; grill, covered, just until surface is cooked but not browned, about 1 minute. Remove from grill; reduce heat to medium-low.

Spread rapini mixture over grilled side of crust; sprinkle with cheese. Grill, covered, until cheese is melted and bubbly and underside is browned, 3 to 8 minutes.

Makes 8 slices.

Before putting pizza dough down on the grill, make sure your barbecue is fully preheated. If dough forms large bubbles while cooking, pop them to flatten.

PER SLICE: about 338 cal, 14 g pro, 20 g total fat (7 g sat. fat), 29 g carb, 4 g fibre, 21 mg chol, 893 mg sodium, 249 mg potassium. % RDI: 31% calcium, 26% iron, 21% vit A, 16% vit C, 44% folate.

Swiss Chard Pizza

Big bunches of freshly picked Swiss chard beckon at harvest time (though nice chard is usually available year round). It makes a wonderful pizza topping when combined with just a few other simple flavourings.

1 bunch **Swiss chard,** about 1½ lb (675 g)

¼ cup **olive oil**

1 **Spanish onion** or large sweet onion, chopped

2 cloves **garlic,** minced

Pinch **salt**

⅓ cup chopped **black olives**

¼ cup lightly toasted **pine nuts**

1 to 1⅓ lb (450 to 600 g) **pizza dough**

2 cups shredded **Fontina cheese,** about 6 oz (170 g)

Pinch **pepper**

Tear chard leaves off stems. In large pot of boiling lightly salted water, boil stems for 6 minutes; add leaves and boil until tender, about 3 minutes. Chill under cold water; drain, squeezing out excess moisture. Chop.

In skillet, heat 3 tbsp of the oil over medium-high heat; sauté onion until lightly browned, 12 to 15 minutes. Add garlic and salt and sauté for 1 minute. Scrape over chard. Add olives and pine nuts; mix well.

On lightly floured surface, stretch dough to roughly 16- x 12-inch (40 x 30 cm) rectangle. Brush with remaining oil. Grill, oiled side down, on greased grill over medium heat until bubbles form on top and grill marked underneath without charring, 3 to 6 minutes. Turn; grill, covered, just until surface is cooked but not browned, about 1 minute. Remove from grill; reduce heat to medium-low.

Spread chard mixture over grilled side of crust; sprinkle with cheese and pepper. Grill, covered, until cheese is melted and bubbly and underside is browned, 3 to 8 minutes.

Makes 8 slices.

PER SLICE: about 358 cal, 12 g pro, 21 g total fat (6 g sat. fat), 33 g carb, 4 g fibre, 25 mg chol, 676 mg sodium, 874 mg potassium. % RDI: 19% calcium, 20% iron, 21% vit A, 10% vit C, 29% folate.

Grilled Pizza Mexicana

Grilled vegetables make a wonderful, earthy salsa that doubles as a pizza sauce. Try this summertime pizza with other toppings as well.

1 lb (450 g) **pizza dough**

2 tsp **olive oil**

8 oz (225 g) **fresh mozzarella cheese,** drained and sliced

GRILLED TOMATO SALSA:

6 **ripe plum tomatoes**

2 **jalapeño peppers**

Half **white onion**

4 cloves **garlic** (unpeeled)

2 soaked **dried chipotle peppers** or canned chipotles in adobo sauce, seeded

1 clove **garlic,** smashed

¾ tsp **salt**

⅓ cup chopped **fresh cilantro**

Grilled Tomato Salsa: Grill tomatoes, jalapeños, onion and unpeeled garlic, covered, on greased grill over medium-high heat, turning often, until tender and charred, 15 to 20 minutes. Let cool enough to handle.

Peel and core tomatoes, discarding juice; place in blender. Peel and seed jalapeños; add to blender. Remove charred layer of onion; chop onion and add to blender. Squeeze garlic from skin into blender. Add chipotles, smashed garlic and salt; blend until minced. Add cilantro; blend until almost puréed.

On lightly floured surface, stretch dough to roughly 16- x 12-inch (40 x 30 cm) rectangle. Brush with oil. Grill, oiled side down, on greased grill over medium heat until bubbles form on top and grill marked underneath without charring, 3 to 6 minutes. Turn; grill, covered, just until surface is cooked but not browned, about 1 minute. Remove from grill.

Spread ¾ cup of the grilled tomato salsa over grilled side of crust; top with cheese. Grill, covered, until cheese is melted and bubbly and underside is browned, 3 to 8 minutes. Serve with remaining salsa to spoon over top.

Makes 8 slices.

TIP

Out of chipotles? Substitute chipotle hot sauce to taste.

PER SLICE: about 265 cal, 12 g pro, 11 g total fat (5 g sat. fat), 31 g carb, 2 g fibre, 23 mg chol, 484 mg sodium, 226 mg potassium. % RDI: 23% calcium, 14% iron, 10% vit A, 13% vit C, 28% folate.

Grilled Corn Pizza

Grilling pizza makes especially good sense when some of the other ingredients are grilled, too, such as the corn and onion here.

1 **cob of corn**

Half **red onion,** thickly sliced

1 to 1⅓ lb (450 to 600 g) **pizza dough**

2 tsp **olive oil**

1½ cups shredded **provolone cheese** or mozzarella cheese, about 5 oz (140 g)

2 **plum tomatoes,** about 6 oz (170 g), thinly sliced

PESTO:

½ cup packed **fresh basil leaves**

2 tbsp grated **Parmesan cheese**

¼ tsp **salt**

2 tbsp **olive oil**

1 clove **garlic,** minced

Husk corn. Grill, covered, on greased grill over medium-high heat, turning occasionally, for 5 minutes. Skewer onion through edges to keep rings intact; add to grill. Grill, covered and turning occasionally, until onion and corn kernels are tender, about 10 minutes. Slice kernels off cob to make ¾ cup. Chop onion.

Pesto: In food processor, finely chop together basil, Parmesan cheese and salt; with motor running, drizzle oil through feed tube in steady stream until smooth and thickened. Stir in garlic.

On lightly floured surface, stretch dough to roughly 16- x 12-inch (40 x 30 cm) rectangle. Brush with oil. Grill, oiled side down, on greased grill over medium heat until bubbles form on top and grill marked underneath without charring, 3 to 6 minutes. Turn; grill, covered, just until surface is cooked but not browned, about 1 minute. Remove from grill.

Spread pesto over grilled side of crust; sprinkle with half of the cheese. Arrange tomatoes, onion and corn over top; sprinkle with remaining cheese. Grill, covered, until cheese is melted and bubbly and underside is browned, 3 to 8 minutes.

Makes 8 slices.

PER SLICE: about 294 cal, 12 g pro, 13 g total fat (5 g sat. fat), 35 g carb, 2 g fibre, 19 mg chol, 565 mg sodium. % RDI: 20% calcium, 12% iron, 10% vit A, 9% vit C, 15% folate.

Smoked Salmon Pizza With Marinated Onion

This fresh and elegant pizza is great to serve for brunch or cut into squares as an appetizer.

½ cup **sour cream**

2 tbsp chopped **fresh dill**

1 tsp **lemon juice**

Pinch each **salt** and **pepper**

1 to 1⅓ lb (450 to 600 g) **pizza dough**

2 tsp **olive oil**

7 oz (200 g) thinly sliced **cold-smoked salmon**

2 tsp drained **capers** (optional)

MARINATED ONION:

⅓ cup **white wine vinegar**

1 tbsp **granulated sugar**

½ tsp **salt**

1 **large red onion,** halved and thinly sliced

Marinated Onion: In small saucepan, bring vinegar, ⅓ cup water, sugar and salt to boil, stirring until sugar is dissolved. In heatproof bowl, pour over onion; let stand for 30 minutes, stirring occasionally. Cover; refrigerate for 4 hours or up to 1 week. Drain before using.

Mix together sour cream, half of the dill, the lemon juice, salt and pepper; set aside in refrigerator.

On lightly floured surface, stretch dough to roughly 16- x 12-inch (40 x 30 cm) rectangle. Brush with oil. Grill, oiled side down, on greased grill over medium heat until bubbles form on top and grill marked underneath without charring, 3 to 6 minutes. Turn; grill, covered, until bubbly and underside is browned, 3 to 5 minutes. Remove from grill.

Spread sour cream mixture over crust; top with salmon. Top with ½ cup drained marinated onion (save remainder for another use); sprinkle with remaining dill, and capers (if using).

Makes 8 slices.

PER SLICE: about 221 cal, 9 g pro, 8 g total fat (3 g sat. fat), 28 g carb, 2 g fibre, 12 mg chol, 500 mg sodium, 156 mg potassium. % RDI: 7% calcium, 14% iron, 2% vit A, 2% vit C, 25% folate.

Zucchini Pizza With Fresh Tomato Sauce

Caciocavallo cheese is a stretched-curd cheese that is creamier than provolone and more flavourful than mozzarella because of its light curing; it has a distinctive shape similar to that of a bottle gourd. Provolone and mozzarella are good substitutes.

1 lb (450 g) **zucchini,** sliced

¾ tsp **salt**

2 cups strained finely chopped peeled seeded **ripe tomatoes,** about 1½ lb (675 g)

4 **green onions,** thinly sliced

2 **hot finger peppers,** seeded and minced

⅓ cup grated **Parmesan cheese**

¼ cup chopped **fresh parsley**

¼ cup **olive oil**

¾ tsp **dried oregano**

Pinch **pepper**

1 to 1⅓ lb (450 to 600 g) **pizza dough**

1½ cups shredded **caciocavallo cheese,** about 5 oz (140 g)

3 oz (85 g) sliced **salami**

Toss zucchini with ½ tsp of the salt; let stand for 20 minutes. Using hands, squeeze out as much moisture as possible without breaking slices.

Meanwhile, mix together tomatoes, onions, hot peppers, Parmesan cheese, half of the parsley, 3 tbsp of the oil, the oregano, pepper and remaining salt.

On lightly floured surface, stretch dough to roughly 16- x 12-inch (40 x 30 cm) rectangle. Brush with remaining oil. Grill, oiled side down, on greased grill over medium heat until bubbles form on top and grill marked underneath without charring, 3 to 6 minutes. Turn; grill, covered, just until surface is cooked but not browned, 1 minute. Remove from grill; reduce heat to medium-low.

Spread tomato mixture over grilled side of crust; top with zucchini. Sprinkle with cheese; top with salami. Grill, covered, until cheese is melted and bubbly and underside is browned, 3 to 8 minutes. Sprinkle with remaining parsley.

Makes 8 slices.

TIP

Use sweet, ripe tomatoes for this fresh sauce; you'll need about 4 field tomatoes or 6 to 8 plum (Roma) tomatoes. Loosen the skin by plunging the tomatoes into boiling water for about 20 seconds.

PER SLICE: about 354 cal, 14 g pro, 20 g total fat (7 g sat. fat), 32 g carb, 3 g fibre, 26 mg chol, 775 mg sodium, 436 mg potassium. % RDI: 26% calcium, 20% iron, 19% vit A, 23% vit C, 34% folate.

Barbecued Chicken Pizza

Grilled chicken and barbecue sauce are fabulous, unexpected pizza toppings. Canned pizza sauce is easy to use, but this homemade sauce is much tastier.

1 **boneless skinless chicken breast**

1 tbsp **vegetable oil**

Pinch each **salt** and **pepper**

2 tbsp **barbecue sauce**

1 to 1⅓ lb (450 to 600 g) **whole wheat pizza dough**

½ cup **Tomato Pizza Sauce** (right)

1¼ cups shredded **Cheddar cheese** or Monterey Jack cheese

⅓ cup diced **sweet red pepper**

⅓ cup thinly sliced **green onions**

Brush chicken with 1 tsp of the oil; sprinkle with salt and pepper. Grill, covered, on greased grill over medium-high heat, turning once, until no longer pink inside, 12 minutes. Let cool slightly; thinly slice. Toss with barbecue sauce.

On floured surface, stretch dough to 16- x 12-inch (40 x 30 cm) rectangle. Brush with remaining oil. Grill, oiled side down, on greased grill over medium heat until bubbles form on top and grill marked underneath, 3 to 6 minutes. Turn; grill, covered, just until surface is cooked but not browned, 1 minute. Remove from grill; reduce heat to medium-low. Spread pizza sauce over grilled side; top with half of the cheese. Sprinkle with pepper, onions and chicken; top with remaining cheese. Grill, covered, until cheese is melted and underside is browned, 3 to 8 minutes.

Makes 8 slices.

Tomato Pizza Sauce

Reserving juice, drain, seed and chop 1 can (28 oz/ 796 mL) tomatoes. In saucepan, heat 2 tbsp olive oil over medium heat. Fry ½ cup finely chopped onion; 2 cloves garlic, minced; and ½ tsp dried oregano, stirring, until onion is translucent, 4 minutes. Add tomatoes and juice; ½ tsp red wine vinegar; ¼ tsp each salt and pepper; and pinch granulated sugar. Simmer until thickened, 15 to 20 minutes. Let cool slightly; purée until smooth.

Makes 2 cups.

PER SLICE: about 253 cal, 14 g pro, 11 g total fat (4 g sat. fat), 30 g carb, 5 g fibre, 26 mg chol, 525 mg sodium, 139 mg potassium. % RDI: 15% calcium, 13% iron, 7% vit A, 23% vit C, 4% folate.

Grilled Steak & Gorgonzola Pizza

Freshly grilled steak works best here, but leftover steak is good, too. Not a fan of Gorgonzola? Sprinkle with 1¼ cups shredded mozzarella instead.

6 oz (170 g) **beef grilling steak**

¼ tsp each **salt** and **pepper**

1 **small red onion,** cut into ½-inch (1 cm) thick slices

1 tbsp **vegetable oil**

1 to 1⅓ lb (450 to 600 g) **pizza dough**

3 oz (85 g) thinly sliced or crumbled **Gorgonzola cheese**

½ cup packed **arugula leaves**

SUN-DRIED TOMATO PESTO:

½ cup **boiling water**

¼ cup **dry-packed sun-dried tomatoes**

2 tbsp **pine nuts**

1½ tbsp **tomato paste**

Pinch each **salt** and **pepper**

2½ tbsp **extra-virgin olive oil**

2 tbsp grated **Parmesan cheese**

Half clove **garlic,** minced

Sun-Dried Tomato Pesto: In heatproof bowl, pour boiling water over tomatoes; soak until softened, 10 minutes. Reserving 2 tbsp soaking liquid, drain. Meanwhile, in dry skillet, toast pine nuts over medium heat, shaking often, until light golden, 3 to 5 minutes. Let cool. In food processor, finely chop together tomatoes, soaking liquid, pine nuts, tomato paste, salt and pepper; with motor running, drizzle oil through feed tube in thin steady stream until smooth and thickened. Pulse in Parmesan cheese and garlic.

Sprinkle steak with half each of the salt and pepper. Grill, covered, on greased grill over medium-high heat, turning once, until medium-rare, 8 minutes. Let stand for 5 minutes; slice thinly. Meanwhile, skewer onion through edges. Brush with 1 tsp of the oil; sprinkle with remaining salt and pepper. Grill, covered and turning once, until softened, 5 minutes. Chop coarsely.

On lightly floured surface, stretch dough to 16- x 12-inch (40 x 30 cm) rectangle. Brush with remaining oil. Grill, oiled side down, on greased grill over medium heat until bubbles form on top and grill marked underneath without charring, 3 to 6 minutes. Turn; grill, covered, just until surface is cooked but not browned, 1 minute. Remove from grill; reduce heat to medium-low. Spread pesto over crust; top with onion, steak and cheese. Grill, covered, until cheese is melted and underside is browned, 3 to 8 minutes. Top with arugula.

Makes 8 slices.

PER SLICE: about 321 cal, 12 g pro, 17 g total fat (5 g sat. fat), 30 g carb, 2 g fibre, 22 mg chol, 593 mg sodium, 283 mg potassium. % RDI: 14% calcium, 19% iron, 5% vit A, 3% vit C, 29% folate.

Caprese Pizza With Bacon

Inspired by Caprese salad, this pizza features its basic components: tomatoes, creamy fresh mozzarella and basil. Look for fresh mozzarella or bocconcini cheeses in sealed bags or tubs of water at deli counters. Be sure to dry them well.

6 slices **bacon,** halved

4 oz (115 g) **fresh mozzarella cheese,** drained well

1 to 1⅓ lb (450 to 600 g) **pizza dough**

2 tsp **extra-virgin olive oil**

1 **tomato,** cut into ¼-inch (5 mm) thick slices

2 tbsp sliced **fresh basil**

BASIL PESTO:

2 tbsp **pine nuts**

1 cup packed **fresh basil leaves**

Pinch each **salt** and **pepper**

2½ tbsp **extra-virgin olive oil**

¼ cup grated **Parmesan cheese**

Half clove **garlic,** minced

Basil Pesto: In dry skillet, toast pine nuts over medium heat, shaking often, until light golden, 3 to 5 minutes. Let cool. In food processor, finely chop together pine nuts, basil, salt and pepper; with motor running, drizzle oil through feed tube in thin steady stream until smooth and thickened. Pulse in Parmesan cheese and garlic.

In skillet, cook bacon over medium heat until still slightly chewy, about 8 minutes. Drain on paper towel–lined plate. Cut mozzarella into ¼-inch (5 mm) thick rounds. Drain on separate paper towel–lined plate; pat dry.

On lightly floured surface, stretch dough to roughly 16- x 12-inch (40 x 30 cm) rectangle. Brush with oil. Grill, oiled side down, on greased grill over medium heat until bubbles form on top and grill marked underneath without charring, 3 to 6 minutes. Turn; grill, covered, just until surface is cooked but not browned, 1 minute. Remove from grill; reduce heat to medium-low.

Spread basil pesto over grilled side of crust; top with tomato, bacon and cheese. Grill, covered, until cheese is melted and bubbly and underside is browned, 3 to 8 minutes. Sprinkle with basil.

Makes 8 slices.

PER SLICE: about 301 cal, 11 g pro, 17 g total fat (5 g sat. fat), 27 g carb, 2 g fibre, 20 mg chol, 520 mg sodium, 187 mg potassium. % RDI: 17% calcium, 15% iron, 7% vit A, 5% vit C, 25% folate.

Sausage & Grilled Pepper Pizza

This simple grilled pepper sauce can be used as the base for many other kinds of pizza – use your imagination and experiment.

2 **sweet red peppers**

2 **Italian sausages,** about 8 oz (225 g) total

2 cloves **garlic,** smashed

3 tbsp **extra-virgin olive oil**

½ tsp **salt**

1 to 1⅓ lb (450 to 600 g) **pizza dough**

1 **green hot pepper,** thinly sliced (or half green sweet pepper, chopped)

¾ cup grated **Romano cheese** or other pecorino cheese

Grill peppers and sausages on greased grill over high heat, turning often, until pepper is charred all over and sausage is firm and almost cooked through. Place peppers in bowl; cover and let cool. Peel and seed peppers. Let sausage cool; slice thinly.

In food processor, purée together grilled peppers, garlic, 2 tbsp of the oil and the salt.

On lightly floured surface, stretch dough to roughly 16- x 12-inch (40 x 30 cm) rectangle. Brush with remaining oil. Grill, oiled side down, on greased grill over medium heat until bubbles form on top and grill marked underneath without charring, 3 to 6 minutes. Turn; grill, covered, just until surface is cooked but not browned, about 1 minute. Remove from grill; reduce heat to medium-low.

Spread pepper sauce over grilled side of crust; top with sausage, hot pepper and cheese. Grill, covered, until cheese is melted and underside is browned, 3 to 8 minutes.

Makes 8 slices.

PER SLICE: about 428 cal, 15 g pro, 18 g total fat (6 g sat. fat), 52 g carb, 2 g fibre, 30 mg chol, 1,001 mg sodium. % RDI: 14% calcium, 21% iron, 14% vit A, 88% vit C, 17% folate.

Grilled Vegetable
Quinoa Salad
(page 499)

salads & sides

Tangy Coleslaw | 475

Indian-Spiced Coleslaw | 477

Creamy Coleslaw | 478

Red Cabbage Coleslaw | 479

Creamy Potato Salad | 480

Sweet Pea & Potato Salad | 481

Dilled Potato & Grilled Corn Salad | 482

Roasted Two-Potato Salad | 484

Warm Potato Salad | 485

Baby Potato Salad
   With Salsa Verde | 486

Smashed Potato Salad | 487

Garlic Beets | 489

Baked Beans | 490

Spanish-Style Baked Beans | 491

Frijoles Borrachos | 494

Baked Chili Black Beans | 495

Grilled Corn Polenta With
   Roasted Red Peppers | 496

Cajun Corn Sauté | 497

Grilled Vegetable Quinoa Salad | 499

Tangy Macaroni Salad | 500

Cool Wild Rice & Mushrooms | 501

Mediterranean Barley Rice Salad | 502

Grilled Vegetable
   & Israeli Couscous Salad | 504

Greek Village Salad | 505

Three-Bean Salad | 506

Green Bean, Mushroom
   & Fennel Salad | 509

Filipino Cucumber Salad | 510

Creamy Cucumber Salad | 512

Carrot & Peanut Salad | 513

Tangy Coleslaw

This pleasingly tart coleslaw, made without mayonnaise and with just a touch of oil, is a good accompaniment to most grilled foods.

8 cups shredded **cabbage**

1¼ tsp **salt**

1 **sweet red pepper,** thinly sliced

Half **red onion,** thinly sliced

1 tbsp chopped **fresh dill**
   (or 1 tsp dried)

¼ cup **red wine vinegar**

1 tbsp **granulated sugar**

1 tbsp **vegetable oil**

1 tsp **dry mustard**

¾ tsp **celery seeds**

¼ tsp **pepper**

Toss cabbage with 1 tsp of the salt. In separate bowl, toss red pepper with remaining salt. Let both stand until cabbage is soft, 1 to 2 hours. Drain cabbage; squeeze out excess moisture. Toss together drained cabbage, undrained red pepper, onion and dill.

Whisk together vinegar, sugar, oil, mustard, celery seeds and pepper; toss with cabbage mixture until coated. Let stand for 20 minutes or, covered and refrigerated, up to 4 days.

Makes 8 servings.

PER SERVING: about 55 cal, 1 g pro, 2 g total fat (trace sat. fat), 9 g carb, 2 g fibre, 0 mg chol, 372 mg sodium. % RDI: 4% calcium, 5% iron, 9% vit A, 105% vit C, 22% folate.

Indian-Spiced Coleslaw

A nice change from regular coleslaw, this salad adds a brightly flavoured accent to almost any grilled meat or poultry.

8 cups shredded **cabbage**

1 cup **carrot** fine julienne or shredded carrots

½ cup thinly sliced **red onion**

2 **green hot peppers,** seeded and thinly sliced

2 tbsp **peanut oil** or vegetable oil

1 tbsp black or brown **mustard seeds**

1 tsp **cumin seeds**

½ cup **lemon juice**

2 tbsp **malt vinegar**

½ tsp **salt**

Pinch **granulated sugar**

⅓ cup chopped **fresh cilantro**

¼ cup chopped **fresh mint**

Toss together cabbage, carrots, onion and hot peppers. In small skillet, heat oil over medium heat; fry mustard and cumin seeds until mustard seeds turn grey and begin to pop. Scrape over cabbage mixture; toss well.

Whisk together lemon juice, vinegar, salt and sugar until sugar is dissolved; toss with cabbage mixture. Let stand for 20 minutes or, covered and refrigerated, up to 4 days. Just before serving, toss in cilantro and mint.

Makes 8 to 12 servings.

PER EACH OF 12 SERVINGS: about 46 cal, 1 g pro, 3 g total fat (trace sat. fat), 5 g carb, 2 g fibre, 0 mg chol, 114 mg sodium. % RDI: 3% calcium, 6% iron, 13% vit A, 33% vit C, 13% folate.

Creamy Coleslaw

Fennel gives this coleslaw an added crunch with just a hint of licorice flavour.

6 cups finely shredded **cabbage**

4 **green onions,** thinly sliced

2 ribs **celery,** thinly sliced

1 **large carrot,** finely diced

Half **fennel bulb,** thinly sliced

Half **sweet red pepper,** thinly sliced

⅓ cup **mayonnaise**

⅓ cup **light sour cream**

1 tbsp **Dijon mustard**

1 tbsp **cider vinegar**

2 tsp **granulated sugar**

½ tsp **celery seeds**

½ tsp each **salt** and **pepper**

Toss together cabbage, green onions, celery, carrot, fennel and red pepper. Mix together mayonnaise, sour cream, mustard, vinegar, sugar, celery seeds, salt and pepper; toss with cabbage mixture until coated. Let stand for 20 minutes or, covered and refrigerated, up to 4 days.

Makes 8 servings.

To make coleslaw prep easy, use a mandoline to slice the hard vegetables paper-thin.

PER SERVING: about 111 cal, 1 g pro, 8 g total fat (2 g sat. fat), 8 g carb, 3 g fibre, 6 mg chol, 258 mg sodium. % RDI: 6% calcium, 5% iron, 46% vit A, 75% vit C, 20% folate.

Red Cabbage Coleslaw

With vibrant slivers of red cabbage and red onion, this crimson coleslaw is a colourful keeper that you can make ahead.

10 cups shredded **red cabbage**

1½ tsp **salt**

Half **red onion,** very thinly sliced

2 **large red apples,** cut into julienne

½ tsp **caraway seeds**

⅓ cup **cider vinegar**

2 tbsp **yellow mustard**

2 tbsp **vegetable oil**

1 tbsp **granulated sugar**

Generous ¼ tsp **pepper**

6 slices crisp cooked **bacon,**
    crumbled

Toss cabbage with salt; let stand until soft, about 2 hours. Drain; squeeze out excess moisture. Toss together cabbage, onion, apples and caraway seeds.

Whisk together vinegar, mustard, oil, sugar and pepper; toss with cabbage mixture until coated. Let stand for 20 minutes or, covered and refrigerated, up to 4 days. Just before serving, toss in bacon.

Makes 8 servings.

PER SERVING: about 135 cal, 4 g pro, 7 g total fat (1 g sat. fat), 18 g carb, 4 g fibre, 4 mg chol, 345 mg sodium. % RDI: 5% calcium, 6% iron, 1% vit A, 90% vit C, 11% folate.

Creamy Potato Salad

Classic and much-loved by all, creamy potato salad is perfect with everything, from backyard burgers to barbecued chicken to slow-grilled ribs.

2 lb (900 g) **potatoes**

2 tbsp **cider vinegar**

½ tsp each **salt** and **pepper**

¾ cup **mayonnaise**

2 tbsp **milk**

1 cup coarsely chopped **celery** (about 2 ribs)

½ cup sliced **green onions** (about 2)

In pot of boiling salted water, cover and cook unpeeled potatoes until tender, 20 to 30 minutes. Drain. While still warm, peel; cut into large bite-size pieces. Gently toss together potatoes, vinegar, salt and pepper until coated. Let cool.

In large bowl, whisk mayonnaise with milk; gently toss in potato mixture, celery and green onions, breaking up potatoes as little as possible. *(Make-ahead: Cover and refrigerate for up to 1 day.)*

Makes 8 servings.

PER SERVING: about 459 cal, 4 g pro, 33 g total fat (5 g sat. fat), 39 g carb, 4 g fibre, 16 mg chol, 966 mg sodium, 802 mg potassium. % RDI: 4% calcium, 8% iron, 6% vit A, 43% vit C, 18% folate.

Sweet Pea & Potato Salad

This salad is also delicious made with fresh peas rather than sugar snaps; use 2 to 3 cups shelled peas.

4 cups **sugar snap peas**

1½ lb (675 g) **small red new potatoes**

1 cup chopped **green onions**

½ tsp each **salt** and **pepper**

2 tbsp **white wine vinegar**

2 tbsp **dry white wine**

2 tsp **Dijon mustard**

1½ cups diced **cucumber**

½ cup diced **radishes**

3 tbsp **vegetable oil**

Pull strings off both edges of peas. In large saucepan of boiling salted water, blanch until tender-crisp, 2 to 3 minutes. Chill under cold water; drain. Cut each pod crosswise into 3 or 4 pieces.

In pot of boiling salted water, cover and cook unpeeled potatoes until tender, 15 to 20 minutes. While still hot, quarter; transfer to large bowl. Toss in onions, salt and pepper. Mix together vinegar, wine and mustard; toss with potato mixture until coated. Let cool. Toss in peas, cucumber, radishes and oil.

Makes 8 to 10 servings.

PER EACH OF 10 SERVINGS: about 123 cal, 4 g pro, 4 g total fat (1 g sat. fat), 18 g carb, 4 g fibre, 0 mg chol, 363 mg sodium. % RDI: 3% calcium, 10% iron, 5% vit A, 37% vit C, 17% folate.

Dilled Potato & Grilled Corn Salad

Grilling the corn "naked" (without the husk) gives it a particularly smoky flavour and attractive grill marks.

4 **cobs of corn,** husked

3 tbsp **vegetable oil**

2 lb (900 g) **small red potatoes** or small white potatoes (about 30), peeled

4 **green onions,** sliced

2 tsp **grainy mustard**

½ tsp **salt**

¼ tsp **pepper**

¼ cup **red wine vinegar**

2 tbsp chopped **fresh dill**

Brush corn with 1 tbsp of the oil. Grill, covered, on greased grill over medium-high heat, turning often, until tender and slightly charred, 10 to 15 minutes. Let cool. Cut off kernels.

Meanwhile, in large saucepan of boiling salted water, cover and cook potatoes until tender, about 15 minutes. Drain and halve.

Toss together corn, potatoes, onions, mustard, salt and pepper; sprinkle with vinegar and toss well. Let cool.

Add remaining oil and dill; toss to coat.

Makes 6 to 8 servings.

PER EACH OF 8 SERVINGS: about 197 cal, 4 g pro, 6 g total fat (1 g sat. fat), 34 g carb, 4 g fibre, 0 mg chol, 400 mg sodium, 641 mg potassium. % RDI: 2% calcium, 10% iron, 2% vit A, 37% vit C, 22% folate.

Roasted Two-Potato Salad

This sunny-coloured potato salad tastes as savoury-sweet as it looks.

2 lb (900 g) **yellow-fleshed potatoes,** peeled and cut into 1-inch (2.5 cm) cubes

1½ lb (675 g) **sweet potatoes,** peeled and cut into 1-inch (2.5 cm) cubes

⅓ cup **extra-virgin olive oil**

½ tsp **dried thyme**

½ tsp each **salt** and **pepper**

¼ cup chopped **fresh parsley**

2 tbsp **lemon juice**

1 tbsp **Dijon mustard**

½ tsp **hot pepper sauce**

4 **green onions,** sliced

4 slices crisp cooked **bacon** (optional), crumbled

Toss together potatoes, sweet potatoes, ¼ cup of the oil, thyme, salt and pepper.

Spread potatoes in large roasting pan; roast in 375°F (190°C) oven, turning halfway through, until tender and golden, about 40 minutes. Let stand for 5 minutes.

In large bowl, toss together potatoes, parsley, lemon juice, mustard, hot pepper sauce, green onions, bacon (if using), and remaining oil. *(Make-ahead: Cover and refrigerate for up to 1 day; bring to room temperature before serving.)*

Makes 8 servings.

PER SERVING: about 216 cal, 3 g pro, 9 g total fat (1 g sat. fat), 31 g carb, 4 g fibre, 0 mg chol, 200 mg sodium, 718 mg potassium. % RDI: 4% calcium, 12% iron, 120% vit A, 45% vit C, 9% folate.

Warm Potato Salad

This simple, classic salad pairs well with just about any grilled meat.

3 lb (1.35 kg) **potatoes,** peeled and cut into large chunks

⅓ cup **extra-virgin olive oil**

3 tbsp **wine vinegar**

1½ tbsp **Dijon mustard** or spicy brown mustard

¾ tsp **salt**

Generous ¼ tsp **pepper**

¾ cup diced **celery**

¾ cup diced **sweet green pepper**

3 tbsp chopped **fresh basil** or parsley

In pot of boiling salted water, cover and cook potatoes until tender, 10 to 15 minutes. Drain; transfer to large bowl. Let cool for 10 minutes.

Whisk together oil, vinegar, mustard, salt and pepper; pour over potatoes. Gently toss in celery, green pepper and basil until coated.

Makes 8 servings.

PER SERVING: about 205 cal, 2 g pro, 11 g total fat (2 g sat. fat), 27 g carb, 2 g fibre, 0 mg chol, 563 mg sodium. % RDI: 2% calcium, 5% iron, 2% vit A, 38% vit C, 8% folate.

Baby Potato Salad With Salsa Verde

Using small waxy new potatoes in this salad means you can leave them whole for a pretty presentation.

3 lb (1.35 kg) **small new potatoes**

1 cup chopped **fresh parsley**

2 **anchovy fillets,** rinsed (or 1 tsp anchovy paste)

¼ cup **extra-virgin olive oil**

4 tsp **wine vinegar**

1 tbsp rinsed drained **capers**

1 clove **garlic,** minced

1 tsp **salt**

½ tsp **pepper**

In pot of boiling salted water, cover and cook unpeeled potatoes until tender, about 15 minutes. Drain. While still warm, peel potatoes; place in large bowl.

Meanwhile, in blender or food processor, purée together parsley, anchovies, ⅓ cup water, oil, vinegar, capers, garlic, salt and pepper; gently toss with warm potatoes until coated. Let cool to room temperature. *(Make-ahead: Cover and refrigerate for up to 1 day; bring to room temperature before serving.)*

Makes 8 servings.

PER SERVING: about 176 cal, 3 g pro, 7 g total fat (1 g sat. fat), 27 g carb, 2 g fibre, 0 mg chol, 618 mg sodium. % RDI: 2% calcium, 7% iron, 4% vit A, 40% vit C, 12% folate.

Smashed Potato Salad

Chunky potatoes and chopped eggs are tasty partners in this picnic-staple salad. You can use sweet or sour gherkin pickles, depending on your preference.

3 **eggs**

4 **large potatoes,** about 1½ lb (675 g), peeled

Half **Vidalia onion** or other sweet onion, finely chopped

2 ribs **celery,** diced

½ cup diced **gherkin pickles**

½ cup **mayonnaise**

2 tbsp **Dijon mustard**

1 tbsp **cider vinegar**

¾ tsp **salt**

½ tsp **pepper**

¼ tsp **sweet paprika**

Place eggs in saucepan; pour in enough cold water to cover eggs by at least 1 inch (2.5 cm). Cover and bring to boil over high heat; remove from heat and let stand for 20 minutes.

Meanwhile, in pot of boiling salted water, cover and cook potatoes until tender, about 15 minutes. Drain; coarsely chop into chunks. Place in large bowl.

Peel and chop eggs. Add to potatoes along with onion, celery and pickles, breaking up slightly with potato masher.

Whisk together mayonnaise, mustard, vinegar, salt, pepper and paprika. Add to potato mixture, mixing well. Cover and refrigerate until chilled, about 1 hour.

Makes 8 servings.

PER SERVING: about 208 cal, 4 g pro, 13 g total fat (2 g sat. fat), 20 g carb, 2 g fibre, 75 mg chol, 634 mg sodium, 315 mg potassium. % RDI: 3% calcium, 6% iron, 5% vit A, 12% vit C, 11% folate.

Garlic Beets

If you buy beets with bushy greens attached, you can whip up a second side: steam the washed greens, covered, in a skillet for 3 minutes, then drizzle with sesame oil.

2 lb (900 g) **beets** (with greens)

2 cloves **garlic**

¼ tsp **salt**

3 tbsp **extra-virgin olive oil**

2 tbsp **red wine vinegar**

Pinch **coarsely ground pepper**

Trim beets, leaving roots and about 1 inch (2.5 cm) of stem attached (reserve greens for another use). In large saucepan of boiling salted water, cook beets until fork-tender, about 40 minutes. Chill under cold running water. Trim off roots and stems; slip off skins. Cut beets into quarters or sixths.

On cutting board, coarsely chop garlic; sprinkle with salt. With flat side of knife or fork, mash into paste. Transfer to bowl; whisk in oil, vinegar and pepper. Toss with beets. Let stand for 1 hour or, covered and refrigerated, up to 24 hours. Serve at room temperature.

Makes 3 cups.

PER ¼ CUP: about 45 cal, 1 g pro, 3 g total fat (1 g sat. fat), 3 g carb, 1 g fibre, 0 mg chol, 151 mg sodium, 103 mg potassium. % RDI: 1% calcium, 2% iron, 2% vit C, 12% folate.

Baked Beans

*Traditional baked beans are a wonderfully satisfying side for any barbecue,
and are particularly tasty with smoked meats.*

1 lb (450 g) **dried navy beans** (2⅓ cups)

⅔ cup **bottled strained tomatoes** (passata)

⅓ cup packed **brown sugar**

⅓ cup **cooking molasses** or blackstrap molasses

1 tbsp **sodium-reduced soy sauce**

1 tsp **dry mustard**

½ tsp **salt**

1 **sweet onion,** chopped

6 oz (170 g) **slab bacon** or salt pork (or a combination), diced

Soak beans overnight in enough water to cover well (for quicker prep, see Tip, below); drain. In large saucepan, combine beans with enough water to cover by 2 inches (5 cm); bring to boil. Reduce heat, cover and simmer until tender, 30 to 40 minutes.

Reserving 2 cups of the cooking liquid, drain beans. Place beans and reserved liquid in bean pot or 12- to 16-cup (3 to 4 L) casserole dish; mix in tomatoes, brown sugar, molasses, soy sauce, mustard and salt. Stir in onion and bacon.

Cover and bake in 300°F (150°C) oven for 2 hours. Uncover and bake until sauce is thickened and coats beans, about 2 hours.

Makes 8 servings.

TIP

If you don't have time to soak your dried beans overnight, boil them for 5 minutes. Remove from heat; cover and let stand for 1 hour. Drain. Continue with recipe.

PER SERVING: about 403 cal, 14 g pro, 13 g total fat (6 g sat. fat), 59 g carb, 10 g fibre, 16 mg chol, 462 mg sodium, 812 mg potassium. % RDI: 13% calcium, 34% iron, 5% vit C, 89% folate.

Spanish-Style Baked Beans

Smoked paprika is a Spanish specialty available at gourmet stores. You can use sweet paprika if it's unavailable, but the dish won't have the same smoky edge.

1 lb (450 g) **dried navy beans** or other white beans (2⅓ cups)

1 can (28 oz/796 mL) **tomatoes,** drained

1 **bay leaf**

1 sprig **fresh rosemary**

2½ tsp **smoked paprika**

1½ tsp **salt**

⅓ cup **extra-virgin olive oil**

3 cups chopped **Spanish onion** or sweet onion

3 cloves **garlic,** minced

Soak beans overnight in enough water to cover well (for quicker prep, see Tip, opposite); drain. In large saucepan, combine beans with enough water to cover by 2 inches (5 cm); bring to boil. Reduce heat, cover and simmer until tender, 30 to 40 minutes.

Reserving 2 cups of the cooking liquid, drain beans. Place beans and 1⅓ cups of the reserved cooking liquid in large bowl. Seed tomatoes; chop coarsely. Add to bowl along with bay leaf, rosemary, paprika and salt; mix well.

In skillet, heat oil over medium heat; sauté onion and garlic until onion is soft, about 10 minutes. Scrape into bowl; mix well.

Scrape bean mixture into bean pot or 12- to 16-cup (3 to 4 L) casserole dish. Cover and bake in 400°F (200°C) oven until simmering, about 25 minutes. Reduce heat to 300°F (150°C); bake for 3 hours, checking occasionally and adding a little more of the reserved cooking liquid if beans are dry.

Makes 8 servings.

PER SERVING: about 308 cal, 14 g pro, 11 g total fat (2 g sat. fat), 44 g carb, 11 g fibre, 0 mg chol, 525 mg sodium. % RDI: 12% calcium, 29% iron, 8% vit A, 23% vit C, 90% folate.

Spanish-Style Baked Beans (page 491)

Frijoles Borrachos

These Northern Mexican–style "drunken beans" are also popular in Tex-Mex cooking. Use any leftover beans for refried beans or as a topping for tostadas or tortilla chips.

1 lb (450 g) **dried pinto beans** (2⅓ cups)

2 **white onions,** chopped

6 slices **bacon,** chopped

4 **jalapeño peppers,** finely chopped

5 cloves **garlic,** minced

1 cup chopped **fresh cilantro**

1 cup chopped canned or peeled **ripe tomatoes**

2 cups **dark beer**

1¼ tsp **salt**

Soak beans overnight in enough water to cover well (for quicker prep, see Tip, page 490); drain. In large saucepan, combine beans, 10 cups water and half of the onions; bring to boil. Reduce heat and simmer over medium heat, adding more water if necessary to keep beans covered, until beans are tender, 1 to 1½ hours.

In large saucepan or Dutch oven, fry bacon over medium-high heat until fat begins to render, 2 to 3 minutes. Add remaining onions; fry until lightly browned, about 8 minutes. Add jalapeños, garlic and cilantro; fry for 2 minutes. Add tomatoes, beans with cooking liquid, beer and salt. Bring to boil; reduce heat to medium and simmer, stirring occasionally, until thickened, 45 to 60 minutes.

Makes 8 servings.

PER SERVING: about 321 cal, 15 g pro, 9 g total fat (5 g sat. fat), 47 g carb, 14 g fibre, 12 mg chol, 522 mg sodium. % RDI: 9% calcium, 32% iron, 3% vit A, 23% vit C, 119% folate.

Baked Chili Black Beans

Various chili peppers flavour these beans: smoky and hot chipotles, bright and fresh jalapeños, and sweet and earthy ancho peppers.

1 lb (450 g) **dried black beans** (2⅓ cups)

1 cup **canned diced tomatoes** with juice

¼ cup **fancy molasses**

3 **canned chipotles in adobo sauce,** seeded and minced

1 tbsp **adobo sauce** from canned chipotles

2 **jalapeño peppers,** seeded and diced

1 **onion,** finely grated

1 clove **garlic,** pressed or minced

2 tbsp + 2 tsp **peanut oil** or vegetable oil

2 tsp **ground coriander**

2 tsp **ancho chili powder**

1 tsp **salt**

1 tsp **cider vinegar**

¼ tsp each **cinnamon, ground cloves** and **ground cumin**

Soak beans overnight in enough water to cover well (for quicker prep, see Tip, page 490); drain. In large saucepan, combine beans and 6 cups water; bring to boil. Reduce heat and simmer until tender, 40 to 50 minutes. Reserving cooking liquid, drain.

Stir together beans, tomatoes and juice, molasses, chipotles, adobo sauce, jalapeños, onion, garlic, 2 tbsp of the oil, coriander, ancho chili powder, salt, vinegar, cinnamon, cloves and cumin. Using remaining oil, grease bottom of 8-cup (2 L) bean pot or lidded casserole dish. Scrape bean mixture into pot; pour in enough of the reserved cooking liquid to just cover beans.

Cover and bake in 400°C (200°C) oven until gently simmering, about 20 minutes; reduce heat to 300°F (150°C) and bake for 4 hours, checking at 2 and 3 hours and adding more of the reserved cooking liquid if necessary (beans should not stick to bottom of pot and should be moist but not wet).

Makes 8 to 10 servings.

PER EACH OF 10 SERVINGS: about 229 cal, 11 g pro, 5 g total fat (1 g sat. fat), 38 g carb, 9 g fibre, 0 mg chol, 283 mg sodium. % RDI: 6% calcium, 23% iron, 6% vit A, 7% vit C, 82% folate.

Grilled Corn Polenta With Roasted Red Peppers

Make polenta special by mixing in fresh corn, grilling it and topping it with sweet and smoky roasted peppers.

¾ tsp **salt**

1 cup **cornmeal**

1 cup **fresh corn kernels**

½ cup grated **Parmesan cheese**

ROASTED RED PEPPERS:

3 **sweet red peppers**

1 tbsp **extra-virgin olive oil**

1 tsp **white wine vinegar**

Pinch **salt**

8 **fresh basil leaves,** thinly sliced

Roasted Red Peppers: Grill red peppers, covered, on greased grill over medium heat, turning often, until charred, 10 to 12 minutes. Place in bowl; cover and let cool. Peel, seed and thinly slice. Toss together peppers, oil, vinegar and salt; stir in basil.

In large saucepan, bring 4 cups water and salt to boil; reduce heat to low. Gradually whisk in cornmeal; cook, stirring often, for 10 minutes.

Add corn; cook until tender-crisp and polenta is thick enough to mound on spoon, 5 to 10 minutes. Stir in cheese. Spread in greased 13- x 9-inch (3 L) baking dish. Let cool until set, about 30 minutes.

Cut polenta into 12 squares. Grill, covered, on greased grill over medium heat, turning once, until grill marked, about 8 minutes. Serve topped with roasted red peppers.

Makes 12 servings.

PER SERVING: about 90 cal, 3 g pro, 3 g total fat (1 g sat. fat), 14 g carb, 2 g fibre, 4 mg chol, 114 mg sodium, 100 mg potassium. % RDI: 5% calcium, 3% iron, 12% vit A, 83% vit C, 15% folate.

Cajun Corn Sauté

This recipe is an adaptation of maque choux, *a Cajun dish often made with cream. This version is lightened up by using broth instead.*

2 tbsp **butter**

1 cup finely chopped **sweet onion**

3 cups **fresh corn kernels**

½ tsp each **granulated sugar** and **smoked paprika**

¼ tsp each **salt, pepper** and **cayenne pepper**

1 cup **sodium-reduced chicken broth**

In large skillet, melt butter over medium heat; cook onion, stirring often, until softened and translucent, about 5 minutes.

Stir in corn, sugar, paprika, salt, pepper and cayenne; cook, stirring, until film forms on pan, 3 to 5 minutes.

Meanwhile, in saucepan, heat broth over medium-high heat. Add ¼ cup to corn mixture, stirring until almost evaporated, 2 to 3 minutes. Repeat 3 times until corn is tender and almost all liquid is absorbed.

Makes 4 servings.

PER SERVING: about 178 cal, 5 g pro, 7 g total fat (4 g sat. fat), 29 g carb, 4 g fibre, 15 mg chol, 352 mg sodium, 307 mg potassium. % RDI: 1% calcium, 6% iron, 9% vit A, 13% vit C, 25% folate.

Grilled Vegetable Quinoa Salad

The amount of water you need to cook quinoa varies, so check package instructions for best results.

1 cup **quinoa**

1 each **sweet red pepper** and **sweet yellow pepper,** quartered

1 **zucchini,** cut lengthwise into ½-inch (1 cm) thick strips

12 **asparagus spears,** trimmed

½ cup **light feta cheese,** crumbled

¼ cup toasted **pumpkin seeds**

3 tbsp chopped **fresh cilantro**

CHIPOTLE VINAIGRETTE:

3 tbsp **olive oil**

2 tbsp **red wine vinegar**

1 **canned chipotle in adobo sauce,** minced

2 tsp **liquid honey**

½ tsp **ground cumin**

¼ tsp each **salt** and **pepper**

Soak quinoa in cold water for 3 minutes; drain in sieve. In saucepan, bring 1½ cups salted water to boil; stir in quinoa and return to boil. Reduce heat to low; cover and simmer until no liquid remains, 12 to 15 minutes. Remove from heat and fluff with fork; cover and let stand for 5 minutes. Spread on small tray and let cool for 10 minutes.

Chipotle Vinaigrette: Meanwhile, whisk together oil, vinegar, chipotle pepper, honey, cumin, salt and pepper.

Toss together red and yellow peppers, zucchini, asparagus and 3 tbsp of the vinaigrette until coated. Grill vegetables, covered, on greased grill over medium heat, turning often, until charred and tender, 4 to 6 minutes for asparagus, 10 to 12 minutes for peppers and zucchini. Cut into large chunks.

Stir together vegetables, remaining dressing, quinoa, half of the feta cheese, the pumpkin seeds and cilantro. Sprinkle with remaining feta. Serve immediately.

Makes 4 to 6 servings.

PER EACH OF 6 SERVINGS: about 258 cal, 9 g pro, 13 g total fat (3 g sat. fat), 28 g carb, 4 g fibre, 6 mg chol, 343 mg sodium, 476 mg potassium. % RDI: 7% calcium, 31% iron, 18% vit A, 110% vit C, 34% folate.

Tangy Macaroni Salad

This salad is equally good with whole wheat or vegetable macaroni.

4 cups **elbow macaroni**

1 cup diced **celery**

¼ cup chopped **pimientos**

DRESSING:

½ cup finely chopped **shallots** or green onions

¼ cup **white wine vinegar**

¾ tsp **salt**

⅔ cup **mayonnaise**

1 tbsp **granulated sugar**

2 tsp **Dijon mustard**

¼ tsp **pepper**

Dressing: In large bowl, combine shallots, vinegar and salt; let stand for 10 minutes. Stir in mayonnaise, sugar, mustard and pepper.

Meanwhile, in large pot of boiling salted water, cook pasta until al dente, 8 to 10 minutes. Drain and rinse under cold water; drain well. Toss together pasta, dressing, celery and pimientos. Cover and refrigerate for 1 to 24 hours.

Makes 12 servings.

PER SERVING: about 230 cal, 5 g pro, 10 g total fat (2 g sat. fat), 29 g carb, 2 g fibre, 5 mg chol, 325 mg sodium, 90 mg potassium. % RDI: 2% calcium, 11% iron, 3% vit A, 10% vit C, 35% folate.

Cool Wild Rice & Mushrooms

Canada's central northern lakes and marshes provide us with the finest fragrant long-grain wild rice, our country's only native cereal.

2 cups **wild rice**

4 cups chopped **mushrooms,** about 10 oz (280 g)

1 **small onion,** chopped

1 rib **celery,** diced

¼ cup **olive oil** or vegetable oil

3 tbsp **sherry vinegar** or wine vinegar

1 tsp **salt**

¼ tsp **pepper**

¼ cup chopped **fresh parsley**

¼ cup chopped **fresh chives**

In saucepan, bring 8 cups water to boil; add rice and boil gently until tender and many of the grains have burst open, 30 to 40 minutes. Drain; place in large bowl.

In separate saucepan, stir together mushrooms, onion, celery, oil, vinegar, salt and pepper; bring to boil. Reduce heat to medium; simmer until mushrooms are tender, about 5 minutes. Toss with rice until coated; let cool. Toss in parsley and chives.

Makes 8 servings.

PER SERVING: about 216 cal, 6 g pro, 8 g total fat (2 g sat. fat), 33 g carb, 3 g fibre, 0 mg chol, 297 mg sodium. % RDI: 2% calcium, 11% iron, 3% vit A, 8% vit C, 21% folate.

Mediterranean Barley Rice Salad

Pearl barley adds bite to this hearty salad. If your feta cheese tastes especially salty, soak it for 30 minutes in cold water before crumbling it.

1 cup **pearl barley,** rinsed

1 cup **basmati rice,** rinsed

3 cups **cherry tomatoes,** halved

Half **large red onion,** cut into 1-inch (2.5 cm) chunks

1 **sweet red pepper,** cut into 1-inch (2.5 cm) chunks

1 **English cucumber**

4 cups **baby spinach,** coarsely chopped

1 pkg (200 g) **feta cheese,** crumbled

DRESSING:

½ cup **extra-virgin olive oil**

½ cup **lemon juice**

1 tsp **dried oregano**

1 tsp **salt**

½ tsp **pepper**

In saucepan of boiling salted water, cook barley until tender, about 20 minutes. Drain and rinse under cold water; drain well. Let stand for 10 minutes to dry. Transfer to large bowl.

In separate saucepan, bring 1½ cups salted water to boil. Add rice; cover, reduce heat and simmer until tender and no liquid remains, about 15 minutes. Let stand for 5 minutes. Add to barley; let cool.

Add tomatoes, onion, red pepper and cucumber to barley mixture, tossing to combine.

Dressing: Whisk together oil, lemon juice, oregano, salt and pepper; pour over salad and toss to coat. Cover and refrigerate for 30 minutes or up to 24 hours.

Just before serving, stir in spinach and feta cheese.

Makes 12 to 16 servings.

PER EACH OF 16 SERVINGS: about 197 cal, 4 g pro, 10 g total fat (3 g sat. fat), 24 g carb, 2 g fibre, 12 mg chol, 554 mg sodium, 234 mg potassium. % RDI: 8% calcium, 8% iron, 14% vit A, 38% vit C, 16% folate.

Grilled Vegetable & Israeli Couscous Salad

Israeli couscous is much larger and more pastalike than instant couscous. If you can't find it, use a small pasta, such as orzo, ditalini, acini di pepe or small shells.

2 cups **Israeli couscous**

1 **eggplant,** sliced

1¼ tsp **salt**

2 cloves **garlic**

½ cup **extra-virgin olive oil**

¼ cup **sherry vinegar**

¼ tsp **granulated sugar**

¼ tsp **pepper**

2 **zucchini,** sliced lengthwise

1 **small red onion,** sliced crosswise into ½-inch (1 cm) rounds

3 **portobello mushroom caps,** gills removed

⅓ cup chopped **fresh parsley**

In saucepan of boiling salted water, cook couscous until tender but firm, about 8 minutes. Drain and rinse under cold water; drain well. Transfer to large bowl.

Meanwhile, toss eggplant with ¼ tsp of the salt; let drain in colander for 10 minutes. Pat dry with paper towel.

On cutting board, coarsely chop garlic; sprinkle with pinch of the remaining salt. With flat side of knife or fork, mash into paste. Transfer to bowl; mix in oil, vinegar, sugar, pepper and remaining salt. Lightly brush some over eggplant, zucchini, onion and mushrooms.

Grill vegetables, covered, on greased grill over medium heat, turning often, until tender, 7 to 10 minutes. Cut into 1-inch (2.5 cm) pieces; add to couscous.

Add remaining oil mixture and parsley to salad; toss to coat. Let stand for 1 hour or, covered and refrigerated, up to 24 hours.

Makes 12 servings.

PER SERVING: about 212 cal, 5 g pro, 10 g total fat (1 g sat. fat), 27 g carb, 3 g fibre, 0 mg chol, 226 mg sodium, 346 mg potassium. % RDI: 2% calcium, 6% iron, 5% vit A, 8% vit C, 15% folate.

Greek Village Salad

This is the true Greek salad, literally called "peasant salad" in Greek, that is served throughout the country. It's a natural fit with almost any barbecued dish. Chop the vegetables fairly coarsely for an authentic result.

Half **red onion,** chopped

1 **English cucumber** or 2 peeled
　field cucumbers

2 **tomatoes,** chopped

1 **sweet green pepper,** chopped

½ cup **Kalamata olives**

¼ cup **extra-virgin olive oil**

2 tbsp **lemon juice**

2 tbsp **red wine vinegar**

1½ tsp **dried oregano** (preferably
　Greek)

¼ tsp **salt**

Pinch **pepper**

5 oz (140 g) **feta cheese,** cubed

Soak onion in cold water for 20 minutes. Drain; place in serving bowl. Cut cucumber lengthwise into quarters (if using field cucumbers, seed) and chop; add to bowl along with tomatoes, pepper and olives.

Whisk together olive oil, lemon juice, vinegar, oregano, salt and pepper; toss with cucumber mixture until coated. Top with feta cheese.

Makes 6 to 8 servings.

PER EACH OF 8 SERVINGS: about 162 cal, 4 g pro, 14 g total fat (4 g sat. fat), 7 g carb, 2 g fibre, 16 mg chol, 559 mg sodium. % RDI: 10% calcium, 5% iron, 6% vit A, 40% vit C, 11% folate.

Three-Bean Salad

This picnic favourite is both colourful and quick to throw together.

1½ cups **green beans** and/or
  yellow beans, cut into
  2-inch (5 cm) pieces

¼ cup **extra-virgin olive oil**

¼ cup **wine vinegar**

1 clove **garlic,** minced

2 tbsp chopped **fresh parsley**

½ tsp **granulated sugar**

½ tsp **salt**

¼ tsp **dried oregano**

¼ tsp **pepper**

1 can (19 oz/540 mL) **chickpeas,**
  drained and rinsed

1 can (19 oz/540 mL) **kidney beans,**
  drained and rinsed

2 **green onions,** thinly sliced

In saucepan of boiling salted water, blanch green and/or yellow beans until tender-crisp, 3 to 5 minutes. Drain; chill under cold water. Drain well; pat dry.

In large bowl, whisk together oil, vinegar, garlic, parsley, sugar, salt, oregano and pepper. Toss in green and/or yellow beans, chickpeas, kidney beans and green onions until coated. *(Make-ahead: Cover and refrigerate for up to 8 hours.)*

Makes 8 servings.

PER SERVING: about 197 cal, 7 g pro, 8 g total fat (1 g sat. fat), 26 g carb, 8 g fibre, 0 mg chol, 505 mg sodium. % RDI: 4% calcium, 13% iron, 2% vit A, 10% vit C, 33% folate.

Green Bean, Mushroom & Fennel Salad

This garlicky salad is sure to be a hit with guests. The ice bath keeps the beans a vibrant, beautiful green.

⅓ cup **extra-virgin olive oil**

¼ cup l**emon juice**

3 tbsp chopped **fresh dill**

1 clove **garlic,** minced

¾ tsp **salt**

¼ tsp **pepper**

1 lb (450 g) **small cremini mushrooms,** quartered

1 lb (450 g) **green beans,** trimmed

Half **fennel bulb,** very thinly sliced

In large bowl, whisk together oil, lemon juice, dill, garlic, salt and pepper. Add mushrooms and toss to coat. Let stand for 15 minutes, stirring occasionally.

Meanwhile, halve green beans diagonally. In saucepan of boiling water, blanch beans until tender-crisp, 3 to 5 minutes. Drain; chill in ice water. Drain well; pat dry.

Add beans and fennel to mushroom mixture; toss to coat well. Serve immediately, or cover and refrigerate for up to 4 hours.

Makes 12 servings.

PER SERVING: about 76 cal, 2 g pro, 6 g total fat (1 g sat. fat), 5 g carb, 2 g fibre, 0 mg chol, 152 mg sodium, 262 mg potassium. % RDI: 2% calcium, 4% iron, 2% vit A, 10% vit C, 9% folate.

Filipino Cucumber Salad

In the Philippines, palm sap vinegar or cane vinegar would replace the unseasoned rice vinegar in this refreshing salad.

2 **English cucumbers** (or 3 or 4 field cucumbers, peeled), thinly sliced

Half **sweet red pepper,** thinly sliced

Half **hot pepper,** thinly sliced

¾ cup **unseasoned rice vinegar**

½ cup thinly sliced **red onion**

¼ cup **lime juice**

2 tbsp finely chopped **fresh cilantro** or mint

2 tbsp **fish sauce**

3 cloves **garlic,** minced

1 tbsp **granulated sugar**

1½ tsp **salt**

¼ tsp **pepper**

Toss together cucumbers, sweet and hot peppers, vinegar, onion, lime juice, cilantro, fish sauce, garlic, sugar, salt and pepper. Let stand, stirring occasionally, for 2 hours or, covered and refrigerated, up to 3 days.

Makes 8 servings.

TIP

If you love fresh herbs, increase the amount to 2 tbsp each finely chopped fresh cilantro and mint.

PER SERVING: about 32 cal, 1 g pro, 0 g total fat (0 g sat. fat), 8 g carb, 1 g fibre, 0 mg chol, 781 mg sodium. % RDI: 2% calcium, 3% iron, 6% vit A, 42% vit C, 9% folate.

Creamy Cucumber Salad

Salting the cucumber helps draw liquid out of it so the flesh stays crunchy and the dressing doesn't get watered down. Soaking the onion makes it milder and crisper.

2 **English cucumbers** (or 3 or 4 field cucumbers, peeled), thinly sliced

1 tsp **salt**

1 **small red onion,** thinly sliced

⅔ cup **sour cream**

⅓ cup **lemon juice**

2 tbsp chopped **fresh dill** or mint (or 1 tsp dried)

1½ tsp **granulated sugar**

Toss cucumber with salt; let stand until soft, about 30 minutes. Handful by handful, squeeze out excess moisture; transfer to large bowl. Meanwhile, in bowl of cold water, soak onion for 30 minutes; drain and add to cucumber.

Whisk together sour cream, lemon juice, dill and sugar; toss with cucumber mixture until coated. Let stand for 15 minutes before serving.

Makes 8 servings.

PER SERVING: about 64 cal, 1 g pro, 3 g total fat (2 g sat. fat), 8 g carb, 1 g fibre, 9 mg chol, 15 mg sodium. % RDI: 4% calcium, 3% iron, 12% vit A, 17% vit C, 9% folate.

Carrot & Peanut Salad

Taking this salad to a potluck? Dress it just before leaving so it stays crisp and fresh. Or pack the dressing separately and toss the salad together when you get there.

¼ cup **peanut oil** or vegetable oil

3 tbsp **lime juice**

2 tbsp **fish sauce**

1 tbsp **granulated sugar**

1 tbsp **unseasoned rice vinegar**

1 to 3 **Thai bird's-eye pepper(s),** minced (or 1 jalapeño pepper, seeded and minced)

1 clove **garlic,** minced

½ tsp **salt**

6 cups shredded **carrots**

1¼ cups thinly sliced **radishes**

¾ cup **unsalted roasted peanuts,** coarsely chopped

⅓ cup chopped **fresh cilantro**

In large bowl, whisk together oil, lime juice, fish sauce, sugar, vinegar, Thai pepper(s), garlic and salt.

Add carrots, radishes, peanuts and cilantro; toss until coated. Let stand for 10 minutes; gently squeeze and drain liquid. Serve immediately or cover and refrigerate for up to 2 hours.

Makes 8 to 10 servings.

PER EACH OF 10 SERVINGS: about 144 cal, 4 g pro, 11 g total fat (2 g sat. fat), 11 g carb, 3 g fibre, 0 mg chol, 440 mg sodium, 333 mg potassium. % RDI: 3% calcium, 3% iron, 80% vit A, 14% vit C, 14% folate.

Simple Guacamole
(page 523)

sauces, marinades & rubs

Fresh Tomato Salsa | 517

Yellow Tomato Salsa | 519

Tomato Mint Salsa | 520

Cherry Tomato Salsa | 521

Simple Guacamole | 523

Grilled Hot Pepper Salsa | 524

Avocado & Green Tomato Salsa | 525

Spice Mixes & Rubs | 526

Black Bean Corn Salsa | 528

Smoky Barbecue Sauce | 529

Hot & Spicy Chipotle
   Barbecue Sauce | 530

Grilling Sauces | 531

Marinades | 533

Molasses Barbecue Sauce | 534

Flavoured Butters | 535

Fresh Tomato Salsa

Enjoy this instant salsa with fish, burgers or pork chops. It's great on grilled meat or fish tacos, as well.

1⅓ cups diced **plum tomatoes**

¼ cup chopped **fresh cilantro**

1 tbsp minced seeded **jalapeño pepper**

1 **green onion,** finely chopped

1 tbsp **lime juice** or wine vinegar

1 tbsp **olive oil** or vegetable oil

¼ tsp each **salt** and **pepper**

Stir together tomatoes, cilantro, jalapeño pepper, green onion, lime juice, oil, salt and pepper.

Makes about 1½ cups.

PER ¼ CUP: about 27 cal, trace pro, 2 g total fat (trace sat. fat), 2 g carb, trace fibre, 0 mg chol, 99 mg sodium. % RDI: 1% iron, 3% vit A, 13% vit C, 2% folate.

Clockwise from top: Yellow Tomato Salsa (opposite), Grilled Hot Pepper Salsa (page 524), Avocado & Green Tomato Salsa (page 525) and Tomato Mint Salsa (page 520)

Yellow Tomato Salsa

Try this attractive, mild-flavoured salsa over grilled chicken or fish. Of course, it's also delicious with tortilla chips.

1 **sweet yellow pepper**

1 lb (450 g) **yellow tomatoes** (about 5), peeled and seeded

2 cloves **garlic,** minced

¼ cup loosely packed **fresh basil** or cilantro

3 tbsp **extra-virgin olive oil**

1 tsp grated **lemon zest**

2 tbsp **lemon juice**

¾ tsp **salt**

¼ tsp **hot pepper sauce**

Grill yellow pepper, covered, on greased grill over high heat, turning often, until charred all over, 10 to 12 minutes. Place in bowl; cover and let cool. Peel, seed and coarsely chop.

In food processor, pulse together grilled pepper, tomatoes, garlic, basil, oil, lemon zest and juice, salt and hot pepper sauce until chunky.

Makes about 2 cups.

To peel and seed tomatoes: Plunge tomatoes into boiling water; boil until skins loosen, about 15 seconds. Drain; chill in cold water and drain again. Peel, core and halve tomatoes. Using small spoon or fingers, scoop or squeeze out seeds.

PER 2 TBSP: about 29 cal, 0 g pro, 3 g total fat (0 g sat. fat), 2 g carb, 0 g fibre, 0 mg chol, 114 mg sodium. % RDI: 1% calcium, 1% iron, 23% vit C, 4% folate.

Tomato Mint Salsa

A perfect salsa for grilled lamb, this also goes well with pork, chicken, liver and seafood.

1 cup chopped **sweet onion**

⅔ cup loosely packed **fresh mint**

⅓ cup chopped **fresh cilantro**

2 **jalapeño peppers,** seeded and chopped

1 tsp grated **fresh ginger**

½ tsp **salt**

¼ tsp **pepper**

Pinch **granulated sugar**

1½ cups coarsely chopped seeded peeled **tomatoes** (see Tip, page 519)

1 tbsp **lemon juice**

In food processor, pulse together onion, mint, cilantro, jalapeños, ginger, salt, pepper and sugar. Pulse in tomatoes and lemon juice until finely chopped.

Makes 2⅓ cups.

Photo, page 518

PER 2 TBSP: about 7 cal, 0 g pro, 0 g total fat (0 g sat. fat), 2 g carb, 0 g fibre, 0 mg chol, 64 mg sodium. % RDI: 1% calcium, 2% iron, 3% vit A, 10% vit C, 3% folate.

Cherry Tomato Salsa

Instead of the usual condiments, try this fresh-tasting salsa on your next burger, such as our Brandy Dijon Beef Burgers (page 83). It's great on steak, too.

2 cups halved **cherry tomatoes**

2 tbsp **extra-virgin olive oil**

½ tsp **salt**

3 tbsp finely diced **dill pickle**

2 tbsp minced **red onion**

1 clove **garlic,** minced

2 tsp **red wine vinegar**

½ tsp **dried oregano**

¼ tsp **hot pepper flakes**

¼ tsp **pepper**

Spread tomatoes on rimmed baking sheet; drizzle with oil and sprinkle with salt. Roast in 450°F (230°C) oven until slightly charred, 15 to 20 minutes.

Transfer tomatoes and juices to bowl; mix in pickle, onion, garlic, vinegar, oregano, hot pepper flakes and pepper.

Makes 1 cup.

Photo, page 82

PER 2 TBSP: about 38 cal, 0 g pro, 4 g total fat (0 g sat. fat), 2 g carb, 0 g fibre, 0 mg chol, 188 mg sodium. % RDI: 1% iron, 2% vit A, 10% vit C, 2% folate.

Simple Guacamole

Guacamole can't get quicker and easier than this! Serve with colourful vegetable crudités and tortilla chips.

3 **ripe avocados,** peeled and pitted

2 tbsp **lime juice**

¼ cup finely diced **white onion**

1 **plum tomato,** seeded and diced

2 tbsp chopped **fresh cilantro**

Pinch **salt**

Using fork, mash avocados with lime juice until smooth. Stir in onion, tomato, cilantro and salt.

Makes about 2 cups.

PER 1 TBSP: about 31 cal, trace pro, 3 g total fat (trace sat. fat), 2 g carb, 1 g fibre, 0 mg chol, 2 mg sodium. % RDI: 1% iron, 3% vit C, 7% folate.

Grilled Hot Pepper Salsa

This is an all-purpose salsa that's good with fish, red or white meat, or even simple chips or crudités. Adjust the heat by using the number of hot peppers that suits your palate. You can use finger hot peppers or jalapeño peppers.

1 head **garlic** (unpeeled)

4 **shallots** (unpeeled)

2 **tomatoes**

2 to 4 **hot peppers**

2 **anchovy fillets,** minced
(or ½ tsp salt)

¼ cup minced **fresh cilantro**
or parsley

2 tbsp **extra-virgin olive oil**

4 tsp **lemon juice**

½ tsp **pepper**

¼ tsp **salt**

Grill garlic and shallots, covered, on greased grill over medium-high heat, turning occasionally, until charred all over and tender inside, 20 to 25 minutes. Grill tomatoes and peppers, covered and turning often, until charred all over, 4 or 5 minutes; let cool.

Squeeze garlic cloves into bowl; mash with fork. Peel shallots, tomatoes and peppers; chop finely and add to bowl. Mix in anchovies, cilantro, oil, lemon juice, pepper and salt.

Makes 1⅓ cups.

Photo, page 518

PER 2 TBSP: about 38 cal, 1 g pro, 3 g total fat (0 g sat. fat), 3 g carb, 0 g fibre, 1 mg chol, 85 mg sodium. % RDI: 1% calcium, 2% iron, 4% vit A, 17% vit C, 2% folate.

Avocado & Green Tomato Salsa

When there are lots of green tomatoes available, make this unique and tangy salsa – it's a natural partner to grilled chicken or shrimp, and nachos, too.

1 **green tomato,** diced

⅓ cup finely diced **sweet onion**

2 tbsp minced **fresh cilantro**

1 tbsp **lime juice**

1 **red hot pepper,** seeded and minced

½ tsp **salt**

1 **avocado,** peeled, pitted and diced

Mix together tomato, onion, cilantro, lime juice, hot pepper and salt.

Just before serving, gently stir in avocado.

Makes about 2⅓ cups.

Photo, page 518

PER 2 TBSP: about 20 cal, 0 g pro, 2 g total fat (0 g sat. fat), 1 g carb, 1 g fibre, 0 mg chol, 64 mg sodium.
% RDI: 1% iron, 2% vit A, 7% vit C, 4% folate.

Spice Mixes & Rubs

Turn everyday meals into something special with your choice of these flavourful seasonings. Each is suitable for 4 servings – 1 lb (450 g) boneless meat or poultry, 1½ lb (675 g) bone-in meat or poultry, or 1 lb (450 g) fish. All of these dry spice mixes can be stored in airtight containers for up to 6 months.

To use, in large bowl, combine 2 tbsp each spice mix and vegetable or olive oil; and 1 clove garlic, minced. Add meat, poultry or fish, turning to coat well. Cover and refrigerate for 15 minutes or up to 4 hours.

African Adobo Spice Mix

2 tbsp smoked paprika or sweet paprika; 1 tbsp ground cumin; 1½ tsp each cinnamon and coarsely ground pepper; 1 tsp hot pepper flakes; ½ tsp salt; and ¼ tsp ground cardamom or cloves

Makes about ¼ cup.

Orange Spice Mix

4 tsp finely grated orange zest, dried for 1 hour; 1 tbsp each dry mustard and ground ginger; 2 tsp ground allspice; ½ tsp salt; and ¼ tsp cayenne pepper

Makes about ¼ cup.

Cajun Spice Mix

3 tbsp dried thyme; 2 tbsp each sweet paprika and packed brown sugar; 1 tbsp each ground cumin, dry mustard and hot pepper flakes; and 1 tsp salt

Makes about ⅓ cup.

Mole Spice Mix

¼ cup chili powder; 2 tbsp cocoa powder; ¾ tsp each salt and pepper; and ½ tsp each cayenne pepper, cinnamon and ground allspice

Makes about ⅓ cup.

Chili Spice Mix

3 tbsp chili powder; 2 tbsp each sweet paprika and packed brown sugar; 1 tbsp ground cumin; 1 tsp garlic powder; and ½ tsp each salt and pepper

Makes about ⅓ cup.

Bombay Spice Mix

3 tbsp each ground coriander and turmeric; 2 tsp ground cumin; 1 tsp salt; and ½ tsp each cayenne pepper and dry mustard

Makes about ⅓ cup.

From top: African Adobo Spice Mix, Orange Spice Mix, Cajun Spice Mix and Mole Spice Mix

Black Bean Corn Salsa

This chunky salsa can play two roles: it's great as a condiment with grilled meats or served as a quick, nutritious side salad.

2 **cobs of corn** (unhusked)

2 **sweet green peppers**

1 cup **cooked black beans**

⅓ cup chopped **fresh cilantro**

¼ cup finely chopped **red onion**

1 **jalapeño pepper,** seeded and diced

3 tbsp **lime juice**

3 tbsp **vegetable oil**

½ tsp each **salt** and **ground cumin**

Trim loose silk from corn; soak cobs in water for 10 minutes. Grill, covered, on greased grill over medium-high heat, turning occasionally, until tender and charred, 10 minutes. Let cool. Husk; cut off kernels.

Meanwhile, grill green peppers, covered, on greased grill over medium-high heat, turning occasionally, until tender and charred, about 10 minutes. Place in bowl; cover and let cool. Peel, seed and chop.

Toss together corn, peppers, black beans, cilantro, onion, jalapeño, lime juice, oil, salt and cumin. Serve immediately or cover and refrigerate for up to 24 hours.

Makes about 4 cups.

TIP
To save time soaking and cooking beans, you can substitute 1 can (19 oz/540 mL) black beans, drained and rinsed. Reduce salt to ¼ tsp.

PER ½ CUP: about 118 cal, 3 g pro, 6 g total fat (1 g sat. fat), 16 g carb, 3 g fibre, 0 mg chol, 151 mg sodium. % RDI: 1% calcium, 6% iron, 2% vit A, 42% vit C, 24% folate.

Smoky Barbecue Sauce

This all-purpose barbecue sauce makes a tasty glaze not only on ribs but also on chicken, steak, pork chops and burgers.

1 tbsp **vegetable oil**

1 **small onion,** finely chopped

2 cloves **garlic,** minced

1 tbsp **smoked paprika**

1 tsp **dry mustard**

¼ tsp **salt**

1 cup **ketchup** or tomato-based chili sauce

½ cup **red wine** or water

2 tbsp packed **brown sugar**

2 tbsp **cider vinegar**

In saucepan, heat oil over medium heat; fry onion, garlic, paprika, mustard and salt, stirring occasionally, until onion is softened, about 3 minutes.

Add ketchup, wine, sugar and vinegar; bring to boil. Reduce heat and simmer until mixture is as thick as ketchup, about 20 minutes.

In food processor or blender, purée mixture until smooth. *(Make-ahead: Refrigerate for up to 1 month.)*

Makes about 1½ cups.

PER 1 TBSP: about 26 cal, trace pro, 1 g total fat (0 g sat. fat), 5 g carb, trace fibre, 0 mg chol, 159 mg sodium. % RDI: 1% iron, 3% vit A, 3% vit C, 1% folate.

Hot & Spicy Chipotle Barbecue Sauce

Make a batch of this all-purpose hot sauce to spice up your grills all summer long.

1 tbsp **vegetable oil**

1 **shallot** or small onion, chopped

2 cloves **garlic,** minced

1 tbsp **sweet paprika**

1 tbsp **chili powder**

¼ tsp each **salt** and **pepper**

1 can (19 oz/540 mL) **tomatoes**

1 can (5½ oz/156 mL) **tomato paste**

⅔ cup **white vinegar**

⅓ cup packed **brown sugar**

2 tbsp **Dijon mustard**

4 **canned chipotles in adobo sauce**

2 tbsp **adobo sauce** from canned chipotles

½ cup **fancy molasses**

In saucepan, heat oil over medium heat; fry shallot, garlic, paprika, chili powder, salt and pepper, stirring occasionally, until shallot is softened, about 5 minutes.

Add tomatoes, tomato paste, vinegar, sugar and mustard; bring to boil. Reduce heat and simmer, stirring occasionally, until thickened and reduced by about one-third, about 1 hour. Let cool.

In blender, combine sauce, chipotles and adobo sauce; purée until smooth. Blend in molasses. *(Make-ahead: Refrigerate for up to 1 month.)*

Makes 4 cups.

PER 1 TBSP: about 20 cal, trace pro, trace total fat (0 g sat. fat), 4 g carb, trace fibre, 0 mg chol, 38 mg sodium, 94 mg potassium. % RDI: 1% calcium, 3% iron, 2% vit A, 3% vit C.

Grilling Sauces

Teriyaki Sauce

In saucepan, stir together ¾ cup chicken or vegetable broth, ½ cup soy sauce, ⅓ cup mirin, 2 tbsp granulated sugar and 3 slices fresh ginger. Bring to boil. Reduce heat; simmer until reduced by half, 20 minutes. Whisk 1 tbsp cornstarch with 1 tbsp cold water; add to pan and cook, stirring, until thick enough to coat back of spoon, about 2 minutes. Discard ginger. Let cool. *(Make-ahead: Refrigerate for up to 2 weeks.)*

Makes 1 cup.

Argentine Chimichurri Verde

In food processor, finely chop together 2 cups packed fresh parsley leaves; ⅓ cup olive oil; ¼ cup packed fresh oregano leaves; ¼ cup wine vinegar; 1 jalapeño pepper, seeded; 4 cloves garlic; and ½ tsp each salt and pepper. *(Make-ahead: Refrigerate for up to 1 day.)*

Makes 1 cup.

Chimichurri Rojo

Whisk together ½ cup sherry vinegar or red wine vinegar; ¼ cup extra-virgin olive oil; 3 tbsp minced fresh parsley; 3 cloves garlic, minced; 4 tsp sweet paprika; 1 tsp ground cumin; ½ tsp each salt and pepper; and ¼ to ½ tsp cayenne pepper. *(Make-ahead: Refrigerate for up to 1 week.)*

Makes about ¾ cup.

Korean Barbecue Sauce

In saucepan, combine 4 cups soy sauce; 2 cups granulated sugar; 1 cup sake or Chinese rice wine (or combination of both); 1 cup mirin; 2 apples (unpeeled and uncored), thinly sliced; 2 onions, thinly sliced; 10 cloves garlic, thinly sliced; 2-inch (5 cm) piece fresh ginger, thinly sliced; and 30 black peppercorns. Bring to boil, stirring until sugar is dissolved. Reduce heat to medium-low and simmer until mixture is reduced by about one-third, 40 to 50 minutes. Cover; let stand overnight at room temperature. Strain. *(Make-ahead: Refrigerate for up to 6 months.)*

Makes about 6 cups.

From top: Moroccan Marinade,
Tikka Marinade, Adobo Marinade
and Honey Garlic Marinade

Marinades

Marinades usually contain an acidic ingredient, such as vinegar, that helps tenderize as it flavours.

In small bowl, stir together ingredients for desired marinade (right).

Each makes ⅓ to ½ cup.

Use ⅓ cup marinade for every 4 servings (1 lb/450 g boneless or 1½ lb/675 g bone-in meat or poultry, or 1 lb/450 g fish).

Cover and marinate meat or poultry, refrigerated, for 4 to 12 hours; marinate fish for no more than 30 minutes.

Moroccan Marinade

3 tbsp olive oil; 2 tbsp each ground cumin, sweet paprika, granulated sugar and lemon juice; 2 cloves garlic, minced; ½ tsp each salt and pepper; and ¼ tsp cinnamon

Tikka Marinade

⅓ cup plain yogurt; 1 tbsp minced fresh ginger; 2 cloves garlic, minced; half jalapeño pepper, minced; 1 tsp each ground cumin and cardamom; and ½ tsp each salt and nutmeg

Adobo Marinade

¼ cup orange juice; 1 tsp grated lime zest; 2 tbsp lime juice; 2 cloves garlic, minced; 1 jalapeño pepper, minced; 2 tsp dried oregano; and 1 tsp ground cumin

Honey Garlic Marinade

¼ cup cider vinegar; 2 tbsp liquid honey; 1 tbsp soy sauce; and 4 cloves garlic, minced

Red Wine Marinade

¼ cup dry red wine; 2 tbsp red wine vinegar; 1 tbsp olive oil; 2 cloves garlic, minced; 1 bay leaf; and ¼ tsp each salt and pepper

Apple Thyme Marinade

2 tbsp each cider vinegar, apple juice and vegetable oil; 1 tbsp chopped fresh thyme (or ½ tsp dried); 1 tbsp grainy or Dijon mustard; and ½ tsp each salt and pepper

Lemon Herb Marinade

¼ cup each lemon juice and extra-virgin olive oil; 2 tbsp chopped fresh rosemary, oregano or parsley; 1 tbsp sherry vinegar or wine vinegar; 2 cloves garlic, minced; ½ tsp each salt and pepper; four 2-inch (5 cm) strips lemon zest; and 2 bay leaves, quartered

Molasses Barbecue Sauce

Add a luscious touch to all your barbecue favourites: during the last few minutes of cooking, brush this sauce over chops, burgers, ribs, poultry or fish.

1 cup **beef broth**

1 cup **tomato-based chili sauce**

½ cup **fancy molasses**

2 tbsp **white vinegar**

4 tsp **yellow mustard**

2 tsp **chili powder**

2 tsp **Worcestershire sauce**

1 tsp **celery seeds,** crushed

1 tsp **ground cumin**

½ tsp each **salt** and **pepper**

In large saucepan, whisk together broth, chili sauce, ⅔ cup water, molasses, vinegar, mustard, chili powder, Worcestershire sauce, celery seeds, cumin, salt and pepper; bring to boil.

Reduce heat and simmer until reduced to about 2 cups, about 20 minutes. *(Make-ahead: Refrigerate for up to 2 weeks.)*

Makes 2 cups.

PER 1 TBSP: about 26 cal, 1 g pro, trace total fat (trace sat. fat), 6 g carb, 1 g fibre, 0 mg chol, 190 mg sodium. % RDI: 2% calcium, 3% iron, 1% vit A, 3% vit C, 1% folate.

Flavoured Butters

Flavoured butters are an inspired addition to barbecued meat, poultry or fish. Place 1 round on each portion of hot food to serve, or melt and brush on food while grilling.

In small bowl, stir together ½ cup salted butter, softened, with ingredients for desired flavour (right) until smooth. Spoon onto plastic wrap; shape into log and wrap tightly. Or pack into small serving bowl, smoothing top. Refrigerate until firm, or for up to 2 weeks.

Slice log into ½-inch (1 cm) thick rounds or serve directly from bowl.

Makes about ½ cup.

Lime & Chili Butter
(all-purpose)
2 tbsp minced fresh cilantro; 1 tsp grated lime zest; 2 tbsp lime juice; and 1 tsp chili powder

Herb Butter
(all-purpose)
¼ cup minced fresh parsley; 2 tbsp minced fresh chives or green onion; 1 tbsp minced fresh basil, dill, tarragon and/or chervil; and pinch pepper

Shallot Peppercorn Butter
(for beef and lamb)
1 shallot, minced, cooked in 1 tsp butter until softened (let cool); 2 tbsp pink peppercorns, crushed; and 1 tbsp dry red wine

Horseradish Butter
(for beef)
4 tsp prepared horseradish and ¼ tsp pepper

Anchovy Butter
(for beef, lamb or fish)
¼ cup minced green onions; 4 anchovy fillets, mashed (or 2 tsp anchovy paste); 1 clove garlic, minced; and ½ tsp grated lemon zest

Caviar Butter
(for fish and steaks)
2 tbsp each minced fresh chives and red lumpfish or other caviar; and 1 clove garlic, minced

Olive Sage Butter
(for poultry, fish and pork)
¼ cup chopped Niçoise or oil-cured olives; 2 tbsp minced fresh sage; and pinch dried oregano

Caper Mustard Butter
(for fish)
2 tbsp each drained capers and Dijon mustard; ½ tsp grated lemon zest; and 1 tsp lemon juice

acknowledgments

This updated edition of *The Barbecue Collection* is the collective work of so many people. Thanks first to the backbone of all *Canadian Living* food projects: the talented staff – past and present – of The Canadian Living Test Kitchen. Special thanks go to Andrew Chase, Camilo Costales and Christine Picheca, who were instrumental in creating the first edition of this book, and to Nicole Young, who developed a series of fresh new recipes for this second edition.

As always, my heartfelt thanks go to food director Annabelle Waugh, whose guidance and fantastic sense of humour make the book-editing process a pleasure. Janet Rowe is another person to whom I owe a large debt of gratitude. Her skillful editing and unwavering patience in the face of 552 pages of content made this project less onerous and much more joyful.

Since a picture is worth a thousand words, I need to thank our creative team of Michael Erb and Chris Bond, who made this edition look fresh, inviting and utterly mouthwatering. They could not have done their jobs so well without the gorgeous new photographs crafted by photographer Edward Pond, food stylist Ashley Denton and prop stylist Catherine Doherty. It's a treat to work with such talented artists. For a list of the other artists who created the rest of the images in these pages, turn to page 552.

A huge book like this needs a talented copy editing team to comb through it and make the inconsistencies disappear. For their skill and perseverance, I'd like to thank copy editors Lisa Fielding and Austen Gilliland, who spruced up the thousands of words in this book and made us all look good.

Thanks also to Gillian Watts, our tireless indexer, who went through each of these pages, line by line, and created an index that will help readers find the recipes they're looking for. Thanks also to Sharyn Joliat of Info Access, who provided the in-depth nutritional analysis at the bottom of every recipe.

No book project we work on would be possible without the support and creativity of our publishers and editor-in-chief. A heartfelt thank you to Transcontinental Books publisher Jean Paré, *Canadian Living* publisher Lynn Chambers and *Canadian Living* editor-in-chief Susan Antonacci for their good humour, encouragement and belief in our cookbooks.

Finally, thanks to our distribution and promotion team at Random House Canada for getting this barbecue tome into bookstores and into the hands of eager grillers across North America.

Happy barbecuing!

– *Christina Anson Mine, project editor*

Index

A

Adana Lamb Kabobs, 39
Adobo Marinade, 533
African Adobo Spice Mix, 526
Ancho Turkey Waves, 62
anchovies
    Anchovy Butter, 535
    Baby Potato Salad With Salsa
        Verde, 486
    Grilled Eggplant With
        Provolone, 447
    Grilled Hot Pepper Salsa, 524
    Grilled Mozzarella Skewers
        With Anchovy Sauce, 452
    Rapini & Garlic Pizza With
        Asiago Cheese, 460
apples and apple juice
    Apple Thyme Marinade, 533
    Basic Brined Rotisserie
        Chicken, 287
    Chicken Drumsticks With
        Apple Stout Barbecue
        Sauce, 302
    Cider & Maple Grilled
        Duck, 341
    Cider-Glazed Apples &
        Onion, 435
    Korean Barbecue Sauce, 531
    Pork, Apple, Sage & Stilton
        Sausages, 144
    Red Cabbage Coleslaw, 479
Arctic char
    Grilled Arctic Char With
        Tahini Sauce, 361
    Whole Arctic Char With Green
        Onion Butter Sauce, 363
Argentine Burgers, 89
Argentine Chimichurri Verde, 531
Armenian Butterflied Leg
    of Lamb, 272

arugula
    Arugula & Beefsteak Salad
        With Tomato
        Vinaigrette, 183
    Flank Steak Sandwiches With
        Pepper Sauce, 105
    Grilled Prosciutto & Fig
        Sandwiches, 121
    Tilapia With Tomatoes &
        Lemon Relish, 384
asparagus
    Grilled Asparagus With Curry
        Yogurt Sauce, 443
    Grilled Chicken & Charred
        Corn Salad, 312
    Grilled Vegetable Quinoa
        Salad, 499
avocado
    Avocado & Green Tomato
        Salsa, 525
    Cumin Flank Steak With
        Avocado Salad, 169
    Guacamole, Simple, 523
    Lime-Grilled Chicken Breasts
        With Avocado Salsa, 296
    Steak Tostadas With
        Avocado & Radish Slaw, 173
    Tilapia Tacos, 379

B

Baby Octopus With Cherry
    Tomatoes, 420
Baby Potato Salad With Salsa
    Verde, 486
Backyard Burgers, Classic, 81
bacon and pancetta
    Armenian Butterflied Leg of
        Lamb, 272
    Baked Beans, 490
    Caprese Pizza With
        Bacon, 470
    Chicken Bacon Brochettes, 54
    Frijoles Borrachos, 494
    Italian Pork Tenderloin
        Brochettes, 27
    Red Cabbage Coleslaw, 479
    Rolled Veal Roast, 249
    Smoky Beef Burgers With
        Chipotle Ketchup, 93
Baked Beans, 490
Baked Chili Black Beans, 495

Balsamic Grilled Peppers, 38
Balsamic Grilled Vegetables, 439
Balsamic Honey Tenderloin, 259
Balsamic Peppercorn Chicken
    Legs, 301
barbecuing. See grilling
Barley Rice Salad,
    Mediterranean, 502
basil (fresh)
    Basil Butter, 433
    Caprese Pizza With
        Bacon, 470
    Grilled Corn Pizza, 463
    Grilled Eggplant With
        Provolone, 447
    Grilled Halloumi & Tomato
        Kabobs, 450
    Grilled Veal Saltimbocca, 22
beans. See also beans, green/
    yellow
    Baked Beans, 490
    Baked Chili Black Beans, 495
    Black Bean Corn Salsa, 528
    Frijoles Borrachos, 494
    Grilled Shrimp With Corn &
        Black Bean Salad, 412
    Spanish-Style Baked
        Beans, 491
    Three-Bean Salad, 506
beans, green/yellow
    Green Bean, Mushroom &
        Fennel Salad, 509
    Grilled Lamb Chops With
        French Bean Salad, 226
    Indonesian Chicken Breast
        Salad, 314
    Three-Bean Salad, 506
beef. See also liver; specific
    cuts (below)
    Texas Barbecue Brisket, 244
beef, ground
    cooking, 102
    Argentine Burgers, 89
    Brandy Dijon Beef Burgers, 83
    Chorizo Patties With
        Pebre, 149
    Classic Backyard Burgers, 81
    Jalapeño Cheeseburgers With
        Tomato Salad, 92
    Lamb Burgers With Grilled
        Vegetables, 116
    Puttanesca Burgers, 85

Rosemary Beef Burgers With
Jalapeño Mayo, 90
Shiitake Beef Burgers, 88
Smoky Beef Burgers With
Chipotle Ketchup, 93
Stuffed Cheddar Burgers, 86
beef flank steak. *See also*
beef steak
Cumin Flank Steak With
Avocado Salad, 169
Flank Steak Sandwiches With
Pepper Sauce, 105
Grilled Flank Steak &
Pebre, 179
Mustard Garlic Flank
Steak, 178
Soy-Marinated Flank
Steak, 180
Steak Tostadas With
Avocado & Radish Slaw, 173
beef ribs
Chipotle-Glazed Beef Short
Ribs, 192
Devilled Beef Ribs, 185
Hot-Smoked Spiced Beef
Back Ribs, 189
Korean Beef Short Ribs, 186
Savoury Beef Short Ribs, 188
Steak House Beef Ribs With
Stout Barbecue Sauce, 191
Texas Barbecued Beef
Ribs, 184
beef roast
Beef & Pork Bratwurst, 142
Beef, Caramelized Shallot &
Thyme Sausages, 145
Beef Tenderloin Roast With
Oyster Mushrooms, 242
Garlicky Prime Rib, 239
Honey Garlic Prime Rib
Roast, 243
Roast Sirloin With Orange
Barbecue Sauce, 241
Rotisserie Prime Rib, 237
Tandoori Barbecued Beef, 246
beef steak. *See also* beef flank
steak
trimming, 177
Arugula & Beefsteak Salad
With Tomato
Vinaigrette, 183

Beef Bulgogi Skewers, 20
Beef Kabobs With
Horseradish Sauce, 21
Beef Satays, 13
Cheesesteak Sandwiches for
Two, 106
Deli-Spiced Steak Kabobs
With Pearl Onions, 17
Gibson Flatiron Steak, 176
Grilled Steak & Gorgonzola
Pizza, 468
Grilled Steak Diable, 175
Grilled Steaks With Roquefort
Cheese Butter, 155
Grilled Tenderloin Steaks With
Mushrooms & Peppers, 159
Korean Steak Barbecue, 166
Mexican-Style Rib Eye
Medallions With
Peppers, 157
Old-Style Red Wine Marinated
"London Broil," 165
Peppercorn-Crusted
Steaks, 153
Peppercorn Thyme
T-Bones, 156
Rib Eye Steaks With Herb
Butter, 160
Rib Steaks With Beer
Marinade, 163
Rib Steak With Cherry Tomato
Salsa, 168
Salt & Pepper Steak With
Green Sauce, 170
Spicy Steak Kabobs, 15
Steak Burgers, 84
Steak Shish Kabobs, 16
Thick-Cut Sirloin Steak, 164
beer
Barbecue Beer Ribs, 211
Beer-Can Chicken With Greek
Spices, 283
Chicken Drumsticks With
Apple Stout Barbecue
Sauce, 302
Frijoles Borrachos, 494
Grilled Brined Whole
Turkey, 333

Rib Steaks With Beer
Marinade, 163
Savoury Beef Short Ribs, 188
Steak House Beef Ribs With
Stout Barbecue Sauce, 191
Texas Barbecue Brisket, 244
Beets, Garlic, 489
bison
Bison Burgers, 98
Deli-Spiced Steak Kabobs
With Pearl Onions, 17
Deli-Style Spiced Bison
Steaks, 197
Smoky Beef Burgers With
Chipotle Ketchup, 93
Blackened Catfish, 385
bok choy
Grilled Salmon Sandwiches
With Bok Choy Slaw, 131
Lemongrass Barbecued
Halibut Fillets, 389
Salmon Kabobs With Baby
Bok Choy, 63
Bombay Spice Mix, 526
brandy
Brandied Mushrooms, 101
Brandy Dijon Beef Burgers, 83
Grilled Steak With Brandy
Butter Sauce, 155
bread and buns (as ingredient).
See also burgers; sandwiches
Cheese-Stuffed Banana
Peppers, 437
Garlic Bread on the Grill, 459
Grilled Halloumi & Tomato
Kabobs, 450
Grilled Mozzarella Skewers
With Anchovy Sauce, 452
Grilled Sausage Spiedini, 38
Italian Pork Tenderloin
Brochettes, 27
Saucy Pulled Pork on
a Bun, 263
Brined Rotisserie Chicken,
Basic, 287
Brined Whole Turkey,
Grilled, 333
buffalo. *See* bison
Buffet-Style Grilled Squid
Salad, 417

bulgur
 Bulgur & Mushroom
  Burgers, 135
 Chicken With Tabbouleh
  Salad, 311
Buns, Hamburger, 94
burgers, 81–100, 109–110, 113–120,
 125, 135–136
 toppings, 101–102
Buttered Clams on the Grill, 425
Buttermilk & Spice Grilled
 Drumsticks, 300
butters (flavoured), 199, 353,
 359, 431, 535

C

cabbage
 Chinese Chicken Breast
  Salad, 315
 Creamy Coleslaw, 478
 Grilled Coleslaw, 35
 Grilled Fish Burritos, 381
 Grilled Salmon Sandwiches
  With Bok Choy Slaw, 131
 Indian-Spiced Coleslaw, 477
 Napa Slaw, 109
 Red Cabbage Coleslaw, 479
 Tangy Coleslaw, 475
Caesar Turkey Brochettes, 60
Cajun Corn Sauté, 497
Cajun Spice Mix, 526
Calves' Liver With Green Onions,
 Grilled, 232
Caper Mustard Butter, 535
Caprese Pizza With Bacon, 470
Carnival Chicken, 288
carrots
 Carrot & Peanut Salad, 513
 Grilled Chicken Banh Mi, 124
 Grilled Fish Burritos, 381
 Indian-Spiced Coleslaw, 477
catfish
 Blackened Catfish, 385
 Spiced Catfish Fillets With
  Thai Mango Relish, 386
 Spiced Tilapia Sandwiches
  With Onion Salad, 132
Caviar Butter, 535
Cedar-Planked Salmon, 365

celery
 Caesar Turkey Brochettes, 60
 Creamy Potato Salad, 480
 Smashed Potato Salad, 487
 Tangy Macaroni Salad, 500
charcoal grilling, 8
Char Siu, Barbecued, 256
Chat Masala for Grilled Corn, 432
cheese. See also specific types
 of cheese (below)
 Grilled Corn Pizza, 463
 Grilled Corn Polenta With
  Roasted Red Peppers, 496
 Grilled Halloumi & Tomato
  Kabobs, 450
 Grilled Prosciutto & Fig
  Sandwiches, 121
 Halloumi With Fresh
  Chilies, 455
 Parmesan-Crusted Turkey
  Scaloppine, 338
 Pork Tenderloin With Romano
  Cheese, 257
 Rapini & Garlic Pizza With
  Asiago Cheese, 460
 Sausage & Grilled Pepper
  Pizza, 471
 Swiss Chard Pizza, 461
 Veal Patty Melts, 104
 Zucchini Pizza With Fresh
  Tomato Sauce, 466
cheese, blue
 Blue Cheese & Horseradish
  Sauce, 102
 Gorgonzola Pork Tenderloin
  Steaks, 260
 Grilled Steak & Gorgonzola
  Pizza, 468
 Grilled Steaks With Roquefort
  Cheese Butter, 155
 Paris Wings With Crudités, 327
 Pork, Apple, Sage & Stilton
  Sausages, 144
 Veal & Gorgonzola Burgers
  With Onions, 99
cheese, Cheddar
 Barbecued Chicken Pizza, 467
 Glazed Cheddar Pork
  Burgers, 110
 Jalapeño Cheeseburgers With
  Tomato Salad, 92
 Stuffed Cheddar Burgers, 86

cheese, feta
 Feta & Lamb Burger Pitas, 119
 Greek Village Salad, 505
 Grilled Vegetable Quinoa
  Salad, 499
 Mediterranean Barley Rice
  Salad, 502
 Stuffed Feta Burgers, 86
cheese, mozzarella
 Bocconcini Chicken
  Burgers, 125
 Caprese Pizza With
  Bacon, 470
 Cheese-Stuffed Banana
  Peppers, 437
 Grilled Chicken
  Mozzarella, 309
 Grilled Mozzarella Skewers
  With Anchovy Sauce, 452
 Grilled Pizza Mexicana, 462
 Stuffed Meatball Sliders, 95
cheese, provolone
 Cheesesteak Sandwiches for
  Two, 106
 Grilled Cubanos, 111
 Grilled Eggplant & Pepper
  Panini, 134
 Grilled Eggplant With
  Provolone, 447
 Italian Stuffed Veal
  Burgers, 100
 Provoleta, 454
Cherry Tomato Salsa, 521
chicken. See also chicken, whole;
 specific parts (below)
 ground (cooking), 102
 Carnival Chicken, 288
 Chicken With Puerto Rican
  Adobo Seasoning, 293
 Chinese Seasoned Chicken
  Kabobs, 55
 Citrus Sesame Chicken, 299
 Crisp & Juicy Barbecued
  Chicken, 298
 Grilled Chicken Banh Mi, 124
 Thai Grilled Chicken, 291
chicken, whole
 Basic Brined Rotisserie
  Chicken, 287
 Beer-Can Chicken With Greek
  Spices, 283

Grilled Chicken With Buttery
Barbecue Sauce, 292
Mediterranean Lemon &
Rosemary Rotisserie
Chickens, 281
Rotisserie Piri-Piri
Chickens, 284
Spatchcock Barbecue
Chicken, 290
Spiced Spatchcock
Chicken, 285
chicken breasts
Barbecued Chicken Pizza, 467
Chicken & Mango Kabobs, 50
Chicken Bacon Brochettes, 54
Chicken Tikka, 52
Chicken With Tabbouleh
Salad, 311
Chinese Chicken Breast
Salad, 315
Flash-Grilled Chicken
Breasts With Oyster
Mushrooms, 306
Grilled Chicken Mozzarella, 309
Grilled Chicken Salad, 312
Grilled Marinated Quails
(variation), 346
Indonesian Chicken Breast
Salad, 314
Lemon Chicken Kabobs, 49
Lime-Grilled Chicken Breasts
With Avocado Salsa, 296
Mango Chicken, 307
Middle Eastern Chicken Breast
Salad, 317
Oregano Chicken With
Tomato Salsa, 295
Peanut & Coconut Chicken
Skewers, 56
Teriyaki Chicken Sandwiches,
Gourmet, 123
chicken thighs and legs
Balsamic Peppercorn Chicken
Legs, 301
Bocconcini Chicken
Burgers, 125
Buttermilk & Spice Grilled
Drumsticks, 300
Chicken Drumsticks With
Apple Stout Barbecue
Sauce, 302

Chicken Teriyaki Skewers, 47
Coriander Chicken, 294
Ginger Soy Chicken
Skewers, 46
Marmalade-Glazed Chicken
Thighs, 59
Quick Korean Chicken, 303
Sticky Glazed Grilled Chicken
With Cucumber Salad, 318
Thai-Style Grilled Chicken
Wraps, 127
chicken wings
Chili Chicken Wings, 324
Five-Spice Chicken
Wings, 320
Indian Hot Wings With Mint
Dipping Sauce, 321
Mexican Wings & Green
Salsa, 328
Paris Wings With Crudités, 327
Three-Pepper Chicken
Wings, 325
Chilean Pickled Onions, 149
chili sauce (as ingredient)
Chili Barbecued Shrimp, 403
Chili Chicken Wings, 324
Molasses Barbecue
Sauce, 534
Smoky Barbecue Sauce, 529
Chili Spice Mix, 526
Chimichurri Rojo, 531
Chimichurri Verde, Argentine, 531
Chinese Chicken Breast
Salad, 315
Chinese Seasoned Chicken
Kabobs, 55
Chinese-Style Grilled Ribs, 216
Chipotle-Glazed Beef Short
Ribs, 192
Chipotle-Glazed Turkey
Thighs, 340
Chipotle Turkey Waves, 62
Chorizo Patties With Pebre, 149
Cider & Maple Grilled Duck, 341
Cider-Glazed Apples & Onion, 435
cilantro
Chicken Cutlets With Cilantro
Peanut Sauce, 304
Coriander Chicken, 294
Curried Pork Burgers, 113
Frijoles Borrachos, 494
Grilled Cilantro Halibut, 390

Grilled Fish Burritos, 381
Lime & Chili Butter, 535
Pebre Sauce, 179
Pickerel With Charmoula, 66
Pickerel With Cherry Tomato
Relish, 375
Salt & Pepper Steak With
Green Sauce, 170
Shrimp Skewers With Cilantro
& Almond Relish, 73
Smoke-Grilled Lamb
Shoulder, 270
Citrus Sesame Chicken, 299
Clams on the Grill, Buttered, 425
coconut and coconut milk
Kerala Grilled Shrimp, 410
Lemongrass Barbecued
Halibut Fillets, 389
Peanut & Coconut Chicken
Skewers, 56
Cod in Grape Leaf Packets, 398
coleslaw. See cabbage
Coriander Pork Skewers With
Red Onion Salsa, 33
corn
butters and sauces for, 431
Black Bean Corn Salsa, 528
Cajun Corn Sauté, 497
Dilled Potato & Grilled Corn
Salad, 482
Grilled Chicken & Charred
Corn Salad, 312
Grilled Corn on the Cob With
Ancho Chili Glaze, 429
Grilled Corn Pizza, 463
Grilled Corn Polenta With
Roasted Red Peppers, 496
Grilled Shrimp With Corn &
Black Bean Salad, 412
Cornish hens
Lemon Pepper Cornish
Hens, 330
Tuscan Cornish Hens, 329
couscous. See pasta and noodles
Cubanos, Grilled, 111

cucumber
    Arugula & Beefsteak Salad
        With Tomato
        Vinaigrette, 183
    Chinese Chicken Breast
        Salad, 315
    Creamy Cucumber Salad, 512
    Filipino Cucumber Salad, 510
    Greek Grilled Squid, 417
    Greek Village Salad, 505
    Indonesian Chicken Breast
        Salad, 314
    Lamb Kabobs With
        Kachumber Salad, 45
    Mediterranean Barley Rice
        Salad, 502
    Quick Pickled Cucumbers, 180
    Sticky Glazed Grilled Chicken
        With Cucumber Salad, 318
    Sweet Pea & Potato Salad, 481
    Tart-Sweet Cucumber
        Slices, 101
    Tzatziki, 25
    Vietnamese Squid Salad, 418
Cumin Flank Steak With
    Avocado Salad, 169
Curried Pork Burgers, 113
Curry Glaze, 68
Curry Shrimp Soft Tacos,
    Grilled, 406

D

daikon. *See* radishes
Deli-Spiced Steak Kabobs With
    Pearl Onions, 17
Deli-Style Spiced Bison
    Steaks, 197
Deli-Style Steak Spice Mix, 17
Devilled Beef Ribs, 185
Dilled Potato & Grilled Corn
    Salad, 482
duck
    Cider & Maple Grilled
        Duck, 341
    Grilled Orange Duck, 342

E

eggplant
    Grilled Eggplant & Pepper
        Panini, 134
    Grilled Eggplant & Tomato
        Sandwiches, 138
    Grilled Eggplant With
        Provolone, 447
    Grilled Vegetable & Israeli
        Couscous Salad, 504
    Lamb Burgers With Grilled
        Vegetables, 116
    Rosemary Grilled
        Scallops, 413
    Soy-Glazed Halibut
        Kabobs, 65
    Whitefish With Grilled
        Ratatouille Salad, 402

F

fennel
    Creamy Coleslaw, 478
    Green Bean, Mushroom &
        Fennel Salad, 509
    Whole Lake Trout With
        Fennel Salad, 351
Filipino Cucumber Salad, 510
fish. *See also* specific types of
    fish and seafood
    about, 102, 364
    Fish Tikka, 383
    Glazed Fish Kabobs, 69
    Misoyaki, 400
    Seafood Kabobs With Saffron
        Aioli, 74
Five-Spice Chicken Wings, 320
flank steak. *See* beef flank steak
Flash-Grilled Chicken Breasts
    With Oyster Mushrooms, 306
Frijoles Borrachos, 494

G

garlic
    Argentine Chimichurri
        Verde, 531
    Beef Bulgogi Skewers, 20
    Chimichurri Rojo, 531
    Garlic Beets, 489

    Garlic Bread on the Grill, 459
    Garlic Flatbread, 456
    Garlicky Prime Rib, 239
    Garlic-Marinated Veal Chops
        With Grilled Potato
        Salad, 196
    Grilled Cubanos, 111
    Grilled Hot Pepper Salsa, 524
    Honey Garlic Marinade, 533
    Korean Barbecue Sauce, 531
    Mustard Garlic Flank
        Steak, 178
    Rapini & Garlic Pizza With
        Asiago Cheese, 460
gas grilling, 8
gin
    Gibson Flatiron Steak, 176
    Turkey Sausages, 142
ginger
    Chinese Seasoned Chicken
        Kabobs, 55
    Ginger Garlic Pork
        Chops, 200
    Ginger Soy Chicken
        Skewers, 46
    Ginger Teriyaki Glaze, 68
    Grilled Pickerel With Ginger &
        Green Onions, 378
    Grilled Pork Chops With
        Pineapple Salsa, 207
    Korean Barbecue Sauce, 531
    Quick Korean Chicken, 303
    Salmon & Scallop Grill, 366
    Tikka Marinade, 533
Glazed Cheddar Pork
    Burgers, 110
Glazed Fish Kabobs, 69
Glazed Salmon Steaks, 374
glazes, 68
Golden Onions, 102
Gourmet Teriyaki Chicken
    Sandwiches, 123
Greek Grilled Squid, 417
Greek-Style Leg of Lamb for a
    Crowd, 276
Greek-Style Seafood Kabobs, 70
Greek Village Salad, 505
Green Bean, Mushroom &
    Fennel Salad, 509
Green Onion Pork Burgers, 109

greens. *See also* arugula; lettuce; radicchio; spinach
    Middle Eastern Chicken Breast Salad, 317
    Rapini & Garlic Pizza With Asiago Cheese, 460
    Swiss Chard Pizza, 461
Green Salsa, 328
Gremolata Rack of Lamb, 221
grilling
    fuel choice, 8
    temperatures, 8
    tools, 9
Guacamole, Simple, 523

H

halibut
    Grilled Cilantro Halibut, 390
    Grilled Halibut With Oyster Mushrooms, 388
    Lemongrass Barbecued Halibut Fillets, 389
    Soy-Glazed Halibut Kabobs, 65
Halloumi With Fresh Chilies, 455
ham. *See* prosciutto and ham
Hamburger Buns, 94
herbs (fresh). *See also* specific herbs
    Caviar Butter, 535
    Cod in Grape Leaf Packets, 398
    Garlic-Marinated Veal Chops With Grilled Potato Salad, 196
    Grilled Lemon Herb Trout for Two, 357
    Grilled Veal Chops With Fines-Herbes Butter, 199
    Herb & Spice Lamb Burgers, 118
    Herb Butter, 535
    Herbed Lamb Kabobs, 43
    Herbed Pork Rib Roast, 252
    Indian-Spiced Coleslaw, 477
    Lemon Herb Marinade, 533
    Pebre Sauce, 179
    Pickerel With Charmoula, 66
    Rib Eye Steaks With Herb Butter, 160

Rotisserie Prime Rib, 237
    Spatchcock Barbecue Chicken, 290
    Trout With Herb Stuffing, 360
honey
    Balsamic Honey Tenderloin, 259
    Honey Garlic Marinade, 533
    Honey Garlic Prime Rib Roast, 243
    Honey-Mustard Pork Kabobs, 28
    Sticky Glazed Grilled Chicken With Cucumber Salad, 318
    Texas Barbecued Beef Ribs, 184
horseradish
    Beef Kabobs With Horseradish Sauce, 21
    Blue Cheese & Horseradish Sauce, 102
    Horseradish Butter, 535
    Horseradish Cream, 170
Hot & Spicy Chipotle Barbecue Sauce, 530
Hot Italian Sausages, 141
Hot Pepper Salsa, Grilled, 524
Hot-Smoked Spiced Beef Back Ribs, 189

I

Indian Hot Wings With Mint Dipping Sauce, 321
Indian-Spiced Coleslaw, 477
Indonesian Chicken Breast Salad, 314
Indonesian Peanut Dressing, 314
Indonesian-Style Ribs, 217
Island Pork Loin & Pineapple Brochettes, 23
Italian Pork Tenderloin Brochettes, 27
Italian Sausage Spiral, 139
Italian Stuffed Veal Burgers, 100

J

Jalapeño Cheeseburgers With Tomato Salad, 92

K

kalbi (cutting), 187
Kerala Grilled Shrimp, 410
ketchup (as ingredient)
    Chili Chicken Wings, 324
    Grilled Chicken With Buttery Barbecue Sauce, 292
    Honey Garlic Prime Rib Roast, 243
    Slow-Grilled Barbecue Pork Ribs, 210
    Texas Barbecued Beef Ribs, 184
Korean Barbecue Sauce, 531
Korean Beef Short Ribs (Kalbi), 186
Korean Chicken, Quick, 303
Korean Grilled Quails, 347
Korean Steak Barbecue, 166

L

lamb. *See also* lamb, ground; liver
    Armenian Butterflied Leg of Lamb, 272
    Beef Satays, 13
    Gremolata Rack of Lamb, 221
    Grilled Lamb Chops With French Bean Salad, 226
    Herbed Lamb Kabobs, 43
    Lamb & Leek Sausages, 146
    Lamb Chops With Orzo Salad, 228
    Lamb Chops With Spinach Biryani, 223
    Lamb Kabobs With Kachumber Salad, 45
    Leg of Lamb With Red Currant Mint Sauce, 277
    Merguez Sausages, 147
    Mojito Rack of Lamb, 225
    Peppered Lamb With Mint Butter, 230
    Rotisserie Greek-Style Leg of Lamb, 276
    Sage Lamb Kabobs, 42

Smoke-Grilled Lamb
Shoulder, 270
Teriyaki Orange Lamb
Chops, 224
Wine-Marinated Leg of
Lamb, 271
lamb, ground, 102
Adana Lamb Kabobs, 39
Feta & Lamb Burger Pitas, 119
Herb & Spice Lamb
Burgers, 118
Lamb Burgers, 115
Lamb Burgers With Grilled
Vegetables, 116
Lamb Koftas on Rosemary, 40
Stuffed Cheddar Burgers
(variation), 86
Last-Minute Turkey
Scaloppine, 339
leeks
Lamb & Leek Sausages, 146
Peach & Leek–Stuffed
Butterflied Pork Loin, 258
lemon
Caper Mustard Butter, 535
Gremolata Rack of Lamb, 221
Grilled Lemon Pork
Chops, 208
Lemon Butter, 431
Lemon Chicken Kabobs, 49
Lemon Dill Salmon
Steaks, 370
Lemon Grilled Potatoes, 434
Lemon Herb Marinade, 533
Lemon Mint Pork
Tenderloin, 265
Lemon Pepper Cornish
Hens, 330
Lemon Pepper
Mayonnaise, 431
Lemon Sage Barbecued
Turkey Breast, 336
Salmon With Lemon &
Onion Relish, 369
Tilapia With Tomatoes &
Lemon Relish, 384
Whole Trout With Lemon
Parsley Butter, 353
Lemongrass Barbecued
Halibut Fillets, 389

lettuce
Grilled Chicken & Charred
Corn Salad, 312
Grilled Lamb Chops With
French Bean Salad, 226
Grilled Shrimp With Corn &
Black Bean Salad, 412
Indonesian Chicken Breast
Salad, 314
Korean Steak Barbecue, 166
Seafood Caesar Salad, 405
lime
Adobo Marinade, 533
Lime & Chili Butter, 535
Lime-Grilled Chicken Breasts
With Avocado Salsa, 296
Shrimp & Mango
Brochettes, 76
liver
Chicken Teriyaki Skewers, 47
Grilled Calves' Liver With
Green Onions, 232
Grilled Liver With Mushrooms
& Onions, 231

M

mango
Chicken & Mango Kabobs, 50
Mango Chicken, 307
Shrimp & Mango
Brochettes, 76
Spiced Catfish Fillets With
Thai Mango Relish, 386
Vietnamese Squid Salad, 418
maple syrup
Chicken Drumsticks With
Apple Stout Barbecue
Sauce, 302
Cider & Maple Grilled
Duck, 341
Glazed Salmon Steaks, 374
Grilled Brined Whole
Turkey, 333
marinades, 533
Marinated Peppers, Grilled, 101
Marinated Sardines, Grilled, 394
Marmalade-Glazed Chicken
Thighs, 59
Masala Salmon, 373

mayonnaise (as ingredient)
Caper Mayonnaise, 123
Dill Pickle Aioli, 130
Green Onion Mayonnaise, 131
Horseradish Cream, 170
Jalapeño Mayo, 90
Lemon Pepper
Mayonnaise, 431
Minty Mayonnaise, 101
Romano Mayo, 138
Smoky Orange Mayonnaise, 431
Tarragon Mayonnaise, 351
Mediterranean Barley Rice
Salad, 502
Mediterranean Lemon &
Rosemary Rotisserie
Chickens, 281
Mediterranean Olive Oil, 431
Merguez Sausages, 147
Mexican Pork Shoulder, 268
Mexican-Style Rib Eye
Medallions With Peppers, 157
Mexican Wings & Green
Salsa, 328
Middle Eastern Chicken
Breast Salad, 317
mint (fresh)
Indian Hot Wings With Mint
Dipping Sauce, 321
Lamb Koftas on Rosemary, 40
Leg of Lamb With Red
Currant Mint Sauce, 277
Lemon Mint Pork
Tenderloin, 265
Minty Mayonnaise, 101
Mojito Rack of Lamb, 225
Peppered Lamb With Mint
Butter, 230
Tomato Mint Salsa, 520
Miso-Orange Grilled Scallops, 77
Misoyaki, 400
Mojito Rack of Lamb, 225
molasses
Baked Chili Black Beans, 495
Chicken Drumsticks With
Apple Stout Barbecue
Sauce, 302
Hot & Spicy Chipotle
Barbecue Sauce, 530
Molasses Barbecue
Sauce, 534

Mole Spice Mix, 526
Moroccan Marinade, 533
mushrooms
    Beef Tenderloin Roast With
        Oyster Mushrooms, 242
    Brandied Mushrooms, 101
    Bulgur & Mushroom
        Burgers, 135
    Chicken Bacon Brochettes, 54
    Flash-Grilled Chicken
        Breasts With Oyster
        Mushrooms, 306
    Green Bean, Mushroom &
        Fennel Salad, 509
    Grilled Halibut With Oyster
        Mushrooms, 388
    Grilled Liver With Mushrooms
        & Onions, 231
    Grilled Portobello & Cheese
        Burgers, 136
    Grilled Tenderloin Steaks With
        Mushrooms & Peppers, 159
    Grilled Tofu & Vegetable
        Antipasto, 448
    Grilled Vegetable & Israeli
        Couscous Salad, 504
    Herbed Lamb Kabobs, 43
    Mushroom-Stuffed Turkey
        Breast Rolls, 337
    Oyster Mushrooms &
        Peppers, 442
    Shiitake Beef Burgers, 88
    Steak Burgers, 84
    Venison Burgers With Red
        Wine Mushrooms, 120
    Wild Rice & Mushrooms,
        Cool, 501
mustard
    Brandy Dijon Beef Burgers, 83
    Caper Mustard Butter, 535
    Honey-Mustard Pork
        Kabobs, 28
    Mustard Cream Sauce, 170
    Mustard Garlic Flank
        Steak, 178

N

Napa Slaw, 109
noodles. *See* pasta and noodles

O

octopus
    Baby Octopus With Cherry
        Tomatoes, 420
    Grilled Octopus, 419
Old-Style Red Wine Marinated
    "London Broil," 165
Olive Oil Potatoes, 434
olives
    Feta & Lamb Burger Pitas, 119
    Greek Grilled Squid, 417
    Greek Village Salad, 505
    Olive Sage Butter, 535
    Swiss Chard Pizza, 461
One Potato, Two Potato, 434
onions. *See also* onions, green
    Balsamic Grilled
        Vegetables, 439
    Cajun Corn Sauté, 497
    Chilean Pickled Onions, 149
    Cider-Glazed Apples &
        Onion, 435
    Coriander Pork Skewers With
        Red Onion Salsa, 33
    Deli-Spiced Steak Kabobs
        With Pearl Onions, 17
    Fresh Tomato & Onion
        Relish, 102
    Golden Onions, 102
    Grilled Liver With Mushrooms
        & Onions, 231
    Grilled Stuffed Squid, 414
    Salmon With Lemon & Onion
        Relish, 369
    Shrimp & Mango
        Brochettes, 76
    Smoked Salmon Pizza With
        Marinated Onion, 465
    Spanish-Style Baked
        Beans, 491
    Spiced Tilapia Sandwiches
        With Onion Salad, 132
    Tilapia Tacos, 379
    Turkish Onion Salad, 39
onions, green
    Chicken Teriyaki Skewers, 47
    Green Onion Pork
        Burgers, 109

    Grilled Calves' Liver With
        Green Onions, 232
    Salmon & Scallop Grill, 366
    Salt & Pepper Steak With
        Green Sauce, 170
    Whole Arctic Char With Green
        Onion Butter Sauce, 363
oranges and orange juice
    Adobo Marinade, 533
    Grilled Orange Duck, 342
    Miso-Orange Grilled
        Scallops, 77
    Orange Spice Mix, 526
    Roast Sirloin With Orange
        Barbecue Sauce, 241
    Teriyaki Orange Lamb
        Chops, 224
oregano (fresh)
    Argentine Chimichurri
        Verde, 531
    Oregano Chicken With
        Tomato Salsa, 295
Oyster Mushrooms &
    Peppers, 442
Oysters With Black Bean
    Sauce, Grilled, 424

P

pancetta. *See* bacon and
    pancetta
Paris Wings With Crudités, 327
parsley (fresh)
    Argentine Burgers, 89
    Argentine Chimichurri
        Verde, 531
    Baby Potato Salad With Salsa
        Verde, 486
    Chicken Cutlets With Cilantro
        Peanut Sauce, 304
    Chicken With Tabbouleh
        Salad, 311
    Chimichurri Rojo, 531
    Gremolata Rack of Lamb, 221
    Herb Butter, 535
    Pebre Sauce, 179
    Pickerel With Charmoula, 66
    Provoleta, 454
    Whole Trout With Lemon
        Parsley Butter, 353

pasta and noodles
  Grilled Vegetable & Israeli
    Couscous Salad, 504
  Lamb Chops With Orzo
    Salad, 228
  Tangy Macaroni Salad, 500
Pattypan Skewers, 444
peaches
  Barbecued Peach Pork
    Chops, 202
  Peach & Leek–Stuffed
    Butterflied Pork Loin, 258
peanuts and peanut butter
  Carrot & Peanut Salad, 513
  Chicken Cutlets With Cilantro
    Peanut Sauce, 304
  Indonesian Peanut
    Dressing, 314
  Peanut & Coconut Chicken
    Skewers, 56
Pebre Sauce, 179
Peppercorn-Crusted Steaks, 153
Peppercorn Thyme T-Bones, 156
Peppered Lamb With Mint
  Butter, 230
peppers. See also peppers, hot;
  peppers, sweet
  Black Bean Corn Salsa, 528
  Grilled Curry Shrimp Soft
    Tacos, 406
  Grilled Turkey Breast With
    Sautéed Banana
    Peppers, 334
  Grilled Vegetable Quinoa
    Salad, 499
  Lemon Chicken Kabobs, 49
  Mexican Pork Shoulder, 268
  Mexican-Style Rib Eye
    Medallions With
    Peppers, 157
  Mexican Wings & Green
    Salsa, 328
  Pork & Poblano Kabobs, 30
  Sausage & Grilled Pepper
    Pizza, 471
  Sweet & Tangy Sausage
    Pepper Kabobs, 36
  Texas Barbecued Beef
    Ribs, 184
  Vietnamese Squid Salad, 418

peppers, hot. See also peppers,
  jalapeño
  Baked Chili Black Beans, 495
  Caesar Turkey Brochettes, 60
  Carnival Chicken, 288
  Carrot & Peanut Salad, 513
  Cheese-Stuffed Banana
    Peppers, 437
  Chipotle-Glazed Beef
    Short Ribs, 192
  Chipotle-Glazed Turkey
    Thighs, 340
  Greek Grilled Squid, 417
  Green Salsa, 328
  Grilled Hot Pepper Salsa, 524
  Grilled Pizza Mexicana, 462
  Grilled Pork Chops With
    Pineapple Salsa, 207
  Halloumi With Fresh
    Chilies, 455
  Hot & Spicy Chipotle
    Barbecue Sauce, 530
  Hot-Smoked Spiced Beef
    Back Ribs, 189
  Indian-Spiced Coleslaw, 477
  Indonesian-Style Ribs, 217
  Island Pork Loin & Pineapple
    Brochettes, 23
  Korean Steak Barbecue, 166
  Peanut & Coconut Chicken
    Skewers, 56
  Rosemary Grilled
    Scallops, 413
  Rotisserie Piri-Piri
    Chickens, 284
  "Shrimp on the Barbi"
    With Chinese Dipping
    Sauce, 409
  Smoky Beef Burgers With
    Chipotle Ketchup, 93
  Smoky Orange
    Mayonnaise, 431
  Spiced Catfish Fillets With
    Thai Mango Relish, 386
  Thai-Style Grilled Chicken
    Wraps, 127
  Thai Sweet Chili Sauce, 76
  Zucchini Pizza With Fresh
    Tomato Sauce, 466

peppers, jalapeño. See also
  peppers, hot
  Adobo Marinade, 533
  Argentine Burgers, 89
  Argentine Chimichurri
    Verde, 531
  Curried Pork Burgers, 113
  Frijoles Borrachos, 494
  Grilled Fish Burritos, 381
  Jalapeño Cheeseburgers With
    Tomato Salad, 92
  Lime-Grilled Chicken Breasts
    With Avocado Salsa, 296
  Minty Mayonnaise, 101
  Pebre Sauce, 179
  Rib Steak With Cherry
    Tomato Salsa, 168
  Rosemary Beef Burgers With
    Jalapeño Mayo, 90
  Salt & Pepper Steak With
    Green Sauce, 170
  Tikka Marinade, 533
  Tilapia Tacos, 379
  Tomato Mint Salsa, 520
  Tuna With Grilled Jalapeño
    Salsa, 395
peppers, sweet
  Balsamic Grilled Peppers, 38
  Balsamic Grilled
    Vegetables, 439
  Beef Bulgogi Skewers, 20
  Chicken & Mango Kabobs, 50
  Chinese Seasoned Chicken
    Kabobs, 55
  Flank Steak Sandwiches With
    Pepper Sauce, 105
  Glazed Fish Kabobs, 69
  Greek-Style Seafood
    Kabobs, 70
  Grilled Corn Polenta With
    Roasted Red Peppers, 496
  Grilled Eggplant & Pepper
    Panini, 134
  Grilled Marinated Peppers, 101
  Grilled Tenderloin Steaks With
    Mushrooms & Peppers, 159
  Grilled Tofu & Vegetable
    Antipasto, 448
  Mediterranean Barley Rice
    Salad, 502

Mexican-Style Rib Eye Medallions With Peppers, 157
Oyster Mushrooms & Peppers, 442
Portuguese Grilled Sardines With Potatoes & Peppers, 392
Shrimp & Mango Brochettes, 76
Spicy Steak Kabobs, 15
Tofu Skewers With Jerk Barbecue Sauce, 35
Yellow Tomato Salsa, 519
Philippine Pork Kabobs, 31
pickerel
Grilled Pickerel With Ginger & Green Onions, 378
Pickerel & Potato Packets, 377
Pickerel With Charmoula, 66
Pickerel With Cherry Tomato Relish, 375
Whitefish With Grilled Ratatouille Salad, 402
pineapple
Grilled Pineapple, 449
Grilled Pork Chops With Pineapple Salsa, 207
Indonesian Chicken Breast Salad, 314
Island Pork Loin & Pineapple Brochettes, 23
Sweet & Sour Shrimp Kabobs, 72
pitas
Feta & Lamb Burger Pitas, 119
Pork Souvlaki, 25
pizza dough
Barbecued Chicken Pizza, 467
Caprese Pizza With Bacon, 470
Grilled Corn Pizza, 463
Grilled Pizza Mexicana, 462
Grilled Steak & Gorgonzola Pizza, 468
Rapini & Garlic Pizza With Asiago Cheese, 460
Sausage & Grilled Pepper Pizza, 471

Smoked Salmon Pizza With Marinated Onion, 465
Swiss Chard Pizza, 461
Zucchini Pizza With Fresh Tomato Sauce, 466
Plum-Glazed Pork Loin, 254
pork. *See also* liver; specific cuts (below)
Baked Beans, 490
Barbecued Peach Pork Chops, 202
Barbecued Pork Belly, 267
Beef & Pork Bratwurst, 142
Beef Satays, 13
Ginger Garlic Pork Chops, 200
Grilled Lemon Pork Chops, 208
Grilled Pork Chops With Pineapple Salsa, 207
Hot Italian Sausages, 141
Island Pork Loin & Pineapple Brochettes, 23
Italian Sausage Spiral, 139
Lamb & Leek Sausages, 146
Philippine Pork Kabobs, 31
Pork & Poblano Kabobs, 30
Pork, Apple, Sage & Stilton Sausages, 144
Pork Chops With Chimichurri Rojo, 204
Pork Souvlaki, 25
Turkey Sausages, 142
pork, ground
cooking, 102
Chorizo Patties With Pebre, 149
Curried Pork Burgers, 113
Glazed Cheddar Pork Burgers, 110
Green Onion Pork Burgers, 109
Juicy Pork Burgers, 114
Puttanesca Burgers, 85
Stuffed Cheddar Burgers (variation), 86
Thai Minced Pork Kabobs, 34
pork ribs
Barbecue Beer Ribs, 211
Chinese-Style Grilled Ribs, 216
Indonesian-Style Ribs, 217
Rosemary Back Ribs, 214

Slow-Grilled Barbecue Pork Ribs, 210
Smoked Garlic Ribs With Fresh Tomato Barbecue Sauce, 220
Whisky Sour Ribs, 213
pork roast
Barbecued Char Siu, 256
Herbed Pork Rib Roast, 252
Mexican Pork Shoulder, 268
Peach & Leek–Stuffed Butterflied Pork Loin, 258
Plum-Glazed Pork Loin, 254
Rotisserie Pork Rib Roast, 251
Saucy Pulled Pork on a Bun, 263
Smoked Pork Loin, 255
pork tenderloin
Balsamic Honey Tenderloin, 259
Coriander Pork Skewers With Red Onion Salsa, 33
Gorgonzola Pork Tenderloin Steaks, 260
Grilled Cubanos, 111
Honey-Mustard Pork Kabobs, 28
Italian Pork Tenderloin Brochettes, 27
Lemon Mint Pork Tenderloin, 265
Pork Souvlaki, 25
Pork Tenderloin With Romano Cheese, 257
Sweet & Sour Pork Tenderloin, 262
Portuguese Grilled Sardines With Potatoes & Peppers, 392
potatoes
Baby Potato Salad With Salsa Verde, 486
Creamy Potato Salad, 480
Dilled Potato & Grilled Corn Salad, 482
Garlic-Marinated Veal Chops With Grilled Potato Salad, 196
Grilled Potato Salad Kabobs, 433
Lemon Grilled Potatoes, 434
Olive Oil Potatoes, 434
Pickerel & Potato Packets, 377

Portuguese Grilled Sardines With Potatoes & Peppers, 392

Roasted Two-Potato Salad, 484

Rosemary Grilled Scallops, 413

Salt & Pepper Potato Packets, 434

Smashed Potato Salad, 487

Sweet Pea & Potato Salad, 481

Warm Potato Salad, 485

poultry. See chicken; Cornish hens; duck; quails; turkey

prosciutto and ham

Grilled Cubanos, 111

Grilled Prosciutto & Fig Sandwiches, 121

Grilled Veal Saltimbocca, 22

Grilled Whitefish BLTs, 130

Italian Stuffed Veal Burgers, 100

Lemon Sage Barbecued Turkey Breast, 336

Peach & Leek–Stuffed Butterflied Pork Loin, 258

Provençal Butter, 431

Provoleta, 454

Puttanesca Burgers, 85

Q

quails

Grilled Marinated Quails, 346

Korean Grilled Quails, 347

Rosemary Skewered Quails, 345

Quick Korean Chicken, 303

Quick Pickled Cucumbers, 180

Quinoa Salad, Grilled Vegetable, 499

R

radicchio

Grilled Radicchio, 440

Middle Eastern Chicken Breast Salad, 317

radishes

Carrot & Peanut Salad, 513

Chinese Chicken Breast Salad, 315

Grilled Chicken Banh Mi, 124

Steak Tostadas With Avocado & Radish Slaw, 173

Sweet Pea & Potato Salad, 481

Rapini & Garlic Pizza With Asiago Cheese, 460

Rib Eye Steaks With Herb Butter, 160

ribs. See beef ribs; pork ribs

Rib Steaks With Beer Marinade, 163

Rib Steak With Cherry Tomato Salsa, 168

rice

Cool Wild Rice & Mushrooms, 501

Lamb Chops With Spinach Biryani, 223

Mediterranean Barley Rice Salad, 502

rosemary (fresh)

Lamb Koftas on Rosemary, 40

Mediterranean Lemon & Rosemary Rotisserie Chickens, 281

Rosemary Back Ribs, 214

Rosemary Beef Burgers With Jalapeño Mayo, 90

Rosemary Grilled Scallops, 413

Rosemary Skewered Quails, 345

Rotisserie Greek-Style Leg of Lamb, 276

Rotisserie Piri-Piri Chickens, 284

Rotisserie Pork Rib Roast, 251

Rotisserie Prime Rib, 237

rubs and spice mixes, 17, 526

S

sage

Olive Sage Butter, 535

Pork, Apple, Sage & Stilton Sausages, 144

Sage Lamb Kabobs, 42

salmon

Cedar-Planked Salmon, 365

Glazed Salmon Steaks, 374

Greek-Style Seafood Kabobs, 70

Grilled Salmon Patties, 129

Grilled Salmon Sandwiches With Bok Choy Slaw, 131

Lemon Dill Salmon Steaks, 370

Masala Salmon, 373

Salmon & Scallop Grill, 366

Salmon Kabobs With Baby Bok Choy, 63

Salmon With Lemon & Onion Relish, 369

Smoked Salmon Pizza With Marinated Onion, 465

Tamarind-Glazed Salmon Kabobs, 64

salsas, 517–521

Salt & Pepper Potato Packets, 434

Salt & Pepper Steak With Green Sauce, 170

sandwiches, 105–106, 121–124, 127, 130–134, 138. See also burgers; pitas; tortillas

sardines

Grilled Marinated Sardines, 394

Portuguese Grilled Sardines With Potatoes & Peppers, 392

sauces, 76, 101–102, 179. See also salsas

barbecue, 529–531, 534

for corn, 431

pizza, 467

Saucy Pulled Pork on a Bun, 263

sausage, 139–149
  making, 140
  Grilled Sausage Spiedini, 38
  Sausage & Grilled Pepper
    Pizza, 471
  Sweet & Tangy Sausage
    Pepper Kabobs, 36
scallops
  Greek-Style Seafood
    Kabobs, 70
  Miso-Orange Grilled
    Scallops, 77
  Rosemary Grilled
    Scallops, 413
  Salmon & Scallop Grill, 366
  Seafood Kabobs With
    Saffron Aioli, 74
seasonings, 17, 526
shallots
  Beef, Caramelized Shallot &
    Thyme Sausages, 145
  Shallot Peppercorn
    Butter, 535
shrimp
  Chili Barbecued Shrimp, 403
  Greek-Style Seafood
    Kabobs, 70
  Grilled Curry Shrimp Soft
    Tacos, 406
  Grilled Shrimp With Corn &
    Black Bean Salad, 412
  Kerala Grilled Shrimp, 410
  Seafood Caesar Salad, 405
  Seafood Kabobs With
    Saffron Aioli, 74
  Shrimp & Mango
    Brochettes, 76
  "Shrimp on the Barbi" With
    Chinese Dipping
    Sauce, 409
  Shrimp Skewers With Cilantro
    & Almond Relish, 73
  Sweet & Sour Shrimp
    Kabobs, 72
Slow-Grilled Barbecue Pork
  Ribs, 210
Smashed Potato Salad, 487
Smoked Garlic Ribs With Fresh
  Tomato Barbecue Sauce, 220
Smoked Pork Loin, 255
Smoked Salmon Pizza With
  Marinated Onion, 465

Smoke-Grilled Lamb
  Shoulder, 270
Smoky Barbecue Sauce, 529
Smoky Beef Burgers With
  Chipotle Ketchup, 93
Smoky Orange Mayonnaise, 431
Souvlaki, Pork, 25
Soy-Glazed Halibut Kabobs, 65
Soy-Marinated Flank Steak, 180
Spanish-Style Baked Beans, 491
Spatchcock Barbecue
  Chicken, 290
Spiced Catfish Fillets With Thai
  Mango Relish, 386
Spiced Olive Oil & Butter, 431
Spiced Spatchcock Chicken, 285
Spiced Tilapia Sandwiches
  With Onion Salad, 132
spice mixes and rubs, 17, 526
Spicy Steak Kabobs, 15
spinach
  Italian Stuffed Veal
    Burgers, 100
  Lamb Chops With Spinach
    Biryani, 223
  Mediterranean Barley
    Rice Salad, 502
squid
  Greek Grilled Squid, 417
  Grilled Stuffed Squid, 414
  Seafood Caesar Salad, 405
  Vietnamese Squid Salad, 418
steak. See beef flank steak;
  beef steak
Sticky Glazed Grilled Chicken
  With Cucumber Salad, 318
Stuffed Cheddar Burgers, 84
Stuffed Meatball Sliders, 95
Stuffed Squid, Grilled, 414
Sweet & Sour Pork
  Tenderloin, 262
Sweet & Sour Shrimp Kabobs, 72
Sweet & Tangy Sausage
  Pepper Kabobs, 36
Sweet Pea & Potato Salad, 481
Swiss Chard Pizza, 461

T

Tacos, Tilapia, 379
Tahini Sauce, 101
Tamarind-Glazed Salmon
  Kabobs, 64
Tandoori Barbecued Beef, 246
Tangy Coleslaw, 475
Tangy Macaroni Salad, 500
Tart-Sweet Cucumber Slices, 101
Teriyaki Chicken Sandwiches,
  Gourmet, 123
Teriyaki Orange Lamb
  Chops, 224
Teriyaki Sauce, 531
Texas Barbecue Brisket, 244
Texas Barbecued Beef Ribs, 184
Thai Chili Sauce, 531
Thai Grilled Chicken, 291
Thai Minced Pork Kabobs, 34
Thai-Style Grilled Chicken
  Wraps, 127
Thai Sweet Chili Sauce, 76
Thick-Cut Sirloin Steak, 164
Three-Bean Salad, 506
Three-Pepper Chicken
  Wings, 325
thyme (fresh)
  Apple Thyme Marinade, 533
  Beef, Caramelized Shallot &
    Thyme Sausages, 145
  Peppercorn Thyme
    T-Bones, 156
Tikka Marinade, 533
tilapia
  Grilled Fish Burritos, 381
  Spiced Tilapia Sandwiches
    With Onion Salad, 132
  Tilapia Tacos, 379
  Tilapia With Tomatoes &
    Lemon Relish, 384
tofu
  Grilled Tofu & Vegetable
    Antipasto, 448
  Indonesian Chicken Breast
    Salad, 314
  Tofu Skewers With Jerk
    Barbecue Sauce, 35
tomatillos
  Green Salsa, 328
  Trout With Tomato Tomatillo
    Salsa, 354

tomatoes. *See also* tomatoes, cherry/grape
 Avocado & Green Tomato Salsa, 525
 Baked Chili Black Beans, 495
 Caprese Pizza With Bacon, 470
 Coriander Pork Skewers With Red Onion Salsa, 33
 Fresh Tomato & Onion Relish, 102
 Fresh Tomato Salsa, 517
 Greek Village Salad, 505
 Grilled Chicken & Charred Corn Salad, 312
 Grilled Corn Pizza, 463
 Grilled Eggplant & Tomato Sandwiches, 138
 Grilled Hot Pepper Salsa, 524
 Grilled Pizza Mexicana, 462
 Guacamole, Simple, 523
 Hot & Spicy Chipotle Barbecue Sauce, 530
 Jalapeño Cheeseburgers With Tomato Salad, 92
 Last-Minute Turkey Scaloppine, 339
 Lime-Grilled Chicken Breasts With Avocado Salsa, 296
 Pebre Sauce, 179
 Roast Sirloin With Orange Barbecue Sauce, 241
 Smoked Garlic Ribs With Fresh Tomato Barbecue Sauce, 220
 Spanish-Style Baked Beans, 491
 Steak House Beef Ribs With Stout Barbecue Sauce, 191
 Sun-Dried Tomato Pesto, 468
 Tofu Skewers With Jerk Barbecue Sauce, 35
 Tomato Mint Salsa, 520
 Tomato Pizza Sauce, 467
 Trout With Tomato Tomatillo Salsa, 354
 Tuna Steaks With Mediterranean Tomato Relish, 397
 Yellow Tomato Salsa, 519
 Zucchini Pizza With Fresh Tomato Sauce, 466

tomatoes, cherry/grape
 Baby Octopus With Cherry Tomatoes, 420
 Cherry Tomato Salsa, 521
 Grilled Eggplant With Provolone, 447
 Grilled Halloumi & Tomato Kabobs, 450
 Lamb Chops With Orzo Salad, 228
 Mediterranean Barley Rice Salad, 502
 Middle Eastern Chicken Breast Salad, 317
 Oregano Chicken With Tomato Salsa, 295
 Pickerel With Cherry Tomato Relish, 375
 Rib Steak With Cherry Tomato Salsa, 168
 Steak Shish Kabobs, 16
 Tilapia With Tomatoes & Lemon Relish, 384
 Whitefish With Grilled Ratatouille Salad, 402

tortillas
 Grilled Curry Shrimp Soft Tacos, 406
 Grilled Fish Burritos, 381
 Steak Tostadas With Avocado & Radish Slaw, 173
 Thai-Style Grilled Chicken Wraps, 127

trout
 Grilled Lemon Herb Trout for Two, 357
 Salmon With Lemon & Onion Relish, 369
 Trout With Herb Stuffing, 360
 Trout With Pink Peppercorn & Tarragon Butter, 359
 Trout With Tomato Tomatillo Salsa, 354
 Whole Lake Trout With Fennel Salad, 351
 Whole Trout With Lemon Parsley Butter, 353

tuna
 Tuna Steaks With Mediterranean Tomato Relish, 397
 Tuna With Grilled Jalapeño Salsa, 395

turkey
 ground (cooking), 102
 Ancho Turkey Waves, 62
 Caesar Turkey Brochettes, 60
 Chipotle-Glazed Turkey Thighs, 340
 Grilled Brined Whole Turkey, 333
 Grilled Turkey Breast With Sautéed Banana Peppers, 334
 Last-Minute Turkey Scaloppine, 339
 Lemon Sage Barbecued Turkey Breast, 336
 Mushroom-Stuffed Turkey Breast Rolls, 337
 Parmesan-Crusted Turkey Scaloppine, 338
Turkish Onion Salad, 39
Tuscan Cornish Hens, 329

V

veal
 cooking (ground), 102
 Argentine Burgers, 89
 Garlic-Marinated Veal Chops With Grilled Potato Salad, 196
 Grilled Veal Chops With Fines-Herbes Butter, 199
 Grilled Veal Saltimbocca, 22
 Italian Stuffed Veal Burgers, 100
 Rolled Veal Roast, 249
 Stuffed Meatball Sliders, 95
 Veal & Gorgonzola Burgers With Onions, 99
 Veal Loin Rib Roast, 250
 Veal Patty Melts, 104

vegetables. *See also* specific
    vegetables
    grilling, 438
    Balsamic Grilled
        Vegetables, 439
    Grilled Tofu & Vegetable
        Antipasto, 448
    Grilled Vegetable & Israeli
        Couscous Salad, 504
    Grilled Vegetable Quinoa
        Salad, 499
    Paris Wings With Crudités, 327
    Shrimp & Mango
        Brochettes, 76
    Sweet Pea & Potato Salad, 481
    Whitefish With Grilled
        Ratatouille Salad, 402
venison
    Grilled Venison Chops, 195
    Venison Burgers With Red
        Wine Mushrooms, 120
Vietnamese Squid Salad, 418

W

Warm Potato Salad, 485
Whiskey Sour Ribs, 213
whitefish
    Grilled Whitefish BLTs, 130
    Pickerel With Cherry Tomato
        Relish, 375
    Whitefish With Grilled
        Ratatouille Salad, 402
Wild Rice & Mushrooms,
    Cool, 501
wine
    Grilled Steaks With
        Roquefort Cheese
        Butter (variation), 155
    Old-Style Red Wine Marinated
        "London Broil," 165
    Red Wine Marinade, 533
    Rotisserie Pork Rib Roast, 251
    Venison Burgers With
        Red Wine Mushrooms, 120
    Wine-Marinated Leg of
        Lamb, 271

Y

Yellow Tomato Salsa, 519
yogurt
    Grilled Asparagus With Curry
        Yogurt Sauce, 443
    Tahini Sauce, 101
    Tandoori Barbecued Beef, 246
    Tikka Marinade, 533
    Tzatziki, 25

Z

zucchini
    Balsamic Grilled
        Vegetables, 439
    Grilled Tofu & Vegetable
        Antipasto, 448
    Grilled Vegetable & Israeli
        Couscous Salad, 504
    Grilled Vegetable Quinoa
        Salad, 499
    Whitefish With Grilled
        Ratatouille Salad, 402
    Zucchini Pizza With Fresh
        Tomato Sauce, 466

Credits

Recipes

All recipes were developed by The Canadian Living Test Kitchen and Andrew Chase, except the following.

Camilo Costales: pages 13, 64, 65, 189, 216, 217, 220, 232, 250, 363, 386, 397, 409, 417, 418, 419 and 424.

Christine Picheca: pages 42, 84, 139, 141, 147, 244, 249, 255, 268, 345, 379, 413, 420, 425, 452, 454, 455 and 480.

Nicole Young: pages 20, 21, 22, 85, 95, 111, 121, 124, 129, 144, 145, 173, 184, 196, 246, 256, 258, 266, 374, 378, 381, 384, 385, 433 and 450.

Photography

Michael Alberstat: pages 148 and 174.

Christopher Campbell: page 273.

Yvonne Duivenvoorden: pages 24, 29, 41, 48, 51, 67, 71, 87, 96, 97, 112, 117, 158, 162, 171, 190, 201, 203, 205, 209, 229, 238, 282, 310, 316, 319, 332, 355, 356, 399, 404, 407, 411, 430, 441, 445, 457, 464, 469, 472, 498, 503, 507, 508 and 527.

Geoff George: pages 44, 161 and 264.

Kevin Hewitt: pages 26, 53, 57, 61, 82, 122, 177, 182, 198, 212, 289, 335, 367, 368, 372, 476, 492, 493, 511 and 518.

Jim Norton: pages 32, 133, 222 and 382.

Edward Pond: pages 1, 4, 5, 6, 7, 10, 18, 19, 37, 58, 78, 91, 103, 128, 137, 150, 172, 227, 234, 240, 247, 253, 261, 267, 269, 313, 348, 352, 358, 371, 376, 380, 391, 393, 426, 436, 451, 488, 514, 522 and 532.

Jodi Pudge: pages 14, 107, 193, 206, 215, 286, 297, 305, 308 and 446.

David Scott: pages 126, 154, 181 and 483.

Michael Visser: page 401.

Felix Wedgwood: pages 75, 108, 143, 167, 187, 194, 218, 219, 233, 248, 274, 275, 278, 322, 323, 326, 331, 343, 344, 362, 387, 396, 408, 415, 416, 421, 422, 423, 453 and 458.

Food styling

Julie Aldis: pages 26, 29, 51, 57, 82, 148, 174, 182, 209, 238, 401 and 518.

Donna Bartolini: pages 48 and 203.

Andrew Chase: pages 133, 143, 218, 219, 233, 274, 275, 278, 322, 323, 331, 343, 362, 382, 387, 399, 411, 415, 416 and 458.

Ashley Denton/Judy Inc.: pages 1, 4, 5, 6, 7, 10, 18, 19, 58, 78, 91, 128, 150, 172, 234, 240, 247, 261, 267, 269, 348, 358, 371, 380, 391, 426, 436, 451, 488, 514, 522 and 532.

Christine Picheca: pages 108, 194, 248, 326, 344, 396, 408, 421, 422, 423 and 453.

Lucie Richard: pages 14, 24, 37, 87, 112, 126, 154, 205, 282, 313, 355, 356, 376, 430, 445, 483, 503, 508 and 527.

Claire Stubbs: pages 32, 41, 67, 71, 96, 97, 103, 107, 117, 137, 158, 162, 171, 190, 193, 201, 206, 215, 222, 227, 229, 253, 286, 297, 305, 308, 310, 316, 319, 332, 352, 393, 404, 407, 441, 446, 457, 464, 469, 472, 498 and 507.

Rosemarie Superville: page 181.

Nicole Young: pages 44, 53, 61, 75, 122, 161, 167, 187, 198, 212, 264, 289, 335, 367, 368, 372, 476, 492, 493 and 511.

Prop styling

Laura Branson: pages 24, 26, 32, 53, 57, 61, 75, 112, 126, 167, 187, 198, 212, 289, 335, 356, 367, 476, 483, 503, 508 and 511.

Catherine Doherty: pages 1, 4, 5, 6, 7, 10, 14, 18, 19, 37, 44, 58, 78, 91, 96, 97, 107, 108, 128, 133, 137, 143, 150, 161, 172, 190, 193, 194, 215, 218, 219, 227, 229, 233, 234, 240, 247, 248, 261, 264, 267, 269, 274, 275, 278, 286, 297, 310, 313, 322, 323, 326, 331, 343, 344, 348, 358, 362, 371, 376, 380, 382, 387, 391, 396, 404, 408, 415, 416, 421, 422, 423, 426, 436, 446, 451, 453, 457, 458, 464, 469, 488, 514, 522 and 532.

Marc-Philippe Gagné: page 316.

Mandy Gyulay: pages 206, 305 and 308.

Maggi Jones: pages 158 and 238.

Oksana Slavutych: pages 29, 48, 51, 67, 71, 87, 103, 117, 148, 154, 162, 174, 181, 203, 205, 209, 253, 282, 332, 352, 355, 399, 401, 411, 430, 441, 445, 507 and 527.

Carolyn Souch/Judy Inc.: pages 82, 122, 368, 492, 493 and 518.

Genevieve Wiseman: pages 41, 171, 182, 201, 222, 319, 393, 407 472 and 498.

Madeleine Wong: page 372.